"Professor Voltaire's commitment to promoting understanding and compassion for individuals with ASD is evident throughout the book. His dedication makes this book an inspiring and invaluable resource for parents and professionals."

Aya Shigeto, PhD, *Developmental Psychologist*

"Professor Voltaire's book is an in-depth exploration of Autism. It contains a treasure trove of information for developmental psychology, researchers, clinicians, students, and parents with autistic children."

Lena E. Hall, PhD

"Professor Voltaire has offered a thoroughly researched and lucidly written account of autism. This book is an invaluable contribution to the growing understanding of autism. It will also be practically helpful for parents, educators, and caregivers working with the ASD population."

Joyce Avotri Wuaku, PhD, *Associate Professor, Medical Sociologist*

Developmental Trajectories, Diagnosis, and Interventions for Autism

This book introduces a developmental psychopathology approach to exploring the concept of autism in terms of three broad domains of development—physical, cognitive, and psychosocial—that are inextricably linked.

Developmental psychopathology focuses on the interplay between normal and abnormal development. The juxtaposition of typical and atypical developmental patterns can better inform clinicians and parents of possible signs of achievement milestones that are missing or falling behind. This book consists of twelve chapters grouped under four parts, with each chapter's core content based on the most recent research findings and ending with the author's reflections on various parts of the chapter and a summary of the main points discussed. A final chapter addresses topics of utmost importance rarely discussed in books on autism.

Appropriate for a wide range of professionals who work with clients who have autism, this book is a unique resource with approaches often overlooked in most books on autism.

Michael Voltaire, PhD, BCBA-D, is a developmental psychologist and a board-certified behavior analyst specializing in typical and atypical development, particularly autism. Dr Voltaire is a full-time faculty member at Nova Southeastern University.

Developmental Trajectories, Diagnosis, and Interventions for Autism

Michael Voltaire, PhD, BCBA-D

Routledge
Taylor & Francis Group

NEW YORK AND LONDON

Designed cover image: Getty Images

First published 2026
by Routledge
605 Third Avenue, New York, NY 10158

and by Routledge
4 Park Square, Milton Park, Abingdon, Oxon, OX14 4RN

*Routledge is an imprint of the Taylor & Francis Group, an informa
business*

ISBN: 978-1-032-37287-7 (hbk)
ISBN: 978-1-032-37286-0 (pbk)
ISBN: 978-1-003-33626-6 (ebk)

DOI: 10.4324/9781003336266

Typeset in Times New Roman
by KnowledgeWorks Global Ltd.

Contents

Foreword

One of my earliest encounters with *Voltaire*, as he is called by friends and colleagues, was about 15 years ago when we were both brand-new Assistant Professors and our Dean asked me to observe one of his classes (a standard practice for new faculty). It was a Developmental Psychology course, and that day's lesson was on the social lives of elderly people. Voltaire was dismantling some of the students' stereotypes about the elderly by presenting data on the high rate of sexually transmitted diseases in eldercare communities. "Trust me!" he concluded in a conspiratorial stage whisper. "They are *doing it*!" The students and I burst out laughing, and I can guarantee they will remember that day's lesson for a long time to come.

Voltaire brings this same distinctive cheeky, jovial, yet informative style to all his interactions and lectures, whether he is giving a talk on the history of Haiti's treatment by European invaders (shocking and horrific—and yet, even here Voltaire finds a humorous approach to the topic), or mentoring younger players on the city league soccer team we play on together—or when discussing Autism Spectrum Disorder (ASD) in this book. When his humorous lecture style is combined with clear, precise prose, the result is a remarkably informative yet enjoyable read.

What most parents want to know more than anything—whether their child is neuro-divergent or neuro-typical—is an answer to some version of this question: *Will my child be okay?* Of course, the answer can mean many different things to different parents. To some parents, "okay" may mean that their child will grow up reasonably content and fulfilled in his or her day-to-day life. Other parents worry about their child's ability to have a successful career, graduate from college, get married, produce offspring, play sports, excel on their SAT scores, and so on. Most parents will be forced to go through the complicated process of recognizing that their child's abilities, interests, or temperament differ in *some* way from what they had envisioned when their child was born. This process may be particularly frightening for parents of children with autism because these parents often do not know what to expect or hope for. It is said that when you know one child with autism, you know one child with autism—meaning that autism spectrum disorder (ASD) presents differently in virtually every case. Yet most parents of a child with ASD will want to know the answer to that key question: *Will my child be okay?* This book is designed to help parents figure out how best to assist and encourage their child to be okay—particularly a neuro-divergent child, but really any child who struggles in some way. This "help" may not enable children to fulfill parents' every dream for their child—but of course we parents must realize that our wishes for our children may not be what they wish for themselves. Often people with ASD have different interests, abilities, and lifestyles than neuro-typical people. Understanding these differences may be the best key to helping not only the neuro-divergent child but also his or her parents.

The author of this book is a long-time expert in the field of autism. Dr. Michael Voltaire (Ph.D., 2005, Florida International University) is a highly qualified developmental psychologist who has worked with children with ASD and their parents for the past two decades. He became a Board-Certified Behavior Analyst in 2005 and has provided services for countless persons with developmental disabilities. In his current role as Associate Professor in the Department of Psychology and Neuroscience at Nova Southeastern University, Voltaire developed the Applied Behavior Analysis (ABA) minor and has trained both undergraduate and graduate students to become ABA therapists. He is the recipient of two internal university grants to conduct research on echolalia in autism and well-being.

This book is divided into four sections. The first section provides an overview of ASD, along with early physical, social, and cognitive trajectories in typical and atypical development, namely autism, and what happens to children with ASD as they enter adulthood, including a discussion of employment opportunities, independent living, and health issues. This information can help parents as well as adolescents with ASD as they transition into adult life. The second section of the book covers the etiology and heterogeneity of autism. The third section of the book discusses screening and assessment of autism. This section can help parents who suspect their child is neuro-divergent, as well as pediatricians and other medical professionals who need to decide whether a child patient's behavior is in the typical range or warrants evaluation by a specialist. The fourth section of the book covers interventions for ASD. This information can help parents who are determining how best to help their child, as well as the medical professionals who advise the parents. The final chapter delves into the early definitions and stigmatization of autism, the current research and treatment available for the condition, and future perspectives and awareness of autism guided by the concept of neurodiversity and how society might view autism in a more favorable light.

So much regarding the causes of and best treatments for ASD are still unknown. This can cause a great deal of anxiety for people with ASD and for those who care most about them—particularly their parents, but also teachers and clinicians. There is no magic bullet to quell these anxieties; frankly, neuro-divergent development can be difficult in a world designed for neuro-typical people. But this masterful book by an expert developmental psychologist will leave readers feeling more in control and better informed about how best to proceed.

R. Weylin Sternglanz
Associate Professor of Psychology
Nova Southeastern University

Preface

Autism spectrum disorder (ASD) is considered one of the most severe and complex neurodevelopmental disorders, affecting approximately 1% of the world population. The Centers for Disease Control and Prevention (CDC) estimates the prevalence of ASD in the United States at 1 in 36 children (CDC, 2020). The idea of authoring this book originated from my graduate training as a developmental psychologist and my experience as a service provider to children diagnosed with autism. The primary aim was to write a comprehensible account of autism based on the most recent research findings. The book is carefully organized into four parts that address essential aspects of autism. I hope the information in the book will be a valuable resource for parents, students, teachers, care workers, therapists, behavior analysts, and other professionals collaborating with people diagnosed with autism.

There are hundreds of books on autism, ranging from those written by parents of children diagnosed with autism to more comprehensive volumes written by autism researchers and practitioners. In contrast, this book is one of the few texts that integrate the three broad domains of development into its content—physical, cognitive, and psychosocial. Many books describe typical symptoms or characteristics of autism but do not delineate expected developmental milestones. After all, we can best understand atypical development by first understanding typical development.

Part I consists of five chapters: (1) *Overview of Autism Spectrum Disorder*, (2) *Physical Development in Autism*, (3) *Social Development in Autism*, (4) *Cognitive Development in Autism, and (5) Life Course of Autism*. It introduces the reader to autism spectrum disorder, its conceptualization, characteristics, and prevalence in the United States and other parts of the world. Part I also explores the broad domains (i.e., physical, cognitive, and social) in terms of typical and atypical development and how autism impacts individuals throughout different life stages, from early childhood into adulthood.

Part II has two chapters: (6) *Autism Etiology* and (7) *Autism Heterogeneity*. It examines the role genetic and environmental factors play in the etiology and heterogeneity of autism. Those factors are inextricably connected and have hindered autism research and treatment.

Part III includes two chapters: (8) *Screening Tools* and (9) *Diagnostic Tools*. It explores a variety of developmental and behavioral screening instruments used to screen and diagnose autism. Screening tools during well-child visits can allow pediatricians to decide whether a child suspected of having autism requires a more in-depth evaluation before a formal diagnosis. Part III also reviews the Diagnostic and Statistical Manual of Mental Disorders (DSM) and the International Classification of Diseases (ICD) and their role in autism diagnosis.

Part IV has three chapters: (10) *Behavioral Interventions*, (11) *Pharmacologic Interventions*, and (12) *Biomedical and Complementary Alternative Treatments for Autism*. It explores various interventions currently available to address the symptoms of autism. Each of the interventions described is examined in terms of their effectiveness and empirical support.

Chapter 13 (*Autism Then, Now, and Moving Forward*) recapitulates the main ideas presented in the book. The concept of *Neurodiversity*, which has gained much traction in recent years, is also examined. Many individuals at the more able end of the spectrum do not consider their unorthodox ways of behaving a disorder. They have argued that what neurotypicals often perceive as eccentric behavior can contribute positively to the overall diversity of human experiences, similar to how biodiversity is crucial for ecological balance that supports all life on planet Earth.

Michael Voltaire, PhD, BCBA-D

Associate Professor

Nova Southeastern University

Acknowledgments

I am grateful to my wife Danielle for giving me the time and space needed to complete this book—her support and patience have been unwavering. She also gave me valuable feedback on many sections of the manuscript. My trusted colleague Dr. Aya Shigeto was the first to read the initial proposal and revise the first sections I wrote. I am thankful for her contribution. My colleague Dr. Weylin Sternglanz also read the book proposal and did not think writing such a book whose content departed radically from published ones was a crazy idea. He wrote the foreword.

Furthermore, Dr. Lena Hall, my former colleague and a published author, commented on numerous parts of the manuscript. I am grateful to my daughter, Saradiah Voltaire-Taylor, for reading and providing feedback on several chapters of the book. Lastly, I want to thank Alexis Alvarez, one of my students, who diligently read many sections of the book, ensuring that every cited reference is accurate. Many other students, including Melissa Bell, Olivia Batista, Varsha Krishnan, and Joshua Ponnuchamy, read parts of the manuscript and revised various reference sections for accuracy.

I want to express my gratitude to the many parents of children on the autism spectrum who collaborated with me in collecting data and implementing programs for skills acquisition and behavior reduction. Their involvement has significantly enhanced the quality of life for their children. I also thank the researchers, clinicians, educators, writers, and parents whose published work and interest in autism have influenced the content of this book. I hope that the subject matter presented is engaging and sparks the interest of anyone concerned with autism spectrum disorder. Finally, I am grateful to the Taylor & Francis Group and their associates and editors for allowing me ample time to complete and submit this manuscript.

Part I

Part I introduces the reader to autism and how the condition affects the three broad domains—physical, social, cognitive—and developmental trajectories of individuals on the autism spectrum. The first chapter, *Overview of Autism Spectrum Disorder*, describes Kanner's and Asperger's observations, their basis for formulating a diagnosis of autism—the condition they thought was rare but is now much more prevalent today. Chapter 2, *Physical Development in Autism*, explores typical and atypical brain development and examines challenges and strengths that individuals with autism may exhibit. Similarly, Chapter 3, *Social Development in Autism*, and Chapter 4, *Cognitive Development in Autism*, explore both typical and atypical development of both domains and the challenges autistic individuals face. Finally, Chapter 5, *Life Course of Autism,* takes a holistic view of how individuals on the autism spectrum transition through different life stages, highlighting the support they need to live as independently as possible.

DOI: 10.4324/9781003336266-1

Chapter 1

Overview of Autism Spectrum Disorder

Chapter Contents

Introduction

Autism is not a recent phenomenon; it has always existed. What used to be a rare condition when first clinically identified in the 1930s and 1940s is now the most prevalent of all neurodevelopmental conditions. Although the Diagnostic and Statistical Manual of Mental Disorders (DSM) has proposed various designations of the disorder since the American Psychiatric Association published the manual in 1952, The DSM-5 (APA, 2013) proposed the umbrella term "Autism Spectrum Disorder," which encompasses a range of symptoms and severity levels. The

DOI: 10.4324/9781003336266-2

previous three diagnostic criteria, designated as the triad of impairments, (1) social interaction difficulties, (2) communication difficulties, and (3) repetitive or restrictive behaviors, are now reduced to two diagnostic criteria: (1) Social communication difficulties and (2) restricted repetitive and/or sensory behaviors or interests.

Although the exact causes of autism are unknown, genetic research points to many genes and gene mutations implicated in the development of the condition. Autism research also identifies various environmental conditions that increase the risk of someone developing autism. The **prevalence** of autism from 1 in 150 children in 2000 to 1 in 36 children in 2024 is attributed to numerous factors, including changes in diagnostic criteria, increased awareness, the development of more accurate **screening** and diagnostic instruments, and environmental factors (Fombonne, 2018).

Identity-First versus Person-First Language

Throughout the book, I will use various terms, nouns, and adjectives (e.g., autism, autistic, autism spectrum disorder, ASD, a condition, a disorder, autism spectrum, high-functioning autism, and low-functioning autism). Many people in the autism community prefer an identity-first language because they identify with the disability. Autism, in their view, is not a condition separate from them but an essential part of who they are. Furthermore, identifying with the disability has been empirically demonstrated to improve the self-esteem and quality of life of many individuals with various disabilities (Gernsbacher, 2017). In contrast, the American Psychological Association, the American Psychiatric Association, and others explicitly instruct writers to put the person first. The rationale is that naming the person first and then the disability reduces the stigma associated with the disability. I will interchangeably use an identity-first designation (e.g., an autistic person) or a person-first designation (e.g., a person with autism or a person on the autism spectrum). The intent is not to disparage persons diagnosed with the condition but to capture the various epithets that parents, clinicians, researchers, and journal editors have used.

Origin of the Term Autism

Eugen Bleuler, a Swiss psychiatrist, coined the term schizophrenia (1950 [1911]) and described the four As he considered deficits associated with cognition, emotion, and memory in individuals who suffer from the disorder: (1) *Affect*: lack of emotional display that is present at the onset of the condition; (2) *Ambivalence*: holding contradictory emotions and attitudes toward the self and others; (3) *Association*: lacking coherence of thoughts, leading to flights of ideas or word salad; and (4) *Autism*: social withdrawal and a preference to live in a fantasy world rather than interacting appropriately with the social world. The word autism has its roots in the Greek words *autos and autismos*, which means self or, more specifically, wholly self-absorbed. Kanner (1943) and Asperger (1944) borrowed the term *autism* to describe conditions they had observed in atypically developing children concerned parents brought to their clinic in the 1930s and 1940s.

Autism and Schizophrenia

Autism and schizophrenia share many symptomatic similarities. It was not until the publication of the DSM-III (APA, 1980) that autism was classified as a separate condition with "distinct developmental trajectories and dissociative features" (Sasson et al., 2011, p. 87). Autism spectrum disorder is classified as a neurodevelopmental disorder, whereas schizophrenia is a psychotic disorder. Despite the difference that characterized both conditions, they share a core phenotype of social and nonsocial cognitive impairments (Boada et al., 2020; Eack et al., 2013). Additionally, both disorders share neurobiological characteristics, including genetic risk factors and abnormalities in brain structure and function, social withdrawal, poor eye contact, and communication impairment. Brain imaging of individuals with autism and those with schizophrenia show brain structural abnormalities (Pina-Camacho et al., 2016).

Initially, autism was considered a form of childhood schizophrenia. During the early 1900s, child psychologists and psychoanalysts used the term "autism" to describe the hallucinations and unconscious fantasy life in infants. The theories of autism were later linked to schizophrenia in adults and psychoanalytic methods of reasoning (Evans, 2013). Researchers identified apparent differences in clinical features and natural histories between the two (Jutla et al., 2022), with autism being characterized by profound social difficulties and early onset, unlike schizophrenia onset during adolescence and early adulthood.

Autism and schizophrenia have a history of diagnosis conflation because of the similarities in social dysfunction and the overlapping symptoms of the two conditions. As a result, clinicians often misidentified autistic children as having schizophrenia. ASD is usually diagnosed in early childhood and follows a stable course. On the other hand, schizophrenia is typically diagnosed in adolescence or adulthood. Hallucinations and delusions characterize this disorder, which tends to worsen over time. Adolescents with ASD are three to six times more likely to develop schizophrenia compared to those without ASD (Jutla, Foss-Feig et al., 2022). Although it may be challenging to predict which adolescents will develop psychosis, ASD may, nevertheless, be a risk factor for them to develop psychotic-like experiences (Jutla et al., 2022).

Childhood Schizophrenia

Compared to autism, childhood schizophrenia is a rare condition that affects children under the age of 13 (Kendhari et al., 2016). Both positive and negative symptoms characterize childhood-onset schizophrenia and schizophrenia among adults. Positive symptoms, such as hallucinations and delusions, are more apparent than negative symptoms, which can be more challenging to evaluate. Some children with schizophrenia may experience cognitive issues related to memory and executive functioning. Academic difficulties, social isolation, withdrawal, disruptive behaviors, and speech and language problems are common among children with schizophrenia (McClellan & Stock, 2013).

Autism Before Sukhareva, Asperger, and Kanner

Before autism was clinically identified, the signs and symptoms suggestive of ASD people displayed were categorized as "madness," "feeble-mindedness," or "schizophrenia" (Grinker, 2007, p. 54). Writers from various eras and cultures have documented accounts that reflect the current characteristics of autism. Challis and Dewey (1971) wrote a narrative about individuals in Old Russia (i.e., the period that preceded the 1917 Russian Revolution) who were considered "blessed fools" ("blessed" in terms of their feeblemindedness) and thus revered by their contemporaries as having prophetic powers. Those "blessed fools" exhibited various symptoms that could indicate a diagnosis of ASD, including insensitivity to pain, nonadherence to social conventions, withdrawal, living on the fringes of society, selective mutism, odd mannerisms, muteness, echolalia, and epilepsy. Challis and Dewey described an account of Pelagija Serebrenikova, a woman considered a "blessed fool" who would collect loose bricks and stones and throw them one by one into a pond. She would repeatedly enter the pond to retrieve them and throw them back into the pond.

Houston and Frith (2000) described the case of Hugh Blair, an 18th-century Scottish Laird (landowner) whose odd behavior would have warranted a diagnosis of autism (e.g., insistence on sameness, deficiency in social understanding and communication, repetitive behavior, and narrow interest). His younger brother (John) successfully obtained a court-granted annulment of his older brother's wedding based on mental incapacity. John wanted to be the sole heir to the large estate. Twenty-nine witnesses testified in court that Hugh was "void of common sense" and a "natural fool." Hugh allegedly engaged in eccentric behaviors, including occupying the same seat every time he attended church services, attending every burial service in Borgue whether he knew the deceased person or not, always wearing the same clothes, being indifferent to social norms and conventions, and collecting twigs and bird feathers. Based on the court case report, Houston and Frith concluded, "The available evidence is rich enough and unambiguous enough to demonstrate that Hugh Blair would be given an unequivocal diagnosis of autism today" (Houston & Frith, 2000, p. 149).

Lane (1976) wrote an account of a feral child who emerged from the woods of a small village in southern France on January 8, 1800. The so-called wild boy of Aveyron (subsequently named Victor) appeared to be 11 or 12 years of age and was marked with numerous body scars, indicating that he had lived in the wilderness and had been exposed to the elements for many years. Victor did not speak any meaningful words and grunted like an animal. It was not unusual for parents to abandon children suspected of having a neurological or developmental impairment in those days. It can only be assumed that Victor was abandoned as a child but somehow managed to defy the odds and survive. Jean-Marc Gaspard Itard (the physician who took on the case as his own) taught Victor a few essential words to socialize him, but his attempts to educate Victor were unsuccessful even after five years. Whether or not Victor had autism is debatable, but many consider the wild boy of Aveyron to be another documented case. Pierre-Joseph Bonnaterre, the first scientist who examined Victor, wrote (Lane, 1976):

> When he is seated, and even when he eats, he lets out a guttural sound, a dull murmur; and he rocks his body in an oscillatory movement from right to left or from front to back (p. 36) ... but he is entirely without the gift of speech and makes himself heard only by cries and inarticulate sounds (p. 37) ... He likes solitude a great deal; crowds irritate him and make him uncomfortable and temperamental; he avoids them as much as possible (p. 43) ... When he wants to go to sleep, he rocks for a little while (p. 45).

Autism Trailblazers

Grunya Sukhareva

It is noteworthy to document early descriptions of autism and compare them with current definitions, especially with the growing number of cases. Over the years, the understanding of autism has evolved significantly. Researchers and clinicians often mention diagnostic substitution as a contributing factor, suggesting that children who might have received different diagnoses for intellectual disabilities or other developmental disorders are now being diagnosed with autism instead.

Long before Kanner and Asperger published in the 1940s their clinical account of what is now termed autism spectrum disorder, Grunya Efimovna Sukhareva, a Russian child psychiatrist, was one of the first clinicians to describe characteristics now recognized as autism. She published a detailed description of autistic traits in 1926 of six boys who presented a clinical picture that was, to a great extent, consistent with current diagnostic criteria (Manouilenko & Bejerot, 2015). In 1921, Sukhareva founded a therapeutic school for children with psychiatric problems in Moscow and published case reports based on her observations over two years. The original report was published in Russian in 1925 and translated and published in German in 1926. Sukhareva provided a vivid description of those characteristics of the children that are akin to the diagnostic criteria delineated in the DSM-5, specifically: "Flattened affective life," "Lack of facial expressiveness and expressive movements," "Find it hard to adapt to other children," "Tic-like behavior,"

"Emotional outbursts." "Strong interests pursued exclusively," "Sensitivity to noise, seeks quietness," and "Sensitivity to smell." Interestingly, Sukhareva suggested that some brain regions (e.g., frontal lobes, basal ganglia, and the cerebellum) were implicated in the manifestation of what she termed "schizoid psychopathy in childhood" (Manouilenko & Bejerot, 2015, p. 480).

Why, then, did her contribution to autism remain unacknowledged? Did Kanner or Asperger read Sukhareva's publication translated into German and opt not to cite it? Sheffer (2018) provides compelling evidence, shedding light on the enigma. Asperger was a budding Austrian pediatrician who was, to some extent, connected to the "Third Reich," which considered Jewish scientists (particularly physicians) as persona non grata. Therefore, acknowledging the work of Sukhareva, who was Jewish, would have been problematic. As for Kanner, it is possible that he read Sukhareva's work and chose not to acknowledge it because he was a Jewish Austrian-born physician who fled Nazi persecution. Perhaps he was more interested in establishing himself as the preeminent child psychiatrist, focusing on the psychiatric problems of children presented to him at the Harriet Lane Clinic at Johns Hopkins University in Baltimore.

Hans Asperger

Hans Asperger (an Austrian pediatrician at the University Children's Hospital in Vienna) observed four boys who displayed behavior patterns that included "lack of empathy, little ability to form friendships, one-sided conversations, intense absorption in a special interest, and clumsy movements." He termed the condition Autistic Psychopathy (i.e., the equivalent of pervasive developmental disorder). Asperger's thesis (1944) and clinical observations lay dormant in obscure archives until Frith (1991) had it translated from German into English. Coincidentally (perhaps not), Asperger introduced his landmark paper as Kanner (1943) introduced his.

> In what follows, I will describe a particularly interesting and highly recognisable type of child. The children I will present all have in common a fundamental disturbance which manifests itself in their physical appearance, expressive functions and, indeed, their whole behaviour. This disturbance results in severe and characteristic difficulties of social integration. In many cases the social problems are so profound that they overshadow everything else.
>
> (Frith, 1991, p. 37)

Fritz V. was born full-term without any complications. While he spoke his first words at around 10 months and subsequently expressed his thoughts like an adult, his motor skills were delayed, and he walked at approximately 14 months. After only a few days, his school referred him to the clinic because he was considered "uneducable" and displayed "severe impairment in social integration."

Fritz was oppositional and defiant from the earliest age, tended to destroy anything within his reach, and engaged in indiscriminate acts of aggression toward other children.

Asperger described Fritz as avoiding eye contact with conversation partners "as if he was not there." His speech lacked the natural melodic flow and came out as a singsong pattern. Fritz seldom responded to questions and instead repeated the question or a single word from the question. His behavior in the clinic was less than exemplary: He was uninterested in playing with other children, and his solitary activities were destructive. For instance, Fritz would chew on building blocks instead of playing with them appropriately. He engaged in repetitive behavior, including tapping rhythmically on his thigh, banging loudly on a table, hitting a wall, hitting another person, or jumping around a room. Psychological testing was virtually impossible to carry out because Fritz would engage in disruptive behaviors, including smacking the experimenter on the hand, dropping to the floor, or refusing to answer any questions. Whereas Fritz's intellectual abilities could not be estimated, he demonstrated superior rote memory and calculating ability. Asperger viewed Fritz's behavior as resulting from a disturbed "regulating mechanism" due to Fritz's inability to understand other people's expressions and react appropriately.

Asperger contemplated two possibilities that could explain Fritz's abnormal behavior: Childhood schizophrenia or post-encephalic state. He quickly refuted the former possibility because Fritz's personality indicated no sign of degradation, severe anxiety, or hallucinations. Even though there is a striking similarity between autistic children and brain-damaged children, he also ruled out the possibility of a post-encephalic state because there were no signs of neurological affectation.

Harro L. was referred to the clinic by his school at the age of 8.5 years because he was deemed unmanageable and had to repeat a grade and be placed with younger students. He was defiant, non-compliant, easily prone to anger, and rarely did what he was told, including homework. He was born with the assistance of forceps, but there was no indication of brain injury. He typically looked absentminded and in deep thought and never formed close relationships with anyone in the ward. His mode of expression was adult-like and reflected a degree of maturity seldom seen in children. Rarely did he respond to questions but talked incessantly about his areas of interest. It was virtually impossible to conduct any testing with him because of his inattention and persistence in engaging in behaviors unrelated to the test questions. Harro never participated in any play activities with other students; instead, he sat in a corner reading a book, indifferent to any surrounding noises.

Ernst K. was 7.5 years old when his school referred him to the Children's Clinic at the University Hospital because of learning and speech difficulties and unmanageable behavior problems. Subsequently, he learned to speak "like an adult." Ernst was particularly clumsy and experienced significant challenges with dressing. He was prone to getting into fights and pinching and stabbing other children with his pen. Everything in his environment needed to be ordered, and any change in his routine resulted in uncontrolled fits of anger. He seldom participated in any play activities with other students. During testing, he was oblivious and rarely responded correctly to any questions.

Hellmuth L. experienced birth complications and had to be resuscitated because of severe asphyxia. As a result, he suffered many recurrent convulsions. His development was delayed, and despite his slow language acquisition, he learned to speak even as a toddler "like a grown-up." Asperger described Hellmuth as "unattractive" with "a massive body ... big face with flabby cheeks ... tiny skull ... little eyes [that] were closely set together." Hellmuth's movements were poorly coordinated. Asperger depicted Hellmuth as "an autistic automaton, impractical and instinctually disturbed." Hellmuth could not relate to other students, frequently engaged in naughty behavior, and showed no genuine connection with others. He generally responded with irrelevant and pedantic answers when questioned about ordinary matters. His mother once explained that he was always "in another world." Asperger thought Hellmuth's condition was organic in origin, unlike the previously described cases, given his medical history of brain **anoxia** at birth (Frith, 1991, pp. 65–67).

Asperger was primarily concerned with addressing the "peculiarities" and "difficulties" of the children he examined. Because of his commitment to their education, he thought that formulating their personality (psychopathy) type would be a necessary step. However, the existing typologies in the literature did not match the characteristics he observed. He cautioned that it would be best to follow the children into adulthood and conduct a more comprehensive study to research the "biological and genetic" basis of their odd behaviors. Unfortunately, Asperger's subsequent work did not investigate any of the students' developmental trajectories.

Asperger was perhaps the first to differentiate autism with and without intellectual disability. Despite the difficulty in social integration (i.e., the hallmark of the condition he observed), those individuals without an intellectual disability, he wrote, have "potential value to society." Conversely, those with intellectual disability fare less favorably and achieve poor developmental outcomes. He examined more than 200 children over ten years (not just the four children he showcased) and most likely noticed a broad range of those children's behavioral manifestations. As a result, Asperger wrote in his thesis:

> We have mentioned repeatedly that autism occurs at different levels of ability. The range encompasses all levels of ability from the highly original genius, through the weird eccentric who lives in a world of his own and achieves very little, down to the most severe contact-disturbed, automaton-like mentally retarded individuals.

(Frith, 1991, p. 74)

Asperger thus described the newly discovered condition as occurring on a continuum of severity. Therefore, the belief that the children Asperger examined displayed behavioral symptoms entirely different from those Kanner observed in Baltimore is unjustified. Why have clinicians and writers persistently differentiated between Kanner's autism and the condition that would subsequently be termed Asperger's Disorder?

One may wonder about the fate of those children that Asperger labeled in his thesis as "mentally retarded individuals." During the Third Reich (regime from 1933–1945), Nazi policy encouraged parents deemed "racially acceptable" to give birth to as many "Aryan" children as possible. Conversely, parents viewed as less than genetically desirable were not encouraged to procreate. Edith Sheffer (2018) provided compelling evidence that children viewed as defective were probably considered as "life unworthy of life"—the Nazi designation of those regarded as flawed—and thus euthanized.

Leo Kanner

Kanner (1943) introduced the term "early infantile autism" to describe the behavioral pattern of a group of children he observed at the Harriet Lane Home for Invalid Children, a now-defunct clinic at Johns Hopkins Children's Hospital in Baltimore. He wrote in the introduction to his seminal paper: "Since 1938, there have come to our attention several children whose condition differs so markedly and uniquely from anything reported so far, that each case merits—and I hope, will eventually receive—a detailed consideration of its fascinating peculiarities" (p. 217). Kanner was referring to 11 children (eight boys and three girls between the ages of 2 and 8) he systematically examined. While these children displayed different symptoms, Kanner observed many common traits that pervaded their natural dispositions and carefully described them.

Donald T. was the first child Kanner (1943) examined at 5 years and 1 month. He was born full-term and walked at 13 months of age. He was breastfed, but feeding him had always been problematic. Donald had a phenomenal memory for faces and names but only learned to ask or answer questions if they were related to his particular interest or obsession. Long before Donald arrived in Baltimore, his father had sent a detailed report of his son's concerning behaviors:

> He seems to be self-satisfied. Donald has no apparent affection when petted. He does not observe anyone coming or going and never seems glad to see his father, mother, or playmate. He seems almost to draw into his shell and live within himself … He was always constantly happy and busy entertaining himself but resented being urged to play with certain things.

During his first visit with Kanner, Donald wandered about the room. He engaged in repetitive finger-crossing in the air, moving his head from side to side while humming a repetitive three-note tune, spinning any items he could find on the floor, and jumping up and down in delight at the sound they made.

During the second visit, six months later, Donald was more engaged with people in the clinic yet exhibited erratic behaviors, including climbing onto tables and desks, giggling incessantly, uttering nonsensical words or phrases, and displaying temper tantrums. During the third visit to the clinic, Donald paid no mind to the three attending physicians who had examined him, walked to a desk, grabbed a pencil and a piece of paper, drew letters of the alphabet, and read them horizontally and vertically. The team of physicians who examined Donald could not come up with a particular diagnosis. Kanner and his associates gathered behavioral observations of ten more children.

Frederick W. was born via cesarean section two weeks before term. While he presented no problems with feeding, his mother reported that he never assumed an "anticipatory posture" that typically developing infants display before being picked up. He sat and walked at about the expected age, 7 and 18 months, respectively. When Frederick was examined at the Harriet Lane Home, he wandered around the room, paid no attention to the three adults present, and was content with being left alone. He responded to questions by repeating them verbatim and was more interested in playing obsessively with objects than interacting with people around him. He had difficulty using personal pronouns (e.g., saying "you" instead of "I") and was able to utter a few words before the age of two.

Richard M. was born after a healthy pregnancy. While he sat at around 8 months of age and walked around his first birthday, he displayed no anticipation or eagerness to be picked up and held. His parents brought him to the clinic at 3 years and 3 months to ascertain whether he was deaf because he did not speak. The intern who examined him wrote, "He seems quite self-sufficient in his play. It is difficult to tell definitely whether he hears, but it seems that he does. He will obey commands, such as 'Sit up' or 'Lie down,' even when he does not see the speaker." Assessing his language acquisition progress, his mother wrote,

> I can't be sure just when he stopped the imitation of word sounds. It seems that he has gone backward mentally gradually for the last two years ... Now that he is making so many sounds, it is disconcerting because it is now evident that he can't talk.

During the first clinical examination, Richard engaged in active play with the surrounding toys and paid no attention to the people in the room. During subsequent testing at the clinic, he took great delight in switching the lights on and off. Richard displayed emotional outbursts because he could not express his desires until he got what he wanted (Kanner, 1943, pp. 225–226).

Paul G. was born at full-term and reached certain developmental milestones (e.g., teething, sitting, walking, and bladder and bowel control) on time but did not tolerate feeding well. He was referred to the clinic at age five for a psychometric assessment due to his incoherent speech, noncompliance, and temper tantrums in response to anyone interfering with his behaviors. Paul was thought to have a severe intellectual disability. He would show no reaction to his name, repeatedly continue in any course of action even when told to stop, and show full-fledged tantrums if told to stop whatever he was doing. Paul developed a proficient vocabulary and good sentence construction, except he never used first-person pronouns. For example, if he wanted candy, he would say, "You want candy." He could not differentiate between people and objects in his immediate environment and rarely looked up at a person's face. When playing with a toy, Paul would utter phrases related to the activity: "The engine is flying" if he was playing with an airplane toy. Some of his utterances were out of context (e.g., "Don't throw the dog off the balcony") and reflected instances of delayed echolalia consisting of regurgitating phrases he had probably heard elsewhere (Kanner, 1943, pp. 226–228).

Barbara K. was referred to the clinic at 8 years and 3 months. She was born normally but could not tolerate breastfeeding or bottle feeding. Consequently, she was tube-fed for one year. Although she developed a good vocabulary, she could not string those words into sentences, had great difficulty conversing, and could not use personal pronouns appropriately, interchanging "you" and "I." Her father described her as "repetitious as a baby, and obsessive," holding things in her hands, repeating phrases, taking stuff to bed, and getting stuck on an idea. During the examination, she displayed no "affective contact" and punctuated conversations with irrelevant phrases related to some preoccupation she had developed, such as "motor transports" and "piggy-back" (Kanner, 1943, pp. 228–229).

Virginia S. was 11 years old when examined at the clinic for the first time. She responded to her name but did not mind the person calling her. She responded to questions with vague utterances, such as "Mamma, baby," with eyes reflecting a blank expression. Before she visited the Harriet Lane Clinic, Virginia had been placed in a state training school for the feebleminded. The physician who examined her several times found no evidence of feeble-mindedness and consequently wrote,

> Virginia stands out from other children [at the training school] because she is absolutely different from any of the others … The child will amuse herself by the hour putting picture puzzles together, sticking to them until they are done.

Another psychologist who examined her commented,

> Not once have I seen her smile. She retires within herself, segregating herself from others. She seems to be in a world of her own, oblivious to all but the center of interest in the presiding situation … When others encroach upon her integrity, she tolerates them with indifference. There was no manifestation of friendliness or interest in people. On the other hand, she finds pleasure in dealing with things about which she shows imagination and initiative.
>
> (Kanner, 1943, pp. 230–231)

Herbert B. was born two weeks early via cesarean section. He was referred to the clinic when he was 3 years and 2 months old to determine whether his intellectual development was delayed. Herbert did not tolerate any food and vomited through the third month. He walked without the expected preliminary crawling around his second birthday. Herbert was quiet and unresponsive to ongoing conversations as if he was deaf and did not acquire meaningful words. He enjoyed engaging in repetitive activities, including pulling blinds up and down and tearing cardboard boxes into pieces and shuffling the pieces around for hours. Any attempts to redirect him from his solitary activities or changes in his daily routine would result in fits of anger. During one examination, he entered the office without showing any interest in anybody in the room and went directly to the Seguin Form Board. He did not respond to questions and was absorbed in whatever activity pleased him.

Alfred L. was born three weeks preterm and did not feed well during the first two months. His mother (a clinical psychologist) summarized the concerns that prompted her to take the child to Dr. Kanner.

> He [Alfred] has gradually shown a marked tendency toward developing one special interest which will completely dominate his day's activities … There has also been the problem of an overattachment to the world of objects and failure to develop the usual amount of social awareness … Language developed slowly; he seemed to have no interest in it … He still confuses pronouns … Since he talked, there has been a tendency to repeat over and over one word or statement. He almost never says a sentence without repeating it … He is upset when the sun sets. He is upset because the moon does not always appear in the sky at night. He prefers to play alone … He reads simple stories to himself.

During the examination, Alfred did not show any interest in anyone in the room but promptly went to a toy cabinet, picked up a toy train, and engaged in solitary play. The administration of any psychometric testing with Alfred was problematic, but he ultimately scored 140 on the Binet test (Kanner, 1943, pp. 233–235).

Charles N. was born full-term and walked when he was around 15 months without preliminary crawling. He was brought to the clinic when he was 4.5 years old. Her mother described him as inactive, "slow and phlegmatic" as a baby and compiled a list of his behavioral manifestations that she deemed concerning. Charles

> would pay no attention to me and show no recognition of me if I enter the room … He walks as if he is in a shadow, lives in a world of his own where he cannot be reached … His entire conversation is a replica of whatever has been said to him … When he is with other people, he does not look at them … He has a wonderful memory for words … vocabulary is good, except for pronouns.

When he entered the clinic, he showed no interest in the people present. He did not respond to his name, and when presented with the Seguin Form Board, he placed the pieces in their appropriate space and took great delight in spinning them and jumping up and down in excitement while the parts were spinning (Kanner, 1943, pp. 235–237).

John F. was 2 years and 4 months old when he was first brought to the clinic. His father's main worries were his son's difficulty in feeding and slow developmental progress. When John entered the clinic, he wandered erratically around the room and did not respond to any questions or commands. Although he acquired some knowledge of the English language, he had difficulty communicating and using the appropriate personal pronoun when referring to himself. He adhered to his routing, and the slightest departure from it resulted in temper tantrums.

Elaine C. was born at term, stood up at around 7 months, walked before her first birthday, and could speak four words when she turned one year old, but her language development stalled for the next four years. Elaine was 7 years 2 months old when first examined at the clinic, much older than other children Kanner examined. Her parents thought that her development was unusual. She preferred to be alone playing with blocks, drawing, or stringing beads and was content in doing so for hours. She was particularly fond of animals and occasionally made unusual sounds while walking on all fours. Elaine's speech progressed, but her utterances were somewhat mechanical. She did not respond to questions during the examination but merely echoed what she heard.

In sum, Kanner and Asperger's pioneering observations paved the way for identifying the common characteristics of autism. Both were equally convinced that the condition they observed differed from schizophrenia despite the similarities between both disorders (e.g., obsessiveness, stereotypy, echolalia). The children Kanner observed did not show any gradual behavioral changes. Their "extreme aloneness" was evident from the first months of life. Childhood schizophrenia follows at least two years of typical development before the behavioral manifestations of the disorder become gradually manifest. In Kanner's view, people with schizophrenia deal with their symptoms by disconnecting from the reality they once experienced. The autistic children, however, are isolated and "total strangers" and not connected to the world from the very start. Although Asperger described in great detail the family history of the four children he examined, he emphasized genetic transmission of the disorder. Despite the similarities of autistic features with those of schizophrenia, Asperger did not observe any "progressive deterioration" typically associated with psychosis. The condition of more than 200 children he examined and diagnosed with "autistic psychopathy" in ten years had not mutated into schizophrenia.

Asperger described the peculiarities of the parents of the children he examined to establish a possible genetic basis for the disorder he discovered. Conversely, Kanner explored the possibility that "a genuine lack of maternal warmth" could likely cause the disorder he identified but acknowledged that those children's aloneness was present at birth. Therefore, he invoked a counterargument and surmised that those children were born without an "innate ability" to connect with people.

Kanner described three defining features of what he termed "an inborn autistic disturbance of affective contact": (1) an inability to relate to other people and a preference to be alone, (2) disturbance and a deficit of language—three of the eleven children he observed possessed fewer than five words, and (3) an anxious obsession with the preservation of sameness. In addition, five of the eleven children Kanner observed had relatively larger heads with no significant observable dysmorphic features, suggesting some anomalies in fetal development. Interestingly, there is evidence now that **macrocephaly** and brain volume are more prevalent in children diagnosed with ASD (Barnard-Brak et al., 2011).

Asperger emphasized the personality, physical characteristics, cognitive capability, social interaction, emotional disposition, biological factors, and the fate of those diagnosed with "autistic psychopathy." Asperger pointed to the distinctiveness and "persistence over time" of the autistic personality, despite individual differences and prominent characteristics that become apparent from "the second year of life." Autistic children have a "paucity of facial and gestural expression." They typically do not gaze at their interlocutors for cues when engaged in conversation. Those without an intellectual disability tend to use creative language and word choice typically developing children seldom use. Autistic children distance themselves from the world around them, and the "personal distance" they create is the hallmark of what Asperger termed "psychopathic clarity of vision," which enables them to zero in on specific areas of interest that can lead to "exceptional achievements," but those with lower "levels of ability" do not achieve much. Regardless of the ability level, learning does not occur naturally via imitation as in typically developing children. Learning must be structured with the help of contrived rules.

Kanner and the Concept of Refrigerator Mother

The concept of "refrigerator mother," while commonly attributed to Bettelheim (1967), originated in Kanner's seminal paper (1943). He described a set of features including "coldness," "obsessiveness," and "lack of genuine warmth" he observed in parents who brought their children to his clinic. Kanner (1949) described a scene he observed during one visit to the Triplett family in Forest, Mississippi:

> I spent an evening with the family. Donald, the patient [case 1], sat down next to his mother on the sofa. She kept moving away from him as though she could not bear the physical proximity. When Donald moved along with her, she finally told him coldly to go and sit on a chair.

> (Kanner, 1949, p. 422)

In the same paper (Kanner, 1949), he wrote:

> Most of the patients [I observed] were exposed from the beginning to parental coldness, obsessiveness, and a mechanical type of attention to material needs only. They were the objects of observation and experiment conducted with an eye on fractional performance rather than with genuine warmth and enjoyment. They were kept neatly in refrigerators which did not defrost.
>
> (Kanner, 1949, p. 425)

Kanner's invention of the concept of "refrigerator mother" propelled his newly conceptualized condition to new heights but at the same time provided the spark for Bettelheim's (1967) writing and publishing of a book whose content blamed the parents of autistic children and exalted the psychogenic view of the condition.

Paradoxically, Kanner (1943, p. 242, my emphasis) wrote:

> The outstanding, '**pathognomonic**,' fundamental disorder in the children's inability to relate themselves in the ordinary way to people and situations from the beginning of life ... There is from the start an extreme autistic aloneness that, whenever possible, disregards, ignores, shuts out anything that comes to the child from the outside.

Kanner (1943, p. 250) concluded with the following assumption: "We must, then, assume that these children have come into the world with [an] innate inability to form the usual, biologically provided affective contact with people, just as other children come into the world with innate physical handicaps."

Kanner's integration of psychogenic explanations in his early descriptions of autism was probably influenced by his mentor, Adolf Meyer, who appointed him to head the first child psychiatric unit in the U.S. at the Henry Phipps Psychiatric Clinic in Baltimore, Maryland. One dominant view held by psychiatrists in the first half of the 1900s is that psychological disorders (e.g., schizophrenia) resulted from mothers' interactions with the affected children. The term "schizophrenogenic mother" evidenced such practice.

The Onset of Autism

The onset of autism is not a discrete event but a process that develops in infancy and persists throughout a person's life. Parents and pediatricians are usually the first to notice early signs of autism before an infant's first birthday. However, symptoms may become more consistently apparent during toddlerhood, in most cases. In some cases, the social and functional impairment associated with the disorder, if mild, may become evident in the preschool years. Infants typically show symptoms of autism within the first year. Symptoms presentation differs from infant to infant. Although ASD symptoms may not become apparent until 24 months or later, some children show symptoms within the first 12 months of age.

It is generally documented that the onset of autism occurs when infants show delays in social development and communication during the first year of life. Conversely, the onset can also occur when children's development proceeds as expected for some period and then regresses. They experience declines in or loss of previously acquired skills (Ozonoff et al., 2008). Barger and colleagues (2013) conducted a **meta-analysis** of the prevalence and onset of regression in ASD. They found that contrary to the long-held documented onset of autism, regressive autism occurs more commonly than previously recognized. Another less generally occurring pattern of onset is marked by a "developmental stagnation." Skills that children acquire remain intact and remain on a developmental plateau and no longer progress toward achieving expected gains (Shumway et al., 2011).

Data from retrospective and prospective studies consistently show that the symptoms of ASD emerge in the first two years of life in children at risk for developing the disorder (Zwaigenbaum et al., 2013). Studies investigating the emergence of early signs of autism have relied on **retrospective studies** (e.g., parent reports and analysis of home movies of children later diagnosed with autism). One problem with such an approach is that it can introduce distorted parental recall and potential biases by viewing selective home videotaping. Therefore, **prospective studies** are better suited to answer questions about the emergence of behavioral signs of autism (Ozonoff & Iosif, 2019). Research studies that use prospective methods have generally reported typical early development followed by development going awry and the onset of symptoms at the end of the first year and continuing in the second year of life.

Early Signs

When do autism symptoms become apparent? Autism is not present "from the beginning of life," as Kanner posited in his influential paper describing the condition (1943, p. 242) but emerges over the first two years of life. ASD symptoms presentation differs among children. Some parents perceive their children as "different" during the first few months of life. Some children show delays in language acquisition during the second year; others develop typically until the second year and then regress (Tsang et al., 2019). Clinicians and researchers have documented their observations and focused on early social behaviors (e.g., shared emotions, social interest, response to name, joint attention, and orientation to faces and eyes) that are expected in typical development. Multiple studies comparing infants not at risk of developing autism to those at higher risk (i.e., in **simplex** or **multiplex families**) found no differences in the emergence of symptoms before 9 months of age. However, starting at 12 months, ASD symptoms become apparent for high-risk infants, who differ significantly from infants on course for optimal development trajectories.

In early childhood, central nervous system viral infections (e.g., enterovirus encephalitis or enterovirus meningitis) can cause mild symptoms (e.g., sore throats, stomach upsets). However, these viral infections can cause some autism-related behavior in rare cases. Marques and colleagues (2014) described a case of a 32-month-old patient with enterovirus encephalitis who exhibited autistic features, aphasia, and persistent stereotypies. The autistic-like behavior associated with those medical conditions usually subsides over time. Thus, quasi-autism or pseudo-autism seems more appropriate than autism *per se* (Boucher, 2022).

Social experiences in early postnatal development guide the formation of neural networks in brain development. The lack of such human contact and cognitive stimulation can result in the brain wiring itself, a process that can go awry. In addition to genetic and environmental influences, psychological deprivation in infancy can also be a risk factor for autism. The English & Romanian Adoptees study (Kumsta et al., 2015) documented a cohort of infants in orphanages who suffered persistent social deprivation. As a result, some children developed marked deficits in social cognition and quasi-autistic features (e.g., cognitive impairment and attention-deficit/hyperactivity disorder).

Autism Prevalence in the United States

Autism is a lifelong neurodevelopmental condition characterized by "persistent deficits in social communication and social interactions" and "restricted, repetitive patterns of behavior, interests, or activities" (APA, 2013). When autism was clinically identified in the 1940s, the disorder was considered a rare condition. The condition Kanner (1943) described—infantile autism—as a rare disorder has been on the rise every decade. Kanner also believed that the characteristics he examined were rare but probably "more frequent than is indicated by the paucity of observed cases" (p. 242). Children who exhibited unusual behaviors before Kanner's clinical descriptions of the disorder were viewed as schizophrenic, feebleminded, idiots, or imbeciles. What has been considered a rare condition is now among the most prevalent of developmental disorders. The frequency of occurrence of autism is calculated in terms of its prevalence. Is autism becoming more common? Is there an epidemic? What is clear is that the prevalence of the disorder has increased in the past three decades.

The first studies on the prevalence of autism were conducted in Europe and the United States in the 1960s and 1970s, respectively (Lotter, 1966; Treffert, 1970). The low prevalence estimate of 2 to 4 cases per 10,000 children led to a belief that autism was a rare childhood disorder. However, in recent decades, the prevalence of autism has increased alarmingly. As a result, the concern that autism has reached an epidemic proportion has been propagated in the media. In 2000, the Centers for Disease Control and Prevention (CDC) established the

Table 1.1 Prevalence of autism in the U.S. since the CDC began monitoring the disorder in 2000

Surveillance Year	Birth Year	Number of ADDM Sites Reporting	Combined Prevalence for 1,000 Children (Range Across ADDM Sites)	This is about 1 in X Children
2022	2014	16	32.2 (9.7–53.1)	1 in 31
2020	2012	11	27.6 (23.1–44.9)	1 in 36
2018	2010	11	23.0 (16.5–38.9)	1 in 44
2016	2008	11	18.5 (18.0–19.1)	1 in 54
2014	2006	11	16.8 (13.1–29.3)	1 in 59
2012	2004	11	14.5 (8.2–24.6)	1 in 69
2010	2002	11	14.7 (5.7–21.9)	1 in 68
2008	2000	14	11.3 (4.8–21.2)	1 in 88
2006	1998	11	9.0 (4.2–12.1)	1 in 110
2004	1996	8	8.0 (4.6–9.8)	1 in 125
2002	1994	14	6.6 (3.3–10.6)	1 in 150
2000	1992	6	6.7 (4.5–9.9)	1 in 150

Autism and Developmental Disabilities Monitoring (ADDM) Network to estimate the prevalence rate among 8-year-old children in the United States in 11 ADDM network sites. The ADDM network consists of several sites across the United States where data is collected on the prevalence of ASD and other developmental disabilities in various communities. The prevalence of autism has increased in each CDC consecutive publication, from 1 in 150 children in 2000 to 1 in 54 in 2016. The 2016 ADDM network findings revealed a higher prevalence of autism compared to previous estimates, raising public health concerns. Black and Hispanic children were evaluated at an older age and were more likely than White children to have an intellectual disability (Maenner et al., 2020). The prevalence rate for the surveillance year 2022 was 1 in 31 children, as shown in the table above. Today, autism has become increasingly more prevalent in the U.S. and worldwide.

Suspected Causes of the Prevalence

There is strong evidence that changes in diagnostic criteria, changes in special education policy, diagnostic substitution (i.e., the inclusion of children with language impairments or learning disabilities), readily available services, and awareness of autism contribute to the increased prevalence of autism (Fombonne, 2009), but do these factors reflect an actual **incidence** of the disorder? Some researchers (e.g., Schieve et al., 2011) have evaluated factors associated with known increased risk factors (e.g., infertility treatment, multiple births, preterm delivery, low birth weight, and cesarian section) and found no conclusive evidence that they cause an actual prevalence increase of autism. Conversely, Thomas Insel, a psychiatrist and neuroscientist who served as director of the

National Institute of Mental Health, suggested that there might be an actual incidence of autism due to environmental factors.

> This whole idea of whether the prevalence is increasing is so contentious for autism, but not for asthma, type 1 diabetes, food allergies—lots of other areas where people kind of accept the fact that there are more kids affected.
>
> (Weintraub, 2011, p. 22)

Can concrete environmental risk factors be ruled out? Certainly not! If environmental factors of relatively recent origin contribute to the incidence of autism, autism researchers must identify those factors. The focus in recent decades has been on genetic causes rather than environmental ones. During the past decade, the Federal government allocated about $1 billion to finding the genetic causes of autism compared to only $40 million to identify possible environmental causes (Weintraub, 2011).

Worldwide and Regional Prevalence Variations

Although the prevalence of autism has been on the rise worldwide in the past several years, most of the estimated rates come from developed regions of Western countries. Data from non-western or non-affluent countries are neither reliable nor consistent (Adak & Halder, 2017). Regional variations in diagnostic practices have probably contributed to the increased prevalence rates of ASD in recent years (Zaroff & Uhm, 2012). Additionally, cultural values and expectations can influence diagnoses that are behaviorally based. For example, Norbury and Sparks (2013) reported a prevalence rate of about two children in 10,000 in Oman compared to approximately 260 children in 10,000 in South Korea.

Studies report rate variations in different sites even when a comparable methodology is used. For example, the Autism and Developmental Disabilities Monitoring (ADDM) Network reported the lowest rates of autism in Missouri (viz. 85, 81, and 96 per 10,000 for 2010, 2012, and 2014, respectively). However, rates were the highest in New Jersey (viz. 197, 221, and 284 per 10,00, respectively, for the same years). Sites that used education and health sources to ascertain cases of autism reported higher rates than sites that only used education records (Christensen et al., 2019).

A previous systematic review of the global prevalence of autism found a medium rate of 62/1000 children (Elsabbagh et al., 2012). Consistent with previous global estimates, boys were more likely to be diagnosed than girls. The review reported rate estimates mainly for children, substantial variability across many world regions, and estimates that were limited or absent in many parts of the world, including Eastern Europe and Africa. More recently, Zeidan and colleagues (2022) conducted a systematic review of 71 studies worldwide since 2012 to estimate the prevalence of autism. They reported a prevalence increase and a high variability worldwide within and across regions (i.e., the median prevalence of 100/10,000—ranging from 1.09/10,000 to 436/10,000).

Compared to global estimates of the prevalence of autism reported (Elsabbagh et al., 2012), it has increased in various countries, namely the United States, South Korea, France, India, and Australia (Zeidan et al., 2022). The prevalence estimates will continue to rise due to (1) methodological factors and diagnostic inconsistencies, (2) surveillance systems' capability to identify "autism" more readily, and (3) continual modification of the disorder's diagnostic criteria.

The definition of autism has evolved significantly and departed from the original descriptions by Kanner and Asperger. Kanner focused on characteristics and behaviors that he viewed as rare, while Asperger described children with similar traits but noted that they did not have severe language deficits. In recent years, our understanding of autism has expanded to include a variety of symptoms, levels of severity, and presentations, which illustrates the diverse nature of the condition. The current framework, as outlined in the DSM-5, recognizes a spectrum of disorders under the umbrella of autism spectrum disorder.

Summary

Autism existed long before its clinical identification and description in the 1940s. In the past, signs and symptoms suggestive of autism were categorized as schizophrenia, madness, or feeble-mindedness. The condition, which used to be rare, has now become the most prevalent of all neurodevelopmental disorders. Its prevalence rate has increased from 1 in 150 children in 2000 to 1 in 31 children in 2022. The term "autism" was coined by Swiss psychiatrist Eugen Bleuler to describe the social withdrawal that affects schizophrenic patients. Although autism and schizophrenia share many similarities, they are two distinct conditions.

In the 1930s and 1940s, researchers Leo Kanner and Hans Asperger used the term "autism" to describe the range of symptoms they observed in the children in their clinics, highlighting the diversity of the condition. Kanner's initial group of eleven children exhibited various debilitating traits, including language difficulties. In contrast, Asperger studied several children who displayed characteristics like those of Kanner's group but showcased four with various developmental deficits while still possessing functional language abilities.

Autism is not apparent from the beginning of life but emerges during infancy. Symptoms presentation differs among infants and toddlers. Parents are usually the first to notice early signs of their infant being "different." Some children show delays in language acquisition; others do not respond to social overtures. Yet others develop typically until the second year and then regress.

The first studies on the prevalence of autism in the 1960s found low estimates, ranging from 2 to 4 cases per 10,000 children. In 2000, the Centers for Disease Control and Prevention established the Autism and Developmental Disabilities Monitoring Network to estimate the prevalence of autism among eight-year-old children in the United States. The reported prevalence of autism has increased from 1 in 150 children in 2000 to the most recent estimate of 1 in 31. Various factors may have contributed to this rising prevalence, including genetic and environmental influences, the expansion of diagnostic criteria, and increased awareness of the condition.

Questions to Ponder for Further Thinking and Learning

1 What are some of the common misconceptions about autism today?
2 How does the prevalence of autism differ across demographic groups, such as age, gender, race, and **socioeconomic status**?
3 What are some of the challenges associated with estimating the prevalence of autism? Consider underdiagnosis, misdiagnosis, and cultural differences in the perception of autism.
4 How does the prevalence of autism vary across different regions of the world, and what might account for these differences?
5 What are some of the implications of the increasing prevalence of autism, both in terms of healthcare and education policy, as well as social attitudes toward individuals with autism?
6 How can we improve our understanding of the prevalence of autism and its impact on individuals and society, and what should future research explore?
7 Suppose Kanner and Asperger were to examine children in their clinic today for eccentric behavior. Would the symptoms they observe differ from what both clinicians observed in the 1940s, and would they call the condition autism?

References

Adak, B., & Halder, S. (2017). Systematic review on prevalence for autism spectrum disorder with respect to gender and socio-economic status. *Journal of Mental Disorders and Treatment, 3*(1), 1–9.

APA (2013). *Diagnostic and statistical manual of mental disorders* (5th ed.). American Psychiatric Association.

APA (1980). *Diagnostic and statistical manual of mental disorders* (3rd ed.). American Psychiatric Association.

Asperger, H. (1944). Die "Autistischen Psychopathen" im Kindesalter. [The "Autistic Psychopaths" in Childhood]. *Archiv für Psychiatrie und Nervenkrankheiten, 117*, 76–136.

Barger, B. D., Campbell, J. M., & McDonough, J. D. (2013). Prevalence and onset of regression within autism spectrum disorders: A meta-analytic review. *Journal of Autism and Developmental Disorders, 43*(4), 817–828.

Barnard-Brak, L., Sulak, T., & Hatz, J. K. (2011). Macrocephaly in children with autism spectrum disorder. *Pediatric Neurology, 44*(2), 97–100.

Bettelheim, B. (1967). *The empty fortress: Infantile autism and the birth of the self.* The Free Press.

Bleuler E. (1950 [1911]). *Dementia praecox or the group of schizophrenias*. International Universities Press.

Boada, L., Lahera, G., Pina-Camacho, L., Merchán-Naranjo, J., Díaz-Caneja, C. M., Bellón, J. M., ... Parellada, M. (2020). Social cognition in autism and schizophrenia spectrum disorders: The same but different? *Journal of Autism and Developmental Disorders, 50*(8), 3046–3059.

Boucher, J. (2022). *Autism spectrum disorders: Characteristics, causes & practical issues* (2nd ed.). SAGE.

Challis, N., & Dewey, H. W. (1971). The blessed fools of Old Russia. *Farhrbucher Fur Geschichte Ostruropas, NS 22*, 1–11.

Christensen, D. L., Maenner, M. J., Bilder, D., Constantino, J. N., Daniels, J., Durkin, M. S., ... Dietz, P. (2019). Prevalence and characteristics of autism spectrum disorder among children aged 4 years—Early autism and developmental disabilities monitoring network, seven sites, United States, 2010, 2012, and 2014. *MMWR Surveillance Summaries, 68*(2), 1–19.

Eack, S. M., Bahorik, A. L., McKnight, S. A., Hogarty, S. S., Greenwald, D. P., Newhill, C. E., ... Minshew, N. J. (2013). Commonalities in social and non-social cognitive impairments in adults with autism spectrum disorder and schizophrenia. *Schizophrenia Research, 148*(1–3), 24–28.

Elsabbagh, M., Divan, G., Koh, Y. J., Kim, Y. S., Kauchali, S., Marcín, C., ... Fombonne, E. (2012). Global prevalence of autism and other pervasive developmental disorders. *Autism Research, 5*(3), 160–179.

Evans, B. (2013). How autism became autism: The radical transformation of a central concept of child development in Britain. *History of the Human Science, 26*(3), 3–31.

Fombonne, E. (2009). Epidemiology of pervasive developmental disorders. *Pediatric Research, 65*(6), 591–598.

Fombonne E. (2018). Editorial: The rising prevalence of autism. *Journal of Child Psychology and Psychiatry, 59*(7), 717–720.

Frith, U. (1991). *Autism and Asperger syndrome*. Cambridge University Press.

Gernsbacher, M. A. (2017). Editorial perspective: The use of person-first language in scholarly writing may accentuate stigma. *Journal of Child Psychology and Psychiatry, 58*(7), 859–861.

Grinker, R. R. (2007). *Unstrange minds: Remapping the world of autism*. Basic Books.

Houston, R., & Frith U. (2000). *Autism in history: The case of Hugh Blair of Borgue*. Blackwell.

Jutla, A., Donohue, M. R., Veenstra-VanderWeele, J., & Foss-Feig, J. H. (2022). Reported autism diagnosis is associated with psychotic-like symptoms in the adolescent brain cognitive development cohort. *European Child & Adolescent Psychiatry, 31*(7), 1–10.

Jutla, A., Foss-Feig, J., & Veenstra-VanderWeele, J. (2022). Autism spectrum disorder and schizophrenia: An updated conceptual review. *Autism Research, 15*(3), 384–412.

Kanner, L. (1943). Autistic disturbances of affective contact. *Nervous Child, 2*, 217–250.

Kanner, L. (1949). Problems of nosology and psychodynamics of early infantile autism. *The American Journal of Orthopsychiatry, 19*(3), 416–426.

Kendhari, J., Shankar, R., & Young-Walker, L. (2016). A review of childhood-onset schizophrenia. *Focus, 14*(3), 328–332.

Kumsta, R., Kreppner, J., Kennedy, M., Knights, N., Rutter, M., & Sonuga-Barke, E. (2015). Psychological consequences of early global deprivation: An overview of findings from the English & Romanian Adoptees study. *European Psychologist, 20*(2), 138–151.

Lane, H. (1976). *The wild boy of Aveyron*. Harvard University Press.

Lotter, V. (1966). Epidemiology of autistic conditions in young children. *Social Psychiatry, 1*, 124–135.

Maenner, M. J., Shaw, K. A., Baio, J., Washington, A., Patrick, M., … Dietz, P. M. (2020). Prevalence of autism spectrum disorder among children aged 8 years—Autism and developmental disabilities monitoring network, 11 sites, 2016. *MMWR Surveillance summaries, 69*(4), 1–12.

Manouilenko, I., & Bejerot, S. (2015). Sukhareva—Prior to Asperger and Kanner. *Nordic Journal of Psychiatry, 69*(6), 479–482.

Marques, F., Brito, M. J., Conde, M., Pinto, M., & Moreira, A. (2014). Autism spectrum disorder secondary to enterovirus encephalitis. *Journal of Child Neurology, 29*(5), 708–714.

McClellan, J., & Stock, S. (2013). Practice parameter for the assessment and treatment of children and adolescents with schizophrenia. *Journal of the American Academy of Child & Adolescent Psychiatry, 52*, 976–990.

Norbury, C. F., & Sparks, A. (2013). Difference or disorder? Cultural issues in understanding neurodevelopmental disorders. *Developmental Psychology, 49*(1), 45–58.

Ozonoff, S., & Iosif, A-M. (2019). Changing conceptualizations of regression: What prospective studies reveal about the onset of autism spectrum disorder. *Neuroscience and Biobehavioral Reviews, 100*, 296–304.

Ozonoff, S., Heung, K., Byrd, R., Hansen, R., & Hertz-Picciotto, I. (2008). The onset of autism: Patterns of symptom emergence in the first years of life. *Autism Research, 1*(6), 320–328.

Pina-Camacho, L., Parellada, M., & Kyriakopoulos, M. (2016). Autism spectrum disorder and schizophrenia: Boundaries and uncertainties. *BJPsych Advances, 22*(5), 316–324.

Sasson, N. J., Pinkham, A. E., Carpenter, K. L., & Belger, A. (2011). The benefit of directly comparing autism and schizophrenia for revealing mechanisms of social cognitive impairment. *Journal of Neurodevelopmental Disorders, 3*(2), 87–100.

Schieve, L. A., Rice, C., Devine, O., Maenner, M. J., Lee, L. C., Fitzgerald, R., … Durkin, M. (2011). Have secular changes in perinatal risk factors contributed to the recent autism prevalence increase? Development and application of a mathematical assessment model. *Annals of Epidemiology, 21*(12), 930–945.

Sheffer, E. (2018). *Asperger's children: The origins of autism in Nazi Vienna.* WW Norton & Company.

Shumway, S., Thurm, A., Swedo, S. E., Deprey, L., Barnett, L. A., Amaral, D. G., … Ozonoff, S. (2011). Brief report: Symptom onset patterns and functional outcomes in young children with autism spectrum disorders. *Journal of Autism and Developmental Disorders, 41*(12), 1727–1732.

Treffert, D. A. (1970). Epidemiology of infantile autism. *Archives of General Psychiatry, 22*(5), 431–438.

Tsang, L. P. M., How, C. H., Yeleswarapu, S. P., & Wong, C. M. (2019). Autism spectrum disorder: Early identification and management in primary care. *Singapore, Medical Journal, 60*(7), 324–328.

Weintraub, K. (2011). The prevalence puzzle: Autism counts. *Nature, 479*(7371), 22–24.

Zaroff, C. M., & Uhm, S. Y. (2012). Prevalence of autism spectrum disorders and influence of country of measurement and ethnicity. *Social Psychiatry and Psychiatric Epidemiology, 47*(3), 39–398.

Zeidan, J., Fombonne, E., Scorah, J., Ibrahim, A. Durkin, M. S., Saxena, S., … Elsabbagh, M. (2022). Global prevalence of autism: A systematic review update. *Official Journal of the International Society for Autism Research, 15*(5), 778–790.

Zwaigenbaum, L., Bryson, S., & Garon, N. (2013). Early identification of autism spectrum disorders. *Behavioural Brain Research, 251*, 133–146.

Chapter 2

Physical Development in Autism

Chapter Contents

DOI: 10.4324/9781003336266-3

Introduction

Physical development begins in *utero* and involves systematic growth and development from the moment of conception and beyond. It follows a systematic sequence of changes and continuities occurring at predictable times and is influenced by numerous factors, including genetics, lifestyles, aging, and diverse environmental interactions. Physical development is particularly noticeable during the first few years of life and plays a crucial role in the overall well-being of children. Delays in achieving developmental milestones (CDC, 2022) such as rolling over, sitting up, **gross motor skills**, progression of motor skills from simple movements to more intentional ones, taking the first step, and walking may indicate potential problems that need to be addressed. This chapter will explore more complex aspects of development, such as early brain development, **brain lateralization**, and sleep issues, and how deficits in these areas are related to autism.

Developmentalists and human development researchers consider three principles that underlie human growth and development: *Cephalocaudal*, *proximodistal*, and *orthogenetic*. According to the cephalocaudal principle, development proceeds from head to tail. During the prenatal stages (i.e., the embryonic and fetal), development begins at the head before proceeding to the arms, trunk, and legs. The head is far ahead in its development compared to the rest of the body and accounts for approximately one-fourth of the newborn's length (Zemel, 2002). The proximodistal principle of development posits that growth proceeds from the center to the outer, as the chest must develop before the arm, hand, and finger can grow. The orthogenetic principle of development suggests that human development proceeds from undifferentiated states to more hierarchically organized ones (Werner, 1957). For example, compared to typical individuals, those on the autism spectrum may have brain organization that differs from the norm, resulting in deficits in social interaction, sensory processing, and communication. Typical development results from these principles following an orderly pattern of growth, and departures from expected courses can result in development going awry and atypical patterns of development and behavior.

The brain is central to physical development, as it controls and coordinates various bodily functions, including reflexes, movement, and balance. It also plays a significant role in the growth and functioning of the nervous system. An unhealthy brain can lead to various physical and intellectual disabilities. Although brain development is never complete, it mostly occurs after birth, with the brain undergoing significant growth during the first few years of life. The process leads to structural and functional changes that result in physical, cognitive, and social abilities.

The underlying causes of autism are not fully understood, but research has pointed to atypicality in brain development and connectivity (Belmonte et al.,

2004; Mohammad-Rezazadeh et al., 2016). For example, numerous studies have found that individuals with autism have brain alterations that impede communication among them and differences in the sizes of specific brain regions (Ha et al., 2015; Lange et al., 2015). Brain enlargement is also common in most children with autism by the age of 2.5 years. The abnormal growth trajectory is particularly pronounced in their frontal and temporal cortices and continues throughout early childhood (Schumann et al., 2010).

Unlike children with **Down syndrome**, autistic children do not typically have **dysmorphic features**. However, in chromosomal abnormalities (e.g., fragile X syndrome or **Rett syndrome**), which are usually linked to autistic characteristics (Kaufmann et al., 2017; Percy, 2011), some individuals may have distinct facial features. For example, children with **Fragile X syndrome** have a long face, large ears, and a prominent jaw. Similarly, children (primarily found in girls) have small head sizes, long faces, broad foreheads, and prominent lower jaws. Although some genetic **syndromes** may be linked to autism, the presence of autism *per se* does not result in identifiable physical characteristics.

Early Brain Development

The brain grows at an amazing rate during development. The process begins in the third gestational week (i.e., during the embryonic stage). It continues into the fetal stage, childhood, adolescence, and throughout the lifespan. The brain produces trillions of neurons (nerve cells) prenatally, but most of its **synapses** (small connecting gaps between neurons) are produced by the **cerebral cortex** after birth. At birth, a baby's brain contains an estimated 100 billion **neurons** (nerve cells/brain cells), but there are only a few connections among them.

The brain weight of a newborn is approximately 25% of a fully developed adult brain (i.e., about three pounds). Brain development begins in *utero* and consists of three neuronal processes: proliferation, migration, and differentiation. It is estimated that neurons proliferate by hundreds of thousands every minute during the prenatal period. As a result, a newborn has around 100 billion neurons. During migration, the neurons move from where they originate to various parts of the brain, where they differentiate, reach their destination, and begin to communicate with surrounding neurons. **Neurogenesis**—the process by which new neurons are formed—is crucial during prenatal development and continues after birth and throughout life. Any disruption of this intricate process can lead to a dysfunction of the nervous system and abnormalities in brain development and functions that can lead to neurodevelopmental disorders such as ASD (Gilbert et al., 2017). Infant brain growth results from synaptic connections that are formed but consolidated because of environmental input.

Gestational Age

Gestation denotes the prenatal stages from conception to birth. Although obstetricians organize pregnancy into three trimesters, embryologists divide prenatal development into germinal, embryonic, and fetal stages. The germinal stage lasts two weeks following conception, and the embryonic stage lasts until the end of the eighth week. Every major organ begins to develop during that stage—a process termed organogenesis. The third and last stage—fetal—is the longest, starting in the ninth week post-conception until birth, and entails most brain development (Sigelman & Rider, 2022).

Gestational age is measured in weeks, starting with a woman's first day of the last menstrual cycle. A typical pregnancy lasts approximately 266 days (38 to 42 weeks). Thus, babies can be born full-term, premature (i.e., infants born before 37 weeks), or post-mature (i.e., infants born after 42 weeks). Most full-term infants weigh between 5.5 to 8.5 pounds. Although some **fetuses** born preterm can survive if they reach the age of viability (i.e., 24 weeks gestation), many are at greater risk for some degree of neurological impairment, including autism. Many risk factors are associated with low birth weight, including stress, inadequate weight gain during pregnancy, tobacco, and inadequate prenatal care. The greater the risk factors experienced during pregnancy, the higher the likelihood of delivering a tiny baby (Rosenberg, 2001). Unsurprisingly, the younger and smaller neonates are, the lower their chances for survival.

Gestational Age and Autism

Several studies have shown that low birth weight (LBW) and preterm birth are associated with autism. Schendel and Bhasin (2008) conducted a retrospective study of 565 children with autism. The criterion for inclusion in the study was whether participants were born prematurely, small for gestational age, or both and whether they had autism co-occurring with other developmental disabilities. The researchers found that babies born below 5.5 pounds had a 2.3-fold increased risk for autism, especially if they also have other developmental conditions. A surprising finding was that girls had a significant fivefold increase in autism.

What is the likelihood that LBW babies and premature babies will have autism? The answer lies in prenatal brain development. The earlier babies are born, the more vulnerable they are to brain injury because brain development is disrupted. Brain development entails a series of complex and organized steps, the first being the neural tube formation during the third gestational week. The neural tube is the primordium (initial foundation) of the central nervous system—the brain and the spinal cord. Other brain development, including primary brain region formation, neuronal migration, and synaptic pruning, occur before the age of viability (Newville et al., 2018). **Myelination** (insulation of neural axons that leads to faster neural impulse transmission) happens during the last

12 weeks of pregnancy. The brain goes through a massive growth spurt, nearly doubling its size (Bouyssi-Kobar, 2016).

Courchesne and colleagues (2020) suggested that autism is a heritable, multistage prenatal disorder that originates prenatally. The condition develops due to autism risk genes expressed in the brain and other organs. As a result, neurogenesis, cell proliferation, and cell migration are disrupted early on and continue into the fetal stage. During the fetal stage and early postnatal period, typical brain development is disrupted, including cortical wiring, **synaptogenesis**, neurite outgrowth, and neural network organization.

Kanner (1943), in his clinical description of infantile autism, noted that five of the eleven children he examined had relatively large heads. Since Kanner's observation, head circumference measurement has interested autism researchers. Many cross-sectional and longitudinal studies have found that many infants who are later diagnosed with autism have an average (or below-average) head circumference at birth. However, before age two, head circumference grows disproportionately and results in above-average circumferences that gradually plateau in brain volumes of typical adolescents and adults.

Brain Myelination

Myelin is a fatty substance that covers and insulates the axons of the neurons, thus speeding up the transmission of neural impulses. The myelination process begins in *utero* and continues for many years after birth. Myelination plays an essential role in development throughout the lifespan. For example, rapid myelination of the brain structures associated with language development facilitates the vocabulary spurt observed in toddlers. Similarly, myelination of the frontal lobes during adolescence makes the emergence of abstract concepts possible (Peters et al., 2014). Cells in the **central nervous system** called **oligodendrocytes** and other **glial cells** called Schwann cells in the **peripheral nervous system** orchestrate myelin production. Damage to the **myelin sheath** slows the transmission of nerve impulses and can result in potential neurological problems.

Brain Myelination and Autism

Oligodendrocyte cells are essential for myelination in the central nervous system. They produce the myelin sheath, which insulates nerve fibers and allows for efficient signal conduction. Research suggests that individuals with autism may have reduced myelination in certain areas of the brain, which potentially reduces communication among different brain regions and results in atypical network connectivity. Disturbances in the oligodendrocyte cells and myelination can lead to major nervous system disorders (Bradl & Lassmann, 2010).

Chen and colleagues (2022) examined intracortical myelin in autistic preschoolers and toddlers. Their findings suggested disrupted brain myelination during the first years of life in autistic children compared to typically developing ones. Similarly, a review of numerous studies of the involvement of myelination and oligodendrocytes in the development of autism indicates that some abnormalities in the brain **white matter** could be associated with the atypical brain development observed in individuals with autism (Galvez-Contreras et al., 2020).

Mouse models of autism have found disruption in the abnormal development of white matter and myelination (Graciarena et al., 2019). Another mouse model of autism investigated myelin development in a model of **idiopathic autism**. The findings suggested that precocious myelination could potentially contribute to the increased volume and connectivity of the white matter observed in young children with ASD (Khanbabaei et al., 2019). This premature myelination may disrupt the typical development of neural circuits and impact cognitive functions such as language, social interaction, and sensory processing.

Neurogenesis

Neurogenesis, the process of generating new neurons in the brain, begins in the developing brain and continues throughout life. The neuron, also known as a nerve cell, comprises the cell body (the main part of the neuron), **dendrites**, **axons**, and synapses. Synapses are where **neurotransmitters** are released to facilitate communication among neurons. Neurons are responsible for processing and transmitting information within the nervous system. Neurogenesis is crucial for embryonic development and is most active during prenatal development and early childhood. It involves stem cell proliferation, migration, and differentiation, ultimately leading to new neurons. The newborn has around 100 billion neurons, about 15% more than it will need as an adult (Sakai, 2020). On average, the adult male human brain contains 86 billion neurons, making trillions of connections (Azevedo et al., 2009). A common finding in autism research is that changes in the growth of dendrites and synapse formation and function during brain development can result in neural network dysfunction that can lead to complex social and cognitive dysfunction (Gilbert & Man, 2017).

The brain undergoes **synaptic pruning** from the early stages of postnatal development till early adulthood, eliminating unnecessary neural connections. Synaptic pruning ensures the preservation of the most efficient and effective neural pathways while removing unnecessary connections. Research suggests that autistic individuals have an overabundance of synapses in the brain due to a lack of synaptic pruning (Tang et al., 2014), which could contribute to atypical brain development (Sakai, 2020).

Neurogenesis and Autism

A large body of literature indicates that a subgroup of children who are subsequently diagnosed with autism have an unusual brain enlargement soon after birth and in infancy (Courchesne et al., 2003; Sparks et al., 2002). Kaushik and Zarbalis (2016) proposed that early brain overgrowth in autism should be viewed as a congenital disability possibly associated with an abnormal pro-liferation of neural cells during the early stages of prenatal development. The brain overgrowth observed in the prefrontal cortex of children diagnosed with autism led autism researchers to investigate postmortem prefrontal tissues of seven autistic children, male children, and six non-autistic controls. Chil-dren with autism had 67% more neurons in the prefrontal cortex (Courchesne et al., 2011).

Brain Lateralization

Brain lateralization occurs during typical development (Toga & Thompson, 2003). It refers to the asymmetrical and specialization of functions of the two hemispheres of the cerebral cortex. The two hemispheres do not develop identi-cally. They control different aspects of thought and behavior and have their re-spective specialization, advantages, and limitations (Gazzaniga, 1998). In most people, the left hemisphere typically controls the right side of the body. It is as-sociated with language processing and analytic reasoning. The right hemisphere controls the left side of the body. It regulates our processing and understanding of the visual-motor and emotional content of information (Kensinger & Choi, 2009). Simply stated, the left hemisphere is often considered the "thinking side" of the brain. In contrast, the right hemisphere is called the brain's "emotional side" (Sigelman & Rider, 2022, p. 115).

The two hemispheres communicate via the **corpus callosum** (Gazzaniga, 1998), a large bundle of more than 200 million myelinated nerve fibers. Brain lateralization occurs early in life and seems to have a genetic basis (Sigelman & Rider, 2022), considering that the left hemisphere processes language in most people and right-handedness is predominant in most people. Gotts and col-leagues (2013) found that the left and right **cerebral hemispheres** display two different types of functional lateralization. The left hemisphere tends to interact more with itself, especially for cortical regions responsible for language and fine motor coordination. Conversely, cortical areas in the right hemisphere involved in visuospatial and attentional processing tend to interact in a more integrated manner with both hemispheres.

Atypical Brain Lateralization

Typical development entails lateralization of brain structure and function. In contrast, atypical lateralization occurs in many neuropsychiatric conditions, in-cluding autism. Atypical left lateralization in the structure and function of brain regions associated with language (e.g., **Broca** and Wernicke areas) is character-istic of autism (Nielsen et al., 2014). Additionally, individuals with ASD show atypical structural and functional lateralization of circuits for motor, auditory, visual face processing, and language functions (Deemyad, 2022).

One important aspect of human brain organization is its left-right brain asymmetry. Atypical brain lateralization is generally associated with developmental disorders and neuropsychiatric conditions, including schizophrenia, autism, and language impairment. Reduced brain lateralization during language processing in individuals with autism is the most consistently reported finding. A study using **functional magnetic resonance imaging (fMRI)** to compare language lateralization between 28 adults with autism and a neurotypical group found that participants with autism showed more active right hemisphere activity and reduced language lateralization during the language comprehension tests (Jouravlev et al., 2020). These findings underscore the need for further research to deepen our understanding of these conditions and develop more effective interventions.

Two specific areas of the brain play a critical role in speech and language: Broca's area (named after the French physician Paul Broca) and Wernicke's area (named after the German physician Karl Wernicke). Broca's area is in the frontal lobe of the left hemisphere and is associated with speech production and articulation. Wernicke's area, situated in the temporal lobe of the left hemisphere, is primarily involved in speech comprehension. One consistent finding across many neuroimaging studies of individuals with autism is the reduced brain network laterality that supports language and social communication.

Many neuroimaging studies have consistently found that autistic individuals have reduced brain network laterality, which affects their language and social communication abilities. Brun and colleagues (2016) analyzed MRI scans of three groups of children: neurotypical children, children with autistic disorder, and children with pervasive developmental disorder not otherwise specified. The researchers discovered that children with autistic disorder had a reduced depth in the sulcal pit of the Sylvian fissure, which is in the Broca area of the brain. **Sulci** are narrow fissures that separate adjacent convolutions of the brain. This cortical abnormality was only observed in children with autistic disorder and was found to be correlated with the social communication impairments that are commonly associated with autism. Postema and colleagues (2021) conducted one of the most extensive studies of 54 international data sets to assess brain asymmetry in autism, compared to a control group. They found significantly altered asymmetries of various brain regions.

Similarly, Persichetti and colleagues (2022) tested the functional laterality across the brain region of individuals with autism and a control group of matched typically developing individuals. They found the typical pattern of left laterality in both groups but found right-hemisphere connectivity in individuals with autism and not typically developing ones. Their findings suggest that the reduced laterality often found in previous studies could result from the unusual left-right symmetry of individuals with autism.

Brain Structure Implications for Autism

Autism is a disorder that results from atypical development of the brain. It is identified by two key behaviors: restricted interests and repetitive behaviors and difficulties in social interactions and communication. These traits are believed to result from changes in how different brain structures are connected. Research studies that utilized magnetic resonance imaging (MRI) have identified certain brain regions, including the **cerebellum**, cerebral cortex, amygdala, dopaminergic pathways, hippocampus, and the corpus callosum—areas that are part of the "**social brain**" (Mapelli et al., 2022)—that are implicated in individuals diagnosed with ASD.

The Cerebellum

The cerebellum (from Latin, little brain), a butterfly-shaped structure located at the base of the skull where the spinal cord connects to the brain, plays an essential role in balance, coordination, and other motor skills. However, technological advances and a growing body of research show that the cerebellum also plays a critical role in cognitive functions (Tiemeier et al., 2010). Currently, the most studied brain structure implicated in autism is the cerebellum (Rogers et al., 2013). Considering that more than 50% of neurons in the brain are in the cerebellum, this brain structure has captured the interest of autism researchers (Sereno et al., 2020). Ongoing research on the role of the cerebellum in autism development has not yielded any clear consensus. Some studies suggest that the cerebellum may play a role in the social and communication deficits seen in autism (Baillieux et al., 2008; Buckner, 2013; Cao et al., 2021). Fatemi and colleagues (2012) found that patients diagnosed with autism or within the autism spectrum show structural and functional abnormalities in the cerebellum. In contrast, other studies suggest that the cerebellum may be more related to motor control and coordination deficits (Bares et al., 2008; Manto et al., 2012).

A meta-analysis of 17 studies found differences in cerebellar structure, namely a decrease in **gray matter**, among individuals with ASD but also in those with ADHD and developmental dyslexia. Further anatomical estimates suggest that different brain regions of the cerebellum affect each disorder (Stoodley, 2014). The cerebellum, which is connected to various brain areas associated with autism, is believed to play a role in the pathophysiology and phenotype of autism spectrum disorder (ASD) due to alterations in its structures and connectivity. Furthermore, **murine models** of autism exhibit the same anatomical alterations that are also commonly found in individuals with autism (Mapelli et al., 2022). In addition to the decrease in gray matter in the cerebellum compared to gray matter in the neurotypical brain, research has found reduced numbers of **Purkinje cells** in the cerebellum of individuals with autism (Fatemi, 2016; Ritvo et al., 1986). Purkinje cells play a vital role in the inhibitory control of neural activity. Thus, the reduction of Purkinje cells can disrupt motor, cognitive, affective, and sensory behaviors (Klein et al., 2016).

The Cerebral Cortex

The cerebral cortex is the brain's outer layer and is responsible for sensory perception, attention, memory, and language functions. The cerebral cortex is the most recently evolved part of the human brain, and the **gyri** (i.e., ridges or bumps) and the sulci (i.e., small grooves) give this four-millimeter outer layer its wrinkled appearance. Some studies have suggested that abnormalities in the cerebral cortex may contribute to the social and communication difficulties that are characteristic of ASD. For example, Gandal and colleagues (2022) examined cortical areas on 112 postmortem samples of individuals with autism and neurotypical controls. They found widespread **transcriptomic (RNA) changes** across the cortex of individuals with autism, affecting **excitatory neurons** and glia in the visual cortex. One study conducted with 112 three-year-old boys and 50 non-autistic boys found that cortical surface area (not cortical thickness) was significantly greater in the autistic group compared to the non-autistic one (Ohta et al., 2016).

There is evidence that abnormality in the **orbitofrontal cortex** (OFC) plays a role in the social and communication difficulties that are characteristic of autism. Structural and functional differences in the cerebral cortex have been identified in individuals with autism. For instance, Girgis and colleagues (2007) found a reduction in gray matter in the right lateral OFC in a group of autistic children, a finding that is not present in neurotypical controls. Cortical thickness has been the most reliable measurable factor for evaluating abnormal brain structures in patients with autism. Alterations in the cortical thickness in the **frontal**, **parietal**, **occipital**, and **temporal** lobes have been found in individuals with autism. Those alterations often relate to specific clinical symptoms autistic individuals exhibit (Ong et al., 2023).

The Amygdala

The **amygdala** is a crucial part of the brain for processing emotions such as fear and anxiety. Studies have indicated that people with autism have differences in the size and functioning of the amygdala when compared to individuals without autism (Schumann et al., 2004). Therefore, researchers have linked the social and emotional challenges experienced by people with autism to variations in the structure and function of the amygdala. One **longitudinal study** examined 45 autistic boys and 25 non-autistic ones to determine whether amygdala growth is disproportionate to overall brain growth. Amygdala volumes and total brain volumes were evaluated in years one and two. Although the amygdala was larger in autistic children when evaluated both times, its size grew faster and was bigger at time two compared to that of non-autistic children (Nordahl et al., 2012). Amygdala hyperactivity and reduced connectivity have been associated with externalizing and disruptive behavior in autistic children (Ibrahim et al., 2019).

The Dopamine Pathways

Dopamine pathways are neural connections in areas of the brain and body where dopamine travels to carry important information. **Dopamine** plays a role in various brain functions, including motivation and reward. Some research suggests that the brains of people with autism may process dopamine differently than neurotypical ones, contributing to the social and behavioral symptoms that are associated with the condition. The dopaminergic system has long been suspected to contribute to motor abnormalities in individuals with autism (Damasio & Maurer, 1978). Kosillo and Bateup (2021) conducted a study on genetic **mouse models** of **syndromic autism**. They aimed to investigate whether dysregulation of dopaminergic pathways can contribute to the behavioral manifestations of autism, such as motor stereotypies, changes in sensorimotor processing, and altered values of social stimuli. The study found considerable evidence suggesting that the dopaminergic system may be dysregulated in syndromic autism.

The Hippocampus

The hippocampus is a brain structure within the temporal lobes. It plays a vital role in learning (Izquierdo, 1975), memory and cognitive map creation (Lisman et al., 2017), emotion regulation (Fetterhoff et al., 2024), and language ability (Covington & Duff, 2016). Damage to the **hippocampus** can result in various neurological and psychiatric disorders (Anand & Dhikav, 2012). Changes in hippocampal structures have been widely reported in autism studies (e.g., Arutiunian et al., 2023; Long et al., 2024). Banker and colleagues (2021) emphasized the significance of the hippocampus and how its dysfunction can lead to autism-related impairments in social interaction, memory, and spatial reasoning. These deficits are more likely to occur when the hippocampus is undergoing developmental strides in infancy, when its dysfunction can coincide with the emergence of autism symptoms.

The Corpus Callosum

The corpus callosum is the most prominent bundle of white matter fibers connecting the brain's two hemispheres. The corpus callosum is "the super-highway of neurons connecting the halves of the brain" (Gazzaniga, 1998, p. 50). It facilitates communication between the two brain hemispheres, enabling them to collaborate and share information. This connection is crucial for various cognitive processes, including language, memory, and perception. Some studies have suggested that there may be differences in the size or structure of the corpus callosum in individuals with autism compared to those without the condition (Egaas et al., 1995; Hardan et al., 2009). One of the most consistently observed structural findings in autism is increased brain volume, including gray and white matter structures, contrasting with a reduced corpus callosum volume (Brambilla et al., 2003). Wolff and colleagues (2015) found a thicker and significantly increased corpus callosum area in children with autism spectrum disorder starting at 6 months. These differences were particularly robust in the anterior corpus callosum. Thus, the structural difference of the corpus callosum is thought to contribute to communication difficulties and other deficits associated with autism.

Agenesis of the corpus callosum (AgCC) is a congenital brain condition in which a person has a missing or partially missing corpus callosum. Lau and colleagues (2013) used the Autism Spectrum Quotient (ASQ) on an AgCC cohort to investigate the association of the condition with the occurrence of autism. They found that the ASQ scores of 45%, 35%, and 18% of children, adolescents, and adults, respectively, exceeded the predetermined threshold scores for autism. One study found that approximately one-third of adults with agenesis of the corpus callosum exhibit an autistic behavior profile, while another third display social and communication impairments (Paul et al., 2014). Although individuals with AgCC have average intelligence, they have communication deficits and difficulties understanding nonliteral language and recognizing and interpreting proverbs (Paul et al., 2003).

Studies have discovered that AgCC can cause variations in the brain's neural connections or **connectome**, which may contribute to autism. For instance, Owen and colleagues (2013) examined the structural connectivity of AgCC in contrast to typical human brains. They found an abnormal decrease in global connectivity but an increase in local connectivity in the brain. Autism researchers have also investigated diverse ways in which the corpus callosum is associated with autism. For example, one study compared the corpus callosum volume and sex difference between children with autism and a control group of neurotypical children. The study found that the corpus callosum volumes were significantly larger in children with autism than those without the condition, owing to axonal overgrowth and pruning irregularities. The study also found that the corpus callosum volumes were substantially larger in autistic females than in autistic males (Zhang et al., 2023). Additionally, a longitudinal study examined the corpus callosum's structural trajectory past early childhood in two groups: one with autism and another without autism. The corpus callosum typically undergoes protracted development from childhood to young adulthood. However, the group with autism showed an atypical **developmental trajectory** starting as early as 10 years (Travers et al., 2015).

The Pineal Gland

The pineal gland is a small endocrine gland located in the epithalamus. It produces melatonin, a hormone that regulates sleep-wake cycles and the circadian rhythm (Shomrat & Nesher, 2019). The amount of melatonin released is directly proportional to the size of the pineal gland (Görgülü & Koç, 2021). Due to its role in releasing melatonin when it gets dark (Booth, 1987), the pineal gland is sometimes called the "third eye" in certain cultures and spiritual practices. However, exposure to blue light emitted by electronic devices can interfere with the amount of melatonin released, thus affecting our ability to fall asleep.

Sleep difficulties are common in individuals with autism, and this has piqued the interest of researchers studying the pineal gland and its relationship with the disorder. There is growing evidence suggesting that the pineal gland/melatonin system may play a role in the development of ASD (Wu et al., 2020). Studies investigating the link between melatonin and autism, however, have yielded mixed results. Some studies have found low levels of melatonin in individuals with autism, which could potentially contribute to their sleep difficulties. However, others have found no differences in melatonin levels between individuals with autism and control groups of individuals without the condition.

Consistent with numerous studies linking the pineal gland and melatonin secretion levels to autism and concomitant sleep disturbances, Rossignol and Fryer (2011) conducted a meta-analysis of 35 studies to investigate autism-related melatonin findings. They found that Melatonin Supplements can help regulate the sleep-wake cycle and improve sleep quality, with minimal side effects and better daytime behavior. In addition to treating sleep disturbances, there is a growing body of literature suggesting that melatonin may have a positive effect on various mental and physical health problems that are commonly associated with ASD, including anxiety, pain and sensory processing, and gastrointestinal issues (Gagnon & Godbout, 2018).

Birth Weight

Newborns at gestational age weigh between 5.5 and 8.75 pounds, which is appropriate. Typically, newborns weigh on average 7–7.5 pounds (Sigelman & Rider, 2022). Newborns weighing less than 5.5 pounds are considered small for gestational age (SGA), whereas those weighing more than 8.75 pounds are considered large for gestational age (LGA). Weighing less than 5.5 pounds is associated with various short- and long-term consequences, including infectious diseases, developmental delays, and death during infancy and childhood (World Health Organization, 2014). Several factors influence the birth weight of newborns. They include the sex and gestational age of the infant and the maternal weight gain during pregnancy (Love & Kinch, 1965). Other factors (e.g., genetics—the size of the parents, maternal health and nutrition, alcohol consumption and smoking during pregnancy, high blood pressure, gestational diabetes, and multiple pregnancies) can affect the weight of the baby.

Birth Weight and Autism

Birth weight is an important factor in determining a child's health and development. Newborns weighing less than 5.5 pounds are considered low birth weight (LBW). Many studies have examined the relationship between autism and birth weight. LBW has been found to be an environmental risk factor for autism. Song and colleagues (2022) conducted a retrospective cohort study using the Korean National Health Insurance claims data. LBW infants were associated with having ADHD. Similarly, infants who were born with SGA had an increased risk of having ASD. Fetal growth that deviates significantly from the average for gestational age is associated with ASD (Whitehouse, 2013).

One prospective study investigated the association between fetal growth, gestational age, and autism in a large population study of more than 40,000 children in Sweden. The researchers found that deviance in fetal growth (i.e., either exceedingly small or very large) is a risk factor for developing ASD. Babies who were born weighing over 4.5 kg (or 9.14 pounds) and those weighing less than 2.5 kg (or 5.5 pounds) showed a higher incidence of autism regardless of whether they were born preterm or post-term (Abel et al., 2013).

Babies that are born prematurely (less than 37 weeks gestation) typically weigh less than 5.5 pounds. They have a 30% increased risk of developing ASD compared to those born full-term (Wang et al., 2017). Similarly, a national cohort study was conducted with more than four million babies born in Sweden during 1973–2013; it included those that were extremely preterm, significantly to moderate preterm, early preterm, and full preterm. Babies who were born preterm and early term had an increased risk of ASD (Crump & Sundquist, 2021). Despite advances in medical technology and practices, up to 5–10% of babies are born after the typical 40-week gestational period. Post-term births are also associated with an increased risk of ASD (Jenabi et al., 2023).

Primitive and Survival Reflexes

Newborns are not passive receptacles of environmental stimulation. Their sensory systems function at birth: They can hear, smell, taste, feel, and see (although without any visual acuity). Newborns come equipped with a set of primitive and **survival reflexes**. Reflexes are unlearned and involuntary responses to environmental stimuli (e.g., startle reaction to a loud sound) that can be varied and complex behavioral patterns that allow infants to interact with the natural environment. Reflexes (primitive or survival) inform us that infants' nervous systems are functioning.

Survival reflexes (e.g., the breathing reflex, the sucking reflex, the swallowing reflex, and the pupillary reflex) persist throughout the lifespan and have clear adaptive value. By contrast, **primitive reflexes** (e.g., the **moro reflex**, grasping reflex, swimming reflex, stepping reflex, asymmetrical **tonic neck reflex**, symmetrical tonic neck reflex, and **tonic labyrinthine reflex**) are either present at birth or emerge in early infancy (Futagi et al., 2009). Primitive reflexes are directed from the **brain stem** and are essential for neonates' survival in the first weeks of life (Goddard, 1995). Their primary function is to allow infants to react to the environment in adaptive ways that ultimately lead to the maturation of the motor system (Pecuch et al., 2021). Primitive reflexes are precursors of adaptive voluntary behaviors that develop in late infancy. However, when they persist beyond infancy, they may indicate infants' potential neurological problems, such as something awry with the nervous system.

Primitive Reflexes and Autism

The process of motor development depends on the inhibition of several primitive reflexes whose persistence can alter the developmental trajectory of gross and **fine motor skills** (Chinello et al., 2018). During the first year of typical development, brain stem reflex responses give way to voluntary responses controlled by the mature central nervous system. Primitive reflexes gradually disappear during the first year, indicating that the nervous system develops typically. Infants' interaction with their environment gradually leads to the development of the higher centers of the cerebral cortex, making voluntary motor behaviors possible (Sigelman & Rider, 2022). However, the retention of the primitive reflexes can disrupt typical development even in healthy preschoolers and lead to social and educational difficulties (Gieysztor et al., 2018), and negatively affect cognitive and motor functions that can influence the emergence of autism (Melillo et al., 2022).

The presence of retained primitive reflexes has been observed as a common feature of children with autism (Nagai et al., 2024). Their persistence beyond infancy could indicate compromised neurology, which may interfere with motor development and learning (Sigafoos et al., 2021) and can play a role in the emergence of autistic behavior (Anderson, 2008). Children with autism often have various motor difficulties, ranging from problems with handwriting to atypical gait (Bhat, 2020) and motoric difficulty that can contribute to social impairments (Bhat et al., 2011). Consequently, they may be reluctant to engage others, thus limiting their social interaction and ability to participate in social activities and learn necessary skills.

Assessing Primitive Reflexes Retention

The activity and integration of the primitive reflexes in the first year contributes to healthy psychomotor development. However, their persistence beyond infancy can lead to learning difficulties (e.g., reading, writing, dyslexia) and coordination deficits. The assessment of primitive reflexes can be helpful in the early detection of infants at risk for neurodevelopmental disorders (Futagi et al., 2009).

Pecuch and colleagues (2021) assessed the presence of three primitive reflexes (i.e., asymmetric tonic reflex, symmetric tonic reflex, and labyrinthine reflex). They found that the presence and activity of these reflexes in childhood resulted in "lower levels of motor efficiency." Similarly, de Bildt and colleagues (2012) examined the presence of the visual rooting reflex (VRR). The rooting reflex (i.e., an infant's involuntary muscle response to mouth stimulation or visual stimulation near the face) has interested neurologists and psychologists. Bildt et al. found that the VRR, in addition to the persistence of the reflex being present in most individuals with autism, was associated with lower IQ and adaptive functioning. Accardo and Barrow (2015) assessed the relationship between toe walking and retainment of the labyrinthine reflex in 61 children diagnosed with autism. Those with abnormal tonic labyrinthine reflexes had moderate to high levels of toe walking, a condition also associated with language disorders (Accardo & Whitman, 1989). Minderaa and colleagues (1985) assessed eight reflexes (i.e., snout, sucking, visual routing, tactile routing, grasp, palmomental, glabellar, and **nucho-cephalic**) in a sample of children and young adults with and without autism. They reported an association between the persistence of the snout and visual rooting reflexes and speech and language deficits in participants with autism.

In sum, primitive reflexes are mediated by the brain stem and consist of involuntary motor responses that begin in *utero* and are present at birth in full-term infants. Primitive reflexes serve adaptive functions, help mediate optimal development, and ensure infants' survival in the neonatal period. However, retained survival reflexes beyond infancy have been associated with various developmental disorders, including attention-deficit/hyperactivity disorder and autism, and, as a result, can derail expected developmental trajectories.

Motor Control

Motor control is essential for daily activities such as walking, grasping, and engaging in sports. It is a complex process guided by the nervous system (i.e., the brain, spinal cord, and peripheral nerves), which integrates sensory information and coordinates and controls body movements (Paulin, 1993). Motor control refers to consciously initiating, directing, and executing voluntary movements with a specific purpose. The motor cortex, located in the frontal lobe, generates signals to direct body movement. The cerebellum is responsible for fine motor movement, determining limb position, balance, and fine-tuning movement. The motor control process develops from infancy and continues through toddlerhood and further into childhood. Motor control encompasses both fine motor and gross motor skills. Fine motor skills involve the coordination of small muscles, such as the hands and fingers, while gross motor skills involve the coordination of larger muscles, such as those in the legs and arms.

Motor Control and Autism

Poor motor control is common among individuals with autism. Children aged 12–60 months with autism had significant motor delays compared to typically developing children. These delays became more prominent with age (Mohd et al., 2021). Studies have shown abnormalities in various brain structures, including the cerebellum, which coordinates movement and balance (Paulin, 1993), and the **basal ganglia**, which helps motor planning and execution (Lanciego et al., 2012). Additionally, studies have found reduced connectivity between the cerebellum and other brain structures (e.g., the motor cortex) associated with motor control (Daskalakis et al., 2004). Motor control problems are not unique to people with autism. People with other conditions, including Down syndrome and cerebral palsy, also experience these difficulties. Consequently, motor control difficulty is not considered a core characteristic of autism but is prevalent in autistic individuals. It is estimated that 87% of individuals with autism experience challenges with their motor skills (Bhat, 2020).

Various motor impairments are present in children and adults with ASDs, specifically gross motor, fine motor, postural control, and difficulty performing purposeful movements or actions. It is important to address motor impairments through timely assessments and effective interventions, as motor delays within the first two years of life can contribute to the social impairments of children with ASDs (Bhat et al., 2011). It is common for young infants to lack control of their head movements, which is also known as **head lag**. However, if this condition continues beyond 6 months, it could be a sign of a neurological disorder or a developmental delay. One study has shown that high-risk infants with autism who experience head lag are significantly more likely to develop autism compared to low-risk infants (Flanagan et al., 2012). Treatments for children with autism who experience motor control difficulties usually involve physical and occupational therapy. Unfortunately, only 32% of autistic children receive treatment for their motor control difficulties (Bhat, 2020).

Motor development can also provide children with new learning opportunities to engage with their environment. Developing gross and fine motor skills can predict later language proficiency during early childhood and beyond (Gonzalez et al., 2019). Motor skills played a significant role in predicting handwriting performance in children with autism. They perform worse on handwriting tasks than a control group matched for age and intelligence without autism (Fuentes et al., 2009). One study found associations between early oral and manual motor skills and later speech fluency. These findings have implications for understanding communication in those with autism (Gernsbacher et al., 2008).

In sum, motor control refers to the ability to perform and coordinate movements smoothly and accurately. Children with autism often experience motor control difficulties, making it challenging to perform daily activities and interact with others. Multiple brain structures are involved in motor control.

Unfortunately, many children with autism who struggle with motor control do not receive appropriate treatment. Occupational and physical therapy can improve motor skills and enhance social and communication abilities.

Autism and Stereotypies

Restricted and repetitive behaviors are one of the core symptoms of autism (APA, 2013). Many individuals with autism engage in **stereotyped behavior** (aka stereotypies or **stimming**). These semi-voluntary repetitive movements (e.g., rocking back and forth, twirling, hand-flapping) are one of the defining characteristics of autism. People on the autism spectrum describe them as "relaxing" and helpful in allowing them to reduce distractions and sensory overstimulation (McCarthy & Brumback, 2021). Adults on the autism spectrum reported "stimming" as a coping and adaptive mechanism that helps them communicate intense emotions. Therefore, they do not support efforts to treat or eliminate these behaviors (Kapp et al., 2019).

Self-stimulatory behaviors are not unique to children on the autism spectrum. They can also be observed in **neurotypical** children (Harris et al., 2008; Miller et al., 2006; Smith & Van Houten, 1996). Similarly, neurotypical adults do "fidget" sometimes when, for example, they jiggle their legs, solve a complex math problem, fiddle with a pen during a boring meeting, or pace the floor incessantly when anxious. Should individuals with autism be discouraged from stimming?

Stereotypies can also take various forms, including **self-injurious behavior** (e.g., hand-biting, head-banging). In such a case, preventing instances of such behavior is desirable. Stereotypies (e.g., flicking one's fingers in front of one's eyes in a classroom) can also interfere with a child's ability to acquire necessary skills (Tereshko et al., 2021). There are two categories of motor stereotypies: primary and secondary. Primary motor stereotypies can occur in typically developing children. Primary motor stereotypies tend to remain stable or more likely disappear with time when children interact with others and are more aware of their social surroundings. Secondary motor stereotypies occur more readily among children who have a developmental condition (e.g., autism, intellectual disabilities) or impaired vision or hearing than among neurotypicals. The frequency of self-injurious behavior is more prevalent in secondary motor stereotypies than in primary motor stereotypies (Péter et al., 2017).

Causes of Stereotypies

Autism pioneers Kanner (1943) and Asperger (1991 [1944]) posited that stereotypies are self-stimulatory behaviors that shut away environmental stimuli and thus disrupt focus and attention. Lovaas and colleagues (1987) thought that self-stimulatory behaviors are automatically maintained by the consequences they produce. Other research, however, suggested that stereotypies in autism result from a faulty modulation of sensory input, namely a dysfunction of connections in the vestibular system with the cerebellum and the brain stem (Ornitz, 1974), leading to sensory processing dysfunctions. One more recent theory proposed that **brain oscillations** in the motor, auditory, and visual regions cause individuals with autism to engage in stereotypies to generate electrical signals that can regulate abnormal brain activity and improve sensory functioning (McCarthy & Brumback, 2021).

Treatment for Stereotypies

Various pharmacological treatments are currently available to treat motor stereotypies and associated self-injurious behaviors in autism. Antipsychotics (e.g., Risperidone, Aripiprazole, and others), selective serotonin reuptake inhibitors (SSRIs), and serotonin and **norepinephrine** reuptake inhibitors (e.g., Fluoxetine, Sertraline, and others) when prescribed are minimally effective in reducing stereotypic motor behaviors and result in sometimes profound side effects (Doyle & McDougle, 2012). Even when these medications were used longitudinally with typically developing children who exhibited motor stereotypies, the frequency, duration, and intensity of stereotypic behaviors were not significantly reduced (Harris et al., 2008).

Can behavioral interventions be effective in reducing stereotypies in autism when engaging in such behaviors interferes with engaging in academic tasks or desirable social interactions? Cunningham and Schreibman (2008) argued for the importance of differentiating between self-stimulatory and motor control stereotypies as they can be maintained by automatic sensory and socially mediated consequences. Therefore, interventions to reduce self-stimulatory behavior and motor stereotypies should first determine the function(s) they serve. There is empirical support for behavioral therapies (e.g., habit reversal and **differential reinforcement** of other behavior) for reducing complex motor stereotypies in non-autistic children (Miller et al., 2006). Can the same procedures be as effective with children on the autism spectrum? Akers and colleagues (2020) reviewed and evaluated 109 studies that used behavioral interventions to reduce motor stereotypy among autistic individuals. They found that altering the environment during intervention sessions by reinforcing competing responses reduced motor stereotypies significantly.

In sum, self-stimulatory behaviors are not unique to individuals on the autism spectrum or diagnosed with other disabilities. Neurotypicals also engage in such behaviors, which may serve different functions. Pharmacological interventions have not been effective in reducing self-stimulatory behavior. In contrast, behavior interventions, including environmental manipulation and reinforcing more "socially desirable responses" can be effective in decreasing self-stimulatory behaviors in typical individuals and those diagnosed with an **intellectual disability**.

Handedness and Autism

Handedness refers to an individual's preference to use one hand (the dominant one) instead of the other (the non-dominant hand). Approximately 90% of the human population is right-hand dominant compared to about 10% of left-handers (Papadatou-Pastou et al., 2020; Scharoun & Bryden, 2014). Ambidexterity (equal preference for either hand) and mixed-handedness (cross-dominant) are rare and occur in only 1% of the population. Human hand preference emerges early during gestational age when fetuses show a preference for right thumb-sucking (Francks, 2019), a preference for head turning to the right rather than to the left, and a predisposition for the right hand in their grasp reflex (Johnson & de Haan, 2015). Brain lateralization plays a role in handedness and language. Most right-handed people have left-hemisphere dominance for language, while left-handed individuals may have more evenly distributed language functions between the two hemispheres.

Individuals with autism have been found to have a higher prevalence of atypical handedness (i.e., left-, mixed-, or non-righthandedness) compared to typically developing individuals. This elevated occurrence of atypical handedness in individuals with ASD may be linked to differences in cerebral structure and language lateralization (Markou et al., 2017; Rysstad & Pedersen, 2016). One study examined handedness (assessed by performance on standardized receptive and expressive language tests) in children with autism, compared to typically developed controls. Participants with autism had lower handedness scores than those in the control group. Interestingly, right-handers in the autistic group had better language performance than their counterparts, non-right-handers (Knaus et al., 2016).

Summary

Physical development begins before birth and follows a systematic sequence of changes and continuities that occur at predictable times. Physical development is influenced by numerous factors, including genetics, lifestyles, aging, and diverse environmental interactions. The brain plays a vital role in physical development, as it controls and coordinates various bodily functions such as reflexes, movement, and balance. Although the underlying causes of autism are not fully understood, research has indicated atypicality in brain development and connectivity. At birth, a baby's brain has an estimated 100 billion neurons, but there are only a few connections among them. Sensory experiences and environmental interactions promote the formation of synapses and cortical networks, shaping brain connectivity and function.

Gestational age plays a crucial role in prenatal development and has implications for various health outcomes, including the risk of autism. Babies born prematurely or with low birth weight face an increased likelihood of autism due to disruptions in prenatal brain development. Neurogenesis, brain myelination, and brain lateralization are important brain processes that, if disrupted, can contribute to neurodevelopmental disorders such as autism. Research studies that used magnetic resonance imaging (MRI) have found certain brain regions, including the cerebellum, cerebral cortex, amygdala, dopaminergic pathways, hippocampus, and corpus callosum, are implicated in individuals diagnosed with autism.

Low birth weight and high birth weight have been linked to autism. Similarly, retained survival reflexes beyond infancy have been associated with various developmental disorders, including attention deficit hyperactivity disorder and autism, and, as a result, can derail expected developmental trajectories. As for motor control, children aged 12–60 months with autism had significant motor delays compared to typically developing children. These delays became more prominent with age. Stereotypies and atypical handedness are also common in individuals with autism.

Questions to Ponder for Further Thinking and Learning

1 How does autism affect gross motor skills development?
2 How does sensory processing disorder impact physical development in children with autism?
3 What are the effects of medication use on physical development in children with autism?
4 How do comorbidities such as ADHD and anxiety impact physical development in children with autism?
5 How can parents and caregivers promote physical development in children with autism?
6 What are the common sleep disorders that children with autism experience, and how do they impact physical development?
7 What are the common fine motor skill difficulties associated with autism?
8 Are there any studies on the relationship between physical fitness and autistic symptoms?
9 What are the common fine motor skill difficulties associated with autism?
10 Can physical therapy help children with autism improve their motor skills?

References

Abel, K. M., Dalman, C., Svensson, A. C., Susser, E., Dal, H., Idring, S., … Magnusson, C. (2013). Deviance in fetal growth and risk of autism spectrum disorder. *The American Journal of Psychiatry, 170*(4), 391–398.

Accardo, P. J., & Barrow, W. (2015). Toe walking in autism: Further observations. *Journal of Child Neurology, 30*(5), 606–609.

Accardo, P. J., & Whitman, B. (1989). Toe walking: A marker for language disorders in the developmentally disabled. *Clinical Pediatrics, 28*(8), 347–350.

Akers, J. S., Davis, T. N., Gerow, S., & Avery, S. (2020). Decreasing motor stereotypy in individuals with autism spectrum disorder: A systematic review. *Research in Autism Spectrum Disorders, 77,* 101611.

Anand, K. S., & Dhikav, V. (2012). Hippocampus in health and disease: An overview. *Annals of Indian Academy of Neurology, 15*(4), 239–246.

Anderson, G. M. (2008). The potential role for emergence in autism. *Autism Research, 1*(1), 18–30.

APA (2013). *Diagnostic and statistical manual of mental disorders: DSM-5* (5th ed.). American Psychiatric Association.

Arutiunian, V., Davydova, E., Pereverzeva, D., Sorokin, A., Tyushkevich, S., Mamokhina, U., ... Dragoy, O. (2023). Reduced grey matter volume of amygdala and hippocampus is associated with the severity of autistic symptoms and language abilities in school-aged children with autism spectrum disorder: An exploratory study. *Brain Structure & Function, 228*(6), 1573–1579.

Asperger, H. (1991[1944]). 'Autistic psychopathy' in childhood. In U. Frith (Ed. & Trans.), *Autism and Asperger syndrome* (pp. 37–92). Cambridge University Press.

Azevedo, F. A., Carvalho, L. R, Grinberg, L. T., Farfel, J. M., Ferretti, R. E., Leite, R. E., ...Herculano-Houzel, S. (2009). Equal numbers of neuronal and nonneuronal cells make the human brain an isometrically scaled-up primate brain. *Journal of Comparative Neurology, 513*(5), 532–541.

Baillieux, H., De Smet, H. J., Paquier, P. F., De Deyn, P. P., & Mariën, P. (2008). Cerebellar neurocognition: Insights into the bottom of the brain. *Clinical Neurology and Neurosurgery, 110*(8), 763–773.

Banker, S. M., Gu, X., Schiller, D., & Foss-Feig, J. H. (2021). Hippocampal contributions to social and cognitive deficits in autism spectrum disorder. *Trends in Neurosciences, 44*(10), 793–807.

Bares, M., Lungu, O. V., Husárová, I., & Gescheidt, T. (2010). Predictive motor timing performance dissociates between early diseases of the cerebellum and Parkinson's disease. *Cerebellum, 9*(1), 124–135.

Belmonte, M. K., Allen, G., Beckel-Mitchener, A., Boulanger, L. M., Carper, R. A., & Webb, S. J. (2004). Autism and abnormal development of brain connectivity. *The Journal of Neuroscience, 24*(42), 9228–9231.

Bhat, A. N. (2020). Is motor impairment in autism spectrum disorder distinct from developmental coordination disorder? A report from the SPARK study. *Physical Therapy, 100*(4), 633–644.

Bhat, A. N., Landa, R. J., & Galloway, J. C. (2011). Current perspectives on motor functioning in infants, children, and adults with autism spectrum disorders. *Physical Therapy, 91*(7), 1116–1129.

Booth, F. M. (1987). The human pineal gland: A review of the "third eye" and the effect of light. *Australian and New Zealand Journal of Ophthalmology, 15*(4), 329–336.

Bouyssi-Kobar, M., du Plessis, A. J., McCarter, R., Brossard-Racine, M., Murnick, J., Tinkleman, L., ... Limperopoulos, C. (2016). Third trimester brain growth in preterm infants compared with in utero healthy fetuses. *Pediatrics, 138*(5), e20161640.

Bradl, M., & Lassmann, H. (2010). Oligodendrocytes: Biology and pathology. *Acta Neuropathologica, 119*(1), 37–53.

Brambilla, P., Hardan, A., di Nemi, S. U., Perez, J., Soares, J. C., & Barale, F. (2003). Brain anatomy and development in autism: Review of structural MRI studies. *Brain Research Bulletin, 61*(6), 557–569.

Brun, L., Auzias, G., Viellard, M., Villeneuve, N., Girard, N., Poinso, F., ... Deruelle, C. (2016). Localized misfolding within Broca's area as a distinctive feature of autistic disorder. *Biological Psychiatry: Cognitive Neuroscience and Neuroimaging, 1*(2), 160–168.

Buckner, R. L. (2013). The cerebellum and cognitive function: 25 years of insight from anatomy and neuroimaging. *Neuron, 80*(3), 807–815.

Cao, S., Nie, J., Zhang, J., Chen, C., Wang, X., Liu, Y., …Wang, K. (2021). The cerebellum is related to cognitive dysfunction in white matter hyperintensities. *Frontiers in Aging Neuroscience, 13,* 670463.

CDC (2022). CDC's Developmental milestones. https://www.cdc.gov/ncbddd/actearly/milestones/index.html. Accessed on January 20, 2024.

Chen, B., Linke, A., Olson, L., Kohli, J., Kinnear, M., Sereno, M., … Fishman, I. (2022). Cortical myelination in toddlers and preschoolers with autism spectrum disorder. *Developmental Neurobiology, 82*(3), 261–274.

Chinello, A., Di Gangi, V., & Valenza, E. (2018). Persistent primary reflexes affect motor acts: Potential implications for autism spectrum disorder. *Research in Developmental Disabilities, 83,* 287–295.

Courchesne, E., Carper, R., & Akshoomoff, N. (2003). Evidence of brain overgrowth in the first year of life in autism. *The Journal of the American Medical Association, 290*(3), 337–344.

Courchesne, E., Gazestani, V. H., & Lewis, N. E. (2020). Prenatal origins of ASD: The when, what, and how of ASD development. *Trends in Neuroscience, 4*(5), 326–342.

Courchesne, E., Mouton, P. R., Calhoun, M. E., Semendeferi, K., Ahrens-Barbeau, C., Hallet, M. J., … Pierce, K. (2011). Neuron number and size in prefrontal cortex of children with autism. *The Journal of the American Medical Association, 306*(18), 2001–2010.

Covington, N. V., & Duff, M. C. (2016). Expanding the language network: Direct contributions from the hippocampus. *Trends in Cognitive Sciences, 20*(12), 869–870.

Crump, C., Sundquist, J., & Sundquist, K. (2021). Preterm or early term birth and risk of autism. *Pediatrics, 148*(3), e2020032300.

Cunningham, A. B., & Schreibman, L. (2008). Stereotypy in autism: The importance of function. *Research in Autism Spectrum Disorders, 2*(3), 469–479.

Damasio, A. R., & Maurer, R. G. (1978). A neurological model for childhood autism. *Archives of Neurology, 35*(12), 777–786.

Daskalakis, Z. J., Paradiso, G. O., Christensen, B. K., Fitzgerald, P. B., Gunraj, C., & Chen, R. (2004). Exploring the connectivity between the cerebellum and motor cortex in humans. *The Journal of Physiology, 557*(Pt 2), 689–700.

de Bildt, A., Mulder, E. J., Van Lang, N. D., de With, S. A., Minderaa, R. B., Stahl, S. S., & Anderson, G. M. (2012). The visual rooting reflex in individuals with autism spectrum disorders and co-occurring intellectual disability. *Autism Research, 5*(1), 67–72.

Deemyad, T. (2022). Lateralized changes in language associated auditory and somatosensory cortices in autism. *Frontiers in Systems Neuroscience, 16,* 787448.

Doyle, C. A., & McDougle, C. J. (2012). Pharmacologic treatments for the behavioral symptoms associated with autism spectrum disorders across the lifespan. *Dialogues in Clinical Neuroscience, 14*(3), 263–279.

Egaas, B., Courchesne, E., & Saitoh, O. (1995). Reduced size of the corpus callosum in autism. *Archives of Neurology, 52*(8), 794–801.

Fatemi, S. H., Aldinger, K. A., Ashwood, P., Bauman, M. L., Blaha, C. D., Blatt, G. J., … Welsh, J. P. (2012). Consensus paper: Pathological role of the cerebellum in autism. *Cerebellum, 11*(3), 777–807.

Fatemi, S. H. (2016). Cerebella pathology in autism. In D. L. Gruol, N. Koibuchi, M. Manto, M. Molinari, J. D. Schmahmann, & Y. Shen (Eds.), *Essentials of cerebellum and cerebellar disorders* (pp. 539–543). Springer International.

Fetterhoff, D., Costa, M., Hellerstedt, R., Johannessen, R., Imbach, L., Sarnthein, J., & Strange, B. A. (2024). Neuronal population representation of human emotional memory. *Cell Reports, 43*(4), 114071.

Flanagan, J. E., Landa, R., Bhat, A., & Bauman, M. (2012). Head lag in infants at risk for autism: A preliminary study. *American Journal of Occupational Therapy, 66*(5), 577–585.

Francks, C. (2019). The genetic bases of brain lateralization. In P. Hagoort (Ed.), *Human language: From genes and brain to behavior* (pp. 595–608). MIT Press.

Fuentes, C. T., Mostofsky, S. H., & Bastian, A. J. (2009). Children with autism show specific handwriting impairments. *Neurology, 73*(19), 1532–1537.

Futagi, Y., Toribe, Y., & Suzuki, Y. (2009). Neurological assessment of early infants. *Current Pediatric Reviews, 5*(2), 65–70.

Gagnon, K., & Godbout, R. (2018). Melatonin and comorbidities in children with autism spectrum disorder. *Current Developmental Disorder Reports, 5*(3), 197–206.

Galvez-Contreras, A. Y., Zarate-Lopez, D., Torres-Chavez, A. L., & Gonzalez-Perez, O. (2020). Role of oligodendrocytes and myelin in the pathophysiology of autism spectrum disorder. *Brain Sciences, 10*(12), 951.

Gandal, M. J., Haney, J. R., Wamsley, B., Yap, C. X., Parhami, S., Emani, P. S., ... Geschwind, D. H. (2022). Broad transcriptomic dysregulation occurs across the cerebral cortex in ASD. *Nature, 611*(7936), 532–539.

Gazzaniga, M. S. (1998). The split brain revisited. *Scientific American, 279*(1), 50–55.

Gernsbacher, M. A., Sauer, E. A., Geye, H. M., Schweigert, E. K., & Hill, G. H. (2008). Infant and toddler oral- and manual-motor skills predict later speech fluency in autism. *Journal of Child Psychology and Psychiatry, 49*(1), 43–50.

Gieysztor, E. Z., Choińska, A. M., & Paprocka-Borowicz, M. (2018). Persistence of primitive reflexes and associated motor problems in healthy preschool children. *Archives of Medical Sciences, 14*(1), 167–173.

Gilbert, J., & Man, H. Y. (2017). Fundamental elements in autism: From neurogenesis and neurite growth to synaptic plasticity. *Frontiers in Cellular Neuroscience, 11*, 359.

Girgis, R. R., Minshew, N. J., Melhem, N. M., Nutche, J. J., Keshavan, M. S., & Hardan, A. Y. (2007). Volumetric alterations of the orbitofrontal cortex in autism. *Progress in Neuro-Psychopharmacology & Biological Psychiatry, 31*(1), 41–45.

Goddard, S. (1995). The role of primitive reflexes in the development of the visual system. *Journal of Behavioral Optometry, 6*(2), 31–35.

Gonzalez, S. L., Alvarez, V., & Nelson, E. L. (2019). Do gross and fine motor skills differentially contribute to language outcomes? A systematic review. *Frontiers in Psychology, 10*, 2670.

Görgülü, F. F., & Koç, A. S. (2021). Is there any relationship between autism and pineal gland volume? *Polish Journal of Radiology, 86*, e225–e231.

Gotts, S. J., Jo, H. J., Wallace, G. L., Saad, Z. S., Cox, R. W., & Martin, A. (2013). Two distinct forms of functional lateralization in the human brain. *Proceedings of the National Academy of Sciences of the United States of America, 110*(36), E3435–E3444.

Graciarena, M., Seiffe, A., Nait-Oumesmar, B., & Depino, A. M. (2019). Hypomyelination and oligodendroglial alterations in a mouse model of autism spectrum disorder. *Frontiers in Cellular Neuroscience, 12*, 517.

Ha, S., Sohn, I. J., Kim, N., Sim, H. J., & Cheon, K. A. (2015). Characteristics of brains in autism spectrum disorder: Structure, function and connectivity across the lifespan. *Experimental Neurobiology, 24*(4), 273–284.

Hardan, A. Y., Pabalan, M., Gupta, N., Bansal, R., Melhem, N. M., Fedorov, S., ... Minshew, N. J. (2009). Corpus callosum volume in children with autism. *Psychiatry Research, 174*(1), 57–61.

Harris, K. M., Mahone, E. M., & Singer, H. S. (2008). Nonautistic motor stereotypies: Clinical features and longitudinal follow-up. *Pediatric Neurology, 38*(4), 267–272.

Ibrahim, K., Eilbott, J. A., Ventola, P., He, G., Pelphrey, K. A., McCarthy, G., & Sukhodolsky, D. G. (2019). Reduced amygdala-prefrontal functional connectivity in children with autism spectrum disorder and co-occurring disruptive behavior. *Biological Psychiatry: Cognitive Neuroscience and Neuroimaging, 4*(12), 1031–1041.

Izquierdo, I. (1975). The hippocampus and learning. *Progress in Neurobiology, 5*(1), 37–75.

Jenabi, E., Farashi, S., Salehi, A. M., & Parsapoor, H. (2023). The association between post-term births and autism spectrum disorders: An updated systematic review and meta-analysis. *European Journal of Medical Research, 28*(1), 316.

Johnson, M. H., & de Haan, M. (2015). *Developmental cognitive neuroscience* (4th ed.). Wiley-Blackwell.

Jouravlev, O., Kell, A. J. E., Mineroff, Z., Haskins, A. J., Ayyash, D., Kanwisher, N., & Fedorenko, E. (2020). Reduced language lateralization in autism and the broader autism phenotype as assessed with robust individual-subjects analyses. *Autism Research, 13*(10), 1746–1761.

Kanner, L. (1943). Autistic disturbances of affective contact. *Nervous Child, 2*, 217–250.

Kapp, S. K., Steward, R., Crane, L., Elliott, D., Elphick, C., Pellicano, E., & Russell, G. (2019). 'People should be allowed to do what they like': Autistic adults' views and experiences of stimming. *Autism, 23*(7), 1782–1792.

Kaufmann, W. E., Kidd, S. A., Andrews, H. F., Budimirovic, D. B., Esler, A., Haas-Givler, B., ... Berry-Kravis, E. (2017). Autism spectrum disorder in fragile X syndrome: Cooccurring conditions and current treatment. *Pediatrics, 139*(Suppl 3), S194–S206.

Kaushik, G., & Zarbalis, K. S. (2016). Prenatal neurogenesis in autism spectrum disorders. *Frontiers in Chemistry, 4*, 12.

Kensinger, E. A., & Choi, E. S. (2009). When side matters: Hemispheric processing and the visual specificity of emotional memories. *Journal of Experimental Psychology, Learning, Memory, and Cognition, 35*(1), 247–253.

Khanbabaei, M., Hughes, E., Ellegood, J., Qiu, L. R., Yip, R., Dobry, J., ... Cheng, N. (2019). Precocious myelination in a mouse model of autism. *Translational Psychiatry, 9*(1), 251.

Klein, A., Ulmer, J., Quinet, S., Mathews, V., & Mark, L. P. (2016). Nonmotor functions of the cerebellum: An introduction. *American Journal of Neuroradiology, 37*, 1005–1009.

Knaus, T. A., Kamps, J., & Foundas, A. L. (2016). Handedness in children with autism spectrum disorder. *Perceptual and Motor Skills, 122*(2), 542–559.

Kosillo, P., & Bateup, H. S. (2021). Dopaminergic dysregulation in syndromic autism spectrum disorders: Insights from genetic mouse models. *Frontiers in Neural Circuits, 15*, 700968.

Lanciego, J. L., Luquin, N., & Obeso, J. A. (2012). Functional neuroanatomy of the basal ganglia. *Cold Spring Harbor Perspectives in Medicine, 2*(12), a009621.

Lange, N., Travers, B. G., Bigler, E. D., Prigge, M. B., Froehlich, A. L., Nielsen, J. A., ...Lainhart, J. E. (2015). Longitudinal volumetric brain changes in autism spectrum disorder ages 6–35 years. *Autism Research, 8*(1), 82–93.

Lau, Y. C., Hinkley, L. B., Bukshpun, P., Strominger, Z. A., Wakahiro, M. L., Baron-Cohen, S., ... Marco, E. J. (2013). Autism traits in individuals with agenesis of the corpus callosum. *Journal of Autism and Developmental Disorders, 43*(5), 1106–1118.

Lisman, J., Buzsáki, G., Eichenbaum, H., Nadel, L., Ranganath, C., & Redish, A. D. (2017). Viewpoints: How the hippocampus contributes to memory, navigation and cognition. *Nature Neuroscience, 20*(11), 1434–1447.

Long, J., Li, H., Liu, Y., Liao, X., Tang, Z., Han, K., ... Zhang, H. (2024). Insights into the structure and function of the hippocampus: Implications for the pathophysiology and treatment of autism spectrum disorder. *Frontiers in Psychiatry, 15*, 1364858.

Lovaas, O. I., Newsom, C., & Hickman, C. (1987). Self-stimulatory behavior and perceptual reinforcement. *Journal of Applied Behavior Analysis, 20*(1), 45–68.

Love, E. J., & Kinch, R. A. (1965). Factors influencing the birth weight in normal pregnancy. *American Journal of Obstetrics and Gynecology, 91*, 342–349.

Manto, M., Bower, J. M., Conforto, A. B., Delgado-García, J. M., da Guarda, S. N., Gerwig, M., ... Timmann, D. (2012). Consensus paper: Roles of the cerebellum in motor control—The diversity of ideas on cerebellar involvement in movement. *Cerebellum, 11*(2), 457–487.

Mapelli, L., Soda, T., D'Angelo, E., & Prestori, F. (2022). The cerebellar involvement in autism spectrum disorders: From the social brain to mouse models. *International Journal of Molecular Science, 23*(7), 3894.

Markou, P., Ahtam, B., & Papadatou-Pastou, M. (2017). Elevated levels of atypical handedness in autism: Meta-analyses. *Neuropsychology Review, 27*, 258–283.

McCarthy, M. J., & Brumback, A. C. (2021). *Seminars in pediatric neurology, 38*, 100897.

Melillo, R., Leisman, G., Machado, C., Machado-Ferrer, Y., Chinchilla-Acosta, M., Kamgang, S., ... Carmeli, E. (2022). Retained primitive reflexes and potential for intervention in autistic spectrum disorders. *Frontiers in Neurology, 13*, 922322.

Miller, J. M., Singer, H. S., Bridges, D. D., & Waranch, H. R. (2006). Behavioral therapy for treatment of stereotypic movements in nonautistic children. *Journal of Child Neurology, 21*(2), 119–125.

Minderaa, R. B., Volkmar, F. R., Hansen, C. R., Harcherik, D. F., Akkerhuis, G. W., & Cohen, D. J. (1985). Brief report: Snout and visual rooting reflexes in infantile autism. *Journal of Autism and Developmental Disorders, 15*(4), 409–416.

Mohammad-Rezazadeh, I., Frohlich, J., Loo, S. K., & Jeste, S. S. (2016). Brain connectivity in autism spectrum disorder. *Current Opinion in Neurology, 29*(2), 137–147.

Mohd, A. M., Ismail, J., & Nor, N. K. (2021). Motor development in children with autism spectrum disorder. *Frontiers in Pediatrics, 9*, 598276.

Nagai, Y., Nomura, K., & Uemura, O. (2024). Primitive reflexes in very low birth weight infants later diagnosed with autism spectrum disorder. *Minerva Pediatrica, 76*(1), 19–23.

Newville, J., Ortega, M., & Maxwell, J. (2018). Babies born early can have brain injury. *Frontiers for Young Minds, 6*(20).

Nielsen, J. A., Zielinski, B. A., Fletcher, P. T., Alexander, A. L., Lange, N., Bigler, E. D., ...Anderson, J. S. (2014). Abnormal lateralization of functional connectivity between language and default mode regions in autism. *Molecular Autism, 5*, 8.

Nordahl, C. W., Scholz, R., Yang, X., Buonocore, M. H., Simon, T., Rogers, S., & Amaral, D. G. (2012). Increased rate of amygdala growth in children aged 2 to 4 years with autism spectrum disorders: A longitudinal study. *Archives of General Psychiatry, 69*(1), 53–61.

Ohta, H., Nordahl, C. W., Iosif, A. M., Lee, A., Rogers, S., & Amaral, D. G. (2016). Increased surface area, but not cortical thickness, in a subset of young boys with autism spectrum disorder. *Autism Research, 9*(2), 232–248.

Ong, L. T., & Fan, S. W. D. (2023). Morphological and functional changes of cerebral cortex in autism spectrum disorder. *Innovations in Clinical Neuroscience, 20*(10–12), 40–47.

Ornitz, E. M. (1974). The modulation of sensory input and motor output in autistic children. *Journal of Autism and Childhood Schizophrenia, 4*(3), 197–215.

Owen, J. P., Li, Y. O., Ziv, E., Strominger, Z., Gold, J., Bukhpun, P., ... Mukherjee, P. (2013). The structural connectome of the human brain in agenesis of the corpus callosum. *Neuroimage, 70*, 340–355.

Papadatou-Pastou, M., Ntolka, E., Schmitz, J., Martin, M., Munafò, M. R., Ocklenburg, S., & Paracchini, S. (2020). Human handedness: A meta-analysis. *Psychological Bulletin, 146*(6), 481–524.

Paul, L. K., Corsello, C., Kennedy, D. P., & Adolphs, R. (2014). Agenesis of the corpus callosum and autism: A comprehensive comparison. *Brain, 137*(Pt 6), 1813–1829.

Paul, L. K., Van Lancker-Sidtis, D., Schieffer, B., Dietrich, R., & Brown, W. S. (2003). Communicative deficits in agenesis of the corpus callosum: Nonliteral language and affective prosody. *Brain and Language, 85*(2), 313–324.

Paulin, M. G. (1993). The role of the cerebellum in motor control and perception. *Brain Behavior and Evolution, 41*(1), 39–50.

Pecuch, A., Gieysztor, E., Wolańska, E., Telenga, M., & Paprocka-Borowicz, M. (2021). Primitive reflex activity in relation to motor skills in healthy preschool children. *Brain Sciences, 11*(8), 967.

Percy, A. K. (2011). Rett syndrome: Exploring the autism link. *Archives of Neurology, 68*(8), 985–989.

Persichetti, A. S., Shao, J., Gotts, S. J., Martin, A. (2022). Maladaptive laterality in cortical networks related to social communication in autism spectrum disorder. *The Journal of Neuroscience, 42*(48), 9045–9052.

Péter, Z., Oliphant, M. E., & Fernandez, T. V. (2017). Motor stereotypies: A pathophysiological review. *Frontiers in Neuroscience, 11*, 171.

Peters, B. D., Ikuta, T., DeRosse, P., John, M., Burdick, K. E., Gruner, P., ... Malhotra, A. K. (2014). Age-related differences in white matter tract microstructure are associated with cognitive performance from childhood to adulthood. *Biological Psychiatry, 75*(3), 248–256.

Postema, M. C., van Rooij, D., Anagnostou, E., Arango, C., Auzias, G., Behrmann, M., ...Francks, C. (2021). Altered structural brain asymmetry in autism spectrum disorder in a study of 54 datasets. *Nature Communication, 12*(1), 7260.

Ritvo, E. R., Freeman, B. J., Scheibel, A. B., Duong, T., Robinson, H., Guthrie, D., & Ritvo, A. (1986). Lower Purkinje cell counts in the cerebella of four autistic subjects: Initial findings of the UCLA-NSAC Autopsy Research Report. *American Journal of Psychiatry, 143*(7), 862–866.

Rogers, T. D., McKimm, E., Dickson, P. E., Goldowitz, D., Blaha, C. D., & Mittleman, G. (2013). Is autism a disease of the cerebellum? An integration of clinical and preclinical research. *Frontiers in Systems Neuroscience, 7*, 15.

Rosenberg, J. (2001). Exposure to multiple risk factors linked to delivery of underweight infants. *Family Planning Perspectives, 33*(5), 238–239.

Rossignol, D. A., & Frye, R. E. (2011). Melatonin in autism spectrum disorders: A systematic review and meta-analysis. *Developmental Medicine and Child Neurology, 53*(9), 783–792.

Rysstad, A. L., & Pedersen, A. V. (2016). Brief report: Non-right-handedness within the autism spectrum disorder. *Journal of Autism and Developmental Disorders, 46*(3), 1110–1117.

Sakai, J. (2020). Core concept: How synaptic pruning shapes neural wiring during development and, possibly, in disease. *Proceedings of the National Academy of Sciences, 117*(28), 16096–16099.

Scharoun, S. M., & Bryden, P. J. (2014). Hand preference, performance abilities, and hand selection in children. *Frontiers in Psychology, 5*, 82.

Schendel, D., & Bhasin, T. K. (2008). Birth weight and gestational age characteristics of children with autism, including a comparison with other developmental disabilities. *Pediatrics, 121*(6), 1155–1164.

Schumann, C. M., Bloss, C. S., Barnes, C. C., Wideman, G. M., Carper, R. A., Akshoomoff, N., ... Courchesne, E. (2010). Longitudinal magnetic resonance imaging study of cortical development through early childhood in autism. *Journal of Neuroscience, 30*(12), 4419–4427.

Schumann, C. M., Hamstra, J., Goodlin-Jones, B. L., Lotspeich, L. J., Kwon, H., Buono-core, M. H., … Amaral, D. G. (2004). The amygdala is enlarged in children but not adolescents with autism; the hippocampus is enlarged at all ages. *Journal of Neuroscience, 24*(28), 6392–6401.

Sereno, M. I., Diedrichsen, J., Tachrount, M., Testa-Silva, G., d'Arceuil, H., & De Zeeuw, C. (2020). The human cerebellum has almost 80% of the surface area of the neocortex. *Proceedings of the National Academy of Sciences U S A., 117*(32), 19538–19543.

Shomrat, T., & Nesher, N. (2019). Updated view on the relation of the pineal gland to autism spectrum disorders. *Frontiers in Endocrinology, 10*, 37.

Sigafoos, J., Roche, L., O'Reilly, M. F., & Lancioni, G. E. (2021). Persistence of primitive reflexes in developmental disorders. *Current Developmental Disorders Reports, 8*, 98–105.

Sigelman, C. K., & Rider, E. A. (2022). *Lifespan human development* (11th ed.). Cengage.

Smith, E. A., & Van Houten, R. (1996). A comparison of the characteristics of self-stimulatory behaviors in "normal" children and children with developmental delays. *Research in Developmental Disabilities, 17*(4), 253–268.

Song, I. G., Kim, H. S., Cho, Y. M., Lim, Y. N., Moon, D. S., Shin, S. H., … Eun, H. S. (2022). Association between birth weight and neurodevelopmental disorders assessed using the Korean National Health Insurance Service claims data. *Scientific Reports, 12*(1), 2080.

Sparks, B. F., Friedman, S. D., Shaw, D. W., Aylward, E. H., Echelard, D., Artru, A. A., … Dager, S. R. (2002). Brain structural abnormalities in young children with autism spectrum disorder. *Neurology, 59*(2), 184–192.

Stoodley, C. J. (2014). Distinct regions of the cerebellum show gray matter decreases in autism, ADHD, and developmental dyslexia. *Frontiers in Systems Neuroscience, 8*, 92.

Tang, G., Gudsnuk, K., Kuo, S. H., Cotrina, M. L., Rosoklija, G., Sosunov, A., … Sulzer, D. (2014). Loss of mTOR-dependent macroautophagy causes autistic-like synaptic pruning deficits. *Neuron, 83*(5), 1131–1143.

Tereshko, L., Ross, R. K., & Frazee, L. (2021). The effects of a procedure to decrease motor stereotypy on social interactions in a child with autism spectrum disorder. *Behavior Analysis in Practice, 14*(2), 367–377.

Tiemeier, H., Lenroot, R. K., Greenstein, D. K., Tran, L., Pierson, R., & Giedd, J. N. (2010). Cerebellum development during childhood and adolescence: A longitudinal morphometric MRI study. *Neuroimage, 49*(1), 63–70.

Toga, A., & Thompson, P. (2003). Mapping brain asymmetry. *Nature Reviews Neuroscience, 4*(1), 37–48.

Travers, B. G., Tromp do, P. M., Adluru, N., Lange, N., Destiche, D., Ennis, C., … Alexander, A. L. (2015). Atypical development of white matter microstructure of the corpus callosum in males with autism: A longitudinal investigation. *Molecular Autism, 6*, 15.

Wang, C., Geng, H., Liu, W., & Zhang, G. (2017). Prenatal, perinatal, and postnatal factors associated with autism: A meta-analysis. *Medicine, 96*(18), e6696.

Werner, H. (1957). The concept of development from a comparative and organismic point of view. In D. B. Harris (Ed.), *The concept of development: An issue in the study of human behavior*. University of Minnesota Press.

Whitehouse, A. J. (2013). Autism spectrum disorders are associated with fetal growth extremely below or above average for gestational age. *Evidence-Based Mental Health, 16*(3), 86.

Wolff, J. J., Gerig, G., Lewis, J. D., Soda, T., Styner, M. A., Vachet, C., … Piven, J. (2015). Altered corpus callosum morphology associated with autism over the first 2 years of life. *Brain, 138*(Pt 7), 2046–2058.

World Health Organization (2014). Global nutrition targets 2025: Low birth weight policy brief. https://www.who.int/publications/i/item/WHO-NMH-NHD-14.5. Accessed on January 12, 2024.

Wu, Z. Y., Huang, S. D., Zou, J. J., Wang, Q. X., Naveed, M., Bao, H. N., … Han, F. (2020). Autism spectrum disorder (ASD): Disturbance of the melatonin system and its implications. *Biomedicine & Pharmacotherapy*, *130*, 110496.

Zemel, B. (2002). Body composition during growth and development. In N. Cameron (Ed.), *Human growth and development* (pp. 271–293). Academic Press.

Zhang, Y., Qin, B., Wang, L., Zhang, K., Song, C., Chen, J., … Li, T. (2023). Corpus callosum volumes in children with autism spectrum disorders: Sex-associated differences. *Journal of Autism and Developmental Disorders*, *53*(6), 2421–2429.

Chapter 3

Social Development in Autism

Chapter Contents

DOI: 10.4324/9781003336266-4

Introduction

Social development refers to our capacity to grow and improve interpersonal and communication skills and form and maintain relationships. The process begins in infancy and in **dyadic interaction**—i.e., interaction involving two people attending to each other. Typically developing infants generally exhibit social smiles and interest in human faces and voices. Their interactions with the primary caregiver may elicit more sustained interactions, including joint attention and turn-taking during vocalizations. During the second half of the first year, they may show **attachment**-related behavior, such as seeking comfort from familiar caregivers, fear of strangers, and separation anxiety. These early social interactions pave the way for future social and emotional development. For infants at risk for developing autism, challenges in social development are common. They may experience difficulties with social communication and interaction, including making eye contact, engaging in back-and-forth interaction, responding to their names, understanding and expressing emotions, and responding to social cues.

Genetics and brain development play an essential role in social development. The social brain consists of a network of several regions (e.g., the amygdala, the prefrontal cortex, and the mirror neuron system) that process and facilitate social interactions. These brain structures are discussed in detail in Chapter 2 (*Physical Development in Autism*). Individuals with autism generally experience difficulties with communication, social interactions, and understanding social cues. Neuroimaging studies have provided evidence of brain activity and connectivity differences in regions associated with social cognition and processing in autistic individuals (Müller & Fishman, 2018).

Emotions

What are the characteristics of an emotion? An emotion denotes a state of mind comprised of functionally distinct components of subjective feelings (e.g., "I am sad"), physiological changes (e.g., watery eyes), and behavioral enactments (e.g., sobbing). Emotions are hard-wired into the brain and readily observable in infants during the first days of life. Indeed, typically developing infants are social beings and exhibit various basic emotions during the first few months of life. These basic emotions evolve into more complex ones. They are vital in motivating and organizing behavior.

Long ago, Darwin (1872) postulated that some facial expressions are universal and essential to communication. Pioneering research on facial emotions conducted by Paul Ekman has furthered Darwin's ideas and has contributed to our conceptualization and understanding of emotions. As a result, Ekman (1973) identified six basic emotions (i.e., anger, fear, disgust, surprise, happiness, and sadness) and, based on cross-cultural research conducted in Papua New Guinea, he concluded that the human ability to express and identify some basic emotions is universal. More recently, Lewis (2008) identified three basic emotions present at birth: contentment, interest, and distress. Because emotions are inextricably linked to brain maturation and cognitive development, contentment develops into joy, interest becomes surprise, and distress gives way to sadness, disgust, anger, and fear. These basic emotions (also termed **primary emotions**) are precursors of more complex ones—such as pride, shame, and guilt—that become more apparent during the second year of life, when infants are capable of self-recognition. It is now established that infants' basic emotions are genetically determined and develop early on due to constant interplay with their primary caregivers (Izard & Akerman, 2000).

The ability to recognize emotions is the *sine qua non* for understanding the intentions and feelings of others, so impairments in emotion discrimination can significantly limit social interactions and development. There is a substantial body of evidence suggesting that neurotypical infants can discriminate facial expressions, namely static displays of facial emotions of happiness, sadness, and surprise (Young-Browne et al., 1977), smiling faces from frowning ones (Barrera & Maurer, 1981), and subtle expressions of anger (Ichikawa & Yamaguchi, 2014). Typically developing preschoolers can readily and accurately discern facial expressions of anger, happiness, and sadness and become more proficient at recognizing fear and surprise (Widen & Russell, 2003). Preadolescents are better than children at recognizing most emotional expressions and perform emotion recognition tasks at a level comparable to that of adults. However, they may have difficulty identifying less intense emotions (Thomas et al., 2007). All in all, facial emotion recognition continues to develop in adolescence and reaches its peak in adulthood.

Emotion Recognition in Autism

It is commonly believed that individuals with autism spectrum disorder (ASD) have difficulties processing and interpreting facial expressions of emotion. **Alexithymia** (a phrase of Greek origin meaning "no words for emotions") denotes a condition characterized by the inability of some individuals to describe their own feelings and emotions. It is estimated that approximately 40–65% of adults with ASD are alexithymic. More recent research based on children's self-reports and parents' ratings indicates that the occurrence of alexithymia is common among children diagnosed with autism spectrum disorder (Griffin et al., 2016). Surprisingly, it has been proposed that deficits in emotional expressions associated with ASD are caused by alexithymia and not autism *per se* (Bird & Cook, 2013).

The inability to understand others' emotions can thwart the establishment of relationships and the development of social reciprocity. Research studies that have investigated emotion recognition impairments in autism have yielded inconsistent results. Some studies have suggested deficits in emotion recognition, whereas others have not. The inconsistency of findings probably lies in the use of disparate methodologies (Bal et al., 2010). All in all, emotional adeptness in individuals diagnosed with ASD may be predicated on age, intelligence, and the context in which the emotional stimuli are presented (Begeer et al., 2008).

Do infants who are later diagnosed with autism show difficulties in recognizing facial emotions? **Prospective studies** that have investigated facial emotion recognition in infants have targeted infants at risk—namely, having an older sibling with autism—who are later diagnosed with autism and compared their emotional response to that of their typically developing counterparts (i.e., infants without a history of autism in their immediate families). Infants at risk for autism have been found to be less likely to respond to their name, more likely to mouth objects, less responsive to visual stimuli, and more likely to react aversively to social stimulation (Baranek, 1999).

Previous research has suggested that different emotions are expressed in specific facial regions. Negative emotions (e.g., anger) are typically expressed on the upper part of the face. In contrast, positive emotions (e.g., joy) are generally expressed on the lower part of the face (Dinberg & Petterson, 2000). Other research findings have suggested that by the end of the first year of life infants who are subsequently diagnosed with ASD are more likely than typically developing ones to exhibit "atypical eye contact" and disengage from a visual stimulus (Zwaigenbaum et al., 2005). All in all, individuals diagnosed with ASD may become more proficient at identifying basic emotions as they become adults but are less likely, however, to recognize more subtle emotions and, consequently, may never acquire the level of emotional competence typical adults possess (Rump et al., 2009).

Emotion Regulation

As humans, we are constantly bombarded with pleasant and unpleasant stimuli that can elicit emotions in ways that are usually viewed by others as either socially desirable or undesirable. For example, we can constructively interact with a neighbor who is playing loud music to mitigate and de-escalate the situation. Alternatively, we may choose to get even with that neighbor by playing much louder music in retaliation for the disruption. Our emotions, if not regulated, can bring out our worst selves. Emotion (aka **affect**) regulation, thus, denotes intrinsic and extrinsic processes in which emotional responses are initiated, maintained, and altered in response to what is considered socially acceptable, to achieve a specific objective (Thompson, 1994). Intrinsic factors that regulate emotions originate within the individual and comprise temperamental disposition, cognitive abilities such as attention, and capacity to exert effortful control. Extrinsic factors include infant-caregiver dyadic interactions, sibling and peer interactions, parental socialization of emotional responses, and cultural expectations of emotional expression (Fox & Calkins, 2003). It has been proposed that **emotion regulation** in parenthood plays a significant role owing to parents' capacity to influence emotion regulation in their children, particularly in early development (Rutherford et al., 2015).

Infants must develop the ability to adapt to environmental uncertainty and challenges. While neonates are born with the capacity to express some basic emotions, those emotions are not well regulated because infants only possess limited affect regulation strategies, so they rely on inborn regulatory mechanisms and caregivers to comfort them when faced with distressful situations (Derryberr & Rothbart, 2001). Alternatively, infants may attempt to reduce painful stimulation by turning away from discomforting situations or becoming more agitated (Mangelsdorf et al., 1995). Infants acquire more competent strategies to express and regulate their emotions as they develop. For example, 12- and 18-month-olds are more likely to calm themselves down or distract themselves when in an aroused state or face a stressful situation (Mangelsdorf et al., 1995). As infants acquire motor capabilities and can walk (typically around the first year of life), they explore and discover novel ways to interact with objects in their immediate environment and alleviate boredom and discomfort in the absence of a caregiver.

The development of language plays a role in emotion regulation. As infants gradually build their vocabulary, they become proficient in the use of language during the preschool years. It is estimated that typical first-graders possess a vocabulary of around 10,000 words (Hoff, 2014) and can not only communicate their needs in socially acceptable ways but also understand and express their emotions and the emotions of others. It has been observed that the frequency of crying, most prevalent in infancy, somewhat declines at the end of the second year and becomes progressively less likely during the third and fourth years of life. One explanation for such decline is the emergence of language during those years as a substitute for articulating emotional experiences more effectively and socially appropriately (Kopp, 1992). Indeed, young children (and adults) can use language effectively to mediate emotional experiences and remind themselves, for example, that the use of words can be a more acceptable alternative to hitting, crying, or aggressive responding.

The process of emotion regulation is also influenced from the start by an infant's **temperament**—the natural disposition to respond predictably to stimuli based on genetic and environmental influences. Infant temperament has been extensively and empirically researched, and many studies have centered specifically on infants' reactions to behavioral dimensions such as mood, sleeping habits, feeding, approach/withdrawal from unfamiliar stimulation, and adaptability to novelty (Thomas & Chess, 1986). Other research has focused not only on reactivity (i.e., response latency to stimulation) but also on the role temperament plays in the development of self-regulation (Rothbart, 2011). For example, infants who display negative reactivity as a temperamental dimension tend to exhibit a high degree of distress when placed in unfamiliar and frustrating situations. Research has suggested a link between negative reactivity and emotion regulation and that distress resulting from frustration at 5 months of age has been associated with poor emotion control and self-soothing behaviors at 10 months of age (Calkins & Johnson, 1998).

Emotion Regulation in Autism

The inability of individuals with autism to form "affective contact" with people was documented many years ago in a landmark publication. It has since remained one of the characteristics of the disorder (Kanner, 1943). While dysfunctional emotional responses are not listed in the DSM-5 as part of the definition or main characteristics of ASD, emotion dysregulation is quite common in autism. There is a preponderance of evidence suggesting that ASD is often accompanied by a variety of behaviors and affective problems, including temper tantrums, aggression, self-injurious behaviors, anxiety, depression, irritability, and attention-deficit/hyperactivity disorder (Lecavalier, 2006).

Emotional experiences can be described as either positive or negative (Watson et al., 1988), and strategies used to regulate one's emotions are generally viewed as adaptive or maladaptive (Aldao & Nolen-Hoeksema, 2012). It has been proposed that emotion regulation can take many forms, such as "cognitive reappraisal" or "expressive suppression." Cognitive reappraisal (an antecedent-focused strategy) has generally been viewed as adaptive. It denotes someone's capacity to reinterpret emotional situations and, as a result, exhibit behavioral responses deemed more socially appropriate. Expressive suppression (a response-focused strategy), on the other hand, is defined as alteration or inhibition of emotional responses and has been viewed as maladaptive owing to the cognitive resources required to alter emotional responses that have been activated (Cutuli, 2014). Individuals with ASD have been found not only less likely to use cognitive reappraisal but more likely to exhibit more significant levels of maladaptive behaviors compared to typically developing individuals (Samson et al., 2015).

It is generally accepted that connectivity among many brain regions of individuals with ASD may be disrupted, resulting in impaired emotional functioning. The amygdala (almond-shaped brain structure located in the temporal lobe of the brain, which plays a central role in the processing of emotional stimuli), along with other frontal cortical regions, has been found to mediate the regulation of negative emotions and to increase the effectiveness of cognitive reappraisal (Banks et al., 2007). Individuals diagnosed with ASD have been found to exhibit a decrease in amygdala activation when engaged in a task requiring cognitive reappraisal (Richey et al., 2015).

It is noteworthy to consider the family environment and family dynamics when examining the implications of emotional displays. The term *expressed emotion* (EE) denotes a qualitative measure of patterns of criticism and emotional over-involvement that relatives display toward a family member afflicted with a disorder (Amaresha & Venkatasubramanian, 2012). Criticism can take the form of blaming the afflicted, whereas emotional over-involvement may entail desiring to do *everything* for the person with the disorder. While the family climate may influence the behavioral manifestation of ASD, it is not to suggest that the family causes ASD. In fact, parents of children with ASD have been found to be as supportive and sensitive as parents of children with other disabilities or parents of typically developing children (van Ijzendoorn et al., 2007). More recently, the construct of EE has been of particular interest to those investigating the developmental trends associated with autism. Research has documented that children with disabilities whose parents exhibit high levels of EE are more likely to exhibit behavior problems (Greenberg et al., 2012). Maternal expressions of warmth toward young adults with ASD, however, have been associated with an abatement of behavioral problems (Smith et al., 2008).

Joint Attention

Joint attention is the precursor of social cognition—the capacity to think about the perceptions, thoughts, emotions, and behaviors of self and other people (Flavell, 1999). Joint attention is considered one of the earliest nonvocal social communication skills, which infants typically acquire within the first year of life. Joint attention (or **shared attention**) denotes the focus that two individuals (e.g., a mother-infant dyad) share on a particular object of interest. Joint attention can be achieved through pointing, eye-gazing, or other nonverbal (e.g., smiling) or verbal indications. Joint attention can be further divided into two classes of behavior: (1) responding to joint attention (RJA), where an infant follows his mother's eye-gaze shift and/or gesture toward an object, and (2) initiating joint attention (IJA) (Bruinsma et al., 2004).

Infants responding to joint attention might react to another person's eye-gaze shift or gesture by attending to the object. Initiating joint attention can take different forms (e.g., pointing, showing, and eye gaze alternation between an object and a caregiver) and serve different purposes (i.e., **protoimperative pointing**—requesting a desired item or **protodeclarative pointing**—sharing an experience with a caregiver or drawing someone's attention to something of interest). Infants' capacity to respond and initiate joint attention strongly predicts later language development (Salo et al., 2018).

Joint Attention and Autism

Infants who will later be diagnosed with autism do engage in dyadic interactions with their primary caregivers. However, they lose this ability between the second half of the first year and the end of the second year (Jones et al., 2014; Zwaigenbaum et al., 2013). Dyadic interaction paves the way for triadic interactions—i.e., interaction involving two people attending to the same object.

Protodeclarative pointing is usually evident in the first half of the second year. Its absence is a reliable indicator that a diagnosis of autism is likely. Infants at risk for developing autism may have difficulties with joint attention, which can lead to problems developing communication and social interaction skills. One longitudinal study involving 32 infants assessed joint initiation at 8 months and responding to joint attention at 12 months and suggests that deficits in these prelinguistic communication skills may be precursors of signs of autism (Montagut-Asunción et al., 2022).

Social Referencing

The ability to orient to environmental stimuli is present early in infancy. Typically developing newborns prefer to orient to social stimuli instead of objects and non-social stimuli. This orienting capacity is essential in social-communicative development (Schietecatte et al., 2012). Social referencing refers to the process by which infants interpret the emotional display of an adult (typically the primary caregiver) to approach or avoid environmental objects, persons, or situations (Campos & Stenberg, 1981; Feinman et al., 1992). For example, if the primary caregiver is wary when a stranger approaches, the infant will avoid interacting with the stranger. Conversely, the infant will approach the stranger if the primary caregiver signals that it is okay to do so. Social referencing emerges during the second half of the first year. Although social referencing is the prerequisite for early communication and language development, it is limited or completely absent in children with autism (Brim et al., 2009; DeQuinzio et al., 2015).

Social Referencing and Autism

Impairment in social communication is one of the earliest signs of autism spectrum disorder (Lauttia et al., 2019). Infants who are subsequently diagnosed with autism have little interest in looking at other people's eyes and faces as typically developing infants do. Initial eye contact gradually declines during the first year of life (Jones & Klin, 2013). Dawson and colleagues (1998) compared the orienting ability of typically developing children and children with Down syndrome to that of children with autism. They found that children with autism more readily failed to orient to environmental stimuli, particularly social stimuli. Retrospective studies (e.g., Osterling & Dawson, 1994) found impaired **social orienting** in children with autism, as evidenced by their failure to turn to the person calling their name. Sivaraman and colleagues (2020) systematically reviewed social referencing skills in children diagnosed with ASD. They found that those children had deficits in "spontaneous looking behaviors" and displayed differential responses to affective cues from their primary caregivers.

One study conducted with children with ASD, intellectual disabilities (ID), and typical development (TD) examined approach-motivation-related brain activity using direct gaze versus downcast gaze (Lauttia et al., 2019). Compared to children with ID and TD, children with ASD showed an atypical pattern of frontal EEG (electroencephalogram measures brain electrical activity) asymmetry for direct gaze. Compared to the **downcast gaze**, the direct gaze elicited more significant approach-related frontal activity in TD children. Conversely, ASD children showed more significant approach-related activity in response to downcast gaze. More recently, Lubomirska and colleagues (2022) developed the Social Referencing Observation Scale (SoROS) to identify children at risk for ASD. They found significant score differences between children with ASD and typically developing children in the control group. In addition, the inter-rater agreement ranged between 80 and 100%, and the SoROS showed reliable **specificity** and **sensitivity** in predicting ASD.

Researchers have proposed various explanations for infants subsequently diagnosed with autism's failure to orient to social stimuli. Courchesne and colleagues (1995) thought that the "rapid shifting of attention" is a prerequisite in early social exchanges, an activity that children with autism might find challenging. Long before Campos and Stenberg (1981) coined the term social referencing, Lovaas and Schreibman (1971) used the term stimulus overselectivity to describe how children on the spectrum attend to a narrow range of stimuli available in the natural environment. Dawson (Dawson, 1991; Dawson & Lewy, 1989) proposed that the impairment in orienting and attention shifting in children with ASD is more evident in social stimuli, including facial expressions, gestures, and speech. The complexity and variability of those stimuli are problematic for children with autism, so they are not typically drawn to them. As a result, they miss the opportunity to engage in early social experiences that provide the basis for social development.

In sum, typically developing infants are naturally attuned to orient to human faces, eyes, and mouths. Based on their caregivers' emotional displays, they can determine how to behave (i.e., whether to avoid or approach stimuli) in ambiguous situations. Infants who are subsequently diagnosed with ASD can orient toward environmental stimuli. However, they prefer attending to non-social stimuli and are less likely to fixate on another person's mouth and eyes. Recent advances in developing screening tools for early ASD detection have resulted in the SoROS, an instrument that when validated will offer clinicians and researchers a tool that can help diagnose autism and initiate an appropriate intervention as early as possible.

Empathy

Empathy—our capacity to take the perspective of others—is at the heart of forming social relationships. Empathy gradually develops through social interactions. We are endowed with the capacity to be empathic (Hoffman, 2000). Newborns can display a primitive sign of empathy. For example, they can become distressed when other infants cry (Eisenberg et al., 2015). This phenomenon is known as **emotional contagion**. Infants and toddlers begin to differentiate their distress from those of others and respond more appropriately to other companions' needs. Empathy becomes more advanced as a cognitive process, as children can put themselves in another person's shoes and take another person's perspective.

Empathy and Autism

It is commonly believed that people with autism lack empathy (and sympathy) because impairment in reciprocal social behavior is one of the main characteristics of ASD. Empathy plays a significant role in human social behavior and developing awareness of our feelings for others and whether we are more likely to care for them and help them (Masten et al., 2011). Some individuals with autism may struggle to recognize and understand the emotions of others, impacting their ability to express empathy in typical ways. Research conducted in the past 40 years shows that the inability to show empathetic responses is not universal among individuals diagnosed with ASD (Mul et al., 2018).

Empathy has a dual-dimensional nature and can be experienced on a cognitive level (aka **theory of mind**) or an affective/emotional level (Healey & Grossman, 2018). Marchetti and colleagues (2020) describe empathy as a "dance between two individuals whose steps move between cognition and affects." People with autism may have difficulty with **cognitive empathy** (i.e., recognizing another person's emotional state and responding to it). However, they do not have any difficulty experiencing **affective empathy** (i.e., instinctual and involuntary responses to the emotions of others). This imbalance between cognitive empathy and **emotional empathy** can lead to an "empathic disequilibrium," which is associated with autistic traits and potential autism diagnosis (Shalev et al., 2022). People with autism may feel other people's emotions more intensely than non-autistic people (Smith, 2009), causing them to become overwhelmed and thus find it difficult to interact with others (Markram & Markram, 2010). Because people with ASD have difficulty discerning another person's emotions, sympathy (i.e., feelings of pity and sorrow for another person's misfortune) is also impaired, so they do not automatically make an appropriate response.

Milton (2012) proposed the "double empathy problem." When two or more individuals with different life experiences and dispositions interact, they may struggle to empathize with one another. In other words, autistic and non-autistic individuals have difficulties understanding each other because of differences in cognitive and affective empathy. For example, it is commonly apparent that individuals with autism fail or struggle to read the emotions of non-autistics (i.e., neurotypicals). Similarly, people without autism have difficulty reading the emotions of those with autism. According to Milton, the deficit typically attributed to autistic people should instead be viewed through the lenses of reciprocity and mutuality. Goodall (2013) disclosed her experience as someone diagnosed with Asperger's and highlighted that the emotional expressions of people on the spectrum are atypical rather than non-existent. Therefore, a neurotypical may have difficulties reading those emotions. She reiterated Milton's "double empathy problem," stating, "If Aspies stopped being labeled as un-empathetic, then maybe our type of empathy can be accepted and valued by the majority and not just those who know us very personally" (p. 126).

Alexithymia (i.e., a reduced ability to recognize, describe, and understand one's emotion) is prevalent in around 10% of the general population. However, it is more prevalent (about 50%) in the ASD population. Alexithymia plays a central and complex role in autism spectrum disorder (Poquérusse et al., 2018). For example, individuals with autism and alexithymia might not know they are experiencing fear, anger, or sadness (Bird & Cook, 2013). The inability of some individuals with autism to understand their emotions and that of others has led them to form an attachment and personification toward non-human agents (White & Remington, 2019). Neuroimaging studies show that alexithymia may be associated with reduced activation in some brain structures related to emotion processing, including the amygdala, mirror neuron system, and the dorsomedial prefrontal cortex (van der Velde et al., 2013). Kinnaird and colleagues (2019) conducted a systematic review of 15 articles and used the Toronto Alexithymia Scale (TAS) to compare a neurotypical group with a group of autistic individuals. They found that a significant percentage of individuals with autism score higher on the TAS than the group of neurotypical ones. The authors concluded that alexithymia is common in autism but not universal.

Attachment

Ethologists have long proposed and demonstrated that some species (including humans) are endowed with innate abilities to respond to certain stimuli in ways that ensure their survival. For example, newly hatched goslings follow and form an attachment to their mothers or a moving object. Within a limited age range they are more sensitive and receptive to environmental influences (Lorenz, 1952). This kind of attachment has been termed "imprinting," a learning phase denoting an innate response that promotes attachment behavior. While infants do not imprint on the first moving object or person they encounter after birth, they form an attachment to the one who provides them with responsive and sensitive care.

John Bowlby, a psychiatrist and psychoanalyst, formulated an influential and time-tested theory of attachment based on evolutionary principles, the behavior of many species in their natural habitats, and concepts derived from the psychodynamic approach. His observations of children experiencing distress when separated from their mothers influenced his formulation. Attachment is conceptualized as an affectional bond an infant develops with a primary caregiver.

Attachment theory has also been characterized as a behavioral activation system through which humans regulate their emotional experiences when dealing with uncertainty (Bowlby, 1969, 1982). Bowlby (1973) also proposed that infants form **internal working models**—i.e., cognitive representations based on interactions with primary caregivers.

Infants typically form an attachment with a primary caregiver (usually the mother) during the second half of the first year. While Bowlby postulated four phases of the attachment process: pre-attachment, attachment-in-the-making, clear-cut attachment, and formation of reciprocal relationships, other researchers have empirically tested attachment formation and delineated four distinct phases and recorded three measures—stranger anxiety, separation anxiety, and social referencing. The first phase (birth–6 weeks) deals with infants' "asocial" responses to various stimuli. The second phase (6 weeks–7 months) identifies "indiscriminate attachment," when infants generally respond and interact with any caregiver. In the third phase (7–9 months), "specific attachment" denotes infants' apparent preference for a particular attachment figure. Infants in that phase are more likely to demonstrate fear of strangers and separation anxiety, thus indicating that an attachment to a particular person has been formed. The fourth phase (10 months onwards) indicates infants' attachment to multiple significant others (Schaffer & Emerson, 1964).

Attachment Types

Ainsworth and colleagues (1978) devised the strange situation procedure (a series of infants' and caregivers' separation and reunion) to measure infants' quality of attachment. Based on infants' patterns of behavior across the separation episodes, Ainsworth et al. described three patterns of infants' attachment to their primary caregivers: (1) secure attachment, (2) resistant attachment, and (3) avoidant attachment. Securely attached infants use the primary caregiver as a secure base for exploration of the environment, a base from which they can return for safety and comfort if frightened. Resistant and avoidant attachment are characterized by strong separation anxiety when reunited with the caregiver and little separation anxiety and avoidance of the attachment figure when reunited, respectively. Subsequent attachment research identified a fourth style (disorganized-disoriented attachment) characterized by infants' confusion, approach/avoidance of caregivers during reunification episodes, and a style associated with later emotional problems (Main & Solomon, 1990).

Factors Influencing the Quality of Attachment

Empirical research demonstrates individual variations in infants' attachment patterns and the role that caregivers' sensitive responsiveness plays in attachment. Gervai (2009) suggested that meta-analyses show parenting behavior accounts for about one-third of the variance in attachment behavior. As a result, he noted that "children's differential susceptibility to the rearing environment [when forming an attachment] depends partly on genetic differences." Infants' temperament has been found to influence the quality of attachment. For example, temperamentally fearful, irritable, or unresponsive infants are more likely to develop insecure attachments (Beckwith et al., 2002). The social context can also influence the development of secure attachments. For example, parents living in poverty or experiencing marital conflict may be, as a result, less sensitive to their infant and thus contribute to their infant's insecure attachments (Roisman & Booth-Laforce, 2014). **Oxytocin** (a hormone produced by the hypothalamus and secreted by the pituitary gland), often called the hormone of attachment, has been found to promote mother-infant attachment and facilitate the birthing process and lactation. A comprehensive cross-disciplinary systematic review found a positive correlation between high oxytocin levels and parent-infant interactions (Scatliffe et al., 2019).

Attachment and Autism

Kanner and Asperger were not interested in the process of attachment formation *per se*. However, they specified in their original description of autism that *impairment in social interaction* was one of the critical features of the disorder. Kanner (1943, p. 248) wrote, "The children of our group [have] all shown their extreme aloneness from the very beginning of life, not responding to anything that comes to them from the outside world." Similarly, Asperger (1991, p. 77) noted:

> It has been my aim to show that the fundamental disorder of autistic individuals is the limitation of their social relationships … their behavior in the social group is the clearest sign of their disorder and the source of conflicts from earliest childhood. These conflicts are especially pronounced in the smallest social unit, that is, the family.
>
> (Frith, 1991, p. 77)

Consistent with their description, the diagnostic criteria for autism spectrum disorder (ASD) listed in the DSM-5 include "persistent deficits in social communication and social interaction across multiple contexts" as one of the core symptoms of autism (APA, 2013).

Measuring Attachment in Autism

Ainsworth and colleagues (1978) developed the Strange Situation Procedure (SSP) to measure infant-caregiver attachment behaviors of typically developing infants between 12 and 24 months. While the signs of ASD (e.g., lack of eye contact) may be visible in infancy, most young children with autism are not diagnosed before age three. Consequently, most attachment studies of young children with autism have used a modified version of the SSP, consisting of one mother-infant separation instead of the conventional sequence of two separations. Thus, young children are observed in a laboratory or home environment, so the caregiver is present during all child-stranger interactions. Although the modified SSP can be stressful, it is no longer "strange," because of the constant caregiver's presence. Furthermore, observations conducted in the modified SSP can yield more ecologically valid data.

As an alternative to the SSP to measure attachment security in children with autism, other studies have used the attachment Q-Sort (AQS), based on a series of observation periods of children aged 1 to 5 years (Waters & Deane, 1985). The method comprises ninety items that capture a broad range of attachment-related behaviors, including social cognition, exploratory behaviors, and affective behaviors. The items (e.g., "child is more interested in people than in things") can be printed individually on cards that are sorted according to a predetermined number of piles (typically nine). The composite score ranges from +1.0 (i.e., very secure) to -1.0 (i.e., very insecure). Because of its unobtrusive data collection format, the AQS has been considered one of the gold standards in assessing attachment security in autism (van Ijzendoorn et al., 2004). Moreover, the heterogeneity of ASD favors using the AQS because the procedure does not make group comparisons. Each observed child serves as their own control, and a composite score determines the attachment's relative security or insecurity.

Autism and Reactive Attachment Disorder

According to the DSM-5, Reactive Attachment Disorder (RAD) denotes a condition in which infants and young children seldom seek an attachment figure's comfort, nurturance, and support. While RAD sufferers can form selective attachments, they rarely do, owing to the lack of opportunity to interact with a potential attachment figure. In fact, they exhibit a lack of positive emotions when interacting with caregivers and typically display poor emotion regulation. Although severe social and physical neglect is believed to be the only known risk factor for the disorder, most severely neglected young children in foster care do not develop RAD. Young children are not diagnosed with RAD until they have reached a minimum developmental age of 9 months, when a selective attachment is likely to form.

Because of the behaviors that children diagnosed with RAD exhibit (e.g., lack of positive emotions, deficits in social interactions, and communication delays), clinicians have found the diagnostic differentiation between autism spectrum disorder (ASD) and RAD challenging, owing to the difficulties with social relationships that characterize both disorders. While RAD has been linked to maltreatment and neglect, ASD has not been associated with such practices. The notion that poor parenting caused autism (Bettelheim, 1967), particularly mothers' lack of sensitivity and responsiveness toward their children, has been put to rest. Quite to the contrary, parents of children with autism spectrum disorder have been found to be as responsive and sensitive as parents of typically developing children (van Ijzendoorn et al., 2007).

Are Autistic Children Able to Form Attachments?

Although the DSM-III (1980) explicitly states that children diagnosed with ASD cannot develop an attachment with their caregivers, empirical research indicates otherwise. Generally speaking, young children with autism can form an attachment to their primary caregivers. However, how they express their attachment behavior differs, depending on the severity of the condition. Children at the lower end of the spectrum are generally less securely attached than those at the higher end (Grzadzinski et al., 2014). Compared to neurotypical adults, those on the spectrum are less likely to form secure attachment relationships (Taylor et al., 2008). In fact, a meta-analysis (i.e., a procedure for combining data from many related studies) conducted on autism and attachment found that children with ASD, despite social impairments usually associated with the disorder, can develop secure attachment even when assessed with the strange situation procedure (Rutgers et al., 2004). Willemsen-Swinkels et al. (2000) reported that 53% of children observed in a modified SSP exhibited attachment behaviors compared to 65% of typically developing children. There is evidence of attachment behaviors that include anguish, searching for the attachment figure (mother) during separation, or exhibiting a preference for the attachment figure over a stranger present in the SSP (Buitelaar, 1995). However, intellectual disability, a condition comorbid with autism, has been shown to relate to attachment insecurity (Rutgers et al., 2004). One recent prospective study used the SSP to assess attachment security at 15 months in high-risk infants later diagnosed with autism. High-risk infants were disproportionally more likely to exhibit insecure resistant attachment behavior than low-risk infants. Additionally, high-risk infants with insecure resistant attachment were nine times more likely to be diagnosed with autism than high-risk infants with secure attachment (Martin et al., 2020).

Although it is estimated that approximately 50% of children diagnosed with ASD are securely attached to their parents (Rutgers et al., 2004), it is well documented that many children on the autism spectrum show attachment behaviors when seeking parental comfort in stressful situations. Many of those children exhibit patterns of disorganized-disoriented attachments (Sigman & Capps, 1997). A disorganized attachment style denotes children who have not developed a coherent attachment pattern with their primary caregiver (Main & Solomon, 1986). Children who exhibit this pattern of behavior are thought to be unable to deal with the experience of anxiety and view the attachment figure as a source of fright instead of comfort.

Theory of Mind

Humans are social and cognitive beings. The psychosocial and cognitive domains develop gradually from infancy and improve in adolescence and adulthood. Such capacity is rooted in our genetic endowment and interactions with our social environments. We become cognizant of others by developing empathy, learning to regulate our emotions, and developing an understanding of others' behavior and intentions in social situations. Social cognition (Flavell, 1985) refers to our capacity to think about the thoughts, perceptions, motives, and behaviors of self and others. Do primates (our closest cousins) have any cognitive capability or social cognition that mirrors human perception?

Many decades ago, Kohler (1925) conducted a series of experiments to investigate whether chimpanzees in captivity could demonstrate any form of insight to solve problems by using tools placed in their cages to access food that was out of their reach. In most trials, the chimpanzees managed to get food outside their range using tools available in the cage. Many years later, Premack and Woodruff (1978) used Kohler's methodology to ascertain whether an adult enculturated research chimpanzee (Sarah) could infer a person's mental state after viewing a video recording of the person's attempts to solve a variety of problems (e.g., not being able to get out of a cage or play an unplugged phonograph). When presented with an array of photographs, Sarah consistently chose the correct picture depicting the right solution to the problem the person encountered. Premack and his colleague coined the term "theory of mind" (ToM) to describe the ability to ascribe mental states such as intent, desires, and emotions to oneself and others.

Theory of Mind Development

A theory of mind begins to form in infancy, and the acquisition of many skills (e.g., imitation, **pretend play**, joint attention, and emotional understanding) can contribute to its development. Typically developing infants acquire those skills gradually, whereas most are lacking in children with autism. Imitation (a form of social learning) denotes observing someone's action and replicating the behavior. Typically developing infants effortlessly interact with adults, making eye contact, smiling, and imitating the actions of others. Facial imitation is essential; it allows infants to distinguish between people and objects in the environment and, thus, respond to them differently.

According to Meltzoff and Gopnik (1993), imitation is essential in understanding others' intentions and developing a theory of mind. Pretend play, a **false belief**, shows that infants understand the difference between symbolic and concrete actions. Joint attention entails sharing a perceptual experience in which infants demonstrate they can attend to other environmental stimuli but can also team up with a partner and attend the same event. Finally, emotional understanding can be observed in infants in their first years of life (Woodward, 2009), and by about 6 months, they prefer actors who demonstrate good intentions toward a neutral person versus actors who show bad intentions (Hamlin & Wynn, 2011).

Theory of Mind Tests

The concept of a theory of mind gave rise to various procedures psychologists developed to test humans' ability to detect others' desires, beliefs, and intentions. Wimmer and Perner (1983) tested the understanding of 36 children participants (3–9-year-olds) regarding a protagonist depicted in two sketches. In one version of a series of experiments, the protagonist (P) placed an object in a location (a). The participants observed an antagonist moving the object to another location (b). The participants were asked to indicate where P would look for the object. Three to four-year-old participants incorrectly reported that P would search for the item in "b." Fifty-seven percent of the 4–6-year-olds and 86% of the 6–9-year-olds correctly pointed to location "a." in both sketches. Their finding and a meta-analysis of 178 separate studies (Wellman et al., 2001) suggest that 4–6-year-olds develop the understanding that people can hold incorrect beliefs that guide their behavior. In other words, they could express what they knew and predict the protagonist's behavior based on his absence of knowledge of the object's new location.

Research has produced a large body of evidence suggesting the presence of cognitive impairment in autism. Baron-Cohen and colleagues (1985) used the Sally-Anne test (a variant of Wimmer and Perner's puppet play model) to evaluate the theory of mind in 20 children diagnosed with autism, 14 children with Down syndrome, and 27 typically developing children. Wimmer and Perner (1983) developed the Sally-Anne test. Approximately 85% of typical 4-year-olds and older children with Down syndrome passed the false-belief task. However, 80% of children diagnosed with autism failed the task. Based on many years of research conducted across various disciplines (e.g., developmental psychopathology, cognitive neuroscience, and evolutionary psychology), Baron-Cohen (1990, 1997) proposed the term "mindblindness" to refer to the inability of persons with autism to attribute mental states (e.g., intentions, beliefs, desires) to themselves and others, thus lacking a theory of mind. More recently, Gernsbacher and Yergeau (2019) critically examined the empirical assertion that people with autism lack a theory of mind. They summarized a large body of data showing that lacking a theory of mind is neither a unique characteristic of people with autism nor specific to autism, and people with autism are not uniquely impaired.

Do Autistic Children Lack a Theory of Mind?

The notion that autistic individuals are deficient in understanding that other people have mental states (e.g., intentions, desires, and beliefs) that guide their behavior is ubiquitous in psychology textbooks and research articles. Some children (and adults) with autism fail false belief tests, but deficiencies in ToM are not so unique to autism. Van Neerven and colleagues (2021) systematically reviewed studies on ToM. They found that deficiencies in ToM are present in individuals suffering from affective disorders (e.g., schizophrenia, bipolar disorder, and major depressive disorder). Similarly, Gernsbacher and Yergeau (2019) questioned the notion that autistic people are uniquely and universally impaired in ToM. Individuals with Down syndrome (Zelazo et al., 1996), children with cerebral palsy (Caillies et al., 2012), and children with communication disorders (van Buijsen et al., 2011) are deficient in ToM.

Gernsbacher and Yergeau (2019) challenged the ToM as it relates to autism based on four criteria: *specificity*, *universality*, *replication*, and *validity*. Many learning-disabled children and adults not on the autism spectrum fail ToM tests, so deficits in ToM are not specific to autism. Many children and adults on the least severe end of the spectrum pass ToM tests (Boucher, 2012), so the universality of ToM deficits related to autism does not hold. Efforts to replicate ToM studies that used different tests have resulted in mixed findings (Bauminger & Kasari, 1999). Various tasks developed to test ToM have yielded neither convergent validity (Lukito et al., 2017) nor predictive validity (Melchers et al., 2015).

Autism and Theory of Mind Training

Acquiring a theory of mind (a set of skills behavior analytic practitioners termed "perspective-taking") is the foundation for all subsequent cognitive development. Teaching skills that include joint attention, pretend play, and imitation emerge in infancy and develop in toddlerhood. Children around the ages of 4–5 understand that other people can have thoughts and beliefs that are different from theirs and consequently can pass the false-belief task. The discovery of mirror neurons has shed light on our capacity to imitate others and gain insight into their mental states. There is overwhelming evidence that the development of pretend play and joint attention skills are deficient in children diagnosed with ASDs. The impairment of these skills can thwart the representational abilities associated with a theory of mind. Efforts to teach perspective-taking and other social skills to children with ASDs have been successful (Fletcher-Watson et al., 2014). Additionally, behavior analytic practitioners have had some success in teaching those skills using instructions, modeling, rehearsal, and feedback.

Play

Play is a crucial aspect of a child's life, particularly from the ages of 2 to 5, known as the play years. Play helps develop physical and social skills and other essential aspects of a child's growth (Lantz, 2001; Pellegrini, 2009). Young children usually prefer specific playmates during the first two years of life. Sociologist Mildred Parten (1932) observed the play activities of preschool children and identified different types of play that become increasingly more social and imaginative as children grow older. These types of play include solitary, parallel, associative, and cooperative. During elementary school, play becomes more rule-governed and focused on skill-building than play activities in preschool (Sigelman & Rider, 2022).

Typically developing children engage in pretend play around their first birthday until age five (Rubin et al., 2015). Social pretend play is another form of play in which children cooperate with others to enact social interactions, such as playing the role of a doctor interacting with a patient. Both pretend play and social play are essential for the development of children, as they help them prepare for more complex social interactions that they will face in the future as adolescents and adults.

Engaging in playful activities is highly beneficial and contributes to the growth of three main development domains: physical, cognitive, and social (Howe & Leach, 2018). Pretend play enhances cognitive and language development (Lillard et al., 2013). On the other hand, social pretend play helps children gain a better understanding of other people's mental states (Howe & Leach, 2018). Play also plays a significant role in developing emotional understanding, emotion regulation, and the ability to handle emotional conflicts (Coplan & Abreau, 2009).

Play and Autism

Play is a pivotal activity for children and is vital to their physical and emotional development. According to Wolfberg (1995), play is an active and enjoyable activity that is voluntary and flexible. Social play refers to the type of play where peers interact and collaborate. According to Jordan (2003), autism affects children's social, emotional, and cognitive development. As a result, children with autism face difficulties in initiating play interactions with others due to their cognitive and affective challenges. Jordan suggested various teaching models that can be used to facilitate social play activities for children with autism. Children on the autism spectrum may face challenges engaging in play, as they prefer to play alone instead of with others. One of the main characteristics of their play behavior is difficulties with communication. They usually find play challenging due to their difficulties understanding social cues from their peers or showing an interest in participating in social interactions. They may have trouble comprehending that their play companions have different thoughts and feelings from theirs, or they may have restricted and unusual interests (e.g., lining up toys instead of playing with them). As a result, neurotypical children may be more likely to exclude them from their play activities.

Play Development in Autism

Can children with autism develop play interests that are like those of neurotypical children? Autistic children engage in play that is meaningful to them, which might not always align with typical play patterns. However, it is possible to teach children on the autism spectrum how to participate in play activities. Wolfberg and Schuler (1993) used a combined quantitative and qualitative approach to promote social and cognitive aspects of play in three children diagnosed with autism. As a result, the participants displayed more social play and reduced stereotypic object play. *Video modeling* is a teaching method that has been proven to be effective in teaching various skills to children with autism, including social and academic skills. Besler and Kurt (2016) conducted a study in which mothers of three children with autism were trained to teach their children to build a model train using Lego bricks. The study found that all three children were able to learn the target skill and were able to apply it to non-teaching situations.

Stahmer and colleagues (2003) reviewed different techniques that have been developed and used to enhance object play skills. These techniques include naturalistic strategies (e.g., pivotal response training) and highly structured ones (e.g., discrete trial training). In naturalistic behavioral methods, therapists and parents systematically arrange the environment to encourage the child to be more interactive, and they make it easier for the child to respond to teaching opportunities in the context of natural surroundings. In highly structured methods, the therapist chooses the play material and instructs the child to respond to specific cues. Complex play skills are broken down into simpler ones, and the child is taught to learn and master the steps sequentially.

In sum, engaging in playful activities is crucial for the development of children. It helps them acquire vital skills such as sharing and cooperating with others. Play also promotes cognitive and emotional growth, allowing children to practice different social roles and make friends. However, most children on the autism spectrum face significant challenges in participating in playful activities. As a result, their play patterns differ from those of neurotypical children, which can be uninviting for their peers. During the past three decades, researchers and clinicians have developed and implemented various methods to enhance play activities for children with autism.

Summary

Social development—our capacity to interact with others and establish social relationships—is the product of genetics, brain development, and societal factors. Typically developing infants are endowed with the capacity to express and recognize emotions, and that ability significantly improves with brain maturation and social interactions. They are naturally drawn to human faces and readily engage with their primary caregivers. These behaviors are precursors of early social and emotional development. Emotions serve important communication functions and guide our behavior and reactions toward others in social situations. Neurotypical infants can express a wide range of emotional expressions, such as smiling, crying, and displaying signs of discomfort and distress. Conversely, infants at risk for developing autism may experience difficulties with social communication and interaction, including making eye contact, engaging in back-and-forth interaction, responding to their names, understanding and expressing emotions, and responding to social cues.

Sharing a perceptual experience with another person, known as joint attention, develops in infancy and is crucial for language development and forming relationships. However, infants at risk for autism may exhibit reduced joint attention, decreased eye contact, reduced responsiveness to social cues, and difficulties following someone else's gaze or pointing to share interest in objects. Joint attention lays the foundation for social referencing, where infants look to caregivers for cues on interacting with strangers. This process solidifies the attachment between infants and their caregivers.

Attachment—the emotional bond between infants and their primary caregivers—is central to their emotional and social development. Infants typically develop a primary attachment to their primary caregiver (usually their mother) during the second half of the first year. Babies begin to prefer familiar caregivers and may display distress when separated from them. Infants who later develop autism may experience challenges in early social interactions and social engagement. However, autistic children can form attachments. How they express their attachment behavior varies depending on the severity of the condition. Children with lower cognitive abilities may face more challenges forming secure attachments than their more capable peers. In comparison to neurotypical children, those on the autism spectrum are less likely to form secure attachment relationships. Early attachment experiences can significantly influence the development of a theory of mind.

Theory of mind (ToM), the capacity to understand and attribute mental states to oneself and others, begins to develop in children at around 4 years of age. The development of ToM can further the capacity to empathize with others. Children with autism experience difficulties in developing a theory of mind, and thus experience challenges understanding and attributing mental states to themselves and others. Although autistic individuals may experience cognitive empathy difficulties, they can express affective empathy. Empathetic children are more likely to engage in cooperative play, take on different roles, and understand their playmates' perspectives.

Play is crucial for the development of children as it contributes to their physical, social, and cognitive growth. Engaging in play activities allows children to express and regulate their emotions. However, children with autism often face challenges related to play due to difficulties with social interaction, communication, and imaginative play. With the proper support, guidance, and play interventions, autistic children can develop their play skills.

Questions to Ponder for Further Thinking and Learning

1   How does social development differ in individuals with autism compared to neurotypical individuals?
2   What are some common social challenges individuals with autism experience?
3   How can early interventions help support social development in children with autism?
4   What effective strategies can clinicians use to teach social skills to individuals with autism?
5   How can technological advances be used to promote and support social development in individuals with autism?
6   What roles do family members and caregivers play in supporting social development in individuals with autism?
7   What resources are available for individuals with autism and their families to help support social development?
8   How can schools and educators support the social development of students with autism?
9   How can employers create a more inclusive workplace for individuals with autism to support their social development?
10   What are some promising areas of research in the field of social development and autism?

References

Ainsworth, M. D. S., Blehar, M. C., Waters, E., & Wall, S. (1978). *Patterns of attachment: A psychological study of the strange situation*. Lawrence Erlbaum.

Aldao, A., & Nolen-Hoeksema, S. (2012). When are adaptive strategies most predictive of psychopathology? *Journal of Abnormal Psychology, 121*(1), 276–281.

Amaresha, A. C., & Venkatasubramanian, G. (2012). Expressed emotion in schizophrenia: An overview. *Indian Journal of Psychological Medicine, 34*(1), 12–20.

APA (2013). *Diagnostic and statistical manual of mental disorders* (5th ed.). American Psychiatric Association.

Asperger, H. (1991). Autistic psychopathy in childhood (U. Frith, Trans.). In U. Frith (Ed.). *Autism and Asperger syndrome* (pp. 37–92). Cambridge University Press.

Bal, E., Harden, E., Lamb, D., Van Hecke, A. V., Denver, J. W., & Porges, S. W. (2010). Emotion recognition in children with autism spectrum disorders: Relations to eye gaze and autonomic state. *Journal of Autism and Developmental Disorders, 40*(3), 358–370.

Banks, S. J., Eddy, K. T., Angstadt, M., Nathan, P. J., & Phan, K. L. (2007). Amygdala-frontal connectivity during emotion regulation. *Social Cognitive and Affective Neuroscience, 2*(4), 303–312.

Baranek, G. (1999). Autism during infancy: A retrospective video analysis of sensory-motor and social behaviors at 9–12 months of age. *Journal of Autism and Developmental Disorders, 29*(3), 213–224.

Baron-Cohen, S. (1990). Autism: A specific cognitive disorder of "mind-blindness." *International Review of Psychiatry, 2*(1), 81–90.

Baron-Cohen, S. (1997). *Mindblindness: An essay on autism and theory of mind*. MIT Press.

Baron-Cohen, S., Leslie, A. M., & Frith, U. (1985). Does the autistic child have a "theory of mind"? *Cognition, 21*(1), 37–46.

Barrera, M. E., & Maurer, D. (1981). The perception of facial expressions by the three-month- old. *Child Development, 52*(1), 203–206.

Bauminger, N., & Kasari, C. (1999). Brief report: Theory of mind in high-functioning children with autism. *Journal of Autism and Developmental Disorders, 29*, 81–86.

Beckwith, L., Rozga, A., & Sigman, M. (2002). Maternal sensitivity and attachment in atypical groups. *Advances in Child Development and Behavior, 30*, 231–274.

Begeer, S., Koot, H. M., Rieffe, C., Terwogt, M. M., & Stegge, H. (2008). Emotional competence in children with autism: Diagnostic criteria and empirical evidence. *Developmental Review, 28*(3), 342–369.

Besler, F., & Kurt, O. (2016). Effectiveness of video modeling provided by mothers in teaching play skills to children with autism. *Educational Sciences: Theory & Practice, 16*(1), 209–230.

Bettelheim, B. (1967). The Empty Fortress: Infantile Autism and the Birth of the Self. Free Press.

Bird, G., & Cook, R. (2013). Mixed emotions: The contribution of alexithymia to the emotional symptoms of autism. *Translational Psychiatry, 3*(7), e285.

Boucher, J. (2012). Putting theory of mind in its place: Psychological explanations of the socio-emotional-communicative impairments in autistic spectrum disorder. *Autism, 16*(3), 226–246.

Bowlby, J. (1969). *Attachment and loss: Vol. 1. Attachment*. Basic Books.

Bowlby, J. (1973). *Attachment and loss: Vol. 2. Separation*. Basic Books.

Bowlby, J. (1982). Attachment and loss: Retrospect and prospect. *American Journal of Orthopsychiatry, 52*(4), 664–678.

Brim, D., Townsend, D. B., DeQuinzio, J. A., & Poulson, C. L. (2009). Analysis of social referencing skills among children with autism. *Research in Autism Spectrum Disorders, 3*(4), 942–958.

Bruinsma, Y., Koegel, R. L., & Koegel, L. K. (2004). Joint attention and children with autism: A review of the literature. *Mental Retardation and Developmental Disabilities Research Reviews, 10*(3), 169–175.

Buitelaar, J. K. (1995). Attachment and social withdrawal in autism: Hypotheses and findings. *Behaviour, 132*(5–6), 319–350.

Caillies, S., Hody, A., & Calmus, A. (2012). Theory of mind and irony comprehension in children with cerebral palsy. *Research in Developmental Disabilities, 33*(5), 1380–1388.

Calkins, S. D., & Johnson, M. C. (1998). Toddler regulation of distress to frustrating events: Temperamental and maternal correlates. *Infant Behavior and Development, 21*(3), 379–395.

Campos, J. J., & Stenberg, C. (1981). Perception, appraisal, and emotion: The onset of social referencing. In M. E. Lamb & L. R. Sherrod (Eds.), *Infant social cognition: Empirical and theoretical considerations*. Erlbaum.

Coplan, R. J., & Abreau, K. A. (2009). Peer interactions and play in early childhood. In K. H. Rubin, W. M. Bukowski & B. Laursen (Eds.), *Handbook of peer interaction, relationships, and groups*. Guilford.

Courchesne, E., Akshoomoff, N. A., Townsend, J., & Saitoh, O. (1995). A model system for the study of attention and the cerebellum: Infantile autism. *Electroencephalography and Clinical Neurophysiology, 44*, 315–325.

Cutuli, D. (2014). Cognitive reappraisal and expressive suppression strategies role in the emotion regulation: An overview on their modulatory effects and neural correlates. *Frontiers in Systems Neuroscience, 8*, 175.

Darwin, C. R. (1872). *The expression of the emotions in man and animals.* Oxford University Press.

Dawson, G. (1991). A psychobiological perspective on the early socio-emotional development of children with autism. In D. Cicchetti & S. L. Toth (Eds.), *Rochester symposium on developmental psychopathology, Vol. 3. models and integrations* (pp. 207–234). University of Rochester Press.

Dawson, G., & Lewy, A. (1989). Arousal, attention, and the socioemotional impairments of individuals with autism. In G. Dawson (Ed.), *Autism: Nature, diagnosis, and treatment* (pp. 49–74). The Guilford Press.

Dawson, G., Meltzoff, A. N., Osterling, J., Rinaldi, J., & Brown, E. (1998). Children with autism fail to orient to naturally occurring social stimuli. *Journal of Autism and Developmental Disorders, 28*(6), 479–485.

DeQuinzio, J. A., Poulson, C. L., Townsend, D. B., & Taylor, B. A. (2015). Social referencing and children with autism. *The Behavior Analyst, 39*(2), 319–331.

Derryberr, D., & Rothbart, M. K. (2001). Early temperament and emotional development. In A. F. Kalverboer & A. Gramsbergen (Eds.), *Handbook of brain and behavior in human development* (pp. 967–988). Kluwer Academic.

Dinberg, U., & Petterson, M. (2000). Facial reaction to happy and angry facial expressions: Evidence for right hemisphere dominance. *Psychophysiology, 37*(5), 693–696.

Eisenberg, N., Spinrad, T. L., & Knafo-Noam, A. (2015). Prosocial development. In M. E. Lamb (Vol. Ed.) & R. M. Lerner (Ed.), *Handbook of child psychology and developmental science: Vol. 3. Socioemotional processes* (pp. 610–656). Wiley.

Ekman, P. (1973). Cross-cultural studies of facial expression. In P. Ekman (Ed.), *Darwin and facial expression: A century of research in review* (pp. 169–222). Academic Press.

Feinman, S., Roberts, D., Hsieh, K. F., Sawyer, D., & Swanson, D. (1992). A critical review of social referencing in infancy. In S. Feinman (Ed.), *Social referencing and the social construction of reality in infancy* (pp. 15–54). Springer.

Flavell, J. H. (1985). *Cognitive development* (2nd ed.). Prentice Hall.

Flavell, J. H. (1999). Cognitive development: Children's knowledge about the mind. *Annual Review of Psychology, 50*, 21–45.

Fletcher-Watson, S., McConnell, F., Manola, E., & McConachie, H. (2014). Interventions based on the Theory of Mind cognitive model for autism spectrum disorder (ASD). *Cochrane Database of Systematic Reviews, 2014*(3), CD008785.

Fox, N. A., & Calkins, S. D. (2003). The development of self-control of emotion: Intrinsic and extrinsic influences. *Motivation and Emotion, 27*(1), 7–26.

Frith, U. (1991). *Autism and Asperger syndrome.* Cambridge University Press.

Gernsbacher, M. A., & Yergeau, M. (2019). Empirical failures of the claim that autistic people lack a theory of mind. *Archives of Scientific Psychology, 7*(1), 102–118.

Gervai, J. (2009). Environmental and genetic influences on early attachment. *Child and Adolescent Psychiatry and Mental Health, 3*, Article 25.

Goodall, E. (2013). *Understanding and facilitating the achievement of autistic potential* (2nd ed.). Healthy Possibilities Pty Ltd.

Greenberg, J., Seltzer, M., Baker, J., Smith L., Warren S. F., Brady, N., & Hong, J. (2012). Family environment and behavior problems in Children, adolescents, and adults with fragile X syndrome. *American Journal on Intellectual and Developmental Disabilities, 117*(4), 331–346.

Griffin, C., Lombardo, M. V., & Auyeung, B. (2016). Alexithymia in children with and without autism spectrum disorders. *Autism Research, 9*(7), 773–780.

Grzadzinski, R. L., Luyster, R., Spencer, A. G., & Lord, C. (2014). Attachment in young children with autism spectrum disorders: An examination of separation and reunion behaviors with both mothers and fathers. *Autism, 18*(2), 85–96.

Hamlin, J. K., & Wynn, K. (2011). Young infants prefer prosocial to antisocial others. *Cognitive Development*, *26*(1), 30–39.

Healey, M. L., & Grossman, M. (2018). Cognitive and affective perspective-taking: Evidence for shared and dissociable anatomical substrates. *Frontiers in Neurology*, *9*, 491.

Hoff, E. (2014). *Language development* (5th ed.). Wadsworth.

Hoffman, M. I. (2000). *Empathy and moral development: Implications for caring and justice*. Cambridge University Press.

Howe, N., & Leach, J. (2018). Children's play and peer relations. In W. M. Bukowski, B. Laursen, & K. H. Rubin (Eds.), *Handbook of peer interactions, relationships, and groups* (2nd ed., pp. 222–242). The Guilford Press.

Ichikawa, H., & Yamaguchi, M. K. (2014). Infants' recognition of subtle anger facial expression. *Japanese Psychological Research*, *56*(1), 15–23.

Izard, C. E., & Ackerman, B. P. (2000). Motivational, organizational, and regulatory functions of discrete emotions. In M. Lewis & J. M. Haviland-Jones (Eds.), *Handbook of emotions* (2nd ed.) Guilford.

Jones, E. J., Gliga, T., Bedford, R., Charman, T., & Johnson, M. H. (2014). Developmental pathways to autism: A review of prospective studies of infants at risk. *Neuroscience and Biobehavioral Reviews*, *39*(100), 1–33.

Jones, W., & Klin, A. (2013). Attention to eyes is present but in decline in 2–6 month-old infants later diagnosed with autism. *Nature*, *504*(7480), 427–431.

Jordan, R. (2003). Social play and autistic spectrum disorders: A perspective on theory, implications and educational approaches. *Autism*, *7*(4), 347–360.

Kanner, L. (1943). Autistic disturbances of affective contact. *Nervous Child*, *2*, 217–250.

Kinnaird, E., Stewart, C., & Tchanturia, K. (2019). Investigating alexithymia in autism: A systematic review and meta-analysis. *European Psychiatry*, *55*, 80–89.

Kohler, W. (1925). *The mentality of apes*. Routledge and Kegan Paul.

Kopp, C. B. (1992). Emotional distress and control in young children. In N. Eisenberg & R. A. Fabes (Eds.), *Emotion and its regulation in early development* (pp. 41–56). Jossey-Bass.

Lantz, J. (2001). Play time: An examination of play intervention strategies for children with autism spectrum disorders. *The Reporter*, *6*(3), 1–7, 24.

Lauttia, J., Helminen, T. M., Leppänen, J. M., Yrttiaho, S., Eriksson, K., Hietanen, J. K., & Kylliäinen, A. (2019). Atypical pattern of frontal EEG asymmetry for direct gaze in young children with autism spectrum disorder. *Journal of Autism and Developmental Disorders*, *49*(9), 3592–3601.

Lecavalier, L. (2006). Behavioral and emotional problems in young people with pervasive developmental disorders: Relative prevalence, effects of subject characteristics, and empirical classification. *Journal of Autism and Developmental Disorders*, *36*(8), 1101–1114.

Lewis, M. (2008). The emergence of human emotions. In M. Lewis, J. M. Haviland-Jones, & L. F. Barrett (Eds.), *Handbook of emotions* (3rd ed., pp. 304–319). The Guilford Press.

Lillard, A. S., Lerner, M. D., Hopkins, E. J., Dore, R. A., Smith, E. D., & Palmquist, C. M. (2013). The impact of pretend play on children's development: A review of the evidence. *Psychological Bulletin*, *139*(1), 1–34.

Lorenz, K. Z. (1952). *King Solomon's ring*. Crowell Company.

Lovaas, O. I., & Schreibman, L. (1971). Stimulus overselectivity of autistic children in a two stimulus situation. *Behaviour Research and Therapy*, *9*(4), 305–310.

Lubomirska, A., Eldevik, S., Eikeseth, S., Riis, S., & Budzińska, A. (2022). The development and validation of The Social Referencing Observation Scale as a screening instrument for autism spectrum disorder. *Behavioral Interventions*, *37*(4), 1043–1057.

Lukito, S., Jones, C. R. G., Pickles, A., Baird, G., Happé, F., Charman, T., & Simonoff, E. (2017). Specificity of executive function and theory of mind performance in relation to attention-deficit/hyperactivity symptoms in autism spectrum disorders. *Molecular Autism, 8,* 60.

Main, M., & Solomon, J. (1986). Discovery of an insecure-disorganized/disoriented attachment pattern. In T. B. Brazelton & M. W. Yogman (Eds.), *Affective development in infancy* (pp. 95–124). Ablex Publishing.

Main, M., & Solomon, J. (1990). Procedures for identifying infants as disorganized/disoriented during the Ainsworth Strange Situation. In M. T. Greenberg, D. Cicchetti, & E. M. Cummings (Eds.), *Attachment in the preschool years: Theory, research, and intervention* (pp. 121–160). The University of Chicago Press.

Mangelsdorf, A. C., Shapiro, J. R., & Marzolf, D. (1995). Developmental and temperamental differences in emotion regulation in infancy. *Child Development, 66*(6), 1817–1828.

Marchetti, A., Miraglia, L., & Di Dio, C. (2020). Toward a socio-material approach to cognitive empathy in autistic spectrum disorder. *Frontiers in Psychology, 10,* 2965.

Markram, K., & Markram, H. (2010). The Intense World Theory—A unifying theory of the neurobiology of autism. *Frontiers in Human Neuroscience, 4,* 224.

Martin, K. B., Haltigan, J. D., Ekas, N., Prince, E. B., & Messinger, D. S. (2020). Attachment security differs by later autism spectrum disorder: A prospective study. *Developmental Science, 23*(5), e12953.

Masten, C. L., Morelli, S. A., & Eisenberger, N. I. (2011). An fMRI investigation of empathy for 'social pain' and subsequent prosocial behavior. *Neuroimage, 55*(1), 381–388.

Melchers, M., Montag, C., Markett, S., & Reuter, M. (2015). Assessment of empathy via self-report and behavioural paradigms: Data on convergent and discriminant validity. *Cognitive Neuropsychiatry, 20*(2), 157–171.

Meltzoff, A., & Gopnik, A. (1993). The role of imitation in understanding persons and developing a theory of mind. In S. Baron- Cohen, H. Tager-Flusberg, & D. J. Cohen (Eds.), *Understanding other minds* (pp. 335–366). Oxford University Press.

Milton, D. E. M. (2012). On the ontological status of autism: The 'double empathy problem.' *Disability & Society, 27*(6), 883–887.

Montagut-Asunción, M., Crespo-Martín, S., Pastor-Cerezuela, G., & D'Ocon-Giménez, A. (2022). Joint attention and its relationship with autism risk markers at 18 months of age. *Children, 9*(4), 556.

Mul, C. L., Stagg, S. D., Herbelin, B., & Aspell, J. E. (2018). The feeling of me feeling for you: Interoception, alexithymia and empathy in autism. *Journal of Autism and Developmental Disorders, 48,* 2953–2967.

Müller, R. A., & Fishman, I. (2018). Brain connectivity and neuroimaging of social networks in autism. *Trends in Cognitive Science, 22*(12), 1103–1116.

Osterling, J., & Dawson, G. (1994). Early recognition of children with autism: A study of first birthday home videotapes. *Journal of Autism and Developmental Disorders, 24*(3), 247–257.

Parten, M. B. (1932). Social participation among preschool children. *Journal of Abnormal and Social Psychology, 27*(3), 243–269.

Pellegrini, A. D. (2009). *The role of play in human development.* Oxford University Press.

Poquérusse, J., Pastore, L., Dellantonio, S., & Esposito, G. (2018). Alexithymia and autism spectrum disorder: A complex relationship. *Frontiers in Psychology, 9,* 1196.

Premack, D., & Woodruff, G. (1978). Does the chimpanzee have a theory of mind? *Behavioral and Brain Sciences, 1*(4), 515–526.

Richey, J. A., Damiano, C. R., Sabatino, A., Rittenberg, A., Petty, C., Bizzell, J., … Dichter, G. S. (2015). Neural mechanisms of emotion regulation in autism spectrum disorder. *Journal of Autism and Developmental Disorders, 45*(11), 3409–3423.

Roisman, G. I., & Booth-LaForce, C. (2014). The Adult Attachment Interview: Psychometrics, stability, and change from infancy, and developmental origins: VIII. *General Discussion: Monographs of the Society for Research in Child Development*, *79*(3), 126–137.

Rothbart, M. K. (2011). *Becoming who we are: Temperament and personality development*. Guilford.

Rubin, K. H., Coplan, R. J., Chen, X., Bowker, J. C., McDonald, K. L., & Heverly-Fitt, S. (2015). Peer relationships. In M. H. Bornstein & M. E. Lamb (Eds.), *Developmental science: An advanced textbook* (7th ed., pp. 587–644). Psychology Press.

Rump, K. M., Giovannelli, J. L., Minshew, N. J., & Strauss, M. S. (2009). The development of emotion recognition in individuals with autism. *Child Development*, *80*(5), 1434–1447.

Rutgers, A. H., Bakermans-Kranenburg, M. J., van Ijzendoorn, M. H., & van Berckelaer-Onnes, I. A. (2004). Autism and attachment: A meta-analytic review. *Journal of Child Psychology and Psychiatry*, *45*, 1123–1134.

Rutherford, H. J. V., Wallace, N. S., Laurent, H. K., & Mayes, L. C. (2015). Emotion regulation in parenthood. *Developmental Review*, *36*, 1–14.

Salo, V. C., Rowe, M. L., & Reeb-Sutherland, B. C. (2018). Exploring infant gesture and joint attention as related constructs and as predictors of later language. *Infancy*, *23*, 432–452.

Samson, A. C., Hardan, A. Y., Lee, I. A., Phillips, J. M., & Gross, J. J. (2015). Maladaptive behavior in autism spectrum disorder: The role of emotion experience and emotion regulation. *Journal of Autism and Developmental Disorders*, *45*(11), 3424–3432.

Scatliffe, N., Casavant, S., Vittner, D., & Cong, X. (2019). Oxytocin and early parent-infant interactions: A systematic review. *International Journal of Nursing Science*, *6*(4), 445–453.

Schaffer, H. R., & Emerson, P. E. (1964). The development of social attachment in infancy. *Monographs of the Society for Research in Child Development*, *29*(3), 1–77.

Schietecatte, I., Roeyers, H., & Warreyn, P. (2012). Can infants' orientation to social stimuli predict later joint attention skills? *British Journal of Developmental Psychology*, *30*(2), 267–282.

Shalev, I., Warrier, V., Greenberg, D. M., Smith, P., Allison, C, Baron-Cohen, S., … Uzefovsky, F. (2022). Reexamining empathy in autism: Empathic disequilibrium as a novel predictor of autism diagnosis and autistic traits. *Autism Research*, *15*(10), 1917–1928.

Sigelman, C. K., & Rider, E. A. (2022). *Life-span human development* (10th ed.). Cengage

Sigman, M., & Capps, L. (1997). *Children with autism: A developmental perspective*. Harvard University Press.

Sivaraman, M., Virues-Ortega, J., & Roeyers, H. (2020). Social referencing skills in children with autism spectrum disorder: A systematic review. *Research in Autism Spectrum Disorders*, *72*, 101528.

Smith, A. (2009). Emotional empathy in autism spectrum conditions: Weak, intact, or heightened? *Journal of Autism and Developmental disorders*, *39*(12), 1749–1754.

Smith, L. E., Greenberg, J. S., Seltzer, M. M., & Hong, J. (2008). Symptoms and behavior problems of adolescents and adults with autism: Effects of mother-child relationship quality, warmth and praise. *American Journal on Mental Retardation*, *113*(5), 387–402.

Stahmer, A. C., Ingersoll, B., & Carter, C. (2003). Behavioral approaches to promoting play. *Autism*, *7*(4), 401–413.

Taylor, E. L., Target, M., & Charman, T. (2008). Attachment in adults with high-functioning autism. *Attachment and Human Development*, *10*(2), 143–163.

Thomas, A., & Chess S. (1986). The New York Longitudinal Study: From infancy to early adult life. In R. Plomin & J. Dunn (Eds.), *The study of temperament: Changes, continuities, and challenges*. Erlbaum.

Thomas, L. A., De Bellis, M. D., Graham, R., & LaBar, K. S. (2007). Development of emotional facial recognition in late childhood and adolescence. *Developmental Science*, *10*(5), 547–558.

Thompson, R. A. (1994). Emotion regulation: A theme in search of definition. *Monographs for the Society for Research in Child Development*, *59*(2–3), 25–52.

van Buijsen, M., Hendriks, A., Ketelaars, M., & Verhoeven, L. (2011). Assessment of theory of mind in children with communication disorders: Role of presentation mode. *Research in Developmental Disabilities*, *32*(3), 1038–1045.

van der Velde, J., Servaas, M. N., Goerlich, K. S., Bruggeman, R., Horton P., & Costafreda, S. G. (2013). Neural correlates of alexithymia: A meta-analysis of emotion processing studies. *Neuroscience & Biobehavioral Reviews*, *37*(7), 1774–1785.

van Ijzendoorn, M. H., Rutgers, A. H., Bakermans-Kranenburg, M. J., van Daalen, E., Dietz, C., Buitelaar, J. K., … van Engeland, H. (2007). Parental sensitivity and attachment in children with autism spectrum disorder: Comparison with children with mental retardation, with language delays, and with typical development. *Child Development*, *78*(2), 597–608.

van Ijzendoorn, M. H., Vereijken, C. M. J. L., Bakermans- Kranenburg, M. J., & Risken-Walraven, J. M. A. (2004). Assessing attachment security with the attachment Q-Sort: Meta-analytic evidence for the validity of the observer AQS. *Child Development*, *75*(4), 1188–1213.

van Neerven, T., Bos, D. J., & van Haren, N. E. M. (2021). Deficiencies in Theory of Mind in patients with schizophrenia, bipolar disorder, and major depressive disorder: A systematic review of secondary literature. *Neuroscience and Biobehavioral Reviews*, *120*, 249–261.

Waters, E., & Deane, K. E. (1985). Defining and assessing individual differences in attachment relationships: Q-methodology and the organization of behavior in infancy and early childhood. *Monographs of the Society for Research in Child Development*, *50*(1/2), 41–65.

Watson, D., Clark, L. A., & Tellegen, A. (1988). Development and validation of brief measures of positive and negative affect: The PANAS Scales. *Journal of Personality and Social Psychology*, *54*(6), 1063–1070.

Wellman, H. M., Cross, D., & Watson, J. (2001). Meta-analysis of theory-of-mind development: The truth about false belief. *Child Development*, *72*(3), 655–684.

White, R. C., & Remington, A. (2019). Object personification in autism: This paper will be very sad if you don't read it. *Autism*, *23*(4), 1042–1045.

Widen, S. C., & Russell, J. A. (2003). A closer look at preschoolers' freely produced labels for facial expressions. *Developmental Psychology*, *39*(1), 114–128.

Willemsen-Swinkels, S. H. N., Bakermans-Kranenburg, M. J., Buitelaar, J. K., van Ijzendoorn, M. H., & van Engeland, H. (2000). Insecure and disorganised attachment in children with a pervasive developmental disorder: Relationship with social interaction and heart rate. *Journal of Child Psychology and Psychiatry*, *41*(6), 759–767.

Wimmer, H., & Perner, J. (1983). Beliefs about beliefs: Representation and constraining function of wrong beliefs in young children's understanding of deception. *Cognition*, *13*(1), 103–128.

Wolfberg, P. J. (1995). Enhancing children's play. In K. A. Quill (Ed.), *Teaching children with autism: Strategies to enhance communication and socialization* (pp. 193–218). Delmar Publishers.

Wolfberg, P. J., & Schuler, A. L. (1993). Integrated play groups: A model for promoting the social and cognitive dimensions of play in children with autism. *Journal of Autism and Developmental Disorders*, *23*(3), 467–489.

Woodward, A. L. (2009). Infants' grasp of others' intentions. *Current Directions in Psychological Science, 18*(1), 53–57.

Young-Browne, G., Rosenfeld, H. M., & Horowitz, F. D. (1977). Infant discrimination of facial expressions. *Child Development, 48*(2), 555–562.

Zelazo, P. D., Burack, J. A., Benedetto, E., & Frye, D. (1996). Theory of mind and rule use in individuals with Down's syndrome: A test of the uniqueness and specificity claims. *Journal of Child Psychology and Psychiatry, and Allied Disciplines, 37*(4), 479–484.

Zwaigenbaum, L., Bryson, S., & Garon, N. (2013). Early identification of autism spectrum disorders. *Behavior and Brain Research, 251*, 133–146.

Zwaigenbaum, L., Bryson, S., Rogers, T., Roberts, W., Brian, J., & Szatmari, P. (2005). Behavioral manifestations of autism in the first year of life. *International Journal of Developmental Neuroscience, 23*(2–3), 143–152.

Chapter 4

Cognitive Development in Autism

Chapter Contents

DOI: 10.4324/9781003336266-5

Introduction

Cognition—the mental process of knowing through which we acquire knowledge and problem-solving—is guided by brain maturation and experience with the world. Newborns do not appear to have any sense of self. They gradually develop an implicit understanding of the self, based on their actions in the immediate environment and daily interactions with their caregivers (Rochat, 2018; Rochat & Striano, 2000). By 2 or 3 months of age, infants can display a sense of agency—their capacity to understand that their actions can affect the world around them. During the second half of the first year, infants develop object or person permanence—the understanding that objects or people continue to exist when they are out of sight. Before this age, infants typically believe that when an object is no longer visible, it ceases to exist. Piaget, the architect of the most elaborate theory of cognitive development, proposed that object permanence emerges during the sensorimotor stage from birth to 2 years of age (Bremner et al., 2015). Object permanence is essential for developing cause-and-effect relationships (e.g., searching for and finding an object hidden from view).

Infants' cognitive development paves the way for memory and language development. As infants' cognitive abilities advance, they acquire the ability to store and recall information and produce sounds that resemble meaningful words. The development of language marks a significant milestone in cognitive development. Infants' ability to make sounds, such as cooing and babbling, develops during the first year of life, laying the groundwork for language development and acquisition.

Neurocognitive impairment, including executive dysfunction and social cognition deficits, is usually linked to autism (Hajri et al., 2022). Infants subsequently diagnosed with autism may show delayed language development and deficits in social communication and interaction, attention, and perception. In addition, they are more likely to focus on visual environmental stimuli than social cues. Compared to typical individuals, those on the autism spectrum often experience difficulties with social cues and executive functioning.

Cognitive Development

Cognitive development is a complex and dynamic process that begins in infancy and continues throughout the lifespan. Typically developing infants develop essential cognitive skills, including attention, memory, and problem-solving. Those skills pave the way for future and more advanced cognitive abilities. In essence, cognition comprises processing, storing, and using information. Infants can respond to familiar voices in the first few months of life, recognize faces, and show preferences for certain stimuli. However, their cognitive abilities evolve gradually during the first couple of years. For example, they begin to develop object permanence—that objects continue to exist even when they are out of sight. As infants grow, their cognitive capabilities, including memory, problem-solving, and social interactions, continue to advance.

Much of what we know about cognitive development has been greatly influenced by the works of Jean Piaget and Lev Vygotsky. Piaget (1952) proposed four invariants—universal stages of cognitive development: sensorimotor, pre-operational, concrete operations, and formal operations. According to Piaget, infants can construct world knowledge through the senses and goal-directed behaviors without social mediation and act on their environment to learn.

In contrast, Vygotsky proposed a sociocultural view of cognitive development, emphasizing the crucial role of a more knowledgeable partner in fostering cognitive development. According to Vygotsky (1978), cognitive development does not proceed universally through invariant stages but through guided participation and cultural interactions, using language and the tools a culture provides. Vygotsky's concept of the "zone of proximal development" highlights the difference between what a learner can assimilate independently and what he can with the guidance of a more competent partner, underscoring the importance of social interaction in cognitive development.

Cognition and Autism

Cognitive impairment is not one of the defining diagnostic criteria for autism in the DSM-5 but is among the most challenging characteristics of autism spectrum disorder. Due to the condition's heterogeneity, the degree of impairment varies from person to person. It includes thinking, learning, and problem-solving difficulties that can affect memory, attention, and executive function. The most recent publication of the Autism and Developmental Disabilities Monitoring Network found approximately 40% of 8-year-olds have an intellectual disability (Maenner et al., 2023), a subtype of cognitive impairment.

The effects of autism on cognition differ significantly from person to person. It can affect memory, learning, sensory perception, and cognitive processing (Al-Mazidi, 2023). Some individuals may struggle with social communication, interpreting nonverbal cues, and understanding and expressing emotions. Others may intensely focus on specific topics or objects and pay attention to detail. Additionally, some individuals may need help with executive functioning, such as planning and organization.

The Emerging of Self

Self-Recognition and Self-Awareness

Newborns typically do not have a sense of self. Their self-awareness develops gradually as they interact with their environment, which is crucial for their early cognitive and social growth. The ability to recognize oneself in a mirror, known as self-recognition, depends on the maturation of specific brain structures (such as the medial frontal cortex and occipital cortex) and cognitive development (Bertenthal & Fischer, 1978; Lewis & Carmody, 2008). Generally, infants start self-recognizing around the second half of their second year. Is self-recognition somewhat impaired in children with intellectual disabilities? Hill and Tomlin (1981) investigated this question. They found that children with Down syndrome were slower to recognize themselves in a mirror, but they were more likely to self-recognize when they reached a **mental age** of approximately 18 months.

Infants typically show signs of self-recognition at around 18 to 24 months of age. The mirror test can be used to assess an infant's self-recognition (Lewis & Brooks-Gunn, 1979). In this test, a small but noticeable mark (such as a dab of red lipstick) is applied to an infant's face, and then the infant is placed in front of a mirror. If the infant tries to wipe off the mark, it suggests self-recognition. However, if the infant looks behind the mirror, it may indicate that they think the reflection is of someone else. This ability to recognize oneself in a mirror is considered a key milestone in developing self-awareness.

Self-awareness is an important aspect of human cognition, encompassing our sense of individuality and being conscious of our thoughts, feelings, and actions. Social interaction plays a significant role in fostering self-awareness. For instance, toddlers who have established a secure attachment with their primary caregivers are more likely to recognize themselves in a mirror than those with less secure attachments (Pipp et al., 1992). Gallup (1979) found that chimpanzees raised in isolation were less likely to recognize themselves in a mirror than those who were raised in the company of others.

Self-Recognition, Self-Awareness, and Autism

Many infants who will later develop autism may have difficulties with self-recognition. Unlike typically developing infants, they may show atypical responses to their reflection in a mirror. Carmody and Lewis (2012) conducted a study using mirror recognition, other-directed pretend play, and the use of personal pronouns to investigate the self-representation abilities in typically developing (TD) children and children with autism spectrum disorder (ASD). They found that TD children were more proficient in recognizing themselves in a mirror—using personal pronouns and engaging in other-directed pretend play—than children with ASD. Thus, it seems that some children with ASD may have less developed self-representation skills.

Empirical evidence supports deficits in self-representation and intrapersonal cognition in individuals with autism. Uddin (2011) reviewed the literature and found that the psychological aspects of self-representation are altered in autism, not the physical ones. The medial **prefrontal cortex** has been identified as a potential brain region where self-related deficits may occur in individuals with autism.

Are autistic individuals aware of their condition? Children with more advanced cognitive abilities may better understand that they are different from their peers and their diagnosis compared to those with more significant cognitive difficulties. Similarly, autistic adults may have varying levels of awareness about their condition, depending on their level of cognitive functioning. Huang and colleagues (2017) reviewed the literature on individuals with autism and their understanding of the self. Researchers generally agree that individuals with autism experience impairments in their psychological self. Those difficulties stem from their deficits in communication and theory of mind, leading to their limited awareness of the self and others.

In sum, self-recognition and self-awareness develop gradually in typically developing infants. They can usually recognize themselves in a mirror in the second half of the second year. In contrast, children who develop autism experience difficulties with self-recognition and self-awareness. The medial prefrontal cortex is believed to play a role in autistic individuals' self-representation. Although individuals with autism may be aware of their diagnosis, those with more advanced cognitive functioning are more likely to understand the challenges that their condition imposes.

Decision-Making

Decision-making involves processing information, weighing options, and choosing a course of action based on reasoning and judgment. Newborns can display goal-directed action oriented toward physical targets. In infancy, decision-making is primarily driven by instinctual responses to sensory stimuli. However, decision-making that is based on desire emerges in late infancy. Kenward and colleagues (2009) found that 24-month-olds were more likely to choose a desired item whose value was increased than their counterparts who chose an item whose value remained unchanged. However, 14- and 19-month-olds displayed no such preference. As children develop and mature, decision-making becomes more complex.

Early brain growth, particularly in the prefrontal cortex, has been linked to autism development. Courchesne and colleagues (2011) examined the postmortem prefrontal tissues of seven autistic children and six neurotypical ones. Compared to the brains of neurotypical children studied, those with autism had 67% more neurons in their prefrontal cortex and heavier brain weight. The prefrontal cortex, one of the last structures to mature, is the brain's executive center, responsible for decision-making, planning, and impulse control (Funahashi, 2017a).

Decision-Making and Autism

Autistic individuals experience difficulties in decision-making. Processing sensory information, challenges in processing sensory information, difficulties understanding social cues, and cognitive inflexibility contribute to poor decision-making. Tei and colleagues (2022) used functional magnetic resonance imaging (fMRI) to investigate decision flexibility in autistic and neurotypical participants who were presented with two moral dilemmas they had to recognize and solve:

(1) cost-benefit analysis (i.e., evaluating the pros and cons of a decision) and (2) mitigating inevitable misconducts (i.e., acting to minimize or reduce the consequences of wrongful actions). The **left inferior frontal gyrus** showed lower activity in the cost-benefit analysis of the autistic participants in comparison to the non-autistic one. There was no significant difference in the left inferior frontal gyrus in the groups in the mitigating inevitable misconduct conditions.

Decision-making capacity is influenced by neurological development and social interactions. The prefrontal cortex has been demonstrated in various studies to be particularly crucial for decision-making during development (Steinbeis & Crone, 2016). Luke and colleagues (2012) used the General Decision-Making Style Inventory to examine the decision-making of 38 adults with autism and 40 neurotypical adults. Adults on the autism spectrum reported more avoidance of decision-making than their counterparts without autism.

Attention

Attention is the selective focus on a particular aspect of information while ignoring other non-relevant stimuli. It is a process that begins in infancy and develops in childhood, adolescence, and adulthood. Attention plays a vital role in developing cognitive processes such as memory, learning, and problem-solving. Newborns have an orienting system, which reacts to environmental stimulation and is quickly captured by what attracts their attention. Older children, however, have a focusing system, which purposely attends to environmental stimulation (Ruff & Rothbart, 1996). Consequently, older children have longer attention spans than younger ones. As a result, they can, for example, sit for more extended class periods. This capacity is associated with ongoing myelination of the brain regions that support attention regulation (Tanner, 1990). The myelination process starts **in utero** and continues to develop throughout the lifespan (de Faria et al., 2019).

Attention Development

How does attention develop? Attention develops gradually over time. Newborns have a limited attention span and are easily distracted. As children grow older, they can focus on specific tasks more readily. Posner and Petersen (1990) proposed a conceptualization of attention consisting of three sets of cognitive processes that function independently: The alerting, orienting, and executive system. Heightened alertness in attention results in quicker selection of a response. Orienting attention refers to focusing on a specific environmental stimulus or location. Executive attention focuses on relevant information, ignores distractions, and switches between different tasks.

Infants' ability to engage with people and objects in their environment influences the development of social communication skills. Any disruption in this early process could diminish the frequency and quality of social interactions and learning experiences, negatively affecting social development. Research with infant siblings (younger boys and girls) at risk for developing autism (i.e., owing to having an older autistic sibling) has found disrupted patterns of social orienting and attention in infants as young as 6 months of age (Elsabbagh et al., 2011). Bradshaw and colleagues (2020) examined early attention in at-risk infants for developing autism. Compared to low-risk infants, those at high risk performed lower on attention tasks at 2 and 3 months of age. Other studies have found that 6-month-old infants later diagnosed with ASD show decreased attention to social scenes and faces compared to typically developing infants (Chawarska et al., 2013; Shic et al., 2014).

Attention and Autism

Infants at risk for developing autism and those diagnosed with ASD often have difficulties spontaneously following gazes and rarely engage in joint attention (Montagut-Asunción et al., 2022; Montenegro et al., 2022). These early signs may help identify infants who might benefit from screening, diagnosis, and early interventions. Autistic children experience attention difficulties, including challenges focusing on specific tasks, being easily distracted, and shifting attention. In fact, Attention-Deficit/Hyperactivity Disorder (ADHD) is one of the most common comorbid disorders associated with autism, with prevalence ranging from 22.5% up to 91.8% (van Steensel et al., 2013). In previous editions of the DSM, children could not receive a dual diagnosis of autism and ADHD. However, the DSM-5 (2013) allows children to receive both diagnoses if they meet the criteria. Given consistent findings of high comorbidity between ADHD and autism, Ma and colleagues (2021) investigated possible **pleiotropic** genes that underlap both disorders. They identified The SHANK 2 gene as a potential key gene influencing the genetic overlap between Autism and ADHD. Shank genes are important for synaptic structure and function. Mutations in these genes can disrupt the functioning of the synapses and have been linked to neurodevelopmental disorders, including autism and ADHD (Woike et al., 2022).

Fan and colleagues (2002) developed the Attention Network Test (ANT) to evaluate alerting, orienting, and executive attention. The person being evaluated responds to visual stimuli presented on a computer screen. Test results provide insights into the tester's ability to remain focused, shift attention, and inhibit distractions. Mutreja and colleagues (2016) used the ANT to evaluate the functioning of the attention system in 52 neurotypical children and 14 autistic children. Compared to the neurotypical participants, those on the autism spectrum demonstrated intact alerting attention but performed less efficiently in orienting and executive attention. Similarly, Ridderinkhof and colleagues (2020) investigated the attention systems of 49 autistic children and 51 neurotypical ones. They found that the speed of the attention systems was similar in both groups, but autistic children were less accurate in their orienting and executive attention. Interestingly, the study also found that a mindfulness-based program did not significantly improve the attention of autistic children but showed some improvement in their orienting and executive attention.

In sum, attention is a process that develops in infancy and continues to be a crucial cognitive process throughout the lifespan. Newborns have limited attention spans and are easily distracted. Myelination of brain regions that support attention regulation makes it possible for children, adolescents, and adults to develop extended attention spans progressively. Many children with autism experience difficulties in staying on task. Additionally, attention-deficit/hyperactivity disorder is one of the most common conditions associated with autism. This interconnectedness of the conditions is an important aspect to consider. One potential gene (i.e., SHANK 2) is believed to influence the genetic overlap between autism and attention deficit.

Memory

Memory denotes our capacity to encode, store, and retrieve necessary information when needed. Memory develops and changes throughout the lifespan. The processes of human memory have captured the interest of various researchers. Ebbinghaus (1964 [1885]) pioneered the scientific study of memory when other psychologists were interested in exploring introspection. He is best known for discovering the forgetting curve. Lashley's (1950) search for the engram (i.e., the neural representation of a memory) suggested that memories are not localized but are widely distributed within and among brain structures. Broadbent (1958) was one of the memory researchers who speculated on how humans process and store information. The advent of the information-processing approach and computers provided a model to conceptualize human memory.

Consistent with the workings of a computer system, Atkinson and Shiffrin (1968) proposed a framework consisting of three components: The **sensory register**, the **short-term memory**, and the **long-term memory**. The sensory register holds sensory information briefly (less than one second). In contrast with long-term memory, with its unlimited storage of information that can be maintained over long periods, short-term memory can hold limited information only briefly. **Working memory** is associated with short-term memory (Baddeley, 2012). However, it lasts longer because data must be maintained, processed, and organized when performing a cognitive task (e.g., completing a multiple-choice test item). Additionally, memory researchers differentiate between **implicit memory** (aka procedural) and **explicit memory** (aka declarative) and how the long-term memory store differentially responds depending on the nature of the task. Explicit memory can be further divided into **episodic memory** and **semantic memory**.

Memory Neural Basis

Memory researchers have made considerable progress in understanding how different brain structures influence memory. The case of Henry Molaison, also known as H.M., is a well-documented example that provides evidence of the connection between brain structures and memory function. H.M. was an epileptic patient who underwent a surgical procedure to remove parts of his medial temporal lobe, including the hippocampus. The procedure effectively treated his seizures but resulted in his development of **anterograde amnesia** (Annese et al., 2014; Squire, 2009).

Various parts of the brain are implicated in different forms of memory. Three brain structures are involved in explicit memory: The hippocampus, the **neocortex**, and the amygdala. The hippocampus is instrumental in creating new episodic memories. The neocortex, the largest part of the cerebral cortex, plays an essential role in higher functions, including sensory perception, spatial reasoning, and language. Some memories that are temporarily stored in the hippocampus can be transferred to the neocortex via the **entorhinal cortex**, which connects the hippocampus to the other brain regions (Annese et al., 2014). The amygdala is associated with events with emotional significance (e.g., being involved in a car crash). The amygdala is also involved in forming new memories, particularly those related to fear, and plays an active role in encoding emotionally arousing experiences. It is also involved in implicit learning or learning acquired through unconscious means, as in Pavlovian/classical conditioning (Hermans et al., 2014).

The basal ganglia, the cerebellum, and the prefrontal cortex are other brain regions involved in implicit memory. The basal ganglia's primary function is to regulate movement. However, recent studies have found that it also plays a role in procedural memory retrieval (Foerde & Shohamy, 2011). Insults to the basal ganglia can lead to difficulties with motor control and problems with memory and cognitive function. The cerebellum has been traditionally linked to coordinating voluntary movement and maintaining posture and balance. It has also been associated with conscious episodic memory retrieval (Andreasen et al., 1999), procedural memory (Mochizuki-Kawai, 2008), and verbal working memory (Tomlinson et al., 2014). Damage to the cerebellum can impair memory and other cognitive processes. The prefrontal cortex plays a significant role in working memory (Funahashi, 2017b; Lara & Wallis, 2015).

Memory Development

Memory development is a continuous process that persists throughout adulthood. In typical infants, long-term memory gradually improves with time. Rovee-Collier and Cuevas (2009) used an operant conditioning procedure to demonstrate that infants positioned in a crib and allowed to move an overhead

mobile with a ribbon attached without slack to the ankle can show long-term recollection of the event. After two 9-minute training sessions, 2-month-old infants
remember how to activate the mobile for up to two days, 3-month-olds for up to
one week, and 6-month-olds for up to two weeks.

Childhood amnesia refers to the inability of adults to recall memories from
infancy, typically before the age of 3 or 4 (Alberini & Travaglia, 2017). Childhood amnesia occurs because the hippocampus, the brain structure responsible
for forming new memories, is not fully developed (Riggins et al., 2018). After
birth, infancy is characterized by the highest rate of neurogenesis, during which
new cells and memories replace older ones (Sigelman & Rider, 2022). As children develop, so does the change in basic capacities—i.e., older children have
more developed brains than younger ones due to myelination and greater brain
capacity.

Autobiographical memories depend primarily on language skills. Researchers have postulated that the lack of language is the mechanism underlying **infantile amnesia** (e.g., Hayne & Simcock, 2009). Infants typically do not
have a sense of self. Self-recognition is apparent during the second half of the
second year when infants can recognize themselves in a mirror. As children
develop a stronger sense of self, their autobiographical memories also increase
(Ross et al., 2020).

Memory and Autism

How does memory develop in toddlers who will be diagnosed with autism? Individuals on the autism spectrum may experience a different pattern of memory
development, such as enhanced memory for details of specific events, yet difficulty remembering the sequence of events in their lives or the context surrounding specific memories. Many individuals on the autism spectrum have reported
having vivid childhood memories. However, studies investigating autobiographical memories have found some deficits in individuals with autism. Zamoscik
and colleagues (2016) conducted a research study to compare the autobiographical memories that autistic individuals reported to those non-autistic individuals
reported. They collected data through an online questionnaire, and the results
revealed that, apart from autistic individuals' recollections of early memories
with more sensory details, people with autism do not differ significantly from
non-autistic individuals in terms of autobiographical memories.

Since autism is a neurodevelopmental condition, disruptions in brain structures must be implicated. Research on working memory has found that the
prefrontal cortex of individuals with autism is one of the brain regions most
disrupted. Infants' abnormal head circumference, later diagnosed as autism, has
been observed for years. It turns out that abnormal brain growth in the prefrontal
lobes can affect the neuronal connectivity and functioning characteristics of autism (Courchesne & Pierce, 2005).

Individuals with autism have difficulties with working memory. Are implicit and explicit memory compromised in autism? There is convincing evidence that explicit memory (aka declarative memory) is mainly intact in many neurodevelopmental disorders, including individuals on the low- and high-functioning end of the autism spectrum. Some individuals across the autism spectrum possess enhanced or even **savant**-like memory. Boucher and colleagues (2012) compared the memory abilities of participants with high-functioning autism (HFA) with those with moderately low-functioning autism (M-LFA). They found declarative memory impairments were more extensive in M-LFA than in HFA individuals. Additionally, recognition was largely unaffected in HFA but moderately impaired in M-LFA.

Research has shown that alterations in various brain structures are associated with memory deficits. One study found that individuals with autism have deficits in spatial working memory, as evidenced by less activation in the dorsolateral prefrontal cortex and the posterior cingulate cortex. When presented with two tasks, focusing on the more relevant one while ignoring the other can be problematic (Luna et al., 2002). The basal ganglia play an essential role in procedural memory, including habit learning and action selection and performance. Research has found that parts of the basal ganglia are structurally and functionally impaired in individuals with autism (Subramanian et al., 2017).

Williams and colleagues (2006) conducted a study with children on the autism spectrum. Compared to neurotypicals, autistic participants showed weaker memory for complex visual and verbal information. The findings suggest that autistic children may have a different way of organizing their memory ability. Another study (Renner et al., 2000) compared the memory performance of children with autism to a neurotypical control group on three memory tasks, including one implicit task and two explicit tasks. The study found no deficits in both implicit and explicit memory abilities. However, children with autism had difficulty remembering the items presented at the beginning of the task (primacy effect) but recalled the items presented at the end (recency effect). The authors suggested that individuals with autism may use different strategies for encoding and retrieving stored information. A meta-analysis conducted by Habib and colleagues (2019) of thirty-four studies assessing phonological (auditory) and visuospatial memories of individuals with autism found significant impairments in both domains compared to non-autistic individuals.

Sleep plays a crucial role in memory consolidation. Sleep difficulties can lead to impaired memory consolidation. Individuals with autism spectrum disorder (ASD) can often experience sleep difficulties. These can include trouble falling asleep, staying asleep, and waking up too early. Some common factors that can contribute to sleep difficulties in people with ASD include sensory sensitivities, anxiety, and irregular sleep routines (Devnani & Hegde, 2015). Sleep deprivation is associated with memory loss, particularly episodic memory (Ashton et al., 2020). It has been found that a 90-minute nap after learning a task can facilitate retention in children and promote the integration of newly learned information with existing knowledge (Urbain et al., 2016).

Savant Syndrome and Autism

Despite memory limitations associated with autism, some individuals on the autism spectrum have memory abilities that surpass those of neurotypicals. They are usually diagnosed with "savant syndrome" and thus capable of incredible memory feats despite having an intellectual disability. John Langdon Down coined the term "savant syndrome" in 1887 to describe individuals with intellectual disabilities who demonstrate exceptional skills or talents in specific areas such as music, art, and math. Darold Treffert provided a modern definition of savant syndrome in the 1970s, which includes individuals with average intelligence or above-average IQ. Savant syndrome is often associated with outstanding memory abilities or "islet memory"—and thus the ability to remember specific details about a particular subject or topic. Savant syndrome is often associated with autism spectrum disorder. However, not every individual on the autism spectrum has savant syndrome and vice versa. Individuals with autism with savant syndrome have a distinct psychological profile compared to those with autism without savant syndrome (Hughes et al., 2018).

Although it is possible for savant syndrome to occur in individuals with other developmental disabilities, approximately one in ten people with autism also have savant syndrome (Treffert, 2009). For example, Kim Peek, who inspired the autistic character in the movie "Rain Man," was diagnosed with Fragile X syndrome (a condition associated with autism). Although he had difficulties with simple tasks such as tying his shoelaces or buttoning his shirt, he possessed a remarkable memory that enabled him to memorize entire books and recall them with incredible accuracy. Another well-known example of an autistic savant is the artist Stephen Wiltshire (diagnosed with autism), who can draw hyper-detailed cityscapes from memory.

In sum, not all individuals on the autism spectrum have memory deficits. Memory is a complex process, and many brain structures are involved, including the hippocampus, prefrontal cortex, amygdala, and basal ganglia. Some individuals might face challenges with specific types of memory, such as working memory, episodic memory, or prospective memory. Conversely, some individuals with autism might have excellent visual and long-term memory capabilities. Individuals on the autism spectrum with "savant syndrome" possess remarkable memory capabilities that can surpass those of neurotypicals in the general population despite challenges in performing simple adaptive tasks.

Intelligence

Since Alfred Binet and Theodore Simon, commissioned by the French government in 1904, developed the forerunner of the modern IQ test to identify students who might not benefit from traditional classroom instruction, other theorists and researchers have investigated the concept of intelligence. Spearman (1927) proposed a two-factor model of intelligence consisting of a general mental ability he termed "*g*" and a second aspect of intelligence or special abilities that he termed "*s*." Terman (1954) developed the Stanford-Binet test, based on Binet-Simon's scales, and introduced the concept of **chronological age** and mental age in IQ testing. Horn and Cattel (1967) proposed the notion of **fluid intelligence**—the ability to use the mind to solve novel problems without actively applying accumulated knowledge—and crystalized intelligence—the application of knowledge acquired through formal education and experience.

Although psychologists disagree on the definition of intelligence, there is agreement that it is the ability to acquire and apply knowledge and skills, including reasoning, understanding, learning, planning, problem-solving, and abstract thinking. Gardner (2000 [1999]) rejected the notion of a single IQ score because, in his view, it cannot capture the complexity of human intelligence. Instead, he argued for adopting multiple intelligences (e.g., musical, linguistic, interpersonal, intrapersonal, existential, bodily-kinesthetic, and naturalist) that the traditional IQ tests do not measure. Sternberg (2011) put forth a theory of successful intelligence consisting of three components—**practical**, **creative**, and **analytic** intelligence—that jointly contribute to intelligent behavior. Intelligence is a multifaceted trait encompassing a wide range of abilities, but no universally accepted formal definition exists.

General intelligence test scores (e.g., the Stanford-Binet and Wechsler scales) form a normal distribution depicting a symmetrical, bell-shaped graph constructed around the average score of 100. Most individuals (i.e., 68%) without an intellectual disability complete an IQ test score near the average, whereas scores higher than 130 and lower than 70 are less common. According to the American Association on Intellectual and Developmental Disabilities, "intelligence is the general mental capacity that involves reasoning, planning, solving problems, thinking abstractly, comprehending complex ideas, learning efficiently, and learning from experience" (Shogren & Turnbull, 2010).

Intelligence and Autism

Autism is a spectrum disorder resulting in individuals with the condition experiencing a wide range of abilities and challenges. Differences in intelligence quotient (IQ) reflect the heterogeneity of ASD. Based on epidemiological and clinical studies, many individuals with ASD score below 70, reflecting a degree of disability denoted as "mildly," "moderately," "severely," or "profoundly" disabled. It is worth noting that low IQ scores have been associated with autism severity (Denisova & Lin, 2023).

Autism spectrum disorder (ASD) is a child-onset heterogeneous condition characterized by (1) persistent deficits in social communication and social interaction and (2) restricted, repetitive patterns of behavior, interests, or activities (APA, 2013). In addition to the two core characteristics of the disorder, autism can manifest itself with or without an intellectual disability. According to the

Autism and Developmental Disabilities Monitoring (ADDM) Network (Maenner et al., 2021), 35% of children diagnosed with autism in the United States have an intellectual disability. Several closely related terms were used in the later part of the 1900s to describe individuals who experienced limitations in physical, social, and cognitive functioning (e.g., mental retardation, developmental disability). In 2007, the American Association on Intellectual and Developmental Disabilities (AAIDD) proposed the term "intellectual disability" as the preferred designation. The AAIDD defines Intellectual disability in terms of three criteria: (1) the disability must originate before age 18, (2) significant limitations in adaptive functioning must also be present, and (3) a score of 70 or lower on standardized IQ tests.

Intellectual disability is not unique to autism. It occurs in 1–3% of individuals in the general population. Autism and intellectual disability can co-occur. Some individuals on the autism spectrum have an intellectual disability (i.e., difficulty with cognitive tasks, learning, and problem-solving). Others have above-average IQ scores. According to the Centers for Disease Control and Prevention (ADDM, 2014), approximately 31% of individuals on the autism spectrum have an intellectual disability.

The idea of autism as a disorder of high intelligence has surfaced in popular literature. Many illustrious individuals (e.g., Mozart, Einstein, Jefferson, and others) have been identified as having a form of autism. Crespi (2016) reviewed a body of research suggesting that autism might be a disorder of high intelligence. More recently, Elon Musk (2021), the CEO of Tesla and SpaceX, hosted Saturday Night Live and disclosed his diagnosis of Asperger's Disorder.

IQ and Autism

IQ scores have increased in people diagnosed with autism. Studies conducted from the 1960s till the 1990s found that one-fifth of people with autism have average intelligence (Fombonne, 1999). However, the Autism and Developmental Disabilities Monitoring Network (ADDM, 2014) found that for 2010 approximately half of the children with autism had IQ scores in the average range (i.e., 85 or higher). More recently, The ADDM (Maenner et al., 2021) reported that 35.2% of children with ASD have an IQ lower than 70, 23.1% are in the borderline range (IQ 71–85), and 41.7% have IQ scores in the average to above average range (i.e., greater than 85). Why have IQ scores among people with autism increased? Given that the diagnostic criteria for autism have changed through the years, more individuals with less severe forms of autism are diagnosed with the condition. Additionally, early diagnoses possibly lead to early interventions when the brain is malleable and more responsive to therapy, which could have led to gains in IQ.

Savant syndrome is a rare condition in which individuals with severe mental disabilities (primarily autism, some other disabilities, or brain injury) demonstrate some "islets of ability" or "splinter skills" in areas including music and calendar calculation (Treffert, 2009). It is estimated that one in ten persons with autism has savant syndrome to some degree. For example, Donald T. (Kanner's case 1) was known for multiplying numbers with lightning speed and flawlessly identifying musical notes that someone played on the piano.

In sum, intelligence is a complex and multifaceted trait that encompasses a wide range of abilities. There is no unifying theory of intelligence that is universally accepted. Two-thirds of typically developing individuals score in the normal range of intelligence (i.e., IQ scores of 85–115). Individuals on the autism spectrum, however, exhibit a wide range of intellectual abilities, including those with intellectual disabilities, those with average intellectual abilities, and those with above-average intellectual abilities. Individuals with autism diagnosed with savant syndrome possess unique cognitive abilities that underlie a form of intelligence that may depart from that of the general population.

Language

Language Acquisition

Language is a communication system in which a person can combine a finite number of words to produce an infinite number of messages. Language acquisition is a complex process that begins in infancy and continues into adulthood. Our capacity to acquire language is rooted in our genetic endowment (Pinker, 1994). All typically developing children acquire a language during the first years of their lives (Gervain, 2020) and acquire their native language with remarkable ease. According to Kuhl (2000), infants can perceptually map essential elements of the language they hear in their environment long before they can even speak. Mastering a language is the most important developmental milestone. Language is a complex system intricately woven with various components. These components include phonemes, morphemes, syntax, semantics, pragmatics, and **prosody** (Sigelman & Rider, 2022).

Typically developing infants begin cooing (i.e., vowel-like sound repetitions) at around 6–8 weeks. Babies begin babbling around 3–4 months (i.e., consonant-vowel repetitious sounds). Cooing and babbling are vital precursors of language and indicators that infants can imitate the sounds of a language they hear. Babbling becomes more distinctive, reflecting the language babies have been listening to. Two-month-old infants prefer the human voice and speech over other sounds (Vouloumanos et al., 2010). Around their first birthday, infants typically utter their first meaningful word. Some infants utter their first meaningful word as early as 8 months; others as late as 15.

A vocabulary spurt occurs during the second half of the second year when infants acquire 30–50 words (Carroll, 2008). By the end of the second year, the vocabulary size increases to 300 words (Camaioni, 2004). Typically developing children acquire words informally by being around people who speak a language they will acquire. It is worth noting that children who have more opportunities to converse with adults have more advanced language skills and show greater activation of Broca's area (Romeo et al., 2018).

Brain Structures Implicated in Language

Language is lateralized in the left hemisphere of the brain. Broca's area (located in the left frontal lobe) is associated with language production. Damage to Broca's area can result in expressive aphasia (Fridriksson et al., 2015). Wernicke's area (located in the left temporal lobe) is responsible for language comprehension. Damage to Wernicke's area can seriously impair language development (Binder, 2015). The angular gyrus (located in the parietal lobe) is involved in semantic processing, number processing, and word reading and comprehension (Seghier, 2013). No less important is the insular cortex, which is also implicated in language processing. Damage to this area can result in difficulties in language comprehension and production (Oh et al., 2014; Woolnough et al., 2019).

Language Development and Autism

Typically developing children tend to have a large vocabulary of thousands of words by age five. In contrast, it is not uncommon for autistic children to have a more limited vocabulary. Communication and social interaction challenges are the hallmarks of autism. As a result, language development and acquisition are often delayed in autistic children. Various factors influence autistic children's capacity to develop language, including brain development and connectivity (Gao et al., 2019), sensory processing difficulties, and anxiety (Khaledi et al., 2022).

Individuals with autism often experience language difficulties. Approximately 25% to 30% of children on the autism spectrum are either minimally verbal or do not develop functional language (Brignell et al., 2018). Cooing and babbling may be absent in infants. The lack or delay of early vocalizations could be an indication that they could experience language difficulties and possibly be diagnosed with autism. Language deficits in autistic individuals vary widely and can present significant challenges. Some may not have any language skills at all, while others may experience a delay in language development. Some may repeat words they hear (i.e., **echolalia**), engage in self-talk, or use stereotypical language (Cui et al., 2023).

Individuals on the autism spectrum may have challenges with the meaning of words. As a result, they can experience difficulties understanding and using language appropriately (Ahtam et al., 2020). Figurative language (e.g., idioms, metaphors, sarcasm, and humor) may be too complex for them to grasp. These difficulties in comprehending the subtleties of language may limit their ability to navigate social situations and establish relationships. Kalandadze and colleagues

(2018) conducted a meta-analysis to assess figurative language comprehension in individuals with autism and non-autistic controls. They found that individuals on the autism spectrum showed a poorer understanding of figurative language compared to non-autistic individuals. Unlike typically developing controls, autistic individuals experienced more difficulties comprehending metaphors than irony and sarcasm.

Interventions for Language Deficits

Various interventions have been developed to help remedy the language deficits in autistic individuals. These interventions aim to increase language comprehension, improve communication (Brignell et al., 2018), and reduce behavioral issues often resulting from people's inability to communicate wants and needs (Tiger et al., 2008). Brignell and colleagues (2018) assessed the effectiveness of communication interventions in children on the autism spectrum with minimally verbal repertoire. They focused on four categories of interventions: (1) verbally-based interventions, (2) augmentative and alternative communication (AAC) interventions, (3) verbal combined with AAC interventions, and (4) comprehensive interventions that focused on communication. They found limited evidence to suggest that interventions based on verbal communication or augmentative and alternative communication (AAC) can improve both verbal and nonverbal communication in children with autism spectrum disorder who have limited verbal abilities.

Picture Exchange Communication System (PECS)

The Picture Exchange Communication System (Bondy & Frost, 1998) was developed to teach children with autism and other intellectual disabilities a form of alternative and augmentative communication. Children with language difficulties are taught to use pictures to request items they want and activities in which they wish to participate. Children using PECS gradually develop the capacity to use images to build more complex communication skills. PECS has been found to be effective in fostering communication skills in children with language difficulties (Malhotra et al., 2010).

The VB-MAPP

The Verbal Behavior Milestones Assessment and Placement Program (VB-MAPP) is an assessment tool developed to assess the language and communication skills of autistic individuals and others diagnosed with an intellectual disability (Sundberg, 2008, 2014). The assessment consists of various components that identify the language deficits of individuals with autism and appropriate treatments that can improve their communication abilities. The VB-MAPP has been found to be effective in enhancing the communication skills of autistic individuals (Barnes et al., 2014).

Applied Behavior Analysis (ABA)

The **Applied Behavior Analysis (ABA)** therapy for language impairments in autism originated in the work of Lovaas (1987). The treatment protocol consists of breaking down communication and language competencies into smaller, more manageable units, teaching them through repetitions, and reinforcing the learner's correct response to each acquired unit or word. There are several variants of ABA therapy for language impairment in autism, including Natural Environment Teaching (NET) and Pivotal Response Training (PRT). Each variant targets a specific aspect of language development, such as word acquisition, sentence structure, and conversation. ABA interventions for language deficits in autism have been found to be effective in improving communication skills, reducing problem behaviors, and improving social interactions (Leblanc et al., 2006).

Speech and Language Pathology

Speech-language pathologists (SLP) use a variety of techniques (e.g., visual aids, sign language, and technology-based interventions) to help autistic individuals overcome their language difficulties and improve their language comprehension, communication skills, and social communication. Speech and language pathology interventions can be effective for children with autism. These interventions can help improve communication skills, social interaction, and overall quality of life for autistic children (Paul, 2008).

In sum, language development is a complex process that comes naturally to typically developing children by simply being around people who speak a language. The brain structures responsible for language production and comprehension, such as the Broca and Wernicke areas, play a significant role in this process. However, many children with autism struggle with language acquisition, experiencing difficulties or delays. Fortunately, there are various treatments available to address these language difficulties. It is important to note that these interventions are most effective when initiated early in a child's development, to take advantage of the brain's malleability and responsiveness to practice.

Summary

Cognitive development, one of the broad domains of development, refers to the growth and change in a person's ability to think and understand. It is the capacity to acquire knowledge and problem-solving skills through learning. This process is complex and dynamic, guided by brain maturation and experience with the world. It begins in infancy and continues throughout the lifespan. Cognitive development includes various processes such as self-development, decision-making, attention, memory, intelligence, and language acquisition.

Newborns typically do not have a fully developed sense of self. However, as they grow and experience the world around them, they gradually develop an understanding of being separate entities from their environment. Infants show a capacity for decision-making through their ability to focus attention and choose between different objects or activities, such as preferring specific toys. They also coo and babble in response to environmental input, preparing to acquire meaningful words and language. Initially captured by environmental stimulation, they gradually develop the capacity to share a perceptual experience with another person, remember familiar faces, and form attachments with familiar faces and objects.

In contrast, many infants who will later develop autism may struggle with self-recognition. Unlike typically developing infants, they may exhibit unusual reactions when seeing their reflection in a mirror, have difficulties spontaneously following someone else's gaze, and rarely engage in joint attention. As they reach school age, they may display a different pattern of memory development, such as having a strong memory for specific event details, struggling to remember the sequence of events in their lives or the context surrounding specific memories, and experiencing challenges with working memory. Despite memory limitations associated with autism, some individuals on the autism spectrum have memory abilities that exceed those of neurotypical individuals. They are often diagnosed with "savant syndrome" and are capable of remarkable memory feats despite having an intellectual disability.

Autistic individuals have a wide range of cognitive abilities. Intelligence quotient can vary widely among autistic children, with some performing above the normal range and others below. In comparison to 1–3% of children with an intellectual disability, 35% of autistic children have an intellectual disability. Autistic children are more likely to have language difficulties compared to children in the general population. It is estimated that around 40% of autistic children do not develop spoken language. Researchers and clinicians have developed various approaches and interventions to help address language deficits in individuals with autism.

Questions to Ponder for Further Thinking and Learning

1 How does cognitive development differ in individuals with autism compared to typically developing individuals?
2 What are some early signs of autism in cognitive development?
3 How can we support cognitive development in individuals with autism?
4 What role does sensory processing play in cognitive development and autism?

5 How do executive functioning skills develop in individuals with autism?
6 What interventions and therapies have shown to be effective in supporting cognitive development in individuals with autism?
7 How can we promote social-emotional learning and cognitive development in autistic children?
8 What is the relationship between cognitive flexibility and autism?
9 How can we support the transition to adulthood for individuals with autism in terms of cognitive development?
10 What future research is needed to understand cognitive development in individuals with autism better?

References

ADDM (2014). Prevalence of autism spectrum disorder among children aged 8 years—Autism and Developmental Disabilities Monitoring Network, 11 sites, United States, 2010. *MMWR Surveillance Summary*, *63*(2), 1–21.

Ahtam, B., Braeutigam, S., & Bailey, A. (2020). Semantic processing in autism spectrum disorders is associated with the timing of language acquisition: A magnetoencephalographic study. *Frontiers in Human Neuroscience*, *14*, 267.

Alberini, C. M., & Travaglia, A. (2017). Infantile amnesia: A critical period of learning to learn and remember. *The Journal of Neuroscience*, *37*(24), 5783–5795.

Al-Mazidi, S. H. (2023). The physiology of cognition in autism spectrum disorder: Current and future challenges. *Cureus*, *15*(10), e46581.

APA (2013). *Diagnostic and statistical manual of mental disorders* (5th ed.). American Psychiatric Association.

Andreasen, N. C., O'Leary, D. S., Paradiso, S., Cizadlo, T., Arndt, S., Watkins, G. L., … Hichwa, R. D. (1999). The cerebellum plays a role in conscious episodic memory retrieval. *Human Brain Mapping*, *8*(4), 226–234.

Annese, J., Schenker-Ahmed, N. M., Bartsch, H., Maechler, P., Sheh, C., Thomas, N., … Corkin, S. (2014). Postmortem examination of patient H.M.'s brain based on histological sectioning and digital 3D reconstruction. *Nature Communication*, *5*, 3122.

Ashton, J. E., Harrington, M. O., Langthorne, D., Ngo, H. V., & Cairney, S. A. (2020). Sleep deprivation induces fragmented memory loss. *Learning & Memory*, *27*(4), 130–135.

Atkinson, R. C., & Shiffrin, R. M. (1968). Human memory: A proposed system and its control processes. In K. W. Spence & J. T. Spence (Eds.), *The psychology of learning and motivation: Vol 2. Advances in research and theory*. Academic Press.

Baddeley, A. (2012). Working memory: Theories, models, and controversies. *Annual Review of Psychology*, *63*, 1–29.

Barnes, C. S., Mellor, J. R., & Rehfeldt, R. A. (2014). Implementing the Verbal Behavior Milestones Assessment and Placement Program (VB-MAPP): Teaching assessment techniques. *Analysis of Verbal Behavior*, *30*(1), 36–47.

Bertenthal, B. I., & Fischer, K. W. (1978). Development of self-recognition in the infant. *Developmental Psychology*, *14*(1), 44–50.

Binder, J. R. (2015). The Wernicke area: Modern evidence and a reinterpretation. *Neurology*, *85*(24), 2170–2175.

Bondy, A. S., & Frost, L. A. (1998). The picture exchange communication system. *Seminars in Speech and Language*, *19*(4), 373–388.

Boucher, J., Mayes, A., & Bigham, S. (2012). Memory in autistic spectrum disorder. *Psychological Bulletin*, *138*(3), 458–496.

Bradshaw, J., Klin, A., Evans, L., Klaiman, C., Saulnier, C., & McCracken, C. (2020). Development of attention from birth to 5 months in infants at risk for autism spectrum disorder. *Development and Psychopathology, 32*(2), 491–501.

Broadbent, D. (1958). *Perception and communication.* Pergamon Press.

Bremner, J. G., Slater, A. M., & Johnson, S. P. (2015). Perception of object persistence: The origins of object permanence in infancy. *Child Development Perspectives, 9*(1), 7–13.

Brignell, A., Chenausky, K. V., Song, H., Zhu, J., Suo, C., & Morgan, A. T. (2018). Communication interventions for autism spectrum disorder in minimally verbal children. *Cochrane Database of Systematic Reviews, 11*(11), CD012324.

Camaioni, L. (2004). Early language. In G. Bremner & A. Fogel (Eds.), *Blackwell handbook of infant development* (pp. 404–426). Blackwell Publishing.

Carmody, D. P., & Lewis, M. (2012). Self-representation in children with and without autism spectrum disorders. *Child Psychiatry & Human Development, 43*(2), 227–237.

Carroll, D. W. (2008). *Psychology of language* (5th ed.). Wadsworth.

Chawarska, K., Macari, S., & Shic, F. (2013). Decreased spontaneous attention to social scenes in 6-month-old infants later diagnosed with autism spectrum disorders. *Biological Psychiatry, 74*(3), 195–203.

Courchesne, E., & Pierce, K. (2005). Brain overgrowth in autism during a critical time in development: Implications for frontal pyramidal neuron and interneuron development and connectivity. *International Journal of Developmental Neuroscience, 23*(2–3), 153–170.

Courchesne, E., Mouton, P. R., Calhoun, M. E., Semendeferi, K., Ahrens-Barbeau, C., Hallet, M. J., … Pierce, K. (2011). Neuron number and size in prefrontal cortex of children with autism. *JAMA, 306*(18), 2001–2010.

Crespi, B. J. (2016). Autism as a disorder of high intelligence. *Frontiers in Neuroscience, 10*, 300.

Cui, M., Ni, Q., & Wang, Q. (2023). Review of intervention methods for language and communication disorders in children with autism spectrum disorders. *PeerJ, 11*, e15735.

de Faria, O., Gonsalvez, D. G., Nicholson, M., & Xiao, J. (2019). Activity-dependent central nervous system myelination throughout life. *Journal of Neurochemistry, 148*(4), 447–461.

Denisova, K., & Lin, Z. (2023). The importance of low IQ to early diagnosis of autism. *Autism Research, 16*(1), 122–142.

Devnani, P. A., & Hegde, A. U. (2015). Autism and sleep disorders. *Journal of Pediatric Neurosciences, 10*(4), 304–307.

Ebbinghaus, H. (1964 [1885]). *Memory: A contribution to experimental psychology.* Dover Publications.

Elsabbagh, M., Holmboe, K., Gliga, T., Mercure, E., Hudry, K., Charman, T., … BASIS Team. (2011). Social and attention factors during infancy and the later emergence of autism characteristics. *Progress in Brain Research, 189*, 195–207.

Fan, J., McCandliss, B. D., Sommer, T., Raz, A., & Posner, M. I. (2002). Testing the efficiency and independence of attentional networks. *Journal of Cognitive Neuroscience, 14*(3), 340–347.

Foerde, K., & Shohamy, D. (2011). The role of the basal ganglia in learning and memory: Insight from Parkinson's disease. *Neurobiology of Learning and Memory, 96*(4), 624–236.

Fombonne, E. (1999). The epidemiology of autism: A review. *Psychological Medicine, 29*(4), 769–786.

Fridriksson, J., Fillmore, P., Guo, D., & Rorden, C. (2015). Chronic Broca's aphasia is caused by damage to Broca's and Wernicke's areas. *Cerebral Cortex, 25*(12), 4689–4696.

Funahashi, S. (2017a). Prefrontal contribution to decision-making under free-choice conditions. *Frontiers in Neuroscience, 11*, 431.

Funahashi, S. (2017b). Working memory in the prefrontal cortex. *Brain Sciences*, *7*(5), 49.

Gallup, G. G. (1979). Self-awareness in primates. *American Scientist*, *67*(4), 417–421.

Gao, Y., Linke, A., Jao, K. R. J., Punyamurthula, S., Jahedi, A., Gates, K., Fishman, I., & Müller, R. A. (2019). The language network in autism: Atypical functional connectivity with default mode and visual regions. *Autism Research*, *12*(9), 1344–1355.

Gardner, H. (2000 [1999]). *Intelligence reframed: Multiple intelligence for the 21st century*. Basic Books.

Gervain, J. (2020). Typical language development. *Handbook of Clinical Neurology*, *173*, 171–183.

Habib, A., Harris, L., Pollick, F., & Melville, C. (2019). A meta-analysis of working memory in individuals with autism spectrum disorders. *PLoS One*, *14*(4), e0216198.

Hajri, M., Abbes, Z., Yahia, H. B., Jelili, S., Halayem, S., Mrabet, A., & Bouden, A. (2022). Cognitive deficits in children with autism spectrum disorders: Toward an integrative approach combining social and non-social cognition. *Frontiers in Psychiatry*, *13*, 917121.

Hayne, H., & Simcock, G. (2009). Memory development in toddlers. In M. L. Courage & N. Cowan (Eds.), *The development of memory in infancy and childhood* (pp. 43–68). New Psychology Press.

Hermans, E. J., Battaglia, F. P., Atsak, P., de Voogd, L. D., Fernández, G., & Roozendaal, B. (2014). How the amygdala affects emotional memory by altering brain network properties. *Neurobiology of Learning and Memory*, *112*, 2–16.

Hill, S. D., & Tomlin, C. (1981). Self-recognition in retarded children. *Child Development*, *52*(1), 145–150.

Horn, J. L., & Cattell, R. B. (1967). Age differences in fluid and crystallized intelligence. *Acta Psychologica*, *26*(2), 107–129.

Huang, A. X., Hughes, T. L., Sutton, L. R., Lawrence, M., Chen, X., Ji, Z., & Zeleke, W. (2017). Understanding the self in individuals with autism spectrum disorders (ASD): A review of literature. *Frontiers in Psychology*, *8*, 1422.

Hughes, J. E. A., Ward, J., Gruffydd, E., Baron-Cohen, S., Smith, P., Allison, C., & Simmer, J. (2018). Savant syndrome has a distinct psychological profile in autism. *Molecular Autism 9*, 53.

Kalandadze, T., Norbury, C., Nærland, T., & Næss, K. B. (2018). Figurative language comprehension in individuals with autism spectrum disorder: A meta-analytic review. *Autism*, *22*(2), 99–117.

Kenward, B., Folke, S., Holmberg, J., Johansson, A., & Gredebäck, G. (2009). Goal directedness and decision making in infants. *Developmental Psychology*, *45*(3), 809–819.

Khaledi, H., Aghaz, A., Mohammadi, A., Dadgar, H., & Meftahi, G. H. (2022). The relationship between communication skills, sensory difficulties, and anxiety in children with autism spectrum disorder. *Middle East Current Psychiatry*, *29*, 69.

Kuhl, P. K. (2000). A new view of language acquisition. *Proceedings of the National Academy of Sciences of the United States of America*, *97*(22), 11850–11857.

Lara, A. H., & Wallis, J. D. (2015). The role of prefrontal cortex in working memory: A mini review. *Frontiers in Systems Neuroscience*, *9*, 173.

Lashley, K. S. (1950). In search of the engram. In *Society for Experimental Biology, Physiological mechanisms in animal behavior. (Society's Symposium IV.)* (pp. 454–482). Academic Press.

Leblanc, L. A., Esch, J., Sidener, T. M., & Firth, A. M. (2006). Behavioral language interventions for children with autism: Comparing applied verbal behavior and naturalistic teaching approaches. *The Analysis of Verbal Behavior*, *22*(1), 49–60.

Lewis, M., & Brooks-Gunn, J. (1979). *Social cognition and the acquisition of self.* Plenum.

Lewis, M., & Carmody, D. P. (2008). Self-representation and brain development. *Developmental Psychology*, *44*(5), 1329–1334.

Lovaas, O. I. (1987). Behavioral treatment and normal educational and intellectual functioning in young autistic children. *Journal of Consulting & Clinical Psychology*, *55*, 3–9.

Luke, L., Clare, I. C., Ring, H., Redley, M., & Watson, P. (2012). Decision-making difficulties experienced by adults with autism spectrum conditions. *Autism*, *16*(6), 612–621.

Luna, B., Minshew, N. J., Garver, K. E., Lazar, N. A., Thulborn, K. R., Eddy, W. F., & Sweeney, J. A. (2002). Neocortical system abnormalities in autism: An fMRI study of spatial working memory. *Neurology*, *59*(6), 834–840.

Ma, S. L., Chen, L. H., Lee, C. C., Lai, K. Y. C., Hung, S. F., Tang, C. P., ... Leung, P. W. L. (2021). Genetic overlap between attention-deficit/hyperactivity disorder and autism spectrum disorder in SHANK2 Gene. *Frontiers in Neuroscience*, *15*, 649588.

Maenner, M. J., Shaw, K. A., Bakian, A. V., Bilder, D. A., Durkin, M. S., Esler, A., ... Cogswell, M. E. (2021). Prevalence and characteristics of autism spectrum disorder among children aged 8 years—Autism and Developmental Disabilities Monitoring Network, 11 sites, United States, 2018. *MMWR Surveillance Summaries*, *70*(11), 1–16.

Maenner, M. J., Warren, Z., Williams, A. R., Amoakohene, E., Bakian, A. V., Bilder, D. A., ... Shaw, K. A. (2023). Prevalence and characteristics of autism spectrum disorder among children aged 8 years—Autism and Developmental Disabilities Monitoring Network, 11 Sites, United States, 2020. *MMWR Surveillance Summaries*, *72*(2), 1–14.

Malhotra, S., Rajender, G., Bhatia, M. S., & Singh, T. B. (2010). Effects of picture exchange communication system on communication and behavioral anomalies in autism. *Indian Journal of Psychological Medicine*, *32*(2), 141–143.

Mochizuki-Kawai, H. (2008). [Neural basis of procedural memory]. *Brain Nerve*, *60*(7), 825–832.

Montagut-Asunción, M., Crespo-Martín, S., Pastor-Cerezuela, G., & D'Ocon-Giménez, A. (2022). Joint attention and its relationship with autism risk markers at 18 months of age. *Children*, *9*(4), 556.

Montenegro, J. T. P., Seguin, D., & Duerden, E. G. (2022). Joint attention in infants at high familial risk for autism spectrum disorder and the association with thalamic and hippocampal macrostructure. *Cerebral Cortex Communications*, *3*(3), tgac029.

Musk, E. *Hosting Saturday Night Live* (May 8, 2021). https://www.youtube.com/watch?v=fCF8I_X1qKI&t=85s. Accessed on January 15, 2025.

Mutreja, R., Craig, C., & O'Boyle, M. W. (2016). Attentional network deficits in children with autism spectrum disorder. *Developmental Neurorehabilitation*, *19*(6), 389–397.

Oh, A., Duerden, E. G., & Pang, E. W. (2014). The role of the insula in speech and language processing. *Brain and Language*, *135*, 96–103.

Paul, R. (2008). Interventions to improve communication in autism. *Child and Adolescent Psychiatry Clinics of North America*, *17*(4), 835–856.

Piaget, J. (1952). *The origins of intelligence in children*. International Universities Press.

Pinker, S. (1994). *The language instinct*. Harper Collins.

Pipp, S., Easterbrooks, M. A., & Harmon, R. J. (1992). The relation between attachment and knowledge of self and mother in one to three-year-old infants. *Child Development*, *63*(3), 738–750.

Posner, M. I., & Petersen, S. E. (1990). The attention system of the human brain. *Annual Review of Neuroscience*, *13*, 25–42.

Renner, P., Klinger, L. G., & Klinger, M. R. (2000). Implicit and explicit memory in autism: Is autism an amnesic disorder? *Journal of Autism and Developmental Disorders*, *30*(1), 3–14.

Ridderinkhof, A., de Bruin, E. I., van den Driesschen, S., & Bögels, S. M. (2020). Attention in children with autism spectrum disorder and the effects of a mindfulness-based program. *Journal of Attention Disorders*, *24*(5), 681–692.

Riggins, T., Geng, F., Botdorf, M., Canada, K., Cox, L., & Hancock, G. R. (2018). Protracted hippocampal development is associated with age-related improvements in memory during early childhood. *Neuroimage, 174*, 127–137.

Rochat, P. (2018). The ontogeny of human self-consciousness. *Current Directions in Psychological Science, 27*(5), 345–350.

Rochat, P., & Striano, T. (2000). Perceived self in infancy. *Infant Behavior & Development, 23*(3–4), 513–530.

Romeo, R. R., Leonard, J. A., Robinson, S. T., West, M. R., Mackey, A. P., Rowe, M. L., & Gabrieli, J. D. E. (2018). Beyond the 30-million-word gap: Children's conversational exposure is associated with language-related brain function. *Psychological Science, 29*(5), 700–710.

Ross, J., Hutchison, J., & Cummingham, S. J. (2020). The me in memory: The role of the self in autobiographical memory development. *Child Development, 91*(2), e299–e314.

Rovee-Collier, C., & Cuevas, K. (2009). The development of infant memory. In M. L. Courage & N. Cowan (Eds.), *The development of memory in infancy and childhood* (pp. 11–42). Psychology Press.

Ruff, H. A., & Rothbart, M. K. (1996). *Attention in early development: Themes and variations.* Oxford University Press.

Seghier, M. L. (2013). The angular gyrus: Multiple functions and multiple subdivisions. *Neuroscientist, 19*(1), 43–61.

Shic, F., Macari, S., & Chawarska, K. (2014). Speech disturbs face scanning in 6-month-old infants who develop autism spectrum disorder. *Biological Psychiatry, 75*(3), 231–237.

Shogren, K. A., & Turnbull, H. R. (2010). Public policy and outcomes for persons with intellectual disability: Extending and expanding the public policy framework of AAIDD's 11th Edition of Intellectual Disability: Definition, Classification, and Systems of Support. *Intellectual Developmental Disabilities, 48*(5), 375–386.

Sigelman, C. K., & Rider, E. A. (2022). *Life-span human development* (10th ed.). Cengage.

Spearman, C. (1927). *The abilities of man.* Macmillan.

Squire, L. R. (2009). The legacy of patient H.M. for neuroscience. *Neuron, 61*(1), 6–9.

Steinbeis, N., & Crone, E. A. (2016). The link between cognitive control and decision-making across child and adolescent development. *Current Opinion in Behavioral Sciences, 10*, 28–32.

Sternberg, R. J. (2011). The theory of successful intelligence. In R. J. Sternberg & S. B. Kaufman (Eds.), *The Cambridge handbook of intelligence* (pp. 504–527). Cambridge University Press.

Subramanian, K., Brandenburg, C., Orsati, F., Soghomonian, J. J., Hussman, J. P., & Blatt, G. J. (2017). Basal ganglia and autism—A translational perspective. *Autism Research, 10*(11), 1751–1775.

Sundberg, M. L. (2008). *Verbal behavior milestones assessment and placement program.* AVB Press.

Sundberg, M. L. (2014). *VB-MAPP: Verbal behavior milestones assessment and placement program: A language and social skills assessment program for children with autism or other developmental disabilities.* AVB Press.

Tanner, J. M. (1990). *Foetus into man: Physical growth from conception to maturity* (2nd ed.). Harvard University Press.

Tei, S., Tanicha, M., Itahashi, T., Aoki, Y. Y., Ohta, H., Qian, C., … Fujino, J. (2022). Decision flexibilities in autism spectrum disorder: An fMRI study of moral dilemmas. *Social Cognitive and Affective Neuroscience, 17*(10), 904–911.

Terman, L. M. (1954). The discovery and encouragement of exceptional talent. *American Psychologist, 9*(6), 221–230.

Tiger, J. H., Hanley, G. P., & Bruzek, J. (2008). Functional communication training: A review and practical guide. *Behavior Analysis in Practice, 1*(1), 16–23.

Tomlinson, S. P., Davis, N. J., Morgan, H. M., & Bracewell, R. M. (2014). Cerebellar contributions to verbal working memory. *Cerebellum, 13*(3), 354–361.

Treffert, D. A. (2009). The savant syndrome: An extraordinary condition. A synopsis: Past, present, and future. Philosophical Transactions of the Royal Society of London. Series B, *Biological Sciences, 364*(1522), 1351–1357.

Uddin, L. Q. (2011). The self in autism: An emerging view from neuroimaging. *Neurocase, 17*(3), 201–208.

Urbain, C., De Tiège, X., Op De Beeck, M., Bourguignon, M., Wens, V., Verheulpen, D., … Peigneux, P. (2016). Sleep in children triggers rapid reorganization of memory-related brain processes. *Neuroimage, 134*, 213–222.

van Steensel, F. J., Bögels, S. M., & de Bruin, E. I. (2013). Psychiatric comorbidity in children with autism spectrum disorders: A comparison with children with ADHD. *Journal of Child and Family Studies, 22*, 368–376.

Vouloumanos, A., Hauser, M. D., Werker, J. F., & Martin, A. (2010). The tuning of human neonates' preference for speech. *Child Development, 81*(2), 517–527.

Vygotsky, L. S. (1978). *Mind and society: The development of higher mental processes* (M. Cole, V. John-Steiner, S. Scribner, & E. Souberman, Eds. & Trans.). Harvard University Press. [original work published 1930, 1933, 1935].

Williams, D. L., Goldstein, G., & Minshew, N. J. (2006). The profile of memory function in children with autism. *Neuropsychology, 20*(1), 21–29.

Woike, D., Wang, E., Tibbe, D., Hassani Nia, F., Failla, A. V., Kibæk, M., … Kreienkamp, H. J. (2022). Mutations affecting the N-terminal domains of SHANK3 point to different pathomechanisms in neurodevelopmental disorders. *Scientific Reports, 12*(1), 902.

Woolnough, O., Forseth, K. J., Rollo, P. S., & Tandon, N. (2019). Uncovering the functional anatomy of the human insula during speech. *Elife, 8*, e53086.

Zamoscik, V., Mier, D., Schmidt, S. N., & Kirsch, P. (2016). Early memories of individuals on the autism spectrum assessed using online self-reports. *Frontiers in Psychiatry, 7*, 79.

Chapter 5

Life Course of Autism

Chapter Contents

DOI: 10.4324/9781003336266-6

Introduction

Children diagnosed with autism will grow up to become adults with autism. Unlike the life course of typical individuals, the life of individuals with autism involves various challenges that they and their families experience from early childhood through adolescence and into adulthood. Each stage of the life course, including diagnosis, early interventions, social interactions, education, employment opportunities, independent living, and romantic relationships, presents its unique challenges, as the experience of having autism varies from person to person. When **emerging adults** with autism turn 21, all the support and accommodations they previously received come to an end. Many parents continue to care for their young adults, especially if there is no planned transition from adolescence to adulthood.

The Life Course Perspective

The life course perspective (Elder et al., 2003) posits that human development is an ongoing affair that does not end in childhood or adolescence but continues throughout consecutive cycles that define developmental trajectories throughout the entire lifespan. Moreover, social and historical context also plays a role in shaping those trajectories. For example, typically developing individuals go through the various phases of their lifespan (i.e., infancy, childhood, adolescence, adulthood, and late adulthood) and the roles associated with each developmental stage. In many parts of the world, those roles include graduation from high school, attending college, employment, marriage, having children, and retirement.

Erikson (1993 [1950]) proposed a lifespan theory of psychosocial development in which he delineated eight *stages* of the lifespan and expected developmental outcomes based on a continuum of exploration and resolution. For example, He proposed *trust vs. mistrust* in infancy. Infants who have their needs met consistently by their caregivers develop a sense of security and confidence, which sets the stage for healthy future relationships and a positive outlook on the world. Similarly, adolescents who resolve the *identity versus role confusion* stage develop a sense of self-understanding, personal identity, and their role in the world. Against this backdrop, healthy psychosocial development can be problematic for individuals on the autism spectrum.

Life Course and Autism

The life course of individuals with autism does not follow a **typical development trajectory** from early childhood development to adulthood and aging. Their experiences present more challenges than opportunities depending on the diagnosis (e.g., early or late) and the severity of the condition. Because autism is a lifelong developmental condition that has no cure, it is fitting to understand the life course of autism and explore its developmental trajectory from infancy, childhood, adolescence, and adulthood. Gaining a comprehensive understanding of autism manifestation across the lifespan will better inform approaches to transitional phases and support systems, including independent living, which can facilitate the development and well-being of individuals with autism.

The Life Course of Kanner's 11 "Autistic" Children

In the introductory paragraph of his seminal report describing the characteristics of 11 children he examined in his clinic in Baltimore, Kanner (1943, p. 217) wrote:

> Since none of the children of this group has as yet attained an age beyond 11 years, this must be considered a preliminary report, to be enlarged upon as the patients grow older and further observation of their development is made.

All the children (eight boys and three girls) Kanner examined were born in the 1930s and were between 2 and 8 years old.

Kanner is considered the founder of child psychiatry. When Adolf Meyer appointed him the head of the Johns Hopkins Clinic (the Harriet Lane Home for Invalid Children) in 1931, he was tasked with establishing the first child psychiatry service in a pediatric hospital. Kanner developed an interest in the non-existing field and wrote the first book about it in English, titled *Child Psychiatry* (1935), which focused on the psychiatric problems of children. The man destined to name a condition that was not in the psychiatric classification system could not label the first child presented to his clinic in Baltimore in 1938. It took Kanner four years and the examination of several more children who exhibited traits like Donald's (the first boy he examined) for Kanner to name the condition autistic disturbances of affective contact.

Twenty-eight years later, Kanner (1971) published a follow-up report of the life course, describing the 11 children he examined at the Children's Psychiatric Clinic of the Johns Hopkins Hospital. He presented the report in the same order in which he described the 11 cases in his original paper, with Donald T. listed first. The follow-up report included each case's synopsis, developmental journeys, and developmental statuses after 28 years. Except for Donald T. (subsequently identified as Donald Triplett), whose case Donvan and Zucker (2016) reviewed and documented extensively in a book, little is known about the other ten cases. Kanner's assessment of the children he examined and their developmental trajectories and outcomes provided a *natural history of the disorder*—i.e., the typical progression and outcomes of the disorder in the absence of treatment (except, perhaps, for medications).

Case 1—Donald T.

Much of what is known about Donald was drawn from a detailed, 33-page description that his father gave to Kanner about his son's unusual behavior. The boy, once described as having feeding issues and "an unusual memory for faces and names," stayed at an institution for about a year before his parents took him to Kanner. Donald had done well compared to some of the other children. At the age of 36, his mother wrote to Kanner to inform him that Donald was

> a bachelor living at home with us ... Since receiving his A.B. degree in 1958, he has worked in the local bank as a teller. ... He owns his second car and likes his independence. ... In college, his major was French, and he showed a particular aptitude for language. ... Lack of initiative seems to be his most serious drawback. He takes very little part in social conversation and shows no interest in the opposite sex. ... While Don is not completely normal, he has taken his place in society very well. ... Don has never had any medication for his emotional trouble. ... I wish I knew what his inner feelings really are. As long as he continues as he is now, we can continue to be thankful.
>
> (Kanner, 1971, pp. 120–122)

Donald T., autism's first child, passed away on June 15, 2023, at the age of 89.

Case 2—Frederick (Wikky) W.

The boy (born in breech presentation) initially described as "self-sufficient" and happy to "stick to the same thing," was enrolled at the **Devereux School** in 1942 until 1965. Because the clinic in Baltimore kept close contact with his parents, the school reported that

> he is, at 26 years, a passive, likeable boy whose chief interest is music. He is able to follow the routine and, though he lives chiefly within his own world, he enjoys those group activities which are of particular interest to him.

After leaving Devereux School, Wikky went to Puerto Rico with his family for one year, where "he picked up a lot of Spanish and worked out a schedule of studying language lessons on records at 4 o'clock every afternoon." Wikky (aka Creighton) had moved with his family to Raleigh, where he had full-time employment in the National Air Pollution Administration office. The acting director complimented Creighton as "an outstanding employee by any standard. Outstanding to me means dependability, reliability, thoroughness, and thoughtfulness toward fellow workers. In each case, Creighton is notable" (Kanner, 1971, pp. 122–124).

Case 3—Richard M.

Richard M. had a typical birth and met developmental milestones on time, including sitting and walking. However, he was never able to communicate verbally. His mother took him to see Kanner in Baltimore twice, but eventually she could not continue caring for him. She placed Richard in a foster home and entrusted him to a woman who had a remarkable talent for dealing with difficult children. Later, Richard's mother moved him to another foster home and then to a State School for Exceptional Children.

At the age of 33, Richard was again transferred to another state institution. Five years later, the superintendent of the state wrote describing Richard's situation:

> At the time of admission, tranquilizers were pushed to the point of toxicity. After about three months, he showed some awareness of his environment and began feeding himself and going to the toilet. He is now being maintained on Compazine, 45 milligrams t.i.d. ... He now resides in a cottage for older residents who can meet their own personal needs. He responds to his name and to simple commands and there is some non-verbal communication with the cottage staff. He continues to be withdrawn and cannot be involved in any structured activities.
>
> (Kanner, 1971, pp. 124–126)

Case 4—Paul G.

Kanner examined Paul when he was 5 years old "for determination of his degree of feeble-mindedness." Despite being born typically, having reached many developmental milestones, having clear enunciation, and a good vocabulary, he seldom responded to any form of address, even when his name was called.

Paul's mother entrusted his care to a woman who ran a small home for "retarded children" and removed him thereafter. Despite contacting Kanner's clinic numerous times and applying for his son's admission to the Devereux School, she decided not to commit Paul to any more psychological examinations. According to Kanner, "mother and child could not be located since then." One can reasonably assume that Paul did not fare well and probably ended up in a state institution (Kanner, 1971, pp. 126–127).

Case 5—Barbara K.

Barbara was first examined at the age of 8. Her father, a physician, provided the following information:

> First child, born normally ... She nursed poorly and was put on bottle after a week. ... She was tube-fed five times daily up to 1 year of age. ... Ordinary vocabulary at 2 years, but always slow at putting words into sentences. ... Repetitious as a baby, and obsessive now; hold things in hands, takes things in hands, takes things to bed with her. She used to say 'you' for herself and 'I' for her mother or me, as if she were saying things we would in talking to her. ... Very timid, fearful of changing things. ... Mostly passive, but passively stubborn at times. ... Inattentive to the point where one wonders if she hears.

Barbara attended the Devereux School for ten years. She was then admitted to Springfield State Hospital. When she was 37 years old, a ward physician noted:

> She still has the stereotyped smile ... the child-like voice when uttering her parrot-like repetitions. ... She still shows a total absence of spontaneous sentence production. ... She is childish, impulsive, subject to temper outbursts with stamping her feet, crying loudly and upsetting other patients. Her memory is completely intact. She likes to hum some melodies monotonously.
>
> (Kanner, 1971, pp. 127–128)

Case 6—Virginia S.

Virginia, born in 1931, attended the State Training School for "retardate children" from 1936. A doctor's report stated:

> Virginia stands out from other children ... does not play with other children and does not seem to be deaf but does not talk. ... [Virginia] will amuse herself by the hour putting picture puzzles together. ... All findings seem to be in the nature of a congenital abnormality.

A psychologist at the training school noted that Virginia

> pays no attention to what is said to her but quickly comprehends whatever is expected. ... She is quiet, solemn, composed. Not once have I seen her smile. She retires within herself, segregating herself from others. ... She is mostly self-sufficient and independent.

As a 40-year-old, she was transferred to the Henryton State Hospital

> in a program for adult retardates, with her primary rehabilitation center being the Home Economics Section. ... She can iron clothes. ... She does not talk, uses noise and gestures. ... She desires to keep to herself rather than associate with other residents.
>
> (Kanner, 1971, pp. 128–130)

Case 7—Herbert B.

Herbert was born before term in 1937 via a Caesarian section. He was thought to be deaf because "he did not register any change of expression when spoken to and made no attempt to speak." He would get upset whenever there was a change in his familiar routine. "When he notices change, he is fussy and cries, but he himself likes to pull blinds up and down, open and close doors, and tear card boxes into small pieces and play with them for hours."

Herbert's mother took him to the clinic in 1941 aged 4.5 and again when he was 5 years of age. When Herbert entered Kanner's office, he displayed an "intelligent physiognomy and good motor coordination." He did not pay attention to anyone but entertained himself with the form board, placing figures into their proper place, removing them, and placing them back again. He was utterly absorbed in his work. He rarely smiled and occasionally made incoherent, monotonous sounds.

Herbert had experienced various placements; first with Mr. and Mrs. Moreland, who were farmers in Maryland. According to Herbert's mother, he was happy at the farm. According to the Moreland family,

> he knows his way around the area of the farm and can go for miles and come back without getting lost. ... He learned to cut wood, uses the power mower. ... He is a manageable child. Occasionally, he get[s] upset if there is a sudden change in plans. ... When mother comes to visit, he gets himself absorbed and does not come toward her.

When Herbert was 33 years old, he was still with the farmers in Maryland. His father wrote: "[Herbert] is essentially unchanged. More than anything else, he seems to enjoy doing jigsaw puzzles, which he can do with the utmost skills" (Kanner, 1971, pp. 130–132).

Case 8—Alfred L.

Alfred's mother brought him to the clinic mainly because

> He has gradually shown a marked tendency toward developing one special interest which will dominate his day's activities. ... There has also been the problem of overattachment to the world of objects and failure to develop the usual amount of social awareness. ... He almost never says a sentence without repeating it. ... He is upset when the sun sets or because the moon does not always appear in the sky at night. ... He prefers to play alone.

Alfred had had his share of medical complications, ranging from colds, bronchitis, chickenpox, impetigo (skin infection), and rheumatoid fever. Before revisiting Kanner's clinic in 1941, Alfred was in 11 different schools, including one where he received *Thorazine* for a short time and a "school for brain-damaged children" his mother founded in 1954. At 38, Alfred was still attending his mother's school (Kanner, 1971, pp. 132–134).

Case 9—Charles N.

Charles's mother's main concern was that he was unresponsive to social interactions. His mother wrote: "The thing that upsets me most is that I can't reach my baby." He was "slow and phlegmatic," lying in his bed "almost as if hypnotized. ... The most impressive thing is his detachment and his inaccessibility. He lives in a world of his own where he cannot be reached. No sense of relationship to persons."

Charles attended the Devereux School but was removed soon after joining and placed in various hospitals, including Bellevue Hospital, New Jersey State Hospital, Arthur Brisbane Child Treatment Center, Atlantic County Hospital, and State Hospital at Ancora. In short, Charles resided in a state hospital from 6 years old, and his condition deteriorated to the point he needed "intensive psychotherapy." The last report describing his condition stated, "This patient is very unpredictable in his behavior. He has a small vocabulary and spends most of his time singing to himself. He is under close supervision and in need of indefinite hospitalization" (Kanner, 1971, pp. 134–136).

Case 10— John F.

John's parents took him to Kanner's Clinic because he had difficulty feeding and was slow in development. Due to the feeding problem, he was frequently hospitalized. Although he had an excellent rote memory, his language was mainly delayed echolalia without alteration of personal pronouns (e.g., "I" for "You"). John attended several schools, including a private nursery school, the Devereux School, the Woods Schools, the Children's House, and the Town and Country School. One can assume that his constant displacement and assignment to various places was due to his lack of progress and skill acquisition. Unfortunately, John passed away before his 30th birthday.

Case 11—Elaine C.

The girl initially described as having "unusual development" had not fared well. After numerous stays at various institutions, she was transferred to the Hudson River State Hospital in 1951. At the age of 39, she was still institutionalized. The last report describing her status indicated that

> She is up and about daily, eats and sleeps well and is acting quite independently. ... Her speech is slow and occasionally unintelligible, and she is manneristic. ... She cannot participate in a conversation, however, except for the immediate needs. If things do not go her way, she becomes acutely disturbed, yelling, hitting her chest with her fist, and her head against the wall. ... She has epileptic seizures occasionally and grand mal type and is receiving antiepileptics and tranquilizers. Her general physical condition is satisfactory.
>
> (Kanner 1971, pp. 138–140)

Kanner (1971) published his follow-up study of the 11 autistic children he examined in the 1930s and 1940s, reminding readers that the examination of those children took place long before the advent of various therapeutic methods, such as operant conditioning, pharmacological interventions, educational conditioning, or psychotherapy, were available. In summarizing the natural history of the condition that afflicted the 11 children, Kanner lamented that the children's admission to State Hospitals was "tantamount to a life sentence." He reported the acknowledgment of a superintendent stating that he accepted patients for "custodial care." Kanner wondered whether these children might have fared better in a different setting. Kanner wrote the following concluding optimistic remark:

> The 30-year follow-up has not indicated too much concrete progress from the time of the original report, beyond the refinement of diagnostic criteria. There has been a hodge-podge of theories, hypotheses, and speculations, and there have been many valiant, well-motivated attempts at alleviating awaiting eventual evaluation. It is expected, with good justification, that the next 30- or 20-year follow-up of other groups of autistic children will be able to present a report of newly obtained factual knowledge and material for a more hopeful **prognosis** than the present chronicle has proved to be.
>
> (Kanner, 1971, p. 145, my emphasis)

Although there is currently no cure for autism, there are various treatment options available to help individuals on the autism spectrum acquire adaptive skills and reduce problematic behavior that interferes with their daily functioning. As Kanner predicted, genetic research and the endeavors of various approaches have given rise to behavioral therapy, which includes applied behavior analysis, speech and language therapy, occupational therapy, and psychopharmacological treatments. It is worth noting that the cohort of children he examined could have fared better had they received appropriate care instead of being committed to state institutions and allowing their condition to run its course.

Autism and Family Dynamic

Family Functioning

Considering the many conditions associated with ASD, it is not surprising that raising a child with autism can be stressful for parents and families as they face demanding caregiving challenges. Many studies have reported higher levels of stress in parents of children diagnosed with ASD compared to parents whose children are diagnosed with other disabilities (Eisenhower et al., 2005; Pisula, 2007). Mothers of children diagnosed with autism, especially those children who require substantial support, have consistently reported poorer physical health, poorer mental health, and lower quality of life than mothers of children developing typically or diagnosed with other developmental disabilities. Parents who participated in a qualitative content analysis study wrote in response to the question: "How has your child in the autism spectrum affected your life and your family's life?" "The stress is constant; there is very little respite from it," "pressure cooker," and "constant burden" (Myers et al., 2009).

Besides having deficits in social communication and social interaction, children with ASD, depending on the severity of the condition, often display maladaptive behaviors that parents might find hard to control. Consequently, parents, especially mothers, may hesitate to take their children out in public for fear of embarrassing situations and negative judgments from others. Conversely, some parents and families of children with ASD have chosen to adopt a more positive outlook, placing less emphasis on traditional measures of success and instead prioritizing their children's unique needs (Green, 2007).

Marital Strain

It is commonly asserted that the divorce rate of parents of children diagnosed with autism hovers around 80%. Having a child diagnosed with ASD can tax family resources, strain family relationships, and add stress to a marriage. Research has found both higher and lower divorce rates among parents of children diagnosed with ASD. A recent study including many participants found no support for a higher-than-average rate of divorce among parents of children with ASD. Parents of children with ASD divorce as often as parents of typically developing children (Freedman et al., 2012). Other researchers have investigated how parents feel about the experience of having a child with ASD. Many parents reported that the experience places a "huge strain on the marriage." Others stated that the burden of constant care and supervision of a child with autism disrupts family life, and not having time to spend together as a couple led to a divorce. A small number of parents, however, reported that parenting a child with autism has made the marital bond stronger (Myers et al., 2009).

Social Isolation

Social isolation and stigma in the family unit of a child diagnosed with ASD have been of interest to researchers (Myers et al., 2009; Kinnear et al., 2016). Parents have reported that outings such as going to the grocery store or restaurants or taking a vacation as a family have been considerably reduced, lest their child display unexpected outbursts. Research findings evaluating the functioning of siblings of children with ASD have been incongruent, reporting both positive and negative outcomes (Benson & Karlof, 2008). The loss of many friends after the diagnosis of autism has further contributed to the family's social isolation. Moreover, strangers are more apt to construe their child's behavior as the result of lack of self-control or ineffective parenting, given that children on the spectrum have no apparent physical abnormality. Other research (e.g., Werner

& Shulman, 2015) has found that parents of children diagnosed with autism reported experiencing more stigma and discrimination than parents caring for children diagnosed with other physical or intellectual disabilities.

Financial Burden

Compared to parents of neurotypical children, parents of children diagnosed with ASD face significant employment and financial hardship because of targeted interventions and related support services that their children need (Lavelle et al., 2014). Because autism is a lifelong disorder, the cost of its management has been estimated at $1.4 million in the United States. Mothers of children with autism are typically more involved than fathers in caregiving and support services that their children need. Mothers are usually less likely to be employed, and if they do, they work fewer hours than mothers of children without disabilities.

While most states in the U.S. have enacted specific autism mandates requiring certain insurers to provide coverage for ASD, out-of-pocket expenses can be a financial drain on the family budget, even when fathers work two jobs to make up for the loss of income of spouses' unemployment or reduced earnings. Moreover, many families of children with ASD do not have health insurance coverage, so they rely on state-funded agencies that seldom have adequate resources to provide needed services. Additionally, many other conditions, including epilepsy, anxiety disorders, language disorders, and intellectual disability, can co-occur with a diagnosis of ASD. Consequently, caring for a child with autism can present insurmountable challenges for parents and families. The financial burden that results from intense, sustained interventions and social isolation commonly associated with autism can take its toll on family dynamics.

Challenges Parents Face

Parents of children with autism face numerous challenges stemming from caregiver burden and their children's difficulties with communication deficits, basic life skills, and **adaptive behaviors** (Kakkar & Srivastava, 2017). Additionally, a diagnosis of autism can create marital stress, as one parent (usually the mother) assumes the responsibility of learning about the condition, and the other works increasingly longer hours to meet the financial obligations of the family. It is not hard to imagine that this state of affairs can lead to frustration and strain on the family relationship.

Greeff and van der Walt (2010) identified several resilience factors that can mitigate the difficulties of parenting a child with autism. They found that higher economic status, a supportive family environment, social support, family belief systems, and coping strategies were the most effective. Coping strategies can take two forms: Problem-focused strategies—i.e., dealing with and managing the problem that causes the stress—and emotion-focused strategies— i.e., managing the emotional response resulting from the experience (Lazarus & Folkman, 1984). One longitudinal research study (Gray, 2006) examined parents of children with autism via in-depth interviews and participant observation and found that coping strategies changed over time; reliance on service providers and family support gradually morphed into more emotion-focused strategies (e.g., social withdrawal, religious faith).

Financial Cost of Autism

There is no cure for autism. Treatment approaches typically target managing and mitigating symptoms, skill development, and support using behavioral, pharmaceutical, psychological, and educational therapies. These treatments are costly. According to the Centers for Disease Control and Prevention (CDC), caring for a child with ASD can cost $17,000 extra yearly and $22,000 if the child also has an intellectual disability. Federal laws require all fifty US states to provide insurance coverage for individuals with an autism diagnosis. The laws governing coverage vary in each state and are subject to updates and amendments over time. For example, Florida (Statute § 627.6686 and § 641.31098) requires insurance companies to cover the cost of well-baby and well-child screening to diagnose and treat ASD through applied behavior analysis and speech, occupational, and physical therapy. Coverage is limited to $36,000 annual expenditure and may not exceed $200,000 in lifetime benefits.

Considering that ASD is a lifelong condition, children diagnosed with ASD grow up to be adults with ASD. The condition can be associated with significant social impairments and long-term health issues requiring high financial costs. The economic burden for the affected person and his family can have lifetime societal and economic implications. The lifetime cost to support a person with ASD and intellectual disability was estimated at $2.4 million in the United States and $1.4 million for a person with autism without intellectual disability (Buescher et al., 2014). Considering the increased estimates of the disorder's prevalence over the past two decades, the annual medical cost associated with ASD will continue to rise. The medical, non-medical, and productivity loss was evaluated at $268 billion and projected to be $461 billion by 2025. If the estimated cost holds, ASD costs will surpass those associated with stroke, hypertension, diabetes, and ADHD. Therefore, early identification and targeted intervention are paramount (Leigh & Du, 2015).

Disabilities in the Classroom

Before the enactment of the Education for All Handicapped Children Act (EHA) in 1975, many children with disabilities were excluded from public schools. They did not receive the same educational opportunities as their non-disabled peers. They were confined in preventoriums, which were established in the early 1900s to prevent the spread of tuberculosis by isolating infected children or those at risk of being infected (Connolly, 2008). Many of these institutions also housed children with disabilities, as there were few other options for their care and education at the time. However, preventoriums were notorious for their poor conditions and lack of individualized care. The EHA was later renamed the Individuals with Disabilities Education Act (IDEA) in 1990 to ensure that all children with disabilities have access to a free, appropriate public education (FAPE) in the least restrictive environment (LRE) possible.

The institutionalization of children with disabilities in the United States is a dark chapter in the country's history. For many decades, children with disabilities were removed from their families and placed in institutions, where they were often subjected to neglect, abuse, and mistreatment. Many of these institutions were overcrowded and underfunded, and the children who lived there did not have basic rights and opportunities. It was not until the 1970s that the deinstitutionalization movement began to gain momentum, and many of these institutions were shut down.

The IDEA consists of four parts: (1) the general provisions of the law, (2) the education of all children with disabilities, (3) a particular focus on infants and toddlers with disabilities, and (4) the administration of national support programs (Hulett, 2009). The IEP, FAPE, and LRE are three main elements of the IDEA.

The Individualized Education Plan (IEP) is a document that outlines the special education services and accommodations that a student with a disability may need to be successful in school. The IEP is developed annually by a team of parents, teachers, and other school staff. Its purpose is to ensure that each student with a disability receives an appropriate education tailored to their unique needs and abilities. The IEP may include goals for academic achievement, social skills, behavior, and services such as speech therapy, occupational therapy, or counseling. It is crucial for the education of children with autism as it outlines any accommodations or modifications necessary to help the student succeed in the classroom, providing them with a customized education suited to their needs and abilities.

Free Appropriate Public Education (FAPE) is a legal term in the United States that refers to the education provided to students with disabilities at public expense, under public supervision and direction, and without charge to the parents. The education must meet the student's needs, as outlined in their Individualized Education Program (IEP). This concept is based on the idea that all children, regardless of their disabilities, have the right to a quality education that prepares them for their future. Ultimately, the goal of FAPE is to provide children with disabilities the same educational opportunities as their non-disabled peers and to help them reach their full potential.

The Least Restrictive Environment (LRE) is a concept outlined in the Individuals with Disabilities Education Act (IDEA). It requires students with disabilities to be educated in settings as similar as possible to those attended by their non-disabled peers. This arrangement means that students with disabilities should have access to the same classrooms, extracurricular activities, and other educational opportunities as their peers to the fullest extent possible. The goal of the LRE is to provide students with disabilities the chance to learn and grow alongside their peers and promote inclusion and diversity in the classroom.

Parents and teachers play a critical role in ensuring that children with disabilities receive a Free Appropriate Public Education (FAPE). Parents also play an essential role in the Individualized Education Plan (IEP) team. Their input can help ensure that the IEP reflects the child's unique needs and abilities. Teachers are responsible for implementing the IEP and providing the necessary accommodations and support to help the child succeed. By working together, parents and teachers can create a supportive and inclusive learning environment that promotes the academic and social success of children with disabilities.

Procedural safeguards are an important aspect of Free Appropriate Public Education (FAPE) as they help ensure that students with disabilities receive the necessary educational services. These safeguards provide parents and students with the right to participate in the decision-making process, access to relevant educational records, and the ability to resolve disputes through mediation or due process. By ensuring that these procedures are in place and followed appropriately, we can ensure that every student receives the education they need and deserve. Overall, the components of the Individuals with Disabilities Education Act (IDEA), such as the Individualized Education Program (IEP), early intervention services, and transition planning, play a crucial role in preparing students for life after high school graduation and setting the stage for promoting a positive life course for students with disabilities.

Autism and Transition to Adulthood

Transitioning from adolescence to adulthood can be challenging, even for neurotypical adolescents. Arnett (2000) proposed the term *emerging adulthood* to capture a developmental period from approximately ages 18 to 25. Late teens in cultures that permit independent exploration can have an extended period of identity searching till their mid-twenties. The transition to adulthood is particularly daunting for adolescents on the autism spectrum, as they need significant support to navigate social situations, find employment, and live independently to the extent it is possible. According to Roux and colleagues (2013), an estimated 50,000 autistic Americans turn 18 each year. The estimated number is probably much more, considering that autism has been more prevalent in recent years. More recent data based on population growth and the increased prevalence of autism estimate the number of autistic youths who turn 18 each year to be more than 100,000.

When U.S. students enrolled in special education turn 16, school systems must develop a transition strategy embedded in the IEP to plan for life after high school, including college, vocational training, employment, independent living, and adult day training or services. The special education services U.S. students receive end when they graduate high school or turn 21. The eligibility for adult services is not guaranteed; it depends on availability and funding. Due to the various challenges and responsibilities young adults with autism face, some professionals use the "falling off a cliff" metaphor to describe the transition.

Some autism researchers have emphasized the importance of revisiting transition planning as early as 6 years old. This proactive approach can help identify ways to make the transition more relevant to the obstacles young adults face after high school graduation (Chiang et al., 2013). Daily living skills such as housekeeping, personal hygiene, cooking, money management, and using public transportation are essential for young adults to live independently. Taylor and Mailick (2014) conducted a ten-year longitudinal study with 161 adults with autism. They found that those with better daily living skills performed more optimally in their jobs and educational activities, highlighting the importance of early planning. Parents must ensure that daily living skills are part of the IEP transition plan, as schools may not always include these skills in the IEP of college-bound students. One study found that half of participants with autism with average and above-average intelligence had deficits in daily living skills (Duncan & Bishop, 2015).

Autism in Adulthood

The College Experience

According to *Autism Speaks* (one of the largest autism advocacy organizations in the world), an estimated 50,000 individuals with autism in the United States turn 18 years old each year. The Individuals with Disabilities Education Act (IDEA) mandates that Special education services be provided to those who are eligible until they graduate from high school or turn 21 years old. When they "age out," they are no longer eligible for special education services and may not receive support as they transition to adulthood. The ever-increasing rate of autism diagnoses justifies the need for services for adults with autism that are currently lacking (Shattuck, Roux et al., 2012).

Earning a college degree is not guaranteed even for neurotypicals. According to the National Center for Education Statistics (2020), approximately 60% of full-time undergraduates complete a bachelor's degree within six years of starting college. However, of the 36% of young adults on the autism spectrum who attempt postsecondary education (Roux et al., 2015), only 38.8% complete their degrees (Jackson et al., 2018). In short, only about 14% of young adults on the spectrum graduate from college.

Autism can present unique challenges for college students. As a result, the rate of postsecondary education for youth with autism is significantly lower than that of the general population. Despite the disability support services colleges and universities provide (e.g., extended test-taking time, quiet study spaces, and note-taking assistance), no more than 40% of postgraduates ever attend college and very few complete a degree. Twenty-six autistic and 158 non-autistic students enrolled at UK universities completed an online questionnaire to examine their social and academic experiences (Gurbuz et al., 2019). The autistic students reported facing significant challenges and experiencing more mental health difficulties compared to their non-autistic counterparts. The challenges primarily revolved around the social aspects of university life, such as social skills, opportunities for social support, and the level of awareness about ASD, among others.

Wei and colleagues (2013) examined whether individuals with autism are more likely than those in the general population to gravitate toward science, technology, engineering, and mathematics (STEM) fields. Despite the lowest college enrollment rates among other disability groups, the findings suggest that students on the autism spectrum had the highest STEM enrollment rates, highlighting their potential for success in these fields. Additionally, Wei and colleagues (2014) also found that college students on the autism spectrum pursuing STEM studies were more likely to complete their education at a two-year community college and twice as likely to transfer to a four-year university than their peers not enrolled in STEM fields.

Many individuals on the autism spectrum can earn a college degree. However, they require various supports to succeed (Vanbergeijk et al., 2008). Completion of postsecondary education is associated with more positive outcomes and employment opportunities. Shattuck, Narendorf and colleagues (2012) examined the rates of postsecondary education and employment in a large sample of participants with ASD, learning disabilities, mental retardation, and speech/language impairment. They found that young adults with ASD tend to have lower rates of employment and education after leaving high school. They are less likely to be employed compared to their peers with other intellectual disabilities. Shockingly, more than half of the youth with ASD do not participate in any job or school activities in the first two years after finishing high school.

In sum, many factors can contribute to college students on the autism spectrum not graduating from college. Difficulties with social interactions and communication, difficulty with keeping up with the academic and social demands of college life, sensory processing issues, and social isolation can all add to the challenges that youth on the autism spectrum experience. Many colleges and universities provide support services and accommodations to help autistic students progress academically and socially. Students may need guidance to access those services. Therefore, with appropriate support and accommodations, individuals on the autism spectrum can attend college and complete their degree.

Romantic Relationships

Individuals with autism face challenges starting and maintaining romantic re-lationships owing to difficulties with social interactions and communication. Donvan and Zucker (2016) provide an account of Donald Triplett, the first child Kanner diagnosed with "infantile autism" in the 1940s. Although Donald never got married, he flirted with women in his entourage. One of his famil-iar routines involved using a rubber band and a paper bullet to hit his target: women he liked but could not marshal enough courage to inform them or initi-ate a conversation.

Although the literature shows that asexuality and lack of sexual attraction or low sexual interest are overrepresented in people with autism spectrum disorder compared with neurotypical samples (Attanasio et al., 2022), a diagnosis of au-tism does not hinder one's ability to be in a relationship. Individuals with autism are fully capable of marrying and having successful relationships. However, re-search suggests they are less likely to be involved in such relationships than their non-autistic peers. Moreover, their involvement in romantic relationships tends to be less fulfilling and shorter in duration (Hancock et al., 2019; Renty & Roeyers, 2006). Additionally, individuals with psychiatric conditions, such as schizophrenia and attention-deficit/hyperactivity disorder, or autism, have a higher tendency to pair up with others who share their diagnosis (Nordsletten et al., 2016). With respect to sexual orientation, George and Stokes (2018) found decreased heterosexuality and increased bisexuality, homosexuality, and asexu-ality in an international online sample of 309 participants with autism, compared to 310 neurotypical individuals.

Research on romantic relationships has traditionally focused on autistic char-acteristics as potential barriers to relationship satisfaction. Yew and colleagues (2023) investigated the role partners play in relationship satisfaction and various factors (e.g., social loneliness, personality traits, sexual satisfaction, partner re-sponsiveness) associated with long-term relationship satisfaction for autistic and non-autistic individuals. The findings suggest that partner responsiveness was a strong predictor of relationship satisfaction for autistic and non-autistic partners. One study found that most high-functioning adults with autism are interested in forming romantic relationships. Interestingly, those who had partners also on the autism spectrum reported higher satisfaction in their relationships compared to those in relationships with non-autistic partners (Strunz et al., 2017).

Driving a Motor Vehicle

Learning to drive and acquiring a driver's license during adolescence is a signifi-cant milestone because it provides mobility and independence. Driving can also improve access to employment and educational and social opportunities, which are limited for autistic people (Daly et al., 2014; Renty & Roeyers, 2006). Adults with autism spectrum disorder (ASD) who have access to community mobility have a five times greater chance of employment compared to those who do not (Dickerson et al., 2024). However, only 33% of adolescents and young adults with autism and without an intellectual disability obtain a driver's license, compared to 83% of their neurotypical counterparts. Additionally, those with autism tend to get their license at a later age (Curry et al., 2018).

Parental expectations have contributed to lower rates of adolescents and young adults obtaining driver's licenses. One online survey found that 70% of parents reported that autism negatively impacts their son or daughter's driving, and a similar proportion was concerned about their child's driving. They find learning to drive challenging due to the complexity of driving demands (Cox et al., 2012). Conversely, young adults with autism have reported their desire to enhance their driving abilities, live independently, and make autonomous decisions (Cheak-Zamora et al., 2022).

Inhibiting Factors

Many factors contribute to the challenges autistic individuals face when learning to operate a motor vehicle: Driving apprehension, sensory overload, and executive dysfunction. Anxiety is prevalent among autistic individuals, so it can interfere with their capacity to focus and develop the necessary skills and confidence behind the wheel. Driving entails processing sensory information, including heightened sensitivity to touch, light, and sound that can interfere with a driver's ability to concentrate and react quickly and appropriately behind the wheel. Executive dysfunction refers to difficulty with organization, planning, and decision-making. Additionally, they may experience distractibility, motor coordination, and difficulties interpreting social cues (Myers et al., 2021). The inability to manage these cognitive facets can be problematic for some individuals with autism to learn the complex skills associated with driving.

Fok and colleagues (2022) found that compared to young adult novice drivers without autism those on the spectrum reported more perceived emotion dysregulation, driving difficulties, and negative emotions. Driving instructors can play a significant role in managing their students' apprehension, sensory issues, and executive dysfunction with patience and support so that they feel at ease and confident while learning to drive.

Driver Training for People with ASD

With the appropriate support and training, many young autistic adults can learn how to drive despite the challenging aspects (e.g., multitasking and processing sensory information) operating a motor vehicle entail. One **qualitative study** interviewed three groups of participants to determine their perception regarding autism and driving: (a) parents of autistic individuals, (b) individuals with autism, and (c) driving instructors who teach individuals with autism. The study identified several themes—namely, supporting the idea that targeted support can help autistic individuals overcome the challenges of learning to drive (Vindin et al., 2021). Virtual reality can create a controlled, comfortable environment to simulate different driving conditions. In one study, virtual reality driving simulation training (VRDST) was used to enhance the driving skills of novice autistic drivers. The participants were randomly assigned to routine training (RT) or VRDST groups. Those who underwent VRDST improved their driving performance significantly compared to participants assigned to RT (Cox et al., 2017).

Driving and community mobility (DCM) entail being able to operate a motor vehicle, use public transportation, and plan and complete trips to various destinations when driving is not an option. Dickerson and colleagues (2024) conducted a study that examined whether a five-day intensive and focused intervention can promote independence in teens and young adults with autism. Thirty-eight young adults participated in the study, which consisted of individualized strategies and driving stimulation. The study results indicate that specifically tailored interventions can enhance driving and community mobility skills and promote greater independence for teens and young adults with autism. Lindsay (2017) systematically reviewed 22 studies and factors that affect driving among individuals with autism. Based on the review's shortcomings, she advocated several strategies clinicians and educators could incorporate into driving instruction: breaking training into shorter teachable units, providing regular and consistent driving instructions, and promoting driving coping strategies.

Employment

Obtaining and sustaining employment has been challenging for many individuals on the autism spectrum despite having completed postsecondary education. Some individuals with autism have IQs over the normal range. Additionally, some can focus and sustain attention for long periods, making them ideal candidates to work in the information technology sector. Research suggests that they are reliable and provide benefits to employers without incurring additional costs (Scott et al., 2017), possess excellent visual skills (Soulieres et al., 2009), and are capable of paying attention to details (Kéïta et al., 2014). The success stories of companies like Specialisterne, which originated in Denmark, among many others (e.g., Microsoft, 2015), have hired exclusively people on the autism spectrum to test software, knowing that their ability to deal with repetitive tasks and sustain focus would make them ideal candidates.

The principle of **inclusion** promotes equity, access, opportunities, and equal rights. Therefore, individuals with disabilities must be afforded the same opportunities to work to the best of their abilities and desires. One main objective of the Individuals with Disabilities Education Act (IDEA, 2004) is to facilitate the transition for adolescents in special education to find employment. However, finding and maintaining a gainful occupation has been problematic for emerging adults with developmental disabilities (Wehman, 2011).

Compared with emerging adults with different disabilities, those with autism do not fare well during the first decade after high school. Approximately 50–52% do not hold a paid job outside the home. Those fortunate enough to get a job work less than full-time and earn lower wages than comparison groups with other disabilities. Young adults with conversational and functional skills are more likely to find employment than those with limited conversational skills. Interestingly, one-fifth of youngsters with limited verbal capability are employed, suggesting that training them to participate in the workplace can be effective (Roux et al., 2013).

Hayward and colleagues (2019) conducted qualitative research to determine factors that attract employees with autism and the likelihood that those factors can also determine retention and job satisfaction. Consistent with hypothesized enablers and facilitators, they found that sensory-friendly environments make it more likely for people with autism to join the workforce. One respondent commented:

> I am very sensitive to the bright, fluorescent lights inside, they give me headaches and make me dizzy. When I first started working at this place my manager did not know about my sensory issues but he noticed how it affects my work so where it was possible, he made adjustments. He lets me wear sunglasses inside now, even when I am talking to members/clients. We explain to them and they are fine about it.
>
> (Hayward, 2019, p. 53)

Others reported that opportunities to minimize contact with others in the workplace reduced stress and anxiety, which are common among people with autism. Two employees reported, "I was able to work independently, with my own office and my work required minimal social interaction." "Finding tasks that can be done alone, since this is much less stressful" (Hayward, 2019, p. 52).

Research has consistently found poorer employment outcomes for young adults with autism. This state of affairs makes it difficult for them to consider living independently and, thus, perpetuates the financial burden of families' continuing financial support of their young adults with autism. Providing work experience for youngsters during high school could pave the way for employment opportunities after high school (Hendricks & Wehman, 2009). Employment preparation during the high school transition years should be specific, consistent with the labor market demands, and in line with the capabilities and skills of youngsters with ASD.

Autistic Adults: Research, Independent Living, and Functioning

Independent living is a fundamental human right for individuals with disabilities, including those with autism. It allows them to lead lives that closely resemble those of individuals without disabilities to the extent their conditions permit. Some autistic adults demonstrate the ability to live independently, while others may require more support. Those who can function independently often exhibit key characteristics such as effective coping mechanisms for social situations, strong communication skills, and the ability to advocate for their needs.

There is abundant research on the transition period into young adulthood but limited research regarding the challenges adults with autism face when they contemplate living independently. There is limited research on autism in adulthood and even fewer studies on the services and support that could promote fulfilling adult lives for autistic individuals. There is a growing recognition that researchers and clinicians need to learn more about the needs and developmental outcomes of older adults with ASD (Wise, 2020). There is also a need for primary care providers to receive adequate training for caring for adults with autism (Bruder et al., 2012). The lack of autism research in adulthood is due to the perception of autism as a condition that primarily affects children (Pellicano et al., 2022). Some of the challenges that the limited research on autistic adult independent functioning has found include financial management, integrated community living and housing, and psychophysical stability and daily living (Ghanouni et al., 2021).

One longitudinal study found that despite young autistic adults encountering difficulties in achieving typical social goals, they may be able to experience better mental health and quality of life. Predictors of better outcomes include childhood IQ, autism traits, and adaptive functioning (Forbes et al., 2023). Another study involving a large sample of autistic adults explored the factors linked to independent living, accommodation satisfaction, and life satisfaction. The study found that older participants, women, and those with higher self-reported IQs were more likely to live independently, be satisfied with their accommodation, and experience higher life satisfaction (Scheeren et al., 2022).

Rowe and Kahn (1997) have defined successful aging as a multidimensional concept encompassing the avoidance of disease and disability, the maintenance of high physical and cognitive function, and sustained engagement in social and productive activities. Gerontologists have used the successful aging model to evaluate outcomes in older adults in the general population. Considering that individuals with autism have various co-occurring conditions that limit their capacity to march into advanced age with the prospect of aging successfully, Klein and Klinger (2024) used the four-domain "aging well" model (Fernández-Ballesteros, 2000) to assess the literature on autism and aging, namely outcomes related to health and functioning, cognitive and physical functioning, positive affect and control, and social participation and engagement. The findings suggest that older adults with autism generally experience poor outcomes, including "increased medical conditions, low adaptive skills, elevated risk of cognitive decline, limited physical activity, high rates of mental health conditions, low quality of life, and reduced social or community participation." Klein and Klinger (2024) advocate for a research agenda that targets personalized support to this growing aging population and one that considers the input of adults on the autism spectrum and their caregivers.

Conventional autism research has primarily focused on the deficits model—i.e., biological functioning that is based on pre-established metrics determined by others. Conversely, Pellicano and colleagues (2022) proposed a research model based on Nussbaum's capabilities approach (2011), which focuses on ten core elements (e.g., life worth living, good health, emotional capability, and so forth). There is abundant literature suggesting that some individuals with autism have the potential to excel in various areas of functioning despite the stereotypes commonly associated with the condition. Pellicano and colleagues' approach allows them to assess the opportunities and difficulties that autistic adults face, the factors influencing them, and how researchers and clinicians could design research and deliver services that can improve the quality of lives of autistic adults.

Medical Complexities and Life Expectancy

Autism is a lifelong neurodevelopmental condition that currently has no cure. The symptoms of the condition can vary widely from one person to another. While a small minority of individuals may no longer meet the criteria for an autism diagnosis and achieve an **optimal outcome**, they may still experience significant social and communication impairments (Fein et al., 2013). Some co-occurring conditions that are characteristic of autism tend to subside in adulthood. Others may persist and, thus, require medical treatment due to their medical complexities. Medical complexities encompass a broad spectrum of co-occurring medical and health issues that individuals with autism may encounter, ranging from immune system dysfunction, sleep disorders, ADHD, depression, anxiety, feeding difficulties, and gastrointestinal problems to sensory sensitivities. As individuals with autism transition into adulthood, these conditions can significantly affect their daily functioning.

Compared to adults without autism, those on the spectrum have significantly higher rates of medical conditions such as immune dysfunction, sleep disorders, seizures, obesity, hypertension, and diabetes. They also experience increased rates of psychiatric disorders, including anxiety, bipolar disorder, schizophrenia, and suicide attempts. Moreover, rare conditions in the general population, like stroke and Parkinson's, are also more common among adults with autism (Croen et al., 2014).

Life expectancy has increased in many parts of the world in recent times. However, for individuals diagnosed with autism, life expectancy is lower than that of the general population. Mouridsen (2013) reviewed published systematic mortality studies and found that mortality was nearly three times higher in the ASD population than in the general population. Autism *per se* was not the most significant **risk factor**. Instead, having an intellectual disability, being a female, and suffering from epilepsy were significant risk factors. More recently, DaWalt and colleagues (2019) identified predictors of mortality over 20 years of 406 adolescents and adults with autism. Over the 20 years, 6.4% of the individuals studied died at a mean age of 39 due to various reasons: Chronic health conditions (e.g., heart disease and cancer), accidents (e.g., accidental poisoning and choking on food), and medication side effect complications.

The prevalence of suicidal ideation and suicide attempts among people with ASD is high. A clinical cohort study (Cassidy et al., 2014) found that people with Asperger's syndrome who were also depressed were significantly more likely to report suicidal ideation or plans to attempt suicide. They also had higher levels of autistic traits than those who did not express suicidal thoughts. Newell and colleagues (2023) conducted a meta-analysis with more than 48,000 participants in 36 primary studies. The findings indicate that suicidal thoughts and behaviors are common among both autistic and possibly autistic individuals without accompanying intellectual disabilities. The findings further underscore the need to investigate potential factors influencing suicidality. The authors highlighted the importance for clinicians and researchers to focus more on possibly autistic individuals to gain a better understanding of and prevent suicide in both groups.

Croen and colleagues (2014) conducted a comprehensive study regarding the prevalence of various health issues in adults with autism. The findings showed that cardiovascular disease, epilepsy, and diabetes are more common in people with ASD than in the general population. Moreover, they also found that the risk of suicide attempts in adults with ASD was five times higher than in adults without ASD. Schendel and colleagues (2016) investigated the mortality patterns among individuals with ASD in a population-based study in Denmark. They found that the mortality risk was two-fold higher during adulthood for those with ASD than their typical counterpart. More significantly, their mortality risk was like that of individuals with neurological or mental/behavioral disorders.

In sum, the mortality rate for individuals on the autism spectrum is higher than that of the general population, not because of autism *per se* but rather due to higher rates of health problems throughout childhood, adolescence, and adulthood. Depression appears to have a significant impact on suicidal thoughts, attempts, and completed suicides among individuals on the autism spectrum. Co-occurring conditions commonly associated with autism also play a crucial role in reducing the life expectancy of individuals on the spectrum. Additionally, the long-term use of prescribed medications and their associated side effects can lead to various debilitating health conditions.

Summary

Children diagnosed with autism will grow up to become adults with autism. Unlike typical individuals, those with autism face various challenges throughout their lives, from early childhood through adolescence and into adulthood. Kanner summarized the 11 children he examined in his clinic in the 1930s and 1940s, noting that allowing the natural history of the condition to run its course resulted in no positive outcomes. Given the many conditions associated with ASD, it is not surprising that raising a child with autism can be stressful for parents and families, in that it can lead to demanding caregiving challenges. Numerous studies have shown that parents of children diagnosed with ASD experience higher levels of stress compared to parents of children with other disabilities. Parenting a child with autism can disrupt the family functioning and cause marital strain, social isolation, and financial burden.

The passage of the Individuals with Disabilities Act in 1975 makes it possible for children with disabilities in the U.S. to have access to free, appropriate public education in the least restrictive environment. This Act ensures that children with autism have the right to an education that meets their individual needs. However, the transition from childhood to adolescence and young adulthood is generally problematic for those on the autism spectrum. Attending and completing postgraduate education, establishing romantic relationships, learning to operate a motor vehicle, finding employment, and living and functioning independently can be challenging.

Autism and its co-occurring conditions tend to persist over time and significantly affect the daily functioning of autistic adults. The life expectancy and mortality rate of individuals on the autism spectrum are considerably lower than those in the general population. Suicidal thoughts and rare conditions in the general population, like stroke and Parkinson's, are also more common.

Questions to Ponder for Further Thinking and Learning

1 What are some of the challenges that individuals with autism face throughout their life course?
2 How do societal attitudes toward autism impact the life course of individuals with autism?
3 What are some effective interventions for supporting autistic individuals across their life course?
4 How do family dynamics change over the life course of an individual with autism?
5 What roles do schools and educational systems play in supporting individuals with autism as they transition into adulthood?
6 How do employment opportunities and workplace accommodations impact the life course of individuals with autism?

7 What are some of the unique experiences and challenges faced by aging individuals with autism?
8 How can we improve healthcare access and quality of care for individuals with autism throughout their life course?

References

Arnett, J. J. (2000). Emerging adulthood: A theory of development from the late teens through the twenties. *American Psychologist, 55*(5), 469–480.

Attanasio, M., Masedu, F., Quattrini, F., Pino, M. C., Vagnetti, R., Valenti, M., & Mazza, M. (2022). Are autism spectrum disorder and asexuality connected? *Archives of Sexual Behavior, 51*(4), 2091–2115.

Benson, P. R., & Karlof, K. L. (2008). Child, parent, and family predictors of latter adjustment in siblings of children with autism. *Research in Autism Spectrum Disorders, 2*(4), 583–600.

Bruder, M. B., Kerins, G., Mazzarella, C., Sims, J., & Stein, N. (2012). Brief report: The medical care of adults with autism spectrum disorders: Identifying the needs. *Journal of Autism and Developmental Disorders, 42*(11), 2498–2504.

Buescher, A. V., Cidav, Z., Knapp, M., & Mandell, D. S. (2014). Costs of autism spectrum disorders in the United Kingdom and the United States. *JAMA Pediatrics, 168*(8) 721–728.

Cassidy, S., Bradley, P., Robinson, J., Allison, C., McHugh, M., & Baron-Cohen, S. (2014). Suicidal ideation and suicide plans or attempts in adults with Asperger's syndrome attending a specialist diagnostic clinic: A clinical cohort study. *Lancet Psychiatry, 1*(2), 142–147.

Cheak-Zamora, N., Tait, A., & Coleman, A. (2022). Assessing and promoting independence in young adults with autism spectrum disorder. *Journal of Developmental and Behavioral Pediatrics, 43*(3), 130–139.

Chiang, H. M., Cheung, Y. K., Li, H., & Tsai, L. Y. (2013). Factors associated with participation in employment for high school leavers with autism. *Journal of Autism and Developmental Disorders, 43*(8), 1832–1842.

Connolly, C. A. (2008). *Saving sickly children: The tuberculosis preventorium in American life, 1909–1970.* Rutgers University Press.

Cox, D. J., Brown, T., Ross, V., Moncrief, M., Schmitt, R., Gaffney, G., & Reeve, R. (2017). Can youth with autism spectrum disorder use virtual reality driving simulation training to evaluate and improve driving performance? An exploratory study. *Journal of Autism Developmental Disorders, 47*(8), 2544–2555.

Cox, N. B., Reeve, R. E., Cox, S. M., & Cox, D. J. (2012). Brief report: Driving and young adults with ASD: Parents' experiences. *Journal of Autism and Developmental Disorders, 42*(10), 2257–2262.

Croen, L., Zerbo, O., Qian, Y., Massolo, M. L., Rich, S., Sidney, S., & Kripke, C. (2014). The health status of adults on the autism spectrum. *Autism, 19*(7), 814–823.

Curry, A. E., Yerys, B. E., Huang, P., & Metzger, K. B. (2018). Longitudinal study of driver licensing rates among adolescents and young adults with autism spectrum disorder. *Autism, 22*(4), 479–488.

Daly, B. P., Nicholls, E. G., Patrick, K. E., Brinckman, D. D., & Schultheis, M. T. (2014). Driving behaviors in adults with autism spectrum disorders. *Journal of Autism and Developmental Disorders, 44*(12), 3119–3128.

DaWalt, L. S., Hong, J., Greenberg, J. S., & Mailick, M. R. (2019). Mortality in individuals with autism spectrum disorder: Predictors over a 20-year period. *Autism: The International Journal of Research and Practice, 23*(7), 1732–1739.

Dickerson, A. E., Turbeville, L., & Wu, Q. (2024). Effectiveness of a driving and community mobility intervention for teens and young adults with autism spectrum disorder. *American Journal of Occupation Therapy*, *78*(1), 7801205110.

Donvan, J., & Zucker, C. (2016). *In a different key: The story of autism*. Crown Publishers.

Duncan, A. W., & Bishop, S. L. (2015). Understanding the gap between cognitive abilities and daily living skills in adolescents with autism spectrum disorders with average intelligence. *Autism*, *19*(1), 64–72.

Eisenhower, A. S., Baker, B. L., & Blacher, J. (2005). Preschool children with intellectual disability: Syndrome specificity, behavior problems, and maternal well-being. *Journal of Intellectual Disability Research*, *49*(Pt 9), 657–671.

Elder, G. H., Johnson, M. K., & Crosnoe, R. (2003). The emergence and development of life course theory. In J. T. Mortimer & M. J. Shanahan (Eds.), *Handbook of the life course* (pp. 3–19). Springer.

Erikson, E. H. (1993 [1950]). *Childhood and society*. W. W. Norton & Company.

Fein, D., Barton, M., Eigsti, I. M., Kelley, E., Naigles, L., Schultz, R. T., ... Tyson, K. (2013). Optimal outcome in individuals with a history of autism. *Journal of Child Psychology and Psychiatry*, *54*(2), 195–205.

Fernández-Ballesteros, R., García, L. F., Abarca, D., Blanc, L., Efklides, A., Kornfeld, R., ... Patricia, S. (2000). Lay concept of aging well: Cross-cultural comparisons. *Journal of the American Geriatrics Society*, *56*(5), 950–952.

Fok, M., Owens, J. M., Ollendick, T. H., & Scarpa, A. (2022). Perceived driving difficulty, negative affect, and emotion dysregulation in self-identified autistic emerging drivers. *Frontiers in Psychology*, *13*, 754776.

Forbes, G., Kent, R., Charman, T., Baird, G., Pickles, A., & Simonoff, E. (2023). How do autistic people fare in adult life and can we predict it from childhood? *Autism Research*, *16*(2), 458–473.

Freedman, B. H., Kalb, L. G., Zablotsky, B., & Stuart, E. A. (2012). Relationship status among parents of children with autism spectrum disorders: A population-based study. *Journal of Autism and Developmental Disorders*, *42*(4), 539–548.

George, R., & Stokes, M. A. (2018). Sexual orientation in autism spectrum disorder. *Autism Research*, *11*(1), 133–141.

Ghanouni, P., Quirke, S., Blok, J., & Casey, A. (2021). Independent living in adults with autism spectrum disorder: Stakeholders' perspectives and experiences. *Research in Developmental Disabilities*, *119*, 104085.

Gray, D. E. (2006). Coping over time: The parents of children with autism. *Journal of Intellectual Disability Research*, *50*(Pt 12), 970–976.

Greeff, A. P., & van der Walt, K.-J. (2010). Resilience in families with an autistic child. *Education and Training in Autism and Developmental Disabilities*, *45*(3), 347–355.

Green, S. E. (2007). "We're tired, not sad": Benefits and burdens of mothering a child with a disability. *Social Science & Medicine*, *64*(1), 150–163.

Gurbuz, E., Hanley, M., & Riby, D. M. (2019). University students with autism: The social and academic experiences of university in the UK. *Journal of Autism and Developmental Disorders*, *49*(2), 617–631.

Hancock, G., Stokes, M. A., & Mesibov, G. (2019). Differences in romantic relationship experiences for individuals with an autism spectrum disorder. *Sexuality and Disability*, *38*, 231–245.

Hayward, S. M., McVilly, K. R., & Stokes, M. A. (2019). Autism and employment: What works. *Research in Autism Spectrum Disorders*, *60*, 48–58.

Hendricks, D. R., & Wehman, P. (2009). Transition from school to adulthood for youth with autism spectrum disorders: Review and recommendations. *Focus on Autism and Other Developmental Disabilities*, *24*(2), 77–88.

Hulett, K. E. (2009). *Legal aspects of special education*. Pearson Education Inc.

IDEA (2004). U.S. Department of Education: Individuals with Disabilities Education Act. PL108-446, Section 1400(c)(14). https://www.congress.gov/108/plaws/publ446/PLAW-108publ446.pdf. Accessed on May 4, 2024.

Jackson, S. L. J., Hart, L., & Volkmar, F. R. (2018). Preface: Special issue—College experiences for students with autism spectrum disorder. *Journal of Autism and Developmental Disorders, 48*(3), 639–642.

Kakkar, J., & Srivastava, P. (2017). Challenges and coping among parents having children with autism spectrum disorder. *Journal of Psychosocial Research, 12*(2), 363–371.

Kanner, L. (1935). *Child psychiatry*. Charles C. Thomas, Publisher Ltd.

Kanner, L. (1943). Autistic disturbances of affective contact. *Nervous Child, 2*, 217–250.

Kanner, L. (1971). Follow-up study of eleven autistic children originally reported in 1943. *Journal of Autism and Childhood Schizophrenia, 1*(2), 119–145.

Kéïta, L., Guy, J., Berthiaume, C., Mottron, L., & Bertone, A. (2014). An early origin for detailed perception in autism spectrum disorder: Biased sensitivity for high-spatial frequency information. *Scientific Reports, 4*, 5475.

Kinnear, S. H., Link, B. G., Ballan, M. S., & Fischbach, R. L. (2016). Understanding the experience of stigma for parents of children with autism spectrum disorder and the role stigma plays in families' lives. *Journal of Autism and Developmental Disorders, 46*(3), 942–953.

Klein, C. B., & Klinger, L. G. (2024). Aging well and autism: A narrative review and recommendations for future research. *Healthcare, 12*(12), 1207.

Lavelle, T. A., Weinstein, M. C., Newhouse, J. P., Munir, K., Kuhlthau, K. A., & Prosser, L. A. (2014). Economic burden of childhood autism spectrum disorders. *Pediatrics, 133*(3), e520–e229.

Lazarus, R., & Folkman, S. (1984). *Stress, appraisal, and coping*. Springer Publishing Co.

Leigh, P. J., & Du, J. (2015). Brief report: Forecasting the economic burden of Autism in 2015 and 2025 in the United States. *Journal of Autism and Developmental Disorders, 45*(12) 4135–4139.

Lindsay, S. (2017). Systematic review of factors affecting driving and motor vehicle transportation among people with autism spectrum disorder. *Disability and Rehabilitation, 39*(9), 837–846.

Microsoft (2015). Microsoft Autism Hiring Program. https://www.microsoftalumni.com/s/1769/19/interior.aspx?gid=2&pgid=1119&sid=1769. Accessed on April 27, 2024.

Mouridsen, S. (2013). Mortality and factors associated with death in autism spectrum disorders. *American Journal of Autism, 1*, 17–25.

Myers, B. J., Mackintosh, V. H., & Goin-Kochel, R. P. (2009). "My greatest joy and my greatest heart ache:" Parents' own words on how having a child in the autism spectrum has affected their lives and their families' lives. *Research in Autism Spectrum Disorders, 3*(3), 670–684.

Myers, R. K., Carey, M. E., Bonsu, J. M., Yerys, B. E., Mollen, C. J., & Curry, A. E. (2021). Behind the wheel: Specialized driving instructors' experiences and strategies for teaching autistic adolescents to drive. *American Journal of Occupation Therapy, 75*(3), 7503180110p1–7503180110p11.

National Center for Education Statistics (2020). https://nces.ed.gov/. Accessed on January 15, 2023.

Newell, V., Phillips, L., Jones, C., Townsend, E., Richards, C., & Cassidy, S. (2023). A systematic review and meta-analysis of suicidality in autistic and possibly autistic people without co-occurring intellectual disability. *Molecular Autism, 14*(1), 12.

Nordsletten, A. E., Larsson, H., Crowley, J. J., Almqvist, C., Lichtenstein, P., & Mataix-Cols, D. (2016). Patterns of nonrandom mating within and across 11 major psychiatric disorders. *JAMA Psychiatry*, *73*(4), 354–361.

Nussbaum, M. (2011). *Creating capabilities*. Harvard University Press.

Pellicano, E., Fatima, U., Hall, G., Heyworth, M., Lawson, W., Lilley, R., ... Stears, M. (2022). A capabilities approach to understanding and supporting autistic adulthood. *Nature Reviews Psychology*, *1*(11), 624–639.

Pisula, E. (2007). A comparative study of stress profiles in mothers of children with autism and those of children with Down's Syndrome. *Journal of Applied Research in Intellectual Disabilities*, *20*(3), 274–278.

Renty, J., & Roeyers, H. (2006). Satisfaction with formal support and education for children with autism spectrum disorder: The voices of the parents. *Child: Care, Health and Development*, *32*(3), 371–385.

Roux, A. M., Shattuck, P. T., Cooper, B. P., Anderson, K. A., Wagner, M., & Narendorf, S. C. (2013). Postsecondary employment experiences among young adults with an autism spectrum disorder. *Journal of the American Academy of Child & Adolescent Psychiatry*, *52*(9), 931–939.

Roux, A. M., Shattuck, P. T., Rast, J. E., Rava, J. A., & Anderson, K. A. (2015). National Autism Indicators Report: Transition into Young Adulthood. Life Course Outcomes Research Program, A. J. Drexel Autism Institute. https://drexel.edu/~/media/Files/autismoutcomes/publications/National%20Autism%20Indicators%20Report%20-%20July%202015.ashx. Accessed on January 25, 2024.

Rowe, J. W., & Kahn, R. L. (1997). Successful aging. *Gerontologist*, *37*(4), 433–440.

Scheeren, A. M., Howlin, P., Bartels, M., Krabbendam, L., & Begeer, S. (2022). The importance of home: Satisfaction with accommodation, neighborhood, and life in adults with autism. *Autism Research*, *15*(3), 519–530.

Schendel, D. E., Overgaard, M., Christensen, J., Hjort, L., Jørgensen, M., Vestergaard, M., & Parner, E. T. (2016). Association of psychiatric and neurologic comorbidity with mortality among persons with autism spectrum disorder in a Danish population. *JAMA Pediatrics*, *170*(3), 243–250.

Scott, M., Jacob, A., Hendrie, D., Parsons, R., Girdler, S., Falkmer, T., & Falkmer, M. (2017). Employers' perception of the costs and the benefits of hiring individuals with autism spectrum disorder in open employment in Australia. *Plos One*, *12*(5), e0177607.

Shattuck, P. T., Narendorf, S. C., Cooper, B., Sterzing, P. R., Wagner, M., & Taylor, J. L. (2012). Postsecondary education and employment among youth with an autism spectrum disorder. *Pediatrics*, *129*(6), 1042–1049.

Shattuck, P. T., Roux, A. M., Hudson, L. E., Taylor, J. L., Maenner, M. J., & Trani, J. F. (2012). Services for adults with an autism spectrum disorder. *Canadian Journal of Psychiatry*, *57*(5), 284–291.

Soulières, I., Dawson, M., Samson, F., Barbeau, E. B., Sahyoun, C. P., Strangman, G. E., ... Mottron, L. (2009). Enhanced visual processing contributes to matrix reasoning in autism. *Human Brain Mapping*, *30*(12), 4080–4107.

Strunz, S., Schermuck, C., Ballerstein, S., Ahlers, C. J., Dziobek, I., & Roepke, S. (2017). Romantic relationships and relationship satisfaction among adults with Asperger syndrome and high-functioning autism. *Journal of Clinical Psychology*, *73*(1), 113–125.

Taylor, J. L., & Mailick, M. R. (2014). A longitudinal examination of 10-year change in vocational and educational activities for adults with autism spectrum disorders. *Developmental Psychology*, *50*(3), 699–708.

Vanbergeijk, E., Klin, A., & Volkmar, F. (2008). Supporting more able students on the autism spectrum: College and beyond. *Journal of Autism and Developmental Disorders*, *38*(7), 1359–1370.

Vindin, P., Wilson, N. J., Lee, H., & Cordier, R. (2021). The experience of learning to drive for people with autism spectrum disorder. *Focus on Autism and Other Developmental Disabilities, 36*(4), 225–236.

Wehman, P. H. (2011). Employment for persons with disabilities: Where are we now and where do we need to go? *Journal of Vocational Rehabilitation, 35*(3), 145–151.

Wei, X., Christiano, E. R., Yu, J. W., Blackorby, J., Shattuck, P., & Newman, L. A. (2014). Postsecondary pathways and persistence for STEM versus non-STEM majors: Among college students with an autism spectrum disorder. *Journal of Autism and Developmental Disorders, 44*(5), 1159–1167.

Wei, X., Yu, J. W., Shattuck, P., McCracken, M., & Blackorby, J. (2013). Science, technology, engineering, and mathematics (STEM) participation among college students with an autism spectrum disorder. *Journal of Autism and Developmental Disorders, 43*(7), 1539–1546.

Werner, S., & Shulman, C. (2015). Does type of disability make a difference in affiliate stigma among family caregivers of individuals with autism, intellectual disability or physical disability? *Journal of Intellectual Disability Research, 59*(3), 272–283.

Wise, E. A. (2020). Aging in autism spectrum disorder. *The American Journal of Geriatric Psychiatry, 28*(3), 339–349.

Yew, R. Y., Hooley, M., & Stokes, M. A. (2023). Factors of relationship satisfaction for autistic and non-autistic partners in long-term relationships. *Autism, 27*(8), 2348–2360.

Part II

Autism spectrum disorder is a complex neurodevelopmental condition that has multiple causes brought about by an interplay of genetic, neurological, and environmental influences. Chapter 6, *Autism Etiology,* examines the various biological, genetic, and environmental factors and provides a comprehensive overview of the current scientific underpinnings of what causes the development of autism. Chapter 7, *Autism Heterogeneity*, highlights autism variability and how it manifests among individuals. The chapter further explores differences in brain structure and function, genetic factors, male-to-female ratio, and co-occurring conditions and how they contribute to the heterogeneous presentation of the disorder.

DOI: 10.4324/9781003336266-7

Chapter 6

Autism Etiology

Chapter Contents

Introduction

Over 2000 years ago, Leucippus (5th-century BC Greek philosopher) stated, "Where there is ignorance, theories abound." The **etiology** of autism is not precisely known. The causes of autism are rooted in genetic and environmental

DOI: 10.4324/9781003336266-8

influences acting either singularly or complementarily (Almandil et al., 2019). Therefore, various theories have been proposed to explain the root causes of autism. Boucher (2022) delineated three criteria that can be used to judge the correctness of a theory: *specificity, universality*, and *primacy*. The **specificity criterion** posits that the causal factor must be specific to the condition and not others. The **universality criterion** necessitates the causal factor must be present in everyone who has the condition. The **primacy criterion** emphasizes that the causal factor must be present before the manifestation of the disorder. In other words, the cause must precede its effect. Despite research conducted during the past several decades and progress made over the last 20 years, no single factor or gene has been found to cause autism spectrum disorder (Waterhouse, 2013). Instead, research points to complex interactions of genetic and environmental factors contributing to its etiology. Moreover, ASD is highly heritable, with estimates ranging from 40–80% (Rylaarsdam & Guemez-Gamboa, 2019).

This chapter explores various factors that contribute to the development of autism, including genetic, environmental, and neurobiological influences. By examining how these components interact, researchers and clinicians can gain a deeper understanding of the origins of autism and improve their methods for diagnosis and treatment.

Theories of Autism

Weak Central Coherence

Central coherence refers to our ability to capture and derive meaning from many details. For example, a person looking at an endless stretch of trees would see a forest, whereas another person with "weak central coherence" would see an infinite collection of trees. Individuals with strong central coherence can process information accurately, whereas those with weak central coherence may struggle to fit disparate details into a coherent whole. The phrase "missing the forest for the trees" illustrates the essence of a weak central coherence.

Before Shah and Frith's study (1983) revealed children with autism performed better on the *Children's Embedded Figures Test* than both neurotypical and non-autistic intellectually disabled individuals, many individuals on the autism spectrum had already demonstrated exceptional visual-spatial abilities, also known as "islets of abilities." Frith (1989) proposed the weak central coherence theory of autism to describe individuals on the autism spectrum with remarkable ability in various areas (e.g., memory, music, and calculation) that surpasses the capacity of cognitively intact individuals. The superior ability individuals with ASD have to process details (i.e., enhanced **local processing**) undermines their capacity to integrate parts into a whole (i.e., **global processing**). Most people prefer to focus on the big picture (central coherence), prioritizing specific details that are relevant to them. However, autistic individuals focus on details and often miss the bigger picture. Focusing on finer details is usually called weak central coherence (WCC) or, better yet, specific solid coherence, a different way of seeing the world. However, detecting details and patterns can be advantageous in some situations. For example, attention to detail can be advantageous when performing specific tasks, including proofreading, manufacturing quality control, or fields requiring meticulous observation and pattern recognition (e.g., beta testing).

Neuroscientists using neuro-imaging technology have found brain structural differences between neurotypical individuals and those with autism. Scher and Shyman (2019) conducted a study that challenged the weak central coherence theory of autism. In the study, a group of participants with autism and a control group of neurotypicals completed a visual search task. The task consisted of searching for a target letter among distractor letters with varying levels of similarity between the target letter and the distractor ones. Compared to the control group, individuals with autism were better at detecting the target letter when the distractor letters were more similar to the target one. The study's findings challenge the "deficit" characterization of a WCC theory. Instead, the authors propose a "superiority" of a strong local coherence.

Contrary to the WCC theory, the study's findings suggest that individuals with autism may have an enhanced capacity to detect local details instead of a reduced capability to process global information. Similarly, Mottron and colleagues (2006) proposed the term "enhanced perceptual functioning" to explain the difference in information processing between autistic and non-autistic individuals. The increased perceptual functioning may be the underlying capacity that fuels the unique ability seen in autistic savants.

Executive Function Impairment

Executive function (considered the epicenter and management system of the brain) refers to various mental skills, including flexible thinking, working memory, and self-control. In conjunction with other brain structures, the frontal lobes control the brain's executive functioning, decision-making, and problem-solving. Dysfunctions of the frontal lobes can result in difficulties in executive functions (e.g., organizing and regulating one's emotions and behavior). Executive function is vital in response inhibition (e.g., acting impulsively) and interference control (Diamond, 2013).

Significant research has been conducted on the relationship between executive function and autism. Some individuals with autism experience challenges in executive function (Demetriou et al., 2019). For example, they may experience difficulties completing tasks that require flexible thinking, working memory, and self-control. They may also experience difficulties switching between tasks, following multi-step instructions, and regulating emotions and behaviors. Substantial research and meta-analyses have confirmed the presence of executive dysfunction in autism.

A meta-analysis of executive function studies conducted between 1980 and 2016 has found that executive dysfunction is common in individuals on the autism spectrum and that it persists throughout development. However, this does not necessarily mean that executive function can be used as a diagnostic tool or to inform treatment for autism, as cautioned by the authors of the study (Demetriou et al., 2018). While executive dysfunction is prevalent in individuals on the spectrum, it is not unique to autism. Another meta-analysis of 42 studies published between 1990 and 2020 found that executive dysfunction is also common in individuals with various neurological disorders (Hemmers et al., 2022). It is important to note that executive function can be impaired by stress, lack of sleep, loneliness, or lack of exercise (Diamond, 2013).

Extreme Male Brain

Baron-Cohen (2002) developed the **extreme male brain** theory of autism. The theory posits that individuals with autism have brains that are wired to understand and analyze systems instead of understanding and responding to social and emotional cues. This extreme form of the male brain and a penchant for analyzing and constructing systems instead of recognizing and responding to the feelings of others leads to the difficulties in social interaction and communication individuals with autism experience. The theory gave rise to the **empathizing-systemizing** (E-S) dichotomy to explain the difference between individuals with autism and those without autism. According to Baron-Cohen, males are more inclined to construct systems to deal with aspects of the environment, whereas females are more prone to empathize.

Autism affects males more frequently than females (Werling & Geschwind, 2013). Unusually high levels of maternal testosterone during pregnancy have been cited in the literature as a risk factor for autism. Testosterone plays a vital role in sexual differentiation during fetal development, as the hormone helps to shape male genitals and other masculine traits (Meulenberg & Hofman, 1991). Small amounts of testosterone in female fetal development contribute to the growth of the ovaries and the development of other feminine characteristics. However, excessive exposure to testosterone in *utero* can lead to various disorders. Baron-Cohen and colleagues (2011) proposed that fetal testosterone levels can influence the systemizing-empathizing dichotomy orientation: High levels correlate positively with scores on the systemizing quotient (Auyeung et al., 2006), whereas low levels correlate with scores on the empathizing quotient (Chapman et al., 2006; Knickmeyer et al., 2006).

Research has found evidence supporting the extreme male brain theory (Greenberg et al., 2018; van Eijk & Zietsch, 2021). It has been observed that autism is four times more prevalent in males than in females (Lord et al., 2020). This difference in diagnosis rates has been used to support the extreme male brain theory of autism (Baron-Cohen et al., 2011). However, some studies challenge this perspective. For instance, Eliot (2019) raised doubts about whether men and women have different brain structures and referred to this putative difference as "neurosexism." Ridley (2019) proposed the most cogent argument against the extreme male brain theory. The concept of autistic behavior is inferred from scores on the Autism Spectrum Questionnaire. Evidence supporting the theory must come from non-behavioral sources such as physiological, anatomical, and biological indices that explain brain differences.

Intense World

People with typical sensory processing abilities can process environmental sensory information effectively. They can filter out background noise in a crowded environment, pay attention, and communicate with others. Additionally, they can tolerate various temperatures and textures and adjust their sensory experiences accordingly. However, many individuals with autism spectrum disorder often encounter challenges related to processing sensory information (Leekam et al., 2007). They commonly experience **hypersensitivity** (over-responsiveness) or **hyposensitivity** (under-responsiveness) toward sensory inputs such as sights, smells, sounds, touch, and taste. For instance, a clock ticking might sound unbearably loud to them. These sensory processing issues may affect their ability to carry out daily activities, as they may feel overwhelmed by the sensory inputs they receive.

Markram and colleagues (2007) proposed the *Intense World Theory*, suggesting that individuals on the autism spectrum perceive their surroundings more intensely than neurotypical individuals. The hyperactivity of the brain's neural circuits amplifies sensory signals, making it challenging for autistic individuals to filter out irrelevant information. Subsequently, Markram and Markram (2010) proposed the *intense world syndrome* as a unifying theory based on a **valproic acid** (VPA) rat model of autism. Rats exposed to VPA during pregnancy results in increased repetitive behaviors, reduced social interactions, and loss of neurons in the cerebellum of the rats' pups. According to Rinaldi and colleagues (2008), a hyper-functional prefrontal cortex may be responsible for the deficits in sociability, repetitive behaviors, and attention experienced by people with autism, as seen in a valproic acid rat model of autism. Previous studies have linked VPA intake during pregnancy to an increased probability of giving birth to a child who will develop autism (Rasalam et al., 2005). According to the Intense World Theory, the activation of a **molecular syndrome** can sensitize gene expression pathways, causing them to respond excessively to environmental stimulation.

Mirror Neurons

Researchers discovered the mirror neuron system (MNS) in the 1990s while studying macaque brains. Neurons in the monkeys' premotor cortex fired when they performed "goal-directed hand movements" (e.g., grasping and holding). Interestingly, the same neurons fired when the monkeys observed the researcher perform the same actions (Di Pellegrino et al., 1992, p. 176). They termed those neurons "mirror neurons." Subsequent research with human participants showed that brain cells in the motor areas are activated when they perform an act and observe someone engaging in the same act (Rizzolatti & Craighero, 2004). Rizzolatti proposed two explanations in support of the functional roles of mirror neurons: (1) mirror neurons make it possible for imitation to take place, and (2) they establish a correspondence between a model performing an action and an observer understanding readily the actor's action (Rizzolatti, 2005). According to Rizzolatti and Fabbri-Destro (2010, p. 227), mirror neurons translate "sensory information describing motor acts done by others into a motor format similar to that the observers themselves generate when they perform those acts." Mirror neuron systems (MNS) are involved in social cognition and may contribute to our capacity to be empathic (Lamm & Majdandžić, 2015) and imitate the actions of others. According to Iacoboni (2009, p. 653), mirror neurons facilitate imitation and solve the "problem of other minds" and allow us to understand the minds of others.

Do individuals with autism have mirror neuron system impairments? Mirror neuron system impairments have been linked to deficits in imitation, empathy, and mentalizing of individuals with autism (e.g., Gallese et al., 2013). The idea of deficits in mirror neuron systems has given rise to the broken mirror hypothesis (Ramachandran & Oberman, 2006), which states that these deficits affect autistic individuals' ability to understand and interpret the actions and emotions of others. Other researchers have supported the broken mirror hypothesis of autism (Dapretto et al., 2006; Williams et al., 2006). However, Fan and colleagues (2010) and Yates and Hobson (2020) have challenged the broken mirror hypothesis of autism and have argued that research has not provided enough evidence to support it.

Chan and Han (2020) conducted a meta-analysis to assess the difference in activation of the MNS of individuals with autism compared to neurotypical controls when they observed biological motion with or without social-emotional components. They concluded that the MNS is impaired in individuals with autism. However, the atypical activation patterns were related to the nature of the biological motion the participant observed. Their findings shed light on the inconsistency and contradictory findings of MNS and autism.

Kanner's and Asperger's Understanding of Autism Etiology

Both Kanner (1943) and Asperger (Frith, 1991) painstakingly described the characteristics of the parents of the children they examined in their respective clinics. However, they had not formulated a clear understanding of the root cause of the condition they observed. Kanner insinuated that parents' disengagement toward their children (i.e., "very few really warmhearted fathers and mothers") could have contributed to the manifestation of the disorder. Kanner also postulated that the "children [he examined] have come into the world with innate inability to form the usual, biologically provided affective contact with people" (p. 250). Therefore, he concluded that parental interactions with their children could not have possibly been the only factor, and further study was warranted to elucidate the components of those children's "emotional reactivity." Asperger, on the other hand, emphasized genetic transmission in terms of **polygenic** (multiple genes) inheritance, **dominant** and **recessive** genes. Perhaps his most compelling argument for a genetic cause of autism is the fact that a child diagnosed with autism spectrum disorder (ASD) could have other siblings who developed typically despite identical parental interactions. Therefore, an exogenous (external) cause of autism would be unlikely. In his view, "Autism does not arise because there are unfavorable developmental influences ... but because there is an inherited disposition" (Frith, 1991, p. 86)

Discredited Theories of Autism

The Refrigerator Mother Theory

The refrigerator mother theory of autism (now widely discredited) originated with Kanner (1949, p. 425), who wrote, "Most of the patients [i.e., the children he examined] were exposed from the beginning to parental coldness. ... They [the children] were kept in refrigerators, which did not defrost." Similarly, in an interview with Time Magazine (1960), Kanner was even more accusatory of the parents and described them as cold and "just happen[ed] to defrost enough to produce a child."

Bruno Bettelheim, an Austrian-born early writer on autism and self-proclaimed child psychologist, immigrated to the United States in 1939. Bettelheim claimed to have earned a graduate degree in psychology at the University of Vienna, Austria. In fact, he obtained a doctorate in art history and inexplicably became the director of the Sonia Shankman Orthogenic School at the University of Chicago (Donvan & Zucker, 2016). In 1955, Bettelheim received a grant from the Ford Foundation, recruited a small cohort of children with autism, and developed and implemented his version of autism treatment based on the notion that bad parenting (particularly mothers) caused autism (Silberman, 2015). He compared children with autism to German concentration camp prisoners, as he was, and equated those children's withdrawal to that of the prisoners coping with a frightening and hostile environment. Bettelheim's ideas (1967) were fundamentally rooted in Freudian psychoanalysis and propelled to new heights Kanner's insinuation of cold parenting as a possible cause for autism. The psychogenic view of autism was born. The origin of autism was then considered psychological, not organic.

Although the "refrigerator mother" theory of autism was widely accepted as a cause of autism, Bernard Rimland, an experimental psychologist and parent of a child diagnosed with autism, challenged the psychogenic cause of autism and instead turned his attention to possible brain dysfunctions resulting in a primarily organic disorder. Rimland (1964) synthesized the somewhat scant research available at the time and proposed the reticular formation—a brain structure associated with the regulation of alertness—as a possible cause in the development of autism. Rimland's challenges to the current understanding of the causes of autism gave impetus to research conducted to establish a genetic influence for the disorder.

Vaccines and Autism

Autism Spectrum Disorder (APA, 2013), once considered a rare disorder, is now widely recognized, with a prevalence rate of 1 in 31 children (CDC, 2022). Although many theories have been proposed to explain the underlying causes of the disorder, there is no single etiology of autism. Research indicates that both genetic and environmental factors play a role in its development. One theory that has received significant attention is the claim that measles-mumps-rubella (MMR) vaccines and the mercury-based preservative **thimerosal** cause autism in children.

The Centers for Disease Control and Prevention recommends two doses of the MMR vaccine. The first dose is routinely administered between 12 and 15 months (when autism usually becomes apparent), and the second is given between 4 and 6 years. The administration of the first dose of the MMR vaccine coincides with the appearance of the first notable signs and symptoms of autism by 15–18 months. Moreover, some infants who achieve expected developmental milestones exhibit some form of regression (Rogers, 2004), usually reported in the second year of life. Thus, the temporal correlation between the administration of the MMR vaccine and the onset of autism makes many increasingly concerned parents seeking answers more likely to connect the two events (Doja & Roberts, 2006), especially in the face of no clear etiology of the disorder.

The controversy surrounding the vaccine-autism hypothesis started with the publication of a study in which Wakefield (1998), a gastroenterologist, and 12 co-authors investigated 12 children at the Royal Free Hospital and School of Medicine, London. The children enrolled in the study supposedly had a history of typical development followed by chronic enterocolitis and regressive developmental disorder. Wakefield's previous attempt to link the lesions seen in Crohn's disease to the measles virus was disproved and put to rest (Davidson, 2017). He subsequently turned his efforts to establishing a connection between the MMR triad vaccine and autism. According to Wakefield, the parents of 8 of the 12 children thought the MMR vaccination caused their children to lose acquired skills, including language. Thus, the authors hastily suggested that the combination of measles-mumps-rubella (MMR) vaccines cause autism in children. More specifically, they stated, "the consequences of an inflamed or dysfunctional intestine may play a part in behavioural changes in some children" (Wakefield et al., 1998, p. 639).

Wakefield's paper did not unequivocally state that MMR vaccines cause autism. In fact, the last sentence in the discussion section read: "In most cases, onset of symptoms was after measles, mumps, and rubella immunisation. Further investigations are needed to examine this syndrome and its possible relation to this vaccine" (p. 641). However, his adamant conviction and elaboration about the connection between MMR vaccines and autism fueled an antivaccine campaign that shook public confidence in their safety. He argued before an American Academy of Pediatrics committee (Halsey & Hyman, 2001) that the administration of monovalent vaccines (i.e., vaccines containing one antigen), compared to the typical triad MMR, could lessen the risk of affecting children's vulnerable immune system, an assertion that research does not support. More significantly, he asserted that the measles virus had caused inflammation and lesions of the colon, resulting in neurotoxic proteins reaching the bloodstream, crossing the blood-brain barrier, disrupting brain development, and causing autism. As a result, hundreds of thousands of parents worldwide turned against the MMR vaccine because of Wakefield's putative link between vaccinations and autism.

Long before the Lancet retracted the study and due to Wakefield's research fraud, ten co-authors withdrew their support of their interpretation of the findings because the study, in their views, did not establish a causal relationship between autism and the MMR vaccine (Murch et al., 2004). Twelve years after the study's publication, the Lancet retracted it (Deer, 2011) based on "several elements [that] are incorrect, contrary to the findings of an earlier investigation." Firstly, the study's participants were not randomly selected but carefully chosen. Secondly, lawyers representing parents contemplating suing vaccine manufacturers funded Wakefield's research. Moreover, thirdly, Britain's General Medical Council (GMC) deemed that the researchers acted unethically and thus performed invasive tests (e.g., lumbar puncture) on those children (Eggertson, 2010). As a result, the GMC revoked Wakefield's license to practice medicine.

Similarly, the thimerosal-autism hypothesis began with the publication of a paper suggesting a link between mercury and autism (Bernard et al., 2001). Thimerosal, an organic compound of ethyl mercury, is used to preserve and prevent multiple-dose vial vaccines from bacterial contamination when syringes puncture vials numerous times (Doja & Roberts, 2006). It is worth noting that MMR vaccines produced as single vials never contained thimerosal. The concerns raised by the possible mercury contamination prompted the Food and Drug Administration to recommend that vaccine manufacturers remove thimerosal from vaccines. Except for a few vaccines (e.g., influenza and hepatitis), thimerosal has been removed in vaccines since 2001, yet the prevalence rate of autism has increased from 1 in 150 children in 2000 to 1 in 31 in 2022.

There is overwhelming scientific evidence that MMR vaccines and the mercury-based preservative thimerosal used in vaccines do not cause autism. Epidemiological research (e.g., Taylor et al., 1999; Wilson et al., 2003) and population-based studies (e.g., Madsen et al., 2002) found no association between autism and the MMR vaccine, even after the removal of thimerosal in vaccines (Madsen et al., 2003). In the face of overwhelming evidence that vaccines do not cause autism, many parents still have concerns regarding vaccine safety. One parent wrote:

> My son was born a healthy child. As time went on and the more he was vaccinated, the more he started to change. Not knowing that mercury was in vaccines until he was four years old … I was outraged that I was not told that the most powerful neurotoxin was going to be injected into my newborn child.
>
> (Doja & Roberts, 2006, p. 343)

The decline in the vaccination rate has resulted in measles breakouts and cases in many parts of the world. Offit (2008) eloquently debunked the myths associated with the vaccines and mercury controversy and cautioned about the harm that can result from bad actors and the manipulation of science in the popular media.

In sum, after hundreds of studies conducted involving thousands of children from various parts of the world, there is no evidence that vaccines cause autism. The thimerosal-causing-autism hypothesis has crumbled in the face of overwhelming evidence based on many epidemiological and retrospective studies. The jury is no longer out; the verdict is in: Vaccines and thimerosal (once used as a preservative in some vaccines) do not cause autism. Thus, it is incumbent on healthcare practitioners to educate parents about the safety of vaccines and the importance of immunization to prevent potential diseases that can affect the well-being of their children.

Genetic Influences of Autism

The interaction of genetic and environmental factors influences human characteristics (including autism). There are three different patterns of inheritance: Single gene-pair inheritance (**monogenic**), multiple gene inheritance (polygenic), and sex-linked (X-linked) inheritance (Turnpenny & Ellard, 2012). Sexually reproducing species have two copies (alleles) of each gene. Alleles can be dominant or recessive. When a pair of genes (one from each parent) influences a human characteristic, the characteristic will be expressed if at least one allele is dominant. Otherwise, two recessive copies will result in the recessive expression of the trait.

Folstein and Rutter (1977) were among the first researchers to investigate the genetics of autism. While only 21 twin pairs participated in their study, the authors reported that 36% of identical (but not fraternal) twins shared a diagnosis of autism. Identical twins (monozygotic) develop from a single egg fertilized by one sperm. Consequently, they share 100% of their genes. Fraternal twins (**dizygotic**) develop from two separate eggs fertilized by two different sperm, so they share 50% of their genes. Family and twin studies have been the bedrock of autism research. Ritvo and colleagues (1985) conducted a study in which they used the UCLA Registry for Genetic Study in Autism and reported a **concordance** (i.e., the presence of a particular trait in a pair of twins) of 95.7% in identical twins (22 of 23 participants) and a concordance of 23.5% in fraternal twins (4 of 17 participants). Bailey and colleagues (1995) examined a British sample of twins with autism and found a concordance of 60% for identical twins but no concordance of the disorder among fraternal twins. Ronald and Hoekstra (2011) reviewed over 30 twin studies published in the past ten years. Their findings consistently showed that identical twins had a higher concordance rate for autism compared to fraternal twins. Additionally, a subsequent meta-analysis indicated that 74–93% of the risk for developing autism is heritable (Tick et al., 2016).

The Human Genome and the Autism Genome Project

The Human Genome Project (HGP) was an international scientific research project aimed at determining the complete nucleotide sequence of DNA (Deoxyribonucleic Acid), which consists of four nucleotide bases: Adenine (A), cytosine (C), guanine (G), and thymine (T). The formation of base pairs follows a consistent pattern: A always pairs with T and G pairs with C. There are approximately 3.1 billion base pairs in the human **genome** (i.e., the complete genetic material present in an organism).

We all carry 20,000–22,000 genes (i.e., units of heredity that determine our characteristics) packed into 23 pairs of chromosomes. Eighty percent of all human genes are expressed in the brain (Waterhouse, 2013). Only about 2% (i.e., the exome) of the letters in the genome code for functional molecules called proteins. Autism researchers have thus focused on the exome. Long stretches of DNA (approximately 98%) do not code for proteins and have been termed "junk DNA." However, whole genome sequencing conducted with a large sample of families with ASD children identified 18 new **candidate** ASD-risk genes (Yuen et al., 2017). The data also showed that participants with the ASD **susceptibility genes** in the genome displayed lower adaptive functioning than participants without the genes.

Despite our genetic differences, the sequence of base pairs in any two individuals is more than 99.9% identical. Our individual differences can be attributed to genes in 0.1% of the sequence (Venter et al., 2001). A single change or substitution in a nucleotide pair of one gene can lead to changes in the function of a gene, which may contribute to various physiological malfunctions. In some cases, these changes have been associated with neurodevelopmental disorders such as autism.

The completion of the HGP set the stage for the study of complex human diseases. It gave rise to the Autism Genome Project (AGP), a large-scale collaborative genetics research project aimed at examining the Human Genome in search of autism-susceptibility genes and the identification of nucleotide variants (https://research.mss.ng/). More than 40 research institutions across North America and Europe cooperated (Hu-Lince et al., 2005). During the first phase of the project (2004–2007), researchers scanned the DNA information of 1,200 families in which at least one child was diagnosed with autism. During the second phase (2007–2010), the organization Autism Speaks joined the project and launched the MSSNG (pronounced "missing") awareness campaign in 2010. The goal of MSSNG was to create an open-source research platform for autism and the world's largest database by collecting the DNA of 10,000 families affected by autism (Autism Genome Project). Autism researchers around the globe would analyze and study the data to find the missing answers. The third phase has added 2,000 genome sequences to the existing database, identified 18 new candidate genes for autism, and found an average of 73.8 *de novo* (i.e., new) single nucleotide variants and 12.6 *de novo* deletions and insertions of copy number variants (i.e., DNA strands in the genome), based on genome sequencing of 5,205 participants (Yuen et al., 2017).

Research conducted during past decades has identified the role of common and rare genetic variations causing autism (Malik et al., 2019). Autism researchers have identified many specific genes, ranging from more than one hundred to over one thousand operating together that cause autism (Betancur, 2011; Casey et al., 2012; Sanders et al., 2012). The Simons Foundation Research Initiative (SFARI) maintains an ASD gene database that reviews the association of each gene suspected to have a connection with ASD. A score ranging from 6 ("not supported") to 1 ("high confidence") is assigned to each gene. As of April 2015, of the 667 genes listed in the database, 16 were identified as having "high confidence" (Loke et al., 2015). Research on families suggests a strong genetic component in the susceptibility to autism spectrum disorder (ASD), and genomic studies are starting to clarify the genetic framework involved. Approximately 5–15% of individuals with ASD have a recognizable genetic cause linked to known chromosomal rearrangements or single-gene disorders (Devlin & Scherer, 2012).

Genome Sequencing and Mutations

Whole-genome sequencing and **microarray technology** (i.e., a grid of DNA segments of known sequence) and **Genome-Wide Association Studies** (GWAS) have made it possible for geneticists to more fully understand human genetic variation—the difference in DNA sequence among individuals. Individuals of a species share similar characteristics, and because of genetic variations, they are seldom identical. Each person carries approximately three million **genetic**

variants. Genetic variants can include copy number variants (CNVs)—i.e., duplication or deletion of numerous pairs in the genome—**single nucleotide polymorphisms (SNPs)**, and *de novo* (not inherited) CNVs. Ninety-five percent of those variants are termed **common variants** and are shared with at least 5% of the population worldwide. In contrast, 5% are shared with no more than 5% of the population, and 1% of those genetic variants (termed **rare variants**) are unique to anyone. Therefore, identifying both common and rare variants provided the grounding for understanding the genetic architecture of ASD (Bourgeron, 2015).

Mutations refer to changes in the structure of a particular gene. Mutations can be spontaneous (i.e., the result of errors in biological processes) or induced by environmental agents that cause changes in DNA structure. Most mutations occur due to errors during cell division (Lewis, 2018). In addition, mutations can be neutral, detrimental, or beneficial. When mutations delete or duplicate long segments of DNA, they are termed copy number variants (CNVs). Many mutations are inherited from parents. These mutations are generally harmless. Occasionally, some mutations occur spontaneously or *de novo* (i.e., they are not inherited) and can occur in the parents' egg or sperm or after fertilization. These mutations are usually harmful and can interfere with the typical course of brain development. Autism researchers have focused primarily on *de novo* mutations to compare the DNA of someone with autism with that of the person's parents or unaffected siblings.

Syndromic and Idiopathic Autism

Syndromic autism (also termed secondary autism) refers to autism that is caused by a single gene mutation located in the X chromosome. The vast majority of autism cases, however, are idiopathic/nonsyndromic (i.e., with no known genetic causes). People with syndromic autism often have dysmorphic features, with an equal male-to-female prevalence ratio. Approximately 10% of individuals diagnosed with ASD have an identifiable genetic syndrome, and the most commonly cited are fragile X syndrome, Rett syndrome, and tuberous sclerosis (Devlin & Scherer, 2012). Fragile X syndrome accounts for approximately 2% of autism cases, and the affected individuals typically have intellectual disability, attention difficulties, developmental delay, and ASD. Rett syndrome (a non-inherited genetic disorder that occurs exclusively in girls) and tuberous sclerosis account for 0.5% and 1% of autism cases, respectively.

It has been challenging for geneticists, however, to identify the genetic causes of autism, given that the majority of autism cases are nonsyndromic (idiopathic) and simplex (i.e., one person affected in a family). Researchers have used data from the Simons Simplex Collection (SSC) to establish *de novo* copy-number variants as the cause of 5–8% of simplex autism cases (Levy et al., 2011; Sanders et al., 2011). The Simons Simplex Collection holds genetic data from more than 2,600 families that have a child diagnosed with ASD. Genetic data for each family also includes information about unaffected biological parents and siblings. Therefore, the identification of *de novo* mutations in affected children, and not in their unaffected siblings or parents, supports the view that rare copy number variants are highly penetrant (i.e., high probability of a trait to be expressed) and are the primary cause of nonsyndromic autism.

Proposed Genetic Mechanism Models for Autism

The genetic complexity of autism has given rise to various genetic mechanism models. Pickles and colleagues (1995) proposed two possible, simplistic patterns resulting in autism: (1) single genes contributing to individual symptoms of the disorder, or (2) a small group of genes acting concurrently and likely to cause all the signs of autism. Since the completion of the Human Genome Project (Collins et al., 2003), researchers have proposed several genetic models of autism based on the hundreds of gene variants and copy number variants (CNVs) found for autism.

Voineagu (2011) proposed a model in which a large group of gene variants causes autism. In contrast, Schaaf and Zoghbi (2011) hypothesized that two separate genetic mechanisms cause syndromic autism and idiopathic autism. Walsh and Bracken (2011) argued that many rare or *de novo* copy number variants cause autism. Epigenetic mechanisms (i.e., environmental effects on gene expression) that can influence gene variants have been proposed as a potential cause of autism (Loke et al., 2015). Finally, a neurobiological view of autism emphasizes overall brain reorganization in early development in terms of "atypical trajectory of brain maturation" instead of focusing on impairments in specific brain regions or systems (Ecker et al., 2015).

Animal Models for Autism

Autism researchers have developed animal models in which specific gene knockouts (i.e., an organism's gene made inoperative) in mice produce evidence of autism-like symptoms. Consistent with the findings that a homozygous mutation of the CNTNAP2 gene (one of the largest genes in the human genome) can cause features of autism (Tan et al., 2010), Peñagarikano and colleagues (2011) created a mouse without the CNTNAP2 genes. The mutant mouse exhibited features resembling those of idiopathic autism, including repetitive and restricted behaviors, abnormal social interaction, and hyperactivity. Mice with only one allele (i.e., a variant form of a given gene) of the knockout gene showed no unusual behaviors.

Oxytocin (OT) is a **neuropeptide** involved in affiliative behavior, facial recognition, mind reading, trust, generosity, and envy (MacDonald & MacDonald, 2010). Autism researchers have detected abnormal levels of plasma OT in children diagnosed with autism (Green et al., 2001). Campbell and colleagues

(2011) investigated the link between oxytocin and autism and found a connection between a common oxytocin receptor (OXTR) gene variant and autism based on a large family study. Consequently, Sala and colleagues (2011) created knockout mice in which the neurotransmitter was eliminated. The mutant mice showed signs and symptoms indicative of autism, including impaired cognitive flexibility when completing a maze-switching task, abnormal sociability, and reduced distress to separation from mothers. In addition, they displayed neuronal hyperexcitability, increasing aggressive behavior, and seizure susceptibility. Interestingly, the intracerebral administration of oxytocin to 3-month-old knockout mice normalized their social and learning behavior.

In sum, it is well established that ASD has a strong genetic component. Research in the 1970s paved the way and provided the impetus for further investigations into the genetic causes of the disorder. The completion of the Human Genome Project made it possible for geneticists to conduct whole genome and exome sequencing and identify potential genes implicated in autism. It is now clear that mutations and copy number variations play a role in autism. Geneticists have now identified high-confidence genes that can cause autism and hundreds of other genetic loci that are linked to the disorder. Researchers have also developed animal models of autism and used primarily knockout mice to explore the ramifications of specific genes that, in humans, are associated with autism.

Environmental Influences on Autism

Prescription Medications and Autism

Medication use during pregnancy has substantially increased in recent years. Recent research findings have indicated that most pregnant women in developed countries take at least one medication, and women in the United States consume at least one medication during the first trimester of pregnancy (Lupattelli et al., 2014; Mitchell et al., 2011). The consumption of various drugs can increase the risk of ASD during prenatal development. Much research conducted on the effects of prescribed medications during pregnancy has identified at least four medications (Thalidomide, Valproic acid, Selective Serotonin Reuptake Inhibitors, and Misoprostol) as potential autism risk factors (Dufour-Rainfray et al., 2011).

Thalidomide was marketed in the late 1950s as a tranquilizer to relieve the morning sickness that many women experience during early pregnancy. While the drug had no ill effects when tested on pregnant rats, thousands of pregnant women who used the drug gave birth to babies with stunted limbs or deformed ears, noses, and hearts. Miller and Strömland (1993) conducted a study with patients in a Swedish thalidomide registry. They found that 30% of the participants (a rate significantly higher than that of the general population) exposed to the drug on the third week of gestation had babies that were subsequently diagnosed with autism. Similarly, Strömland and colleagues (1994) conducted a study to determine the effects of thalidomide on the postnatal development of one hundred adults who had been exposed to the drug in *utero*. Five percent of the participants had autism, a rate 30 times higher than the general population. Evidence derived from neuroanatomy shows that exposure to thalidomide early in development can affect brain development and increase the risk of autism. Given that the brain stem begins developing first, Rodier (2002) theorized that the root of autism might originate in early brain development.

Valproic acid (sodium valproate) is used primarily to treat epilepsy and bipolar disorder. Valproate (VPA) is a teratogen (an agent which causes malformations of an **embryo**). Despite VPA's capacity to treat epilepsy and other ailments, women with epilepsy who consumed the drug during the first trimester of pregnancy were more likely to give birth to babies with congenital malformation than women who ingested no drugs or took other medications for their seizures (Jentink et al., 2010). There is ample evidence showing that prenatal exposure to VAP is associated with cognitive deficits in children exposed to the drug in *utero* (Meador et al., 2009). Bromley and colleagues (2013) examined the effect of different antiepileptic drug treatments and the prevalence of ASD in women with epilepsy and a control group without epilepsy. The researchers found that exposure to VPA in *utero* (but not other antiepileptic medications) increased the prevalence of neurodevelopmental disorders, particularly ASD.

Depression is common during pregnancy, and approximately 18% of pregnant women experience depression during pregnancy. **Selective serotonin reuptake inhibitors** (SSRIs) are a group of drugs that are the most commonly prescribed to treat the symptoms of depression during pregnancy (Andrade et al., 2008). The association between maternal use of antidepressants during pregnancy and autism is somewhat established. To date, there are no autism-defining metabolic biomarkers. However, changes in levels of one particular neurotransmitter—serotonin—have interested autism researchers. Numerous research studies have also indicated elevated platelet serotonin levels in approximately 33% of children diagnosed with autism (e.g., Gentile, 2015).

Whitaker-Azmitia (2005) reviewed the literature on the effects of serotonin on prenatal development and explored the proposition that high serotonin levels in the bloodstream (also termed hyperserotonemia) in some children with autism might lead to some of the cellular changes observed in the brain. Based on research conducted with rats and animal models that mimicked hyperserotonemia in those rodents, Whitaker-Azmitia theorized that the excess of serotonin levels during early development could set the stage for the development of autism. A more recent population-based study conducted with 145,456 children found an association between maternal use of antidepressants during pregnancy and the risk of an autism diagnosis in children (Boukhris et al., 2016).

Research indicates several factors that may cause an increased risk of autism if women use antidepressants during pregnancy. First, animal models of the effect of serotonin on brain development found that the neurotransmitter can exert modifying influences on developmental processes prenatally and postnatally, particularly cell division, cell differentiation, and neuronal migration (Tordjman et al., 2013), processes whose disruption can compromise healthy brain development. Second, the SSRIs cross the placental barrier when the blood-brain barrier is not entirely formed and enters the fetus. The high level of serotonin in the blood can penetrate the brain of the developing fetus. It can persist throughout fetal development and set the stage for the symptoms of autism (Whitaker-Azmitia, 2005). The loss of serotonin innervations results in the atypical capacity of the brain of children with autism to synthesize serotonin (Chandana et al., 2005).

Misoprostol is a drug used to prevent and treat gastric ulcers, and because it can cause uterine contractions, the drug has been used in self-induced abortion. Exposure to misoprostol does not always result in abortion. Consequently, babies born after a failed abortion, despite exposure to misoprostol, often show congenital malformations, including Moebius syndrome, a rare genetic condition of brain-stem dysfunction characterized by weakness or paralysis of the facial muscles. Exposure to misoprostol during the first two months of pregnancy can interfere with brain development. Several research studies have found an association between Moebius syndrome and an increased incidence of autism (Gillberg & Steffenburg, 1989; Johansson et al., 2001; Miller & Strömland, 1999). Amid the prevalent use of misoprostol for self-induced abortion in Brazil, Bandim and colleagues (2003) investigated the effect of the medication on 23 babies born with Moebius sequence. Five participants met the DSM-IV criteria for autism, and two children showed significant impairments in social interactions and language skills and engaged in repetitive and stereotypical behaviors.

Parental Age at Conception and Autism

The prevalence of autism has increased since the disorder's identification and description in the 1940s. Clinicians and researchers have pointed to the changing diagnostic criteria, increased awareness, and improved assessment of the disorder as likely causes. Although autism has a strong genetic basis, genes do not operate in a vacuum and cannot alone explain the increased prevalence of the disorder. Various environmental factors, including environmental toxins, early socialization, and prenatal and perinatal influences, have been investigated as likely causes. One of the most consistent findings in the **epidemiology** of autism is that advanced parental age (particularly paternal age) at birth is a risk factor for parents to have a child with autism. Durkin and colleagues (2008) reviewed data from 10 U.S. sites participating in the CDC's Autism and Developmental Disabilities Monitoring Network. They found that parental advanced age at birth is a risk factor for autism.

Karimi and colleagues (2017) reviewed various studies examining the role of environmental factors in autism development. They found that parental age is one of the most significant risk factors for autism. As parents age, the risks associated with childbirth increase. The risk is particularly true for women who have children at an advanced age, as they are more likely to experience complications during pregnancy and labor, such as high blood pressure and gestational diabetes. Moreover, babies born to older parents have a higher likelihood of having a chromosomal abnormality, like Down syndrome or other disorders. Parents' age *per se* does not cause autism but can be a risk factor when parents are too young or too old. The Centers for Disease Control and Prevention reports that fetal mortality rates are higher when mothers are very young or very old. With the availability of assistive reproductive technology, women can now have children later in life, even in their late 30s or early 40s. As a result, more women are delaying childbirth and having their first child at an older age (Matthews & Hamilton, 2009).

Research conducted in various parts of the world investigated advanced paternal age as a risk factor for autism. One study reviewed the medical records of 132,000 Israeli adolescents and found that men in their 40s have a sixfold increased risk of having a child with autism (Reichenberg et al., 2006). Wu and colleagues (2017) conducted a meta-analysis of 27 studies to explore the link between advanced parental age and the likelihood of their children developing autism. The study found that participants in the lowest age range had a lower risk of having children with autism. In contrast, those who belonged to the highest parental age category had an increased risk of having children with autism. Parental age at conception has been implicated in the severity of the disorder. A recent study based on a clinical sample of children diagnosed with autism found that advanced paternal age was not only found to be a risk factor for autism but was also found to be related to the severity of autism symptoms in boys (Rieske & Matson, 2020).

In addition to increased risk factors for autism, advanced parental age is associated with various other adverse outcomes. Shelton and colleagues (2010) reported that compared to younger fathers, paternal advanced age is a risk factor for neurocognitive deficits, schizophrenia, childhood cancer, low birth weight, and alteration in the chemical structure of their children's DNA. Similarly, they found that advanced maternal age is a risk factor for infertility, low birth weight, congenital disabilities, and increased chromosomal copy number variations (Shelton et al., 2010).

Prenatal and Perinatal Influences

Environmental risk factors can operate prenatally when the embryo and fetus develop. For example, a mother who takes certain medications (e.g., thalidomide during the third week of gestation) increases the risk that her baby might develop autism. Karimi and colleagues (2017) highlighted various environmental factors that may increase the risk of children developing autism. Maternal health issues during pregnancy, including infections, exposure to toxins, nutritional deficiencies, and certain medications, could affect fetal brain development and potentially cause autism. Similarly, perinatal factors can also increase the risk of developing autism. For example, anoxia around the time of birth and low Apgar scores have been associated with the disorder. Postnatal factors (e.g., exposure to toxins and heavy metals, including mercury and lead) can also contribute to the development of autism.

Apgar Test

The Apgar test (developed by Virginia Apgar) is a simple and rapid method for assessing newborn viability (Apgar, 1953). The test is administered immediately and 5 minutes after birth and evaluates the newborn's reflex irritability, muscle tone, heart rate, respiration effort, and color (Sigelman & Rider, 2022). Therefore, each index can yield a score of 0, 1, or 2. Newborns who score at least 7 are generally healthy. Those who score four or lower because of various issues, including shallow or irregular breathing, slow heart rate, and low muscle tone, require medical attention.

Apgar Scores and Autism

Although low Apgar scores have been associated with several neuropsychiatric disorders (e.g., intellectual disabilities and cerebral palsy), findings of studies examining the association between autism and low Apgar scores have been inconsistent. Modabbernia and colleagues (2019) investigated the link between low Apgar scores at 5 minutes and the risk for autism in a multinational sample of over 33,000 cases of autism. They found that compared to optimal scores of at least seven low Apgar scores (1–3) and intermediate scores (4–6) were associated with higher autism rates. A more recent nationwide registry-based cohort study in Denmark found that infants whose 5-minute Apgar scores were sup-optimal (i.e., 7–9) had an increased risk of developing neurodevelopmental disorders, including intellectual disability, attention- deficit/hyperactivity disorders, and autism (He et al., 2022).

Summary

Various theories have been proposed to explain the complexity of autism. The weak central coherence, executive function impairment, the extreme male brain hypothesis, and the mirror neuron systems provide valuable insights into the diverse cognitive profiles of individuals with autism. Additionally, the intense world theory emphasizes the heightened sensory challenges that many autistic individuals experience. Both Kanner and Asperger held contrasting views on the causes of the condition they examined and described. Kanner suggested that emotionally cold and distant parenting behaviors could negatively impact a child's development and contribute to the emergence of autistic traits. In contrast, Asperger emphasized the idea of a genetic and biological predisposition to autism traits. Bettelheim's theory linking cold parenting to the cause of autism and the widely popularized view that vaccines cause autism have both been debunked by overwhelming scientific evidence to the contrary.

The Human Genome Project and advancements in genome sequencing technologies have significantly improved the understanding of the genetic factors that influence autism. Research shows that common and rare genetic variants contribute to the risk of developing autism. Syndromic forms of autism are linked to identifiable genetic causes. In contrast, the causes of idiopathic autism remain less understood. Furthermore, animal models of autism have been crucial in helping researchers explore the underlying mechanisms of the disorder.

Research on the environmental influences of autism has identified several key factors: (a) advanced parental age, which increases the likelihood of genetic mutations; (b) prescribed medications that can impact the central nervous system and disrupt fetal development; and (c) prenatal and perinatal factors, including nutritional deficiencies and low Apgar scores.

Questions to Ponder for Further Thinking and Learning

1 Do genetic factors play a more critical role than environmental ones in the development of autism?
2 How does prenatal and early childhood exposure to toxins and pollutants affect the risk of developing autism?
3 What roles do genetic mutations and variations in brain development play in the onset of autism?
4 How do cultural factors and socioeconomic status influence the development of autism?
5 How can research into the causes of autism inform our understanding of neurodevelopmental disorders more broadly?
6 Will the Research Domain Criteria (RDoC) advance the understanding of the genetic and neurological causes of autism?

References

Almandil, N. B., Alkuroud, D. N., AbdulAzeez, S., AlSulaiman, A., Elaissari, A., & Borgio, J. F. (2019). Environmental and genetic factors in autism spectrum disorders: Special emphasis on data from Arabian studies. *International Journal of Environmental Research and Public Health, 16*(4), 658.

APA (2013). *Diagnostic and statistical manual of mental disorders* (5th ed.). American Psychiatric Association.

Andrade, S. E., Raebel, M. A., Brown, J., Lane, K., Livingston, J., Boudrea, D., ... Platt, R. (2008). Use of antidepressant medications during pregnancy: A multisite study. *American Journal of Obstetrics and Gynecology, 198*(2), 194.e1–5.

Apgar, V. (1953). A proposal for a new method of evaluation of the newborn infant. *Current Researches in Anesthesia & Analgesia, 32*(4), 260–267.

Auyeung, B., Baron-Cohen, S., Chapman, E., Knickmeyer, R. C., Taylor, K., & Hackett, G. (2006). Foetal testosterone and the child systemizing quotient. *European Journal of Endocrinology, 155* (s1), S123–S130.

Bailey, A., Le Couteur, A., Gottesman, I., Bolton, P., Simonoff, E., Yuzda, E., & Rutter, M. (1995). Autism as a strongly genetic disorder: Evidence from a British twin study. *Psychological Medicine, 25*(1), 63–77.

Bandim, J. M., Ventura, L. O., Miller, M. T., Almeida, H. C., & Costa, A. E. C. (2003). Autism and Moebius sequence: An exploratory study of children in northern Brazil. *Arquivos de Neuro-Psiquiatria, 61*(2-A), 181–185.

Baron-Cohen, S. (2002). The extreme male brain theory of autism. *Trends in Cognitive Sciences, 6*(6), 248–254.

Baron-Cohen, S., Lombardo, M. V., Auyeung, B., Ashwin, E., Chakrabarti, B., & Knickmeyer, R. (2011). Why are autism spectrum conditions more prevalent in males? *PLOS Biology, 9*(6), e10011081.

Bernard, S., Enayati, A., Redwood, L., Roger, H., & Binstock, T. (2001). Autism: A novel form of mercury poisoning. *Medical Hypotheses, 56*(4), 462–471.

Betancur, C. (2011). Etiological heterogeneity in autism spectrum disorders: More than 100 genetic and genomic disorders and still counting. *Brain Research, 1380*, 42–77.

Bettelheim, B. (1967). *The empty fortress: Infantile autism and the birth of the self.* Free Press.

Boucher, J. (2022). *Autism spectrum disorders: Characteristics, causes & practical issues* (3rd ed.). SAGE Publications.

Boukhris, T., Shehy, O., Mottron, L., & Bérard, A. (2016). Antidepressant use during pregnancy and the risk of autism spectrum disorder in children. *JAMA Pediatrics, 170*(2), 117–124.

Bourgeron, T. (2015). From the genetic architecture to synaptic plasticity in autism spectrum disorder. *Nature Reviews Neuroscience, 16*, 551–563.

Bromley, R. L., Mawer, G. E., Briggs, M., Cheyne, C., Clayton-Smith, J., Garcia-Finana, M., … Baker, G. A. (2013). The prevalence of neurodevelopmental disorders in children prenatally exposed to antiepileptic drugs. *Journal of Neurology, Neurosurgery & Psychiatry, 84*, 637–643.

Campbell, D. B., Datta, D., Jones, S. T., Batey Lee, E., Sutcliffe, J. S., … Levitt, P. (2011). Association of oxytocin receptor (OXTR) gene variants with multiple phenotype domains of autism spectrum disorder. *Journal of Neurodevelopmental Disorders, 3*(2), 101–112.

Casey, J. P., Magalhaes, T., Conroy, J. M., Regan, R., Shah, N., Anney, R., … Ennis, S. (2012). A novel approach of homozygous haplotype sharing identifies candidate genes in autism spectrum disorder. *Human Genetics, 131*, 565–579.

CDC (2020). U.S. Centers for Disease Control and Prevention. Data and Statistics on Autism Spectrum Disorder. https://www.cdc.gov/autism/data-research/?CDC_AAref_Val=https://www.cdc.gov/ncbddd/autism/data.html. Accessed on March 27, 2023.

Chan, M. M. Y., & Han, Y. M. Y. (2020). Differential mirror neuron system (MNS) activation during action observation with and without social-emotional components in autism: A meta-analysis of neuroimaging studies. *Molecular Autism, 11*(1), 72.

Chandana, S. R., Behen, M. E., Juhász, C., Muzik, O., Rotherme, R. D., Mangner, T. J., … Chugani, D. C. (2005). Significance of abnormalities in developmental trajectory and asymmetry of cortical serotonin synthesis in autism. *International Journal of Developmental Neuroscience, 23*(2–3), 171–182.

Chapman, E., Baron-Cohen, S., Auyeung, B., Knickmeyer, R. C., Taylor, K., & Hackett, G. (2006). Fetal testosterone and empathy: Evidence from the empathy quotient (EQ) and the "reading the mind in the eyes" test. *Social Neuroscience, 1*(2), 135–148.

Collins, F., Morgan, M., & Patrinos, A. (2003). The Human Genome Project: Lessons from large-scale biology. *Science, 300*(5617), 286–290.

Dapretto, M., Davies, M. S., Pfeifer, J. H., Scott, A. A., Sigman, M., Bookheimer, S. Y., & Iacoboni, M. (2006). Understanding emotions in others: Mirror neuron dysfunction in children with autism spectrum disorders. *Nature Neuroscience, 9*(1), 28–30.

Davidson, M. (2017). Vaccination as a cause of autism—Myths and controversies. *Dialogues in Clinical Neuroscience, 19*(4), 403–407.

Deer, B. (2011). How the case against the MMR vaccine was fixed. *British Medical Journal, 342*, c5347.

Demetriou, E. A., DeMayo, M. M., & Guastella, A. J. (2019). Executive function in autism spectrum disorder: History, theoretical models, empirical findings, and potential as an endophenotype. *Frontiers in Psychiatry, 10*, 753.

Demetriou, E. A., Lampit, A., Quintana, D. S., Naismith, S. L., Song, Y. J. C., Pye, … Guastella, A. J. (2018). Autism spectrum disorders: A meta-analysis of executive function. *Molecular Psychiatry, 23*(5),1198–1204.

Devlin, B., & Scherer, S. W. (2012). Genetic architecture of autism spectrum disorder. *Current Opinion in Genetics & Development, 22*(3), 229–237.

Diamond, A. (2013). Executive functions. *Annual Review of Psychology, 64*, 135–68.

Di Pellegrino, G., Fadiga, L., Fogassi, L., Gallese, V., & Rizzolatti, G. (1992). Understanding motor events: A neurophysiological study. *Experimental Brain Research, 91*, 176–180.

Doja, A., & Roberts, W. (2006). Immunizations and autism: A review of the literature. *Canadian Journal of Neurological Sciences, 33*(4), 341–346.

Donvan, J., & Zucker, C. (2016). *In a different key: The story of autism.* Crown Publishers.

Dufour-Rainfray, D., Vourc'h, P., Tourlet, S., Guilloteau, D., Chalon, S., & Andres, C. R. (2011). Fetal exposure to teratogens: Evidence of genes involved in autism. *Neuroscience and Biobehavioral Reviews, 35*, 1254–1265.

Durkin, M. S., Maenner, M. J., Newschaffer, C. J., Lee L. C., Cunniff, C. M., Daniels, J. L., … Schieve, L. A. (2008). Advanced parental age and the risk of autism spectrum disorder. *American Journal of Epidemiology, 168*(11), 1268–1276.

Ecker, C., Bookheimer, S. Y., & Murphy, D. G. (2015). Neuroimaging in autism spectrum disorder: Brain structure and function across the lifespan. *Lancet Neurology, 14*(11), 1121–1134.

Eggertson, L. (2010). Lancet retracts 12-year-old article linking autism to MMR vaccines. *Canadian Medical Association Journal, 182*(4), E199–E200.

Eliot, L. (2019). Neurosexism: The myth that men and women have different brain. *Nature, 566*(7745), 453–454.

Fan, Y. T., Decety, J., Yang, C. Y., Liu, J. L., & Cheng, Y. (2010). Unbroken mirror neurons in autism spectrum disorders. *Journal of Child Psychology and Psychiatry, 51*(9), 981–988.

Folstein, S., & Rutter, M. (1977). Infantile autism: A genetic study of 21 twin pairs. *Journal of Child Psychology and Psychiatry, 18*, 297–321.

Frith, U. (1989). *Autism: Explaining the enigma.* Blackwell, Oxford.

Frith, U. (1991). *Autism and Asperger syndrome.* Cambridge University Press.

Gallese, V., Rochat, M. J., & Berchio, C. (2013). The mirror mechanism and its potential role in autism spectrum disorder. *Developmental Medicine and Child Neurology, 55*(1), 15–22.

Gentile, S. (2015). Prenatal antidepressant exposure and the risk of autism spectrum disorders in children: Are we looking at the fall of Gods? *Journal of Affective Disorders, 182*, 132–137.

Gillberg, C. & Steffenburg, S. (1989). Autistic behaviour in moebius syndrome. *Acta Paediatrica Scandinavica, 78*(2), 314–316.

Green, L., Fein, D., Modahl, C., Feinstein, C., Waterhouse, L., & Morris, M. (2001). Oxytocin and autistic disorder: Alterations in peptide forms. *Biological Psychiatry*, *50*, 609–613.

Greenberg, D. M., Warrier, V., Allison, C., & Baron-Cohen, S. (2018). Testing the empathizing-systemizing theory of sex differences and the extreme male brain theory of autism in half a million people. *Proceedings of the National Academy of Sciences of the United States of America*, *115*(48), 12152–12157.

Halsey, N. A., & Hyman, S. L. (2001). Measles-mumps-rubella vaccine and autistic spectrum disorder: Report from the New Challenges in Childhood Immunizations Conference convened in Oak Brook, Illinois. *Pediatrics*, *107*(5), E84.

He, H., Yu, Y., Wang, H., Obel, C. L., Li., F, & Li, J. (2022). Five-minute Apgar score and the risk of mental disorders during the first four decades of life: A nationwide registry-based cohort study in Denmark. *Frontiers in Medicine*, *8*, 796544.

Hemmers, J., Baethge, C., Vogeley, K., & Falter-Wagner, C. M. (2022). Are executive dysfunctions relevant for the autism-specific cognitive profile? *Frontiers in Psychiatry*, *13*, 886588.

Hu-Lince, D., Craig, D. W., Huentelman, M. J., & Stephan, D. A. (2005). The Autism Genome Project: Goal and strategies. *The American Journal of Pharmacogenomics*, *5*(4), 233–246.

Iacoboni, M. (2009). Imitation, empathy, and mirror neurons. *Annual Review of Psychology*, *60*, 653–670.

Jentink, J., Loane, M. A., Dolk, H., Barisic, I., Garne, E., Morris, J. K., & de Jong-van den Berg, L. T. W. (2010). Valproic acid monotherapy in pregnancy and major congenital malformations. *New England Journal of Medicine*, *362*(23), 2185–2193.

Johansson, M., Wentz, E., Fernell, E., Stromland, K., Miller, M. T., & Gillberg, C. (2001). Autistic spectrum disorders in mobius sequence: A comprehensive study of 25 individuals. *Developmental Medicine & Child Neurology*, *43*(5), 338–345.

Kanner, L. (1943). Autistic disturbances of affective contact. *Nervous Child*, *2*, 217–250.

Kanner, L. (1949). Problems of nosology and psychodynamics of early infantile autism. *American Journal of Orthopsychiatry*, *19*(3), 416–426.

Karimi, P., Kamali, E., Mousavi, S. M., & Karahmadi, M. (2017). Environmental factors influencing the risk of autism. *Journal of Research in Medical Sciences*, *22*, 27.

Knickmeyer, R. C., Baron-Cohen, S., Raggatt, P., Taylor, K., & Hackett, G. (2006). Fetal testosterone and empathy. *Hormones and Behavior*, *49*(3), 282–292.

Lamm, C., & Majdandžić, J. (2015). The role of shared neural activations, mirror neurons, and morality in empathy—A critical comment. *Neuroscience Research*, *90*, 15–24.

Leekam, S. R., Nieto, C., Libby, S. J., Wing, L., & Gould, J. (2007). Describing the sensory abnormalities of children and adults with autism. *Journal of Autism and Developmental Disorders*, *37*(5), 894–910.

Levy, D., Ronemus, M., Yamrom, B., Lee, Y., Leotta, A., … Wigler, M. (2011). Rare de novo and transmitted copy-number variation in autistic spectrum disorders. *Neuron*, *70*(5), 886–897.

Lewis, R. (2018). *Human genetics: Concepts and applications*. McGraw-Hill.

Loke, Y. J., Hannan, A. J., & Craig, J. M. (2015). The role of epigenetic changes in autism spectrum disorders. *Frontiers in Neurology*, *6*, 107.

Lord, C., Brugha, T. S., Charman, T., Cusack, J., Dumas, G., Frazier, T., … Veenstra-VanderWeele, J. (2020). Autism spectrum disorder. *Nature Reviews Disease Primers*, *6*(1), 5.

Lupattelli, A., Spigset, O., Twigg, M. J., Zagorodnikova, K., Mardby, A. C., Moretti, M. E., … Nordeng, H. (2014). Medication use in pregnancy: A cross-sectional, multinational web-based study. *American Journal of Obstetrics and Gynecology*, *4*(2), e004365.

MacDonald, K., & MacDonald, T. M. (2010). The peptide that binds: A systematic review of oxytocin and its prosocial effects in humans. *Harvard Review of Psychiatry*, *18*, 1–21.

Madsen, K. M., Hviid, A., Vestergaard, M., Schendel, D., Wohlfahrt, J., Thorsen, P., ... Melbye, M. (2002). A population-based study of measles, mumps, and rubella vaccination and autism. *The New England Journal of Medicine*, *347*(19), 1477–1482.

Madsen, K. M., Lauritsen, M. B., Pedersen, C. B., Thorsen, P., Plesner, A. M., Andersen, P. H., & Mortensen, P. B. (2003). Thimerosal and the occurrence of autism: Negative ecological evidence from Danish population-based data. *Pediatrics*, *112*(3), 604–606.

Malik, S., Khan, Y. S., Sahl, R., Elzamzamy, K., & Nazeer, A. (2019). Genetics of autism spectrum disorder: An update. *Psychiatric Annals*, *49*(3), 109–114.

Markram, H., Rinaldi, T., & Markram, K. (2007). The intense world syndrome—An alternative hypothesis for autism. *Frontiers in Neuroscience*, *1*(1), 77–96.

Markram, K., & Markram, H. (2010). The intense world theory—A unifying theory of the neurobiology of autism. *Frontiers in Human Neuroscience*, *4*, 224.

Matthews, T. J., & Hamilton, B. E. (2009). Delayed childbearing: More women are having their first child later in life. *NCHS data brief*, *21*, 1–8.

Meador, K. J., Baker, G. A., Browning, N., Clayton-Smith, J., Combs-Cantrell, D. T., Cohen, M. ... Loring, D. W. (2009). Cognitive function at 3 years of age after fetal exposure to antiepileptic drugs. *The New England Journal of Medicine*, *360*(16), 1597–1605.

Meulenberg, P. M., & Hofman, J. A. (1991). Maternal testosterone and fetal sex. *Journal of Steroid Biochemistry and Molecular Biology*, *39*(1), 51–54.

Miller, M. T., & Strömland, K. (1993). Thalidomide embryopathy: An insight into autism? *Teratology*, *47*, 387–388.

Miller, M. T., & Strömland, K. (1999). The mobius sequence: A relook. *JAAPOS*, *3*(4), 199–208.

Mitchell, A. A., Gilboa, S. M., Werler, M. M., Kelley, K. E., Louik, C., Hernandez-Diaz, S., & National Birth Defects Prevention Study. (2011). Medication use during pregnancy, with particular focus on prescription drugs: 1976–2008. *American Journal of Obstetrics and Gynecology*, *205*(1), 51. e1–e8.

Modabbernia, A., Sandin, S., Gross, R., Leonard, H., Gissler, M., Parner, E. T., ...Reichenberg, A. (2019). Apgar score and risk of autism. *European Journal of Epidemiology*, *34*(2), 105–114.

Mottron, L., Dawson, M., Soulieres, I., Hubert, B., & Burack, J. (2006). Enhanced perceptual functioning in autism: An update, and eight principles of autistic perception. *Journal of Autism and Developmental Disorders*, *36*(1), 27–43.

Murch, S. H., Anthony, A., Casson, D. H., Malik, M., Berelowitz, M., Dhillon, A. P., ... Walker-Smith, J. A. (2004). Retraction of an interpretation. *Lancet*, *363*(9411), 750.

Offit, P. A. (2008). *Autism's false prophets: Bad science, risky medicine, and the search for a cure*. Columbia University Press.

Peñagarikano, O, Abrahams, B. S., Herman, E. I., Winden, K. D., Gdalyahu, A., Dong, H., ... Geschwind, D. H. (2011). Absence of CNTNAP2 leads to epilepsy, neuronal migration abnormalities, and core autism-related deficits. *Cell*, *147*(1), 235–246.

Pickles, A., Bolton, P., Macdonald, H., Bailey, A., Le Couteur, A., Sim, C. H., & Rutter, M. (1995). Latent-class analysis of recurrence risks for complex phenotypes with selection and measurement error: A twin and family history study of autism. *American Journal of Human Genetics*, *57*, 717–726.

Ramachandran, V. S., & Oberman, L. M. (2006). Broken mirrors: A theory of autism. *Scientific American*, *295*(5), 62–69.

Rasalam, A. D., Hailey, H., Williams, J. H., Moore, S. J., Turnpenny, P. D., Lloyd, D. J., & Dean, J. C. (2005). Characteristics of fetal anticonvulsant syndrome associated autistic disorder. *Developmental Medicine & Child Neurology, 47*(8), 551–555.

Reichenberg, A., Gross, R., Weiser, M., Bresnahan, M., Silverman, J., Harlap, S., … Susser, E. (2006). Advancing paternal age and autism. *Archives of General Psychiatry, 63*(9), 1026–1032.

Ridley, R. (2019). Some difficulties behind the concept of the 'Extreme male brain' in autism research: A theoretical review. *Research in Autism Spectrum Disorders, 57,* 19–27.

Rieske, R. D., & Matson, J. L. (2020). Parental age at conception and the relationship with severity of autism symptoms. *Developmental Neurorehabilitation, 23*(5), 265–270.

Rimland, B. (1964). *Infantile autism: The syndrome and its implications for a neural theory of behavior.* Appleton-Century-Crofts.

Rinaldi, T., Perrodin, C., & Markram, H. (2008). Hyper-connectivity and hyper-plasticity in the medial prefrontal cortex in the valproic acid animal model of autism. *Frontiers in Neural Circuits, 2,* 4.

Ritvo, E. R, Freeman, B. J., Mason-Brothers, A., Mo, A., & Ritvo, A. M. (1985). Concordance for the syndrome of autism in 40 pairs of afflicted twins. *The American Journal of Psychiatry, 142*(1), 74–77.

Rizzolatti, G. (2005). The mirror neuron system and its function in humans. *Anatomy and Embryology, 210*(5–6), 419–421.

Rizzolatti, G., & Craighero, L. (2004). The mirror-neuron system. *Annual Review of Neuroscience, 27,* 169–192.

Rizzolatti, G., & Fabbri-Destro, M. (2010). Mirror neurons: From discovery to autism. *Experimental Brain Research, 200*(3–4), 223–237.

Rodier, P. M. (2002). Converging evidence for brain stem injury in autism. *Development and Psychopathology, 14,* 537–557.

Rogers, S. J. (2004). Developmental regression in autism spectrum disorders. *Mental Retardation and Developmental Disabilities Research Reviews, 10*(2), 139–143.

Ronald, A., & Hoekstra, R. A. (2011). Autism spectrum disorders and autistic traits: A decade of new twin studies. *American Journal of Medical Genetics. Part B, Neuropsychiatric Genetics, 156B*(3), 255–274.

Rylaarsdam, L., & Guemez-Gamboa, A. (2019). Genetic causes and modifiers of autism spectrum disorder. *Frontiers in Cellular Neuroscience, 13,* 385.

Sala, M., Braida, D., Lentini, D., Busnelli, M., Bulgheroni, E., Capurro, V., … Chini, B. (2011). Pharmacologic rescue of impaired cognitive flexibility, social deficits, increased aggression, and seizure susceptibility in oxytocin receptor null mice: A neurobehavioral model of autism. *Biological Psychiatry, 69*(9), 875–882.

Sanders, S. J., Ercan-Sencicek, A. G., Hus, V., Luo, R., Murtha, M. T., Moreno-De-Luca, D., … State, M. W. (2011). Multiple recurrent de novo CNVs, including duplications of the 7q11.23 Williams syndrome region, are strongly associated with autism. *Neuron, 70*(5), 863–885.

Sanders, S. J., Murtha, M. T., Gupta, A. R., Murdoch, J. D., Raubeson, M. J., Willsey, A. J., … State, M. W. (2012). De novo mutations revealed by whole-exome sequencing are strongly associated with autism. *Nature, 485*(7397), 237–241.

Schaaf, C. P., & Zoghbi, H. Y. (2011). Solving the autism puzzle a few pieces at a time. *Neuron, 70,* 806–808.

Scher, L. J., & Shyman, E. (2019). Challenging weak central coherence: A brief exploration of neurological evidence from visual processing and linguistic studies in autism spectrum disorder. *Annals of Behavioral Neuroscience, 2*(1), 136–143.

Shah, A., & Frith, U. (1983). An islet of ability in autistic children: A research note. *Journal of Child Psychology and Psychiatry*, *24*(4), 613–620.

Shelton, J. F., Tancredi, D. J., & Hertz-Picciotto, I. (2010). Independent and dependent contributions of advanced maternal and paternal ages to autism risk. *Autism Research*, *3*(1), 30–39.

Sigelman, C. K., & Rider, E. A. (2022). *Life-span human development* (10th ed.). Cengage.

Silberman, S. (2015). *NeuroTribes: The legacy of autism and the future of neurodiversity*. Avery.

Strömland, K., Nordin, V., Miller, M., Akerstrom, B., & Gillberg, C. (1994). Autism in Thalidomide: A population study. *Developmental Medicine and Child Neurology*, *36*(4), 351–356.

Tan, G. C., Doke, T. F., Ashburner, J., Wood, N. W., & Frackowiak, R. S. (2010). Normal variation in fronto-occipital circuitry and cerebellar structure with an autism-associated polymorphism of CNTNAP2. *Neuroimage*, *53*(3), 1030–1042.

Taylor, B., Miller, E., Farrington, C. P., Petropoulos, M. C., Favot-Mayaud, I., Li, J., & Waight, P. A. (1999). Autism and measles, mumps, and rubella vaccine: No epidemiological evidence for a causal association. *Lancet*, *353*(9169), 2026–2029.

Tick, B., Bolton, B., Happe, F., Rutter, M., & Rijsdijk, F. (2016). Heritability of autism spectrum disorders: A meta-analysis of twin studies. *Journal of Child Psychology and Psychiatry*, *57*, 585–595.

Tordjman, S., Anderson, G. M., Cohen, D., Kermarrec, S., Carlier, M., Touitou, Y., … Verloes, A. (2013). Presence of autism, hypersertonemia, and severe expressive language impairment in Williams-Beuren syndrome. *Molecular Autism*, *4*(1), 29.

Turnpenny, P. D., & Ellard, S. (2012). *Emery's elements of medical genetics* (14th ed.). Elsevier.

van Eijk, L., & Zietsch, B. P. (2021). Testing the extreme male brain hypothesis: Is autism spectrum disorder associated with a more male-typical brain? *Autism Research*, *14*(8), 1597–1608.

Venter, J. C., Adams, M. D., Myers, E. W., Li, P. W., Mural, R. J., Sutton, G. G., … Zhu, X. (2001). The sequence of the human genome. *Science*, *291*(5507), 1304–1351.

Voineagu, I., Wang, X., Johnston, P., Lowe, J. K., Tian, Y., Horvath, S., … Geschwind, D. H. (2011). Transcriptomic analysis of autistic brain reveals convergent molecular pathology. *Nature*, *474*(7351), 380–384.

Wakefield, A. J., Murch, S. H., Anthony, A., Linnell, J., Casson, D. M., Malik, M., … Walker-Smith, J. A. (1998). Lleal-lymphoid-nodular hyperplasia, non-specific colitis, and pervasive developmental disorder in children. *The Lancet*, *351*(9103), 637–641.

Walsh, K. M., & Bracken, M. B. (2011). Copy number variation in the dosage-sensitive 16p11.2 interval accounts for only a small proportion of autism incidence: A systematic review and meta-analysis. *Genetics in Medicine*, *13*(5), 377–384.

Waterhouse, L. (2013). *Rethinking autism: Variation and complexity*. Academic Press.

Werling, D. M., & Geschwind, D. H. (2013). Sex differences in autism spectrum disorders. *Current Opinion in Neurology*, *26*(2), 146–153.

Whitaker-Azmitia, P. M. (2005). Behavioral and cellular consequences of increasing serotonergic activity during brain development: A role in autism? *International Journal of Developmental Neuroscience*, *23*(1), 75–83.

Williams, J. H., Waiter, G. D., Gilchrist, A., Perrett, D. I., Murray, A. D., & Whiten, A. (2006). Neural mechanisms of imitation and 'mirror neuron' functioning in autistic spectrum disorder. *Neuropsychologia*, *44*(4), 610–621.

Wilson, K., Mills, E., Ross, C., McGowan, J., & Jada, A. (2003). Association of autistic spectrum disorder and the measles, mumps, and rubella vaccine: A systematic review of current epidemiological evidence. *Archives of Pediatrics and Adolescent Medicine*, *157*(7), 628–634.

Wu, S., Wu., F, Ding, Y., Hou, J., Bi, J., & Zhang, Z. (2017). Advanced parental age and autism risk in children: A systematic review and meta-analysis. *Acta Psychiatrica Scandinavica, 135*(1), 29–41.

Yates, L., & Hobson, H. (2020). Continuing to look in the mirror: A review of neuroscientific evidence for the broken mirror hypothesis, EP-M model and STORM model of autism spectrum conditions. *Autism, 24*(8), 1945–1959.

Yuen, R. K. C., Merico, D., Bookman, M., Howel, J. L., Thiruvahindrapuram, B., Patel, R. V., … Scherer, S. W. (2017). Whole genome sequencing resource identifies 18 new candidate genes for autism spectrum disorder. *Nature Neuroscience, 20*(4), 602–611.

Chapter 7

Autism Heterogeneity

Chapter Contents

Introduction

Autism is a complex condition that affects individuals in numerous ways. The **heterogeneity** of the condition results in a wide range of symptoms and varying severity levels of co-occurring conditions that can be present in people with autism. For example, some individuals may experience difficulties with social interactions and communication, while others may display restricted and repetitive behavior, interests, or activity patterns. In addition, some individuals with autism may also have intellectual disabilities, while others have average or above-average intelligence and function at the more able end of the spectrum.

DOI: 10.4324/9781003336266-9

Due to the heterogeneity and complexity of the condition, it is challenging to conceptualize it as a single disorder, define its pathophysiology, and design and implement interventions that can be universally effective.

The heterogeneity of autism is a significant hurdle in developing biomarkers and autism-specific medications. Many autism biomarkers have been identified, but no autism-specific ones have been found (McPartland, 2021; Shen et al., 2020). Individuals with autism exhibit a wide range of symptoms that are often treated with psychotropic drugs that do not effectively reduce the core symptoms of the disorder. Stephen Shore, an autism advocate who is on the spectrum, once famously said: "If you've met one person with autism, you've met one person with autism." Until the heterogeneity of autism is better understood and its diagnosis is redefined, it will be challenging to develop effective medications (Waterhouse, 2013).

Various factors contribute to autism heterogeneity. Research suggests that genetic factors such as gene mutations, chromosomal abnormality, copy number variations, and environmental factors, including maternal infections during pregnancy, prenatal exposure to toxins, and complications during birth, play a role in the development of autism. Other factors, such as individual variations in brain development, cognition, and behavior, may play a role in the heterogeneity of autism.

Heterogeneity

Heterogeneity—the presence of differences or variations within a group—is common in the natural environment. Heterogeneity can be observed in ecosystems and variations among species. Similarly, psychiatric conditions generally show a degree of heterogeneity. However, the heterogeneity of behaviors observed in autism surpasses that of other disorders (Boucher, 2011; Waterhouse, 2013). In the context of autism, heterogeneity refers to the differences in symptoms, behaviors, and abilities among autistic individuals. For instance, some individuals may have strong communication skills, while others may be nonverbal. Some may exhibit **maladaptive behaviors**, while others may have a focused interest in specific topics. Additionally, some individuals may be able to perform daily living activities independently, while others may require constant supervision.

When Kanner examined Donald T. (the first child he diagnosed with *infantile autism*) in 1938 at the Children's Psychiatric Clinic of the Johns Hopkins Hospital in Baltimore, Donald presented a clinical profile that, to some degree, differed from that of the other ten children Kanner examined (the children's characteristics are described in Chapter 1). The condition's heterogeneity was then apparent, even though Kanner formulated two defining characteristics that always must be present to justify a diagnosis of ASD: (a) an extreme aloneness from the beginning of life and (b) a desire for the preservation of sameness. It is worth noting that Kanner described a unitary condition that excluded children whose IQ was below 40 or had dysmorphic features, except macrocephaly (Folstein, 2006).

The heterogeneity of autism has played a significant role in the formulation of diagnostic criteria in both the Diagnostic and Statistical Manual of Mental Disorders (DSM) and the International Classification of Diseases (ICD). In the DSM-III, infantile autism was categorized as one of the types under the broader classification of Pervasive Developmental Disorders. The DSM-IV introduced different subtypes of autism, but the DSM-5 consolidated these subtypes under the umbrella term "autism spectrum disorder" to better acknowledge the range of symptoms and abilities among individuals diagnosed with autism and treatment options (Masi et al., 2017). Both the DSM and ICD now recognize the variability in how autism symptoms can present, which further highlights its heterogeneous nature. The revision and refinement of diagnostic criteria for autism and the incorporation of broader criteria have led to an increased prevalence of autism diagnoses (Wazana et al., 2007). These changes acknowledge various symptoms and abilities associated with autism. As a result, more individuals can now be recognized and diagnosed with the condition. This inclusivity reflects the complex nature of autism and its varied presentations in different individuals.

It is now well established that heterogeneity (i.e., diversity and variability) is a hallmark of autism. Individuals with autism share many common impairments but also a broad clinical variability and symptomatic expressions that run the gamut of IQ and language functions. Moreover, they exhibit wide variability in social and behavioral functioning. Stephen Shore, a professor of special education and autism advocate who is on the spectrum, once famously said, "If you've met one person with autism, you've met one person with autism." His statement exemplifies the great diversity of persons on the autism spectrum. In an interview with *Lime Connect* (a global not-for-profit organization with a mission to rebrand disability through achievement), Dr. Shore explained the heterogeneity of autism as follows:

> While the commonalities of people on the autism spectrum include differences in communication, social interaction, sensory receptivity, and highly-focused interests … these characteristics blend together differently for each individual … Autism is an extension of the diversity found in the human gene pool.
>
> (IBCCES, n.d.)

The many etiologies of autism necessarily result in its heterogeneity. Therefore, autism cannot be considered a single disorder. Geschwind and Levitt (2007) proposed a unifying model of the condition-development disconnection syndromes. According to this model, higher-order association areas of the brain, which typically connect to the frontal lobe, are partially disconnected during development. This idea of developmental disconnection helps explain the specific neurobehavioral features observed in autism, their emergence during development, and the diversity in the causes, behaviors, and cognitive profiles associated with autism.

Autism Heterogeneity Causal Factors

The causes of autism (discussed in Chapter 6) and the condition's varied expressions are interconnected. Therefore, different underlying factors can singularly or conjointly lead to diverse presentations affecting individuals with the condition. Genetic factors, neurological differences, comorbid conditions, and gender differences can all contribute to the heterogeneity of autism.

Genetic Factors

Genetic factors play a role in autism. Unlike sickle cell disease, which results from a gene mutation, autism is a polygenic disorder caused by numerous gene variants. Despite the view of autism researchers that there are a modest number of identified autism loci, research has identified more than 100 gene variants associated with autism (Betancur, 2011). In addition to autism, these genes are also linked to intellectual disability, suggesting that both conditions share an underlying genetic basis. There is also a genetic overlap between autism and epilepsy in many cases. Betancur's findings show that autism is not a singular clinical condition; instead, it is a behavioral expression of numerous genetic and genomic disorders, potentially amounting to tens or even hundreds. The saying "If you have met one person with autism, you have met one person with autism" emphasizes the unique nature of the condition. A single factor or gene does not cause autism but results from complex interactions between genetics and environmental factors. Genetic factors contributing to autism likely involve various gene variants, chromosome deletions or duplications, and combinations of different gene and chromosomal variations (Waterhouse, 2013).

Idiopathic and syndromic autism have different presentations. Idiopathic autism does not have an identified genetic or environmental cause, while syndromic autism, such as that seen in Fragile X syndrome, is linked to specific genetic conditions. As a result, the physical characteristics of individuals with idiopathic autism can differ significantly from those with syndromic autism. For example, people with Fragile X syndrome may exhibit features such as an elongated face and large ears. In contrast, individuals with idiopathic autism may show the core symptoms of autism without any distinctive physical traits. Syndromic autism provides valuable insights into the underlying molecular mechanisms that may also be relevant for idiopathic (nonsyndromic) autism. By studying the distinct features and genetic factors involved in syndromic autism, researchers can gain a better understanding of the broader **neurodevelopmental disorders**, including those forms of autism that do not have an identifiable genetic syndrome (Ziats et al., 2021).

Neurological Differences

The neurological factors that play a role in autism etiology (discussed in Chapter 6) also play a role in its heterogeneity. Differences in brain structures and function, atypical neural connectivity, and dysregulation in neurotransmitter systems interacting with environmental influences can all contribute to the heterogeneity manifested in autism.

The variability in autism brain difference is considerable. Head size varies among individuals with autism. **Macrocephaly** is sometimes observed in a subset of children with autism, particularly in early childhood. The increase in head size is thought to be connected to various developmental differences that can lead to autism. Still, a smaller head size than average is not typically recognized as a defining characteristic of autism (Stigler et al., 2011).

Many genetic loci are associated with autism, meaning that specific genetic variations can result in different neurological profiles and affect brain development, synaptic function, and neurotransmitter systems. Disruptions in neurotransmitter systems, such as those involving serotonin, dopamine, and glutamate, can influence mood regulation, social behavior, and cognitive functioning, leading to various symptoms and challenges.

Autism and Co-occurring Conditions

Creating subgroups has not addressed the inherent heterogeneity of autism. Some researchers in the field have suggested rethinking the concept of autism as a single syndrome, advocating for the view that it should be considered "the autisms," which recognizes multiple distinct disorders within the spectrum (Geschwind & Levitt, 2007). The DSM-5 (APA, 2013) subsumed all the subtypes of the conditions described in previous editions of the manual into a new designation, *autism spectrum disorder*, which recognizes the heterogeneity and complexity of the disorder, whose symptoms fall into a continuum that varies from person to person. Consequently, in addition to the two defining conditions of the disorder, social and communication deficits and restricted and repetitive interest and behavior, **comorbidity** or co-occurring conditions are frequent in autism. Various medical, genetic, and psychiatric co-occurring conditions are associated with autism in a much higher proportion than in the general population. Waterhouse (2013) described four disorders commonly associated with autism: (1) intellectual disability, (2) epilepsy, (3) language impairment, and (4) attention-deficit/hyperactivity disorder. She views those four disorders as concurrent symptoms instead of comorbidities.

Intellectual Disability

Intellectual disability (ID) is common among individuals diagnosed with ASD. Approximately 55–70% of individuals with ASD have some form of intellectual disability and impaired adaptive outcome (Charman et al., 2011). Because ID is so prevalent among individuals diagnosed with ASD, making a differential diagnosis is challenging. Van Bokhoven (2011, p. 86) suggested that these two conditions might share a "common molecular etiology at the single-gene level."

The relationship between *epilepsy* and ASD has been documented for decades. Studies have reported a highly variable rate of epilepsy, ranging from 2% to up to 46%, compared to a rate of 1.2% in the U.S. general population. One study (Viscidi, 2014) examined 6,000 autistic children and found that 12.5% have epilepsy, but the percentage rose to 26% among adolescents. One more recent study (Ewen et al., 2019) conducted with 7,000 participants with autism found a rate of 10%.

Language Impairment

Language impairment *per se* is no longer a diagnostic criterion in the DSM-5. Instead, "Persistent deficits in social communication and social interaction" is now one of the defining diagnostic criteria of ASD. DSM-5 (APA, 2013) introduced a new diagnosis, **Social (Pragmatic) Communication Disorder**, whose symptoms are not attributable to autism. Nevertheless, individuals diagnosed with ASD exhibit a continuum ranging from muteness/nonfunctional communication to total expressive language capacity. Approximately 25–50% of individuals with autism do not have language (Eigsti et al., 2011), and language delay is prevalent in nearly all individuals diagnosed with autism (Stefanatos & Baron, 2011). Approximately 30% of children with autism are minimally verbal despite receiving years of language interventions and adequate opportunities to acquire language (Tager-Flushberg & Kasari, 2013).

Attention-Deficit/Hyperactivity Disorder

Under the DSM-IV, **Attention-Deficit/Hyperactivity Disorder** (ADHD) and autism could not be diagnosed in the same person. However, in the DSM-5 and under the new umbrella term "autism spectrum disorder," the two conditions can be diagnosed concurrently in the same person. Symptoms of ASD and ADHD often co-occur (Leitner, 2014). Between 30% and 50% of individuals diagnosed with ASD (especially preschoolers) show symptoms of ADHD. Similarly, approximately two-thirds of individuals with ASD show characteristics of ADHD (Davis & Kollins, 2012). Both conditions are neurodevelopmental disorders that could partly originate from similar genetic factors (Rommelse et al., 2010).

Other Co-occurring Conditions

The most common gastrointestinal (GI) dysfunctions are chronic constipation, diarrhea, and abdominal pain. In addition, bloody stools, vomiting, and gastroesophageal reflux are also prevalent in some autistic individuals (Coury et al., 2012).

Gastrointestinal abnormalities are worth considering not only because of their prevalence in autism but also because they correlate with the severity of many autism-related behavioral problems (Hsiao, 2014). Kanner (1943), in his seminal article describing symptoms of autism, reported that seven out of the 11 children he examined in his clinic exhibited eating/feeding or dietary problems. Immune dysfunction is also common in ASD. A large body of research supports widespread immune dysregulation, increased **cytokine** production (i.e., substances secreted by specific immune system cells that affect other cells), and brain-reactive antibodies in individuals with ASD (Enstrom et al., 2009).

Other co-occurring conditions are also associated with ASD, including sleep disorders, mood disorders, anxiety, sensory issues, irritability, self-injury, tantrums, and aggression. According to the American Academy of Pediatrics, 25 to 50% of children have trouble sleeping. Sleep difficulty, however, is more prevalent in children with ASD and those with a dual diagnosis of developmental delays and ASD. For example, one study found that approximately 80% of preschoolers with ASD have sleep problems (Reynolds et al., 2019). In addition, compared to typically developing children, children with ASD take (on average) 11 minutes longer to fall asleep and spend about 15% of their sleeping in **rapid eye movement (REM)** compared to their typically developing counterparts, who spend 23% in REM during their sleeping time.

The brain's accurate processing and integration of our sensory system and sensory experiences result in a coherent view of our perception. However, many adults and children with ASD and other developmental disabilities have a dysfunctional sensory system. As a result, they may be prone to have *sensory interests* (e.g., fixate on the movement of a ceiling fan for hours). Conversely, they may experience *sensory sensitivities* (e.g., unusual reactions to noise) (Frazier & Hardan, 2016). The high prevalence of sensory issues prompted the inclusion of "Sensory Processing Disorder" (SPD) in the DSM-5 (APA, 2013) in terms of "Hyper- or hypo-reactivity to sensory input or unusual interest in sensory aspects of environment; (such as apparent indifference to pain/heat/cold, adverse response to specific sounds or textures, excessive smelling or touching of objects, fascination with lights or spinning object)." Sensory abnormalities have a cascading effect that can disrupt normal functioning in many developmental domains. Some researchers (Marco et al., 2011) have argued that sensory dysfunction might be at the root of ASD core features. For example, language delays may be caused by poor auditory processing. Similarly, emotional comprehension and reciprocity may be prompted by impaired visual processing.

Mood Instability

Mood instability is also typical in individuals diagnosed with ASD. Irritability is often the primary reason for children with ASD to go into primary care for evaluation and treatment (Robb, 2010). Irritability usually triggers concomitant behavior, including deliberate self-injury, temper tantrums, fluctuating moods, and aggression toward others (Johnson et al., 2007). Sensory input and processing environmental events may be overwhelming for some individuals with ASD, mainly if language impairment is concomitant with the condition. Tantrums and meltdowns may be corollaries of their inability to deal with the bombardment of sensory stimulation.

Male-to-Female Ratio

Both Kanner and Asperger documented case studies with a skewed sex ratio of boys to girls—8:3 and 4:0, respectively. Asperger wrote:

> While we have never met a girl with the fully fledged picture of autism, we have, however, seen several mothers of autistic children whose behavior had decidedly autistic features. It is difficult to explain the observation. It may be only chance that there are no autistic girls among our cases, or it could be that autistic traits in the female become evident after puberty. We just do not know.
>
> (Frith, 1991, p. 85)

Autism is more commonly diagnosed in boys than in girls. Most studies, including the DSM-5 (APA, 2013), have reported a male-to-female ratio of 4:1. However, Loomes and colleagues (2017) conducted a systematic review through a meta-analysis of 54 prevalence studies to investigate the proportion of boys and girls on the spectrum disorder. Contrary to the male-to-female ratio often reported, the study found the ratio closer to 3:1. Furthermore, the researchers found a disparity between active and passive case ascertainment. In other words, studies in the meta-analysis that actively evaluate the presentation of ASD criteria, irrespective of previously ascertained ASD cases, identified more female cases of ASD (i.e., 24 girls per 100 cases) compared to studies that passively relied on once-established ASD diagnoses (i.e., 18 girls per 100 cases). They explained the ratio disparity in terms of "diagnostic gender bias." Girls are less likely than boys not to receive a clinical ASD diagnosis even when they meet the criteria for the disorder.

There is growing support that autism symptoms present differently in females than in males because females have more effective strategies to mask their symptoms in social situations, thus contributing to the disparity in prevalence rates of autism in both genders (Green et al., 2019). Diagnosticians may be missing out on girls and women because their symptoms presentation differs from those observed in boys and men (Gould & Ashton-Smith, 2011).

Why are girls less likely than boys to receive an autism diagnosis? Are females less susceptible to developing autism or present the symptoms differently? Autism researchers and clinicians have proposed various mechanisms to explain the low prevalence of ASD in females compared to that of males. One dominant view is the female protective effect—i.e., being female—reduces the likelihood of developing autism. There is supporting evidence of the Female Autism Phenotype (e.g., displaying fewer repetitive behaviors such as rocking back and forth or hand flapping). Females, more so than males, can "camouflage" autistic characteristics (Hull et al., 2020). Environmental factors have also been linked to the preponderance of males with autism. Prenatal use and exposure to medications such as SSRI have been found to increase the susceptibility of males developing autism more readily than females (Harrington et al., 2014).

Many studies have found that girls without intellectual disabilities have less severe symptoms of the conditions than boys (e.g., Hiller et al., 2016) and are thus more able to mask the difficulties associated with the disorder's social challenges. As a result, if they are diagnosed, it is usually much later, when they become adults. Moreover, despite the difficulties with social relationships associated with autism, there is supportive evidence that females have less social impairment than males and, thus, are more inclined than males to form friendships (Head et al., 2014).

Various research investigating autism genetic causes found that *de novo* **mutations** (i.e., deletions and duplications) play a role in autism. Females have greater protection from these genetic mutations than males (Levy et al., 2011). Additionally, it has been suggested that the genes in the paternal **X chromosome** raise the threshold for autism "phenotypic expression." Only females inherit a paternal X chromosome, so compared to males, they are naturally protected (Skuse, 2000). Another possibility is that females have an inherent biological constitution that protects them from developing autism—i.e., a "female protective effect." In other words, females must have greater genetic and/or environmental risks than males to exhibit similar autistic features, and girls who are diagnosed have a "greater etiological load" than diagnosed males (Robinson et al., 2013).

In sum, autism researchers and clinicians could explain the discrepant autism prevalence ratio between males and females in terms of a female protective effect that reduces their susceptibility to developing autism. Females could express their ASD symptoms in ways that diagnostic instruments do not capture. It could also be that females, particularly those without an intellectual disability, could "camouflage" their symptoms, making an autism diagnosis less likely.

The Broader Autism Phenotype

Kendell (1968) introduced the concept of "zone of rarity" to refer to the gap between the features of a biological disorder with a precise diagnosis and other conditions that do not result in a diagnosis. Many psychological and mental health conditions are commonly classified by a predetermined score or criteria that must cross the threshold into a diagnosis. However, the threshold is unclear, for many people who score below the threshold may experience some difficulties that are not severe enough to meet a formal diagnosis. Autism has no natural boundaries and, as a result, lacks a clear zone of rarity.

The **broader autism phenotype (BAP)** concept illustrates the diversity and heterogeneity found in autism. It highlights that it is not a one-size-fits-all condition but rather encompasses a wide range of characteristics and behaviors. Both genetic and neurological factors likely play a significant role in the BAP. Parents, siblings, and extended family members of individuals diagnosed with ASD may exhibit signs and symptoms suggestive of the disorder, albeit not severe enough to warrant a clinical ASD diagnosis. Autism researchers have introduced the term broader autism phenotype (BAP) to describe family members who display milder features of autism that are not associated with any functional impairment. The BAP traits may be linked to specific genetic factors (**genotype**) that influence the expression of autism-related characteristics (**phenotype**).

Because the key features that make up the BAP are unclearly defined, autism researchers have formulated different sets of behaviors constituting it. Losh and colleagues (2008), based on their analysis of family symptom data, proposed four characteristics associated with the BAP— anxiety, language deficits, social problems, and rigidity—whereas Bernier and colleagues (2012) underscored and included in their BAP delineation: lack of expressiveness, poor social motivation, and limited and restricted interests. Moreover, other researchers have reported a preference for non-social activities, emotional inexpressiveness, and lack of tact in interactions with family members of individuals diagnosed with ASD.

Heterogeneity and Autism Research and Treatment

Research

Despite seven decades of rigorous investigations, autism researchers have not yet identified the neurobiological and environmental causes that lead to the full range of behaviors individuals with autism exhibit (Whitehouse & Stanley, 2013). More research has shown that there are numerous neural and genetic factors involved in autism. However, to date, not a single, unique brain deficit has been found to define autism. The disorder results from a complex interplay of differences in brain structure and function that can vary significantly among individuals with autism. The heterogeneity of autism is so entrenched that a one-size-fits-all approach in research and clinical practice is untenable. Some researchers have even suggested that only artificial intelligence with explanatory power to develop effective drug regimens and behavioral interventions can identify significant subgroups (Erden et al., 2021; Suran, 2022).

The heterogeneity of autism has impeded research progress in determining the precise genetic and neurological cause of the condition. First, the DSM-5 diagnostic criteria and its umbrella term "autism spectrum disorder," which encompasses a wide range of symptoms and severity levels, make it challenging to establish standardized measures for research. For example, researchers often face challenges in identifying and recruiting participants on the autism spectrum with similar characteristics or biological mechanisms, as many research protocols require more homogeneous groups to draw reliable conclusions. What works for one group of participants may be ineffective for another. Second, research has adhered to the DSM-5 model of "building a body of knowledge about autism as a unitary entity" (Waterhouse, 2022). Autism researchers must abandon the notion that autism is a **unitary disorder** in order to find "neurobiological treatment targets" (Waterhouse & Gillberg, 2014, p. 1788).

Genetic studies involving thousands of participants with autism have shown that different subtypes of autism have unique genetic profiles. For instance, individuals with *de novo* mutations tend to have lower IQ scores and higher rates of epilepsy compared to those with common variants (Weiner et al., 2017). Waterhouse (2022) proposed that identifying potential transdiagnostic **endophenotypes** (i.e., endophenotypes are not bound by the specific criteria of any single diagnosis) could help reduce the heterogeneity observed in autism. Researchers may need to examine autism symptoms beyond the traditional DSM-5 diagnostic framework and broaden the range of phenotypes.

Treatment

The heterogeneity of autism has hindered progress in diagnosis and treatments despite the significant advancements that have been made in identifying genetic risk factors. Jeste and Geschwind (2014) proposed three themes that technologies can use to identify various phenotypes within the autism spectrum: Single-gene disorders, gender bias in autism, and genetics and neurological comorbidities. The heterogeneity of autism has also hindered the development of biomarkers and the development of autism-specific drugs. People on the autism spectrum typically display a wide variety of symptoms that are usually treated with psychotropic medications that are not effective at reducing the core symptoms of autism, namely *impaired social interaction* (Rutter, 2011). The diversity within autism spectrum disorder must inform treatment approaches. Clinical trials testing drugs to treat autism have not been successful due to the condition's heterogeneity and the presence of other co-occurring conditions. Despite dozens of clinical trials based on genomics and systems biology, no pharmacologic treatments have been identified to manage the core symptoms of social deficits and restricted/repetitive behavior (Baribeau &Anagnostou, 2022). Until the heterogeneity of autism is understood, effective medications cannot be delivered (Waterhouse, 2013). Despite significant advancements in the understanding of autism biology, clinical trials aimed at addressing the core symptoms of autism have not produced favorable outcomes. The underlying variability in the causes of autism presents ongoing challenges for these trials. Beversdorf and colleagues (2023) have suggested a **precision medicine** approach to clinical drug development.

Individual differences in genetics, brain structure, and function have impeded the development of effective treatment for autism despite more than two decades of neuroscience research. McCracken and colleagues (2021, p. 4) reported "Two decades of increases in intervention research funding with advances in the basic neuroscience understanding of ASD has not produced progress in pharmacological interventions for ASD core deficits."

Summary

The causes of autism are complex, and its characteristics can vary widely among individuals. All areas of development are affected in some way. People with autism may exhibit different physical traits and face varying challenges. Some individuals might struggle with motor coordination, sensory sensitivities, or other health issues, while others may show no noticeable physical differences. Cognitive abilities also vary significantly among autistic individuals. Some may have intellectual disabilities, while others possess average or above-average intelligence. Children on the autism spectrum may attend special education classes or be integrated into mainstream classrooms. Social interactions can also differ from one person to another. Some individuals find it challenging to interpret social cues, while others may have developed social skills but still struggle to form and maintain relationships. This wide range of differences is why autism is referred to as a spectrum rather than a single, uniform disorder.

Autism is more commonly diagnosed in boys than in girls. Both Kanner and Asperger have documented a skewed sex ratio of boys to girls. Some authors have proposed that females are more able to "camouflage" their autistic characteristics, while others have suggested a female **protective factor** advantage due to having two X sex chromosomes. Additionally, autism is not a single disorder but manifests itself differently in each individual, hence the term "spectrum." Many other conditions are associated with autism, including anxiety disorders, epilepsy, intellectual disability, attention-deficit/hyperactivity disorder, gastrointestinal issues, and sleep disturbances. Although these conditions do not affect everyone on the autism spectrum, they are more prevalent among individuals with the condition than among those in the general population.

Autism is neither a unitary disorder nor an all-or-nothing phenomenon. However, it manifests itself in a continuum with ASD traits at one end and typical development at the other. The severity of the disorder and The BAP characteristics also manifest themselves along a continuum. Therefore, the study of the concept of the broader autism phenotype and the reduction of complex phenotypes into simpler endophenotypes can elucidate the genetics of ASD and further researchers' and clinicians' understanding of the boundary between ASD and typical development.

Questions to Ponder for Further Thinking and Learning

1   How can we better recognize and value the diverse strengths and abilities of individuals with autism, including those with exceptional skills in music, art, or math?
2   How can we better support individuals with autism who have co-occurring conditions such as anxiety, depression, or ADHD?
3   How can we identify and diagnose autism in individuals who may not fit the traditional diagnostic criteria but still experience significant challenges in social communication and interaction?
4   What causes the heterogeneity of autism? Is it due more readily to genetic factors than environmental ones?
5   Should autism researchers abandon the search for a unifying genetic cause of autism and acknowledge that "autisms" rather than "autism" is a more appropriate designation?
6   Should autism researchers be more committed to researching idiopathic autism than syndromic autism (e.g., tuberous sclerosis, fragile X syndrome, Rett syndrome, and Angelman syndrome), given that syndromic autism has a known cause?

References

APA (2013). *Diagnostic and statistical manual of mental disorders* (5th ed.). American Psychiatric Association.

Baribeau, D., & Anagnostou, E. (2022). Novel treatments for autism spectrum disorder based on genomics and systems biology. *Pharmacology & Therapeutics, 230*, 107939.

Bernier, R., Gerdts, J., Munson, J., Dawson, G., & Estes, A. (2012). Evidence for broader autism phenotype characteristics in parents from multiple-incidence autism families. *Autism Research, 5*(1), 13–20.

Betancur, C. (2011). Etiological heterogeneity in autism spectrum disorders: More than 100 genetic and genomic disorders and still counting. *Brain Research, 1380*, 42–77.

Beversdorf, D. Q., Anagnostou, E., Hardan, A., Wang, P., Erickson, C. A., Frazier, T. W., & Veenstra-VanderWeele, J. (2023). Editorial: Precision medicine approaches for heterogeneous conditions such as autism spectrum disorders (The need for a biomarker exploration phase in clinical trials—Phase 2m). *Frontiers in Psychiatry, 13*, 1079006.

Boucher, J. (2011). Redefining the concept of autism as a unitary disorder: Multiple causal deficits of a single kind? In D. Fein (Ed.), *The neuropsychology of autism* (pp. 469–482). Oxford University Press.

Charman, T., Pickles, A., Simonoff, E., Chandler, S., Loucas, T., & Baird, G. (2011). IQ in children with autism spectrum disorders: Data from the Special Needs and Autism Project (SNAP). *Psychological Medicine, 41*(3), 619–627.

Coury, D. L., Ashwood, P., Fasano, A., Fuchs, G., Geraghty, M., Kaul, A., ... Jones, N. E. (2012). *Pediatrics, 130* (Supplement 2), S160–S168.

Davis, N. O., & Kollins, S. H. (2012). Treatment for co-occurring attention deficit/hyperactivity disorder and autism spectrum disorder. *Neurotherapeutics, 9*(3), 518–530.

Eigsti, I. M., de Marcheta, A. B., Schuh, J. M., & Kelley, E. (2011). Language acquisition in autism spectrum disorders: A developmental review. *Research in Autism Spectrum Disorders, 5*(2), 681–691.

Enstrom, A. M., Van de Water, J. A., & Ashwood, P. (2009). Autoimmunity in autism. *Current Opinion in Investigational Drugs*, *10*(5), 463–473.

Erden, Y. J., Hummerstone, H., & Rainey, S. (2021). Automating autism assessment: What AI can bring to the diagnostic process. *Journal of Evaluation in Clinical Practice*, *27*(3), 485–490.

Ewen, J. B., Marvin, A. R., Law, K., & Lipkin, P. H. (2019). Epilepsy and autism severity: A study of 6,975 children. *Autism Research*, *12*(8), 1251–1259.

Folstein, D. E. (2006). The clinical spectrum of autism. *Clinical Neuroscience Research*, *6*(3–4), 113–117.

Frazier, T. W., & Hardan, A.W. (2016). Empirically-identified restricted repetitive behavior domains: Informing DSM-6. Paper presented at the International Meeting for Autism Research, Baltimore, Maryland. https://imfar.confex.com/imfar/2016/webprogram/Paper22807.html. Accessed on February 12, 2024.

Frith, U. (1991). *Autism and Asperger syndrome*. Cambridge University Press.

Geschwind, D. H., & Levitt, P. (2007). Autism spectrum disorders: Development disconnection syndromes. *Current Opinion in Neurobiology*, *17*(1), 103–111.

Gould, J., & Ashton-Smith, J. (2011). Missed diagnosis or misdiagnosis? Girls and women on the autism spectrum. *Good Autism Practice*, *12*(1), 34–41.

Green, R. M., Travers, A. M., Howe, Y., & McDougle, C. (2019). Women and autism spectrum disorder: Diagnosis and implications for treatment of adolescents and adults. *Current Psychiatry Reports*, *21*(4), 22.

Harrington, R. A., Lee, L. C., Crum, R. M., Zimmerman, A. W., & Hertz-Picciotto, I. (2014). Prenatal SSRI use and offspring with autism spectrum disorder or developmental delay. *Pediatrics*, *133*(5), e1241–e1248.

Head, A. M., McGillivray, J. A., & Stokes, M. A. (2014). Gender differences in emotionality and sociability in children with autism spectrum disorders. *Molecular Autism*, *5*, 19.

Hiller, R. M., Young, R. L., & Weber, N. (2016). Sex differences in pre-diagnosis concerns for children later diagnosed with autism spectrum disorder. *Autism*, *20*(1), 75–84.

Hsiao, E. Y. (2014). Gastrointestinal issues in autism spectrum disorder. *Harvard Review of Psychiatry*, *22*(2), 104–111.

Hull, L., Petrides, K. V., & Mandy, W. (2020). The female autism phenotype and camouflaging: A narrative review. *Review Journal of Autism and Developmental Disorders*, *7*(4), 306–317.

IBCCES (n.d.). Interview with Dr. Stephen Shore: Autism advocate and on the spectrum. https://ibcces.org/blog/2018/03/23/12748/. Accessed on December 1, 2023.

Jeste, S. S., & Geschwind, D. H. (2014). Disentangling the heterogeneity of autism spectrum disorder through genetic findings. *Nature Reviews Neurology*, *10*(2), 74–81.

Johnson, C. P., Myers, S. M., & American Academy of Pediatrics Council of Children with Disabilities. (2007). Identification and evaluation of children with autism spectrum disorders. *Pediatrics*, *120*(5), 1183–1215.

Kanner, L. (1943). Autistic disturbances of affective contact. *Nervous Child, 2*, 217–250.

Kendell, R. E. (1968). *The classification of depressive illnesses (Institute of Psychiatry, Maudsley Monograph, No. 18)*. Oxford University Press.

Leitner, Y. (2014). The co-occurrence of autism and attention deficit hyperactivity disorder in children—What do we know? *Frontiers in Human Neuroscience*, *8*, Article 268.

Levy, D., Ronemus, M., Yamrom, B., Lee, Y. H., Leotta, A., Kendall, J., … Wigler, M. (2011). Rare de novo and transmitted copy-number variation in autistic spectrum disorders. *Neuron*, *70*(5), 886–897.

Loomes, R., Hull, L., & Mandy, W. P. L. (2017). What is the male-to-female ratio in autism spectrum disorder? A systematic review and meta-analysis. *Journal of the American Academy of Child & Adolescent Psychiatry*, *56*(6), 466–474.

Losh, M., Childress, D., Lam, K., & Piven, J. (2008). Defining key features of the broad autism phenotype: A comparison across parents of multiple- and single-incidence autism families. *American Journal of Medical Genetics B Neuropsychiatric Genetics*, *147B*(4), 424–433.

Marco, E. J., Hinkley, L. B. N., Hill, S. S., & Nagarajan, S. S. (2011). Sensory processing in autism: A review of neurophysiologic findings. *Pediatric Research*, *69*, 48R–54R.

Masi, A., DeMayo, M. M., Glozier, N., & Guastella, A. J. (2017). An overview of autism spectrum disorder, heterogeneity and treatment options. *Neuroscience Bulletin*, *33*(2), 183–93.

McCracken, J. T., Anagnostou, E., Arango, C., Dawson, G., Farchione, T., Mantua, V., ...ISCTM/ECNP ASD Working Group. (2021). Drug development for autism spectrum disorder (ASD): Progress, challenges, and future directions. *European Neuropsychopharmacology*, *48*, 3–31.

McPartland, J. C. (2021). Refining biomarker evaluation in ASD. *European Neuropsychopharmacology*, *48*, 34–36.

Reynolds, A. M., Soke, G. N., Sabourin, K. R., Hepburn, S., Katz, T., Wiggins, L. D., ... & Levy, S. E. (2019). Sleep problems in 2- to 5-year-olds with autism spectrum disorder and other developmental delays. *Pediatrics*, *143*(3), e20180492.

Robb, A. S. (2010). Managing irritability and aggression in autism spectrum disorders in children and adolescents. *Developmental Disabilities Research Reviews*, *16*(3), 258–264.

Robinson, E. B., Lichtenstein, P., Anckarsäter, H., Happé, F., & Ronald, A. (2013). Examining and interpreting the female protective effect against autistic behavior. *Proceedings of the National Academy of Sciences of the United States of America*, *110*(13), 5258–5262.

Rommelse, N. N., Franke, B., Geurts, H. M., Hartman, C. A., & Buitelaar, J. K. (2010). Shared heritability of attention-deficit/hyperactivity disorder and autism spectrum disorder. *European Child and Adolescent Psychiatry*, *19*(3), 281–295.

Rutter, M. L. (2011). Progress in understanding autism: 2007–2010. *Journal of Autism and Developmental Disorders*, *41*(4), 395–404.

Shen, L., Liu, X., Zhang, H., Lin, J., Feng, C., & Iqbal, J. (2020). Biomarkers in autism spectrum disorders: Current progress. *Clinica Chimica Acta*, *502*, 41–54.

Skuse, D. H. (2000). Imprinting, the X-chromosome, and the male brain: Explaining sex differences in the liability to autism. *Pediatric Research*, *47*(1), 9–16.

Stefanatos, G. A., & Baron, I. S. (2011). The ontogenesis of language impairment in autism: A neuropsychological perspective. *Neuropsychology Review*, *21*(3), 252–270.

Stigler, K. A., McDonald, B. C., Anand, A., Saykin, A. J., & McDougle, C. J. (2011). Structural and functional magnetic resonance imaging of autism spectrum disorders. *Brain Research*, *1380*, 146–161.

Suran, M. (2022). New NIH program for artificial intelligence in research. *JAMA*, *328*, 1580.

Tager-Flushberg, H., & Kasari, C. (2013). Minimally verbal school-aged children with autism spectrum disorder: The neglected end of the spectrum. *Autism Research*, *6*(6), 468–478.

van Bokhoven, H. (2011). Genetic and epigenetic networks in intellectual disabilities. *Annual Review of Genetics*, *45*, 81–104.

Viscidi, E. W., Johnson, A. L., Spence, S. J., Buka, S. L., Morrow, E. M., & Triche, E. W. (2014). The association between epilepsy and autism symptoms and maladaptive behaviors in children with autism spectrum disorder. *Autism*, *18*(8), 996–1006.

Waterhouse, L. (2013). *Rethinking autism: Variation and complexity*. Academic Press.

Waterhouse, L. (2022). Heterogeneity thwarts autism explanatory power: A proposal for endophenotypes. *Frontiers in Psychiatry*, *13*, 947653.

Waterhouse, L., & Gillberg, C. (2014). Why autism must be taken apart. *Journal of Autism and Developmental Disorders, 44*(7), 1788–1792.

Wazana, A., Bresnahan, M., & Kline, J. (2007). The autism epidemic: Fact or artifact? *Journal of the American Academy of Child & Adolescent Psychiatry, 46*(6), 721–730.

Weiner, D. J., Wigdor, E. M., Ripke, S., Walters, R. K., Kosmicki, J. A., Grove, J., ... Robinson, E. B. (2017). Polygenic transmission disequilibrium confirms that common and rare variation act additively to create risk for autism spectrum disorders. *Nature Genetics, 49*(7), 978–985.

Whitehouse, A. J. O., & Stanley, F. J. (2013). Is autism one or multiple disorders? *The Medical Journal of Australia, 198*(6), 302–303.

Ziats, C. A., Patterson, W. G., & Friez, M. (2021). Syndromic autism revisited: Review of the literature and lessons learned. *Pediatric Neurology, 114*, 21–25.

Part III

The understanding of autism has evolved since its clinical identification in the 1940s. The development of screening and diagnostic tools has also progressed in response to ongoing research and newly developed treatment methods. Chapter 8, titled *Screening Tools*, discusses various instruments pediatricians and parents can use to identify early signs of autism. Early identification can indicate whether a more thorough evaluation is necessary. Chapter 9, *Diagnostic Tools*, focuses on more comprehensive assessments, which include structured interviews with parents, observational assessments, and the administration of standardized tests that trained professionals can use to diagnose autism.

DOI: 10.4324/9781003336266-10

Chapter 8

Screening Tools

Chapter Contents

Introduction

Autism Spectrum disorder (ASD) is one of the most pervasive neurodevelopmental disorders, yet its neurobiology is poorly understood. The heterogeneity of the condition precludes the development of effective and reliable **biomarkers**. Researchers and clinicians rely primarily on behavioral observations to identify individuals at risk for developing the disorder. Therefore, screening tools are the first step toward establishing a reliable diagnosis.

Signs of autism appear early in infancy. Infants who are subsequently diagnosed with autism show behaviors, starting in the first year of life, that their typically developing counterparts do not show. They are less likely to orient to human faces, seldom respond to their names, and hardly show positive emotions or make eye contact. When attempting to communicate, they use fewer gestures and rarely point to engage another person or indicate what they want (Zwaigenbaum et al., 2013). Additionally, they show little interest in people, avoid most forms of physical contact, and have communication deficits.

DOI: 10.4324/9781003336266-11

Parents are typically the first to notice behaviors that indicate that something may be going awry. They usually communicate their concerns to their children's pediatricians, who play an essential role in the early identification of autism. However, because there are no biological markers or medical tests to diagnose the disorder, early screening is a valuable tool to indicate whether clinicians should conduct further assessments to confirm a diagnosis of autism. Screening tools can help determine whether an infant, a toddler, or a child is at risk for developing autism. In addition to regular developmental surveillance and screening, the American Academy of Pediatrics (AAP) recommends screening all infants for autism spectrum disorder at the 18- and 24-month well-child visits (Johnson et al., 2007).

Although the American Academy of Pediatrics (AAP) recommends universal screening during well-child visits and specifically for autism at 18 and 24 months (Johnson et al., 2007), the US Preventive Service Task Force (USP-STF) published a report emphasizing the limited evidence supporting universal screening for autism during well-child visits of asymptomatic infants and toddlers (Siu et al., 2016). The lack of synchronicity between the AAP and the USPSTF regarding universal screening for autism has engendered doubts and controversies among parents and healthcare professionals serving the autism community (Coury, 2015).

Psychometric Properties of Screening Tools

Validity refers to the accuracy of a test—the extent to which it measures what it purports to measure. Validity is measured by sensitivity and specificity. *Sensitivity* refers to how well a test or a screening tool detects a specific disease or condition. For example, a test with 80% sensitivity will correctly identify 80% of people with the disease or the condition. Thus, the test will miss 20% of people (i.e., **false negative**) with the disease or the condition that should have tested positive. Highly sensitive tests identify a few false negative cases.

Conversely, *specificity* describes a test's ability to identify individuals without a disease or a condition accurately. For example, a test with 100% specificity correctly identifies all individuals without a disease or a condition. Furthermore, a test with 75% specificity identifies 75% of people without the condition but incorrectly reports 25% (i.e., false positive) of individuals as having the disease. Sensitivity and specificity are generally stable for a given test. However, they are inversely related: When the value of one increases, that of the other decreases. It has been suggested that the sensitivity and specificity of tools for population screening applications should exceed 0.70 to merit any consideration (Dumont-Mathieu & Fein, 2005).

Positive Predictive Value (PPV) refers to the likelihood that a person who tests positive for a disease or a condition has the disease or the condition. More specifically, the PPV for autism screening test is a ratio of children screening positive who subsequently receive an ASD diagnosis over the total number of children who were screened positive. **Negative Predictive Value** (NPV) describes the likelihood that a person who tests negative for a disease or condition does not have the disease or condition. In the case of ASD, NPV is the ratio of children who will develop autism over the total number of children a screening tool identified as not at risk for developing autism.

Unlike diagnostic instruments that are designed to confirm a diagnosis of autism, screening tools are structured to identify individuals who may be at risk for autism. Therefore, they are constructed to identify as many potential cases as possible, even if it results in a higher number of false positives. However, these tools must be **reliable** and valid. They must produce consistent results across different populations and detect what they intend to identify.

Effectiveness of Screening Tools

Many developmental screening instruments have been developed for children under three, but the CDC does not endorse any specific ones. They can be administered by trained paraprofessionals in fewer than 15 minutes, and most tools are adequate and have specificities and sensitivities above 70%. Screening for autism requires parents' participation because their concerns have been shown to predict their children's developmental delays and disabilities in 70 to 80% of cases (Glascoe, 2002; Squires et al., 1996).

Selecting a Screening Level

Consistent with the AAP recommendation to screen children at 9, 18, and 30 months during regular well-child visits, *Level I (primary) screens* (aka broadband screeners) do not screen for autism *per se*. They are used with infants in general populations going to pediatricians' or family physicians' offices, regardless of known preexisting risk factors. For example, the M-CHAT-R/F (Robins et al., 2014) is the most used Level I screening instrument in the United States and Europe. The tool screens all children, not just for autism but also for their risk level for other developmental disabilities. Level I screeners are generally quick and inexpensive to administer during well-child visits.

Level II (secondary) screens are specifically for autism and can differentiate children with signs of autism from those with other developmental conditions. Level II screening instruments identify children with possible autism features or those at high risk for various developmental disabilities so that they can undergo more comprehensive evaluation procedures. For example, the Screening Tool for Autism in Toddlers and Young Children (STAT) is one Level II screening instrument with adequate **predictive validity**. Children who are younger siblings of children already diagnosed with autism are more likely to be diagnosed with the disorder (Ozonoff et al., 2011). Children with a genetic condition (e.g., **Angelman syndrome**, **tuberous sclerosis**, Fragile X, or Down syndrome) are more likely to be diagnosed with ASD (Moss & Howlin, 2009).

Autism Screening Instruments

Baron-Cohen and colleagues (1992) developed the first screening tool—The CHecklist for Autism in Toddlers—to identify the early signs of autism in 18-month-olds. Other researchers and clinicians have since published various other measures to identify the emergence of the disorder. Towle and Patrick (2016) systematically reviewed two Level I screening instruments: *Infant-Toddler Checklist* (ITC), *First Year Inventory* (FYI), and three Level II screening instruments: *Screening Test for Autism in Two-Year-Olds* (STAT), *Parent Observation of Early Milestones Scale* (POEMS), and *Autism Detection in Early Childhood* (ADEC). They concluded that (1) screening tools still need further development, and (2) autism surveillance and monitoring in the first year is important, but screening instruments should be used only for high-risk children.

Level I Screening Instruments

CHecklist for Autism in Toddlers (CHAT)

Baron-Cohen and colleagues (1992) developed the instrument to test 18-month-old participants at high risk for developing autism. One study selected high-risk infants for ASD and random 18-month-olds. The participants were tested on joint attention, pretend play, protodeclarative pointing, social interest, and social play. The four participants who failed to perform on at least two items received a diagnosis of autism by 30 months. The instrument was found to have low sensitivity (8%) based on the follow-up of a screened cohort of 18-month-olds (Baird et al., 2000).

The Infant-Toddler Checklist (ITC)

The Infant-Toddler Checklist (ITC) can identify signs of developmental delays that appear during an infant's first year before uttering the first meaningful word. Long before infants can speak, they emit sounds that are precursors of language. For example, Infants coo—i.e., they repeat vowel-like sounds such as "oooooh" and "aaaaah" at around 6–8 weeks of age. Between 4 and 6 months, they babble—i.e., utter consonant-vowel sounds such as "baba" or "dadadada." A parent (or a primary caregiver) can complete the ITC with infants at 6–24 months who show communication delays. The ITC is a broadband screener structured to identify infants and toddlers with communication delays, including children with autism (Wetherby et al., 2008).

The ITC comprises three broad developmental domains: Communication, expressive speech, and symbolic capacity. The instrument's 24 questions are further defined by six constructs (i.e., emotion and eye gaze, gestures, sounds, words, understanding, and object use). However, the screener does not reliably distinguish children with autism from those with other developmental disabilities.

First Year Inventory (FYI)

The First Year Inventory (FYI) is a parent-report questionnaire structured to identify 12-month-old infants who might be at risk for developing autism or other developmental disabilities. The instrument consists of two developmental domains: Social communication and sensory regulatory functions, which are further defined by eight constructs (i.e., social-affective engagement, social orienting and receptive communication, expressive communication, imitation, reactivity, regulatory patterns, sensory processing, and repetitive behavior). The instrument's 63 items were constructed based on retrospective video analysis of 9–12-month-old infants subsequently diagnosed with autism and prospective studies of diagnostic outcomes in 1-year-old infants.

The instrument's validation was conducted in various studies and included at least one of its developers. Reznick and colleagues (2007) conducted a normative survey of a large community sample. They found that boys had higher risk scores than girls and a small number of participants (modest sensitivity) with elevated risk for developing autism. Longitudinal studies to determine whether FYI can reliably predict autism are warranted. Watson and colleagues (2007) evaluated the FYI's construct validity. Parents' retrospective responses of preschoolers with ASD, other developmental disabilities, and typical development indicated significantly higher risk ratings for children with autism than those in the other two groups. Turner-Brown and colleagues (2013) performed a longitudinal follow-up of a community sample of 699 children at 3 years. Their parents completed the FYI when they were 12 months old. The findings suggest that FYI is a promising instrument for identifying infants who will develop autism.

More recently, Lee and colleagues (2021) examined the FYI's construct validity and compared it to other established tools in a cohort of high-risk infant siblings of children with ASD. The validity of an instrument is linked to the instrument's effectiveness and reliability. Except for the sensory-regulatory domain, which showed minimal consistency with other instruments, perhaps due to the FYI domain's unique feature, the social communication domain showed significant commonality with different Level I screeners.

Early Screening of Autistic Traits Questionnaire (ESAT)

The 19-item questionnaire is designed for 14-month-old infants. Health practitioners typically administer the questionnaire at well-baby visits. If a parent answers "no" to more than three questions, the child is eligible for ongoing screening and will undergo a diagnostic evaluation. The instrument was found to have a low positive predictive value of 0.25 (Dietz et al., 2006). Based on a review of broadband screening tools (Zwaigenbaum et al., 2015), additional data is needed before recommending the use of the ESAT as a screening tool.

Modified Checklist for Autism in Toddlers (M-CHAT-R/F)

Robins and Dumont-Mathieu (2006) developed the M-CHAT based on the CHAT. Subsequently, Robins and her colleagues (2014) updated the M-CHAT and added R/F (Revised with Follow up). The instrument is structured for toddlers between 16–30 months and consists of 20 questions that can be scored in less than 2 minutes. For example, one question testing for joint attention is phrased as follows: "If you point to something across the room, does your child look at it?" The instrument has high sensitivity, which results in high false positive rates. Therefore, not all children identified as at risk will develop autism. The follow-up questions can reduce the false positive rates. However, even children who still fail the M-CHAT-R/F may not develop autism but may be at risk for developing other related developmental disorders. Because of its ease of administration, the M-CHAT is an instrument that pediatricians in many parts of the world use to screen for ASD. A positive result usually leads to a recommendation for further evaluation. Screening tools are just that! Screening tools have their limitations.

Aishworiya and colleagues (2023) conducted a meta-analysis that included 15 studies conducted between 2014 and 2021 with more than 49,000 children from 10 countries and found that the positive predictive value (i.e., the probability of obtaining a diagnosis of autism following a positive screen) was 57.7%. The positive predictive value was higher (75.6%) for children at higher risk (e.g., those with an autistic sibling) but significantly lower (51.2%) for those not identified as at risk. The negative predictive value was 72.5%—i.e., approximately 25% of children who did not fail the test were diagnosed with autism when further assessed. M-CHAT-R/F had good sensitivity, poor specificity, and negative predictive value. The authors support using the instrument as a screening tool for autism.

Autism Spectrum Quotient

The Autism Spectrum Quotient (ASD/AQ) is an adult self-report questionnaire. The instrument contains 50 questions that assess five core areas: (1) communication, (2) social skills, (3) imagination, (4) attention to detail, and (5) attention switching (Baron-Cohen et al., 2001). The AQ has been developed to measure the extent to which typically developing adults with average and above intelligence have autistic characteristics. Therefore, the instrument may identify functioning adults with Asperger syndrome or high-functioning autism. One study tested the AQ's diagnostic validity and found that it has "good discriminative validity" and "good screening properties" (Woodbury-Smith, 2005).

The AQ has been adapted to quantify autism traits in children and adolescents. The AQ-Child was administered to a cohort of autistic children and a cohort selected from the general population. Composite scores from the two groups indicated a significant difference between them. The study results showed that the screener has good test-retest reliability, high internal consistency, high sensitivity (95%), and high specificity (95%). However, it is not known how the instrument would perform in population screening (Auyeung et al., 2008). Another study evaluated three groups of adolescents: One group with classic autism, another with Asperger's disorder, and a third group of typically developing adolescents. There was no marked difference between the classic autism group and the Asperger group, but they scored significantly higher on autism traits than the control group (Baron-Cohen et al., 2006). The AQ can readily quantify where an individual falls on the autism-normalcy continuum.

DISCO Signposting Set

The DISCO Signposting Set (DISCO) questionnaire contains 14 items selected from the DISCO (Carrington et al., 2014). The Diagnostic Interview for Social Communication Disorder (DISCO) was developed in the 1970s to conduct research in the epidemiology of autism. The signposting set of 14 highly discriminating items was selected from the DISCO because of their predictive validity with individuals with autism compared to those with intellectual disabilities or language impairments (Carrington et al., 2014). Eleven items are related to social-communication disorders, and the remaining three items target the sub-domains of "stereotyped or repetitive motor movement, use of objects or speech" or "**insistence on sameness**, inflexible adherence to routines, or ritualised patterns of verbal or non-verbal behaviours" (Carrington et al., 2015, p. 46).

A clinician interviews a parent (or caregiver) or the adult to be assessed and scores the assessment. The DISCO Signposting Set interview informs clinicians about supplementing the assessment with a more detailed clinical evaluation. One study with the DISCO Signposting Set indicated high specificity, sensitivity, and strong concordance with the DSM-5 diagnostic criteria (Carrington et al., 2015).

Social Communication Questionnaire

The Social Communication Questionnaire (SCQ) contains 40 questions (e.g., Difficulty in expressing needs or desires; is usually aloof and likes being left alone; difficulty in expressing needs or desires; yes-or-no) chosen from the Autism Diagnostic Interview-Revised—ADI-R (Rutter et al., 2003). Parents, caregivers, or people familiar with the developmental history and current behavior of the person being assessed complete the questionnaire. The instrument can quickly be completed in less than 10 minutes and scored in less than 5 minutes. In addition to its ease of application, the survey can inform clinicians and guide their clinical evaluations.

Social Responsiveness Scale

The Social Responsiveness Scale (SRS-2) is designed to identify the presence and severity of social impairment associated with ASD. The 65-item questionnaire encompasses a broad age range (3–99 years) that parents, caregivers, teachers, or others familiar with the person being assessed can complete in 15–20 minutes. The instrument is formatted for different age ranges. Each of the four formats comprises 65 questions: Preschool (ages 2.5–4.5); school-age (ages 4–18); adult (aged 19 or older); and adult self-report. The survey's total score not only captures the severity of social deficits but also provides scores on five subscales: Social awareness, social cognition, social motivation, social communication, and restricted interests and repetitive behavior. Two of the five subscales (i.e., social communication and restricted interests, and repetitive behavior) are consistent with the DSM-5. One study compared the SRS with the ADI-R and found a correlation of 0.7 and an inter-rater reliability of 0.8 (Constantino et al., 2003).

Quantitative CHecklist for Autism in Toddlers (Q-CHAT)

The Quantitative CHecklist for Autism in Toddlers (Q-CHAT) is based on a major revision of the CHAT (Baron-Cohen et al., 1992). The instrument measures autistic traits in children 18–24 months and contains 25 questions (e.g., "If you or someone else in the family is visibly upset, does your child show signs of wanting to comfort them—e.g., stroking their hair, hugging them?"). A preliminary report comparing a cohort of typical toddlers with a cohort of toddlers diagnosed with autism found that toddlers with ASD scored higher on the Q-CHAT than those in the control group. Boys in the control group scored higher on the instruments than girls (Allison et al., 2008).

Level II Screening Instruments

Parent Observation of Early Milestones Scale (POEMS)

The Parent Observation of Early Milestones Scale (POEMS) contains 61 items that caregivers can rate on a checklist to monitor the development of baby siblings of children with autism. The instrument tracks the emergence of ASD features based on behaviors that are characteristic of young children with autism (e.g., early social and communication deficits, difficulties with new foods, sleeping, and toileting). Feldman and colleagues (2012) reported adequate psychometric properties of the instrument. Another study found that high-risk children (i.e., baby siblings of children with autism) consistently scored significantly higher on the measures at 12, 18, 24, 30, and 36 months of age (Feldman et al., 2015). As a recently developed tool, future investigations, including multi-center studies of the instrument, are warranted to determine its sensitivity and specificity levels (Towle & Patrick, 2016).

Brewer and colleagues (2020) examined in peer-reviewed journals five Level II screeners (i.e., the ADEC, the BISCUIT, the RITA-T, the STAT, and the SORF) and their implementation. They reported limitations of the screeners in terms of reliability, sample sizes, and limited participation of independent researchers.

Autism Detection in Early Childhood (ADEC)

The Autism Detection in Early Childhood (ADEC) is a play-based screener that assesses the presence of ASD in children 12–36 months of age. The instrument contains 16 items that are based on three domains: (1) difficulties interacting with others and objects, (2) stereotyped and repetitive movements, and (3) unusual responses to environmental stimuli. Play-like sessions involve the tester, the child being assessed, and a parent or caregiver. The instrument is easy to administer by personnel with minimal training and experience with autism.

One study that compared a cohort of children with autism with another comprised of typically developing children found that the instrument has high internal consistency, adequate interrater reliability, and test-retest reliability (Nah et al., 2014). Hedley and colleagues (2015) examined the psychometric property of the ADEC and found that it has good sensitivity but poor specificity. Similarly, Dix and colleagues (2015) identified three behaviors that predict autism: gaze switching, gaze monitoring, and response to name. The instrument had good sensitivity and moderate specificity at 87.5% and 62%, respectively. The ADEC shows promise as a screening tool, as it can differentiate between children with autism and those who have developmental delays, namely specific communication disorders.

Baby and Infant Screen for Children with aUtIsm Traits (BISCUIT)

The Baby and Infant Screen for Children with aUtIsm Traits (BISCUIT) is an informant interview with the child's primary caregiver. It comprises a triad of assessments structured for infants and toddlers (17–37 months). Part 1 assesses the core symptoms of autism (e.g., verbal communication, eye contact). Part 2 evaluates comorbid conditions (e.g., eating difficulties, **obsessive-compulsive disorder**, and attention deficit activity disorder). Part 3 evaluates problem behaviors (e.g., self-injurious and stereotypic behaviors). Studies evaluating the psychometric properties of the instruments have been carried out by the instrument's developing team. They have reported adequate validity, sensitivity, and specificity (Matson et al., 2009; Matson et al., 2010; Horovitz & Matson, 2014).

Rapid Interactive (Screening) Test for Autism in Toddlers (RITA-T)

The Rapid Interactive (Screening) Test for Autism in Toddlers (RITA-T) is structured for infants and toddlers aged 18–36 months. The screener can be administered and scored in about 10 minutes with minimal administrator training required. The instrument includes nine semi-structured play-based activities that are based on defined constructs based on the DSM-IV-TR and the DSM-5 (e.g., joint attention, communication, social awareness), generally delayed in children with autism.

One study evaluated the instrument's performance in distinguishing toddlers with ASD from toddlers with developmental delays and typically developing toddlers. RITA-T had a sensitivity of 1.00, a specificity of 0.84, and a positive predictive value of 0.88 for identifying autism in high-risk toddler cohorts (Choueiri & Wagner, 2015). Another study conducted with a larger cohort referred to a pediatric care center examined the discriminative psychometric properties of the instrument and found that it had a sensitivity of 0.97, specificity of 0.71, positive predictive value of 0.95, and negative predictive value of 0.79 (Lemay et al., 2020).

Screening Tool for Autism in Toddlers and Young Children (STAT)

The Screening Tool for Autism in Toddlers and Young Children (STAT) is an interactive tool based on observing 24- to 36-month-old-children's communication, imitation, and social-communicative behavior in play. It is designed to be administered to children suspected of having developmental problems. It comprises 12 activities that can be completed in 20 minutes. The instrument has high sensitivity and specificity, 92% and 85%, respectively (Stone et al., 2004). One exploratory study found that the STAT could also be used with infants 14 to 23 months (Stone et al., 2008). Unlike parent questionnaires (e.g., M-CHAT), the administration of the STAT requires training and a higher level of expertise.

Systematic Observation of Red Flags (SORF)

The Systematic Observation of Red Flags (SORF) is an observation-based screener structured to identify signs of autism in toddlers. The instrument is based on the DSM-5 diagnostic criteria: (1) Impairment in social communication and social interaction and (2) restricted repetitive behavior, interests, and activities. The instrument can be administered to infants 16 to 24 months of age. Each diagnostic criterion comprises 11 questions (e.g., Repetitive speech or intonation; less interest in people than objects; flat affect or reduced facial expression). Studies that investigated the psychometric properties of the SORF found that poor eye gaze, limited pointing, and less interest in people than objects could be identified even in video-recorded clips of parent-child interaction in the home (Dow et al., 2020) and good discrimination, sensitivity, and specificity of the instrument when administered to children with autism and typically developing ones (Dow et al., 2017).

ASD Assessment Scale/Screening Questionnaire (ASSQ)

The ASD Assessment Scale/Screening Questionnaire (ASSQ) is an experimental instrument based on the DSM-5 diagnostic criteria for autism. The instrument consists of a 27-question assessment intended for completion by parents or teachers of children or adolescents aged 6 to 17. It is specifically designed as an initial screening tool for autism spectrum disorder (ASD), particularly for individuals with high or average IQ or those with mild intellectual disabilities.

The questionnaire targets young children's Social Interaction Difficulties (e.g., ignores when called, pervasive ignoring, not turning head to voice), Speech and Language Delay (e.g., no spontaneous initiation of speech and communication), and Abnormal Symbolic Play (e.g., obsessed with objects or topics—trains, weather, numbers, dates).

The Gilliam Autism Rating Scale (GARS)

Eric Gilliam developed the Gilliam Autism Rating Scale (GARS) in the 1990s as a diagnostic tool to help identify autism in individuals between the ages of 3 and 22. The instrument has been revised numerous times (e.g., GARS-2 and GAR-3). GARS-3 contains 56 questions that are structured to assess behavior associated with autism. Clinicians, parents, and teachers can administer the assessment in approximately 20 to 30 minutes.

The GARS-3 assessment provides four probability levels regarding the likelihood of autism: Level 0: An autism index score of 54 or lower indicates a low probability of autism. Level 1: An autism index score between 55 and 70 suggests the presence of autism that requires minimal support. Level 2: An autism index score between 71 and 100 indicates a strong likelihood of autism, which requires substantial support. Level 3: An autism index score of 101 or higher confirms the presence of autism. These indexes help quantify the severity of the symptoms and the likelihood of an autism spectrum disorder diagnosis. GARS is helpful for screening and assessing autism symptoms; however, comprehensive evaluations, including clinical assessments and additional testing, are essential for accurately diagnosing autism spectrum disorder.

Computer-Aided Screening

The use of digital and information technology is worth exploring to improve the accuracy and speed of ASD screening administration. One prospective study compared the effectiveness of the M-CHAT administered electronically versus in a paper format in an outpatient clinic setting. The electronic completion of the instrument resulted in fewer false-positive findings (3%) compared with the paper format (11%). More importantly, parents rated their experience with electronic completion positively (Harrington et al., 2013). Based on findings that autistic individuals have more interest in scanning non-feature areas of the face than core areas—i.e., eyes, nose, and mouth—(Pelphrey et al., 2002) and preliminary evidence (Vabalas & Freeth, 2016) that individuals with "high autistic traits" showed reduced visual exploration (i.e., shorter and less frequent saccades) than typical individuals during face-to-face interaction, one recent report explored the combination of visualization, eye tracking, and machine learning to develop an objective screening tool for autism (Cilia et al., 2021).

Systematic Review and Evaluation of Screening Instruments

One comprehensive review of 37 different autism screening tools classifies them into three categories: (1) screening tools for infants and toddlers, (2) screening tools for adolescents and adults, and (3) hybrid screening—screeners that encompass at least three of the following groups: infants, toddlers, adolescents, and adults (Thabtah & Peebles, 2019). Petrocchi and colleagues (2020) systematically reviewed Level I and II screening tools and their psychometric properties (i.e., validity, negative predictive value, positive predictive value, sensitivity, and specificity) for detecting autism under 24 months of age. Although they highlighted the need to validate the measures in the studies they had reviewed, they identified the M-CHAT, the First Year Inventory (FYI), and the Quantitative CHecklist for Autism in Toddlers (Q-CHAT) as "promising measures" that clinicians and researchers can use to detect autism systematically. Fekar-Gharamaleki and colleagues (2021) reviewed 19 autism screening tests. They found that the Autism Spectrum Quotient had the shortest administration time. The Gilliam autism rating scale takes longer to administer. They also found CARS-2 (Children Autism Rating Scale, Second Edition) the most widely used and validated assessment for autism.

Levy and colleagues (2020) systematically reviewed the psychometric properties of various autism screening tools implemented in primary care and primary care-life settings. They found significant evidence that they can be used to identify percentages of infants and toddlers between 16 and 40 months of age with autism in the general population. Many studies (e.g., Chlebowski et al., 2013; Wetherby et al., 2008) have found the positive predictive value (PPV) of screeners as approximately 50% and much higher PPV (approximately 95%) in their ability to identify other developmental conditions (Chlebowski et al., 2013).

García-Primo and colleagues (2014) identified 18 screening procedures for autism. They acknowledged how various factors and settings can influence the performance of those tools, making it difficult to determine which tool is most effective. They identified several factors that can facilitate researchers' and clinicians' choice of a particular screener and better inform them of the various factors in the screening process. Among the more pressing recommendations are (1) age at screening—screening at a younger age can result in higher rates of false positives and difficulty differentiating ASD from other developmental disorders; (2) level of functioning and autism severity—children not identified as at risk for autism but subsequently diagnosed with autism may be those who function at the less severe end of the spectrum. Therefore, the characteristics of the sample used must be considered when evaluating the psychometric properties of screening instruments; (3) parental non-compliance rate—socio-economic, ethnocultural, and age-related factors can determine parental compliance and non-compliance with screening. Even with compliant parents, limiting the number of assessments a child has to complete may make parents more amenable to completing the process. The stigma associated with a diagnosis of autism may cause less-educated parents not to have their children assessed and potentially receive a diagnosis.

Zwaigenbaum and colleagues (2015) reviewed the effectiveness of screening tools in peer-reviewed articles. They concluded that screening infants and toddlers aged 18–24 months in large community samples can lead to early detection of autism. They also proposed various strategies regarding early screening that researchers and clinicians should consider: (1) although early autism-specific can be informative, such practice is associated with higher false-positive rates than screening performed after 24 months; (2) there is overwhelming evidence indicating that siblings of children with autism have a higher-than-average risk of developing the disorder. Therefore, they should receive more targeted screening, clinical diagnostic evaluation, and treatment; and (3) considering the diversity of screening instruments that have been developed, more independent reviews of those instruments are warranted. Autism researchers and clinicians must undertake rigorous research methodology to establish adequate validity, sensitivity, specificity, and predictive values of those instruments.

Summary

Screening instruments for autism can identify infants, toddlers, and others at risk for developing autism. Although researchers and clinicians do not use screeners to establish a diagnosis of autism, the information those instruments provide can inform them whether to conduct more systematic assessments to diagnose autism. In addition to regular developmental surveillance and screening, the American Academy of Pediatrics (AAP) recommends screening all infants for autism spectrum disorder at the 18- and 24-month well-child visits. Screeners are categorized as Level I and Level II. Level I screeners are not autism-specific. They are used in large-scale screening to identify at-risk children for various developmental disorders (including autism) in the general population. Level II screeners help researchers and clinicians distinguish children with signs of autism from others at risk for other developmental conditions.

Screening tools must have adequate psychometric properties indicating validity, sensitivity, specificity, and predictive value. The instruments described in this chapter are by no means exhaustive. They are some of the screeners researchers and clinicians use to evaluate infants and young children. The Checklist for Autism in Toddlers (CHAT) was the first screening tool developed in the 1990s to assess 18-month-olds' risk for autism. The Modified Checklist for Autism in Toddlers (M-CHAT), the Modified Checklist for Toddlers, Revised with Follow-up M-CHAT-R/F, and the Quantitative CHecklist for Autism in Toddlers (Q-CHAT) are derivatives of the initial CHAT and adapted to be more effective or to screen different populations. Except for the Autism Spectrum Quotient (ASD/AQ), an adult self-report questionnaire, the Level I and Level II screeners described in the chapter are structured for infants and toddlers and have varying degrees of psychometric properties.

Extensive reviews of existing screening instruments by their own developers and research teams caution researchers and clinicians to be mindful that more independent reviews are warranted. Computer technology and artificial intelligence will undoubtedly enhance the development of more accurate screening tools. More importantly, screening instruments must be continually revised to reflect potential changes in the diagnostic criteria described in the ever-evolving DSM and the ICD.

Questions to Ponder for Further Thinking and Learning

1   Compare Level I to Level II screeners presented in the chapter and discuss their role in helping formulate an autism diagnosis.
2   Considering that a diagnosis of autism may lead to stigma, and therefore isolation and confusion, why is it necessary to diagnose a person with autistic characteristics?
3   Siblings of children with autism have a higher risk of developing autism and other developmental disorders. Should they be screened more than children in the general population? If you were a clinician, which instrument described in the chapter would you use to screen a child at risk for developing autism?
4   A diagnosis of autism is based on DSM and ICD criteria that are constantly evolving. Should screening tools be periodically revised to reflect the most recent diagnostic criteria?
5   Must researchers and clinicians combine forces to develop more effective screening tools with high psychometric properties instead of working in isolation and developing newer screening tools?
6   Should researchers and clinicians endeavor to use technological advances, artificial intelligence, and machine learning to develop more effective screening tools?

References

Aishworiya, R., Ma, V. K., Hagerman, R., & Feldman, H. M. (2023). Meta-analysis of the Modified Checklist for Autism in Toddlers, Revised/Follow-up for screening. *Pediatrics*, *151*(6), e2022059393.

Allison, C., Baron-Cohen, S., Wheelwright, S., Charman, T., Richler, J., Pasco, G., & Brayne, C. (2008). The Q-CHAT (Quantitative CHecklist for Autism in Toddlers): A normally distributed quantitative measure of autistic traits at 18–24 months of age: Preliminary report. *Journal of Autism and Developmental Disorders*, *38*(8), 1414–1425.

Auyeung, B., Baron-Cohen, S., Wheelwright, S., & Allison, C. (2008). The Autism spectrum quotient: Children's version (AQ-Child). *Journal of Autism and Developmental Disorders*, *38*(7), 1230–1240.

Baird, G., Charman, T., Baron-Cohen, S., Cox, A., Swettenham, J., Wheelwright, S., & Drew, A. (2000). A screening instrument for autism at 18 months of age: A 6-year follow-up study. *Journal of the American Academy of Child & Adolescent Psychiatry*, *39*(6), 694–702.

Baron-Cohen, S., Allen, J., & Gillberg, C. (1992) Can autism be detected at 18 months? The needle, the haystack, and the CHAT. *British Journal of Psychiatry*, *161*, 839–843.

Baron-Cohen, S., Hoekstra, R. A., Knickmeyer, R., & Wheelwright, S. (2006). The autism-spectrum quotient (AQ)—Adolescent version. *Journal of Autism and Developmental Disorders*, *36*(3), 343–350.

Baron-Cohen, S., Wheelwright, S., Skinner, R., Martin, J., & Clubley, E. (2001). The autism-spectrum quotient (AQ): Evidence from Asperger syndrome/high-functioning autism, males and females, scientists and mathematicians. *Journal of Autism and Developmental Disorders*, *31*(1), 5–17.

Brewer, N., Young, R. L., & Lucas, C. A. (2020). Autism screening in early childhood: Discriminating autism from other developmental concerns. *Frontiers in Neurology*, *11*, 594381.

Carrington, S. J., Kent, R. G., Maljaars, J., Le Couteur, A., Gould, J., Wing, L., ... Leekam, S. R. (2014). *DSM-5* autism spectrum disorder: In search of essential behaviours for diagnosis. *Research in Autism Spectrum Disorders*, *8*(6), 701–715.

Carrington, S., Leekam, S., Kent, R., Maljaars, J., Gould, J., Wing, L., ... Noens, I. (2015). Signposting for diagnosis of autism spectrum disorder using the Diagnostic Interview for Social and Communication Disorders (DISCO). *Research in Autism Spectrum Disorders*, *9*, 45–52.

Chlebowski, C., Robins, D. L., Barton, M. L., & Fein, D. (2013). Large-scale use of the modified checklist for autism in low-risk toddlers. *Pediatrics*, *131*(4), e1121–e1127.

Choueiri, R., & Wagner, S. (2015). A new interactive screening test for autism spectrum disorders in toddlers. *The Journal of Pediatrics*, *167*(2), 460–466.

Cilia, F., Carette, R., Elbattah, M., Dequen, G., Guérin, J. L., Bosche, J., ... Le Driant, B. (2021). Computer-aided screening of autism spectrum disorder: Eye-tracking study using data visualization and deep learning. *JMIR Human Factors*, *8*(4), e27706.

Constantino, J. N., Davis, S. A., Todd, R. D., Schindler, M. K., Gross, M. M., Brophy, S. L., ... Reich, W. (2003). Validation of a brief quantitative measure of autistic traits: Comparison of the social responsiveness scale with the autism diagnostic interview-revised. *Journal of Autism and Developmental Disorders*, *33*(4), 427–433.

Coury, D. L. (2015). Babies, bathwater, and screening for autism spectrum disorder: Comments on the USPSTF recommendations for autism spectrum disorder screening. *Journal of Developmental and Behavioral Pediatrics*, *36*(9), 661–663.

Dietz, C., Swinkels, S., van Daalen, E., van Engeland, H., & Buitelaar, J. K. (2006). Screening for autistic spectrum disorder in children aged 14–15 months. II: Population screening with the Early Screening of Autistic Traits Questionnaire (ESAT). Design and general findings. *Journal of Autism and Developmental Disorders*, *36*(6), 713–722.

Dix, L., Fallows, R., & Murphy, G. (2015). Effectiveness of the ADEC as a Level 2 screening test for young children with suspected autism spectrum disorders in a clinical setting. *Journal of Intellectual and Developmental Disability*, *40*(2), 179–188.

Dow, D., Day, T. N., Kutta, T. J., Nottke, C., & Wetherby, A. M. (2020). Screening for autism spectrum disorder in a naturalistic home setting using the systematic observation of red flags (SORF) at 18–24 months. *Autism Research*, *13*(1), 122–133.

Dow, D., Guthrie, W., Stronach, S. T., & Wetherby, A. M. (2017). Psychometric analysis of the Systematic Observation of Red Flags for autism spectrum disorder in toddlers. *Autism*, *21*(3), 301–309.

Dumont-Mathieu, T., & Fein, D. (2005). Screening for autism in young children: The Modified Checklist for Autism in Toddlers (M-CHAT) and other measures. *Mental Retardation and Development Disabilities Research Reviews*, *11*(3), 253–262.

Fekar-Gharamaleki, F., Bahrami, B., & Masumi, J. (2021). Autism screening tests: A narrative review. *Journal of Public Health Research*, *11*(1), 2308.

Feldman, M. A., Hendry, A. M., Ward, R. A., Hudson, M., & Liu, X. (2015). Behavioral development and sociodemographics of infants and young children at higher and lower risk for autism spectrum disorders. *Journal of Autism and Developmental Disorders*, *45*(5), 1167–1175.

Feldman, M. A., Ward, R. A., Savona, D., Regehr, K., Parker, K., Hudson, M., ... Holden, J. J. (2012). Development and initial validation of a parent report measure of the behavioral development of infants at risk for autism spectrum disorders. *Journal of Autism and Developmental Disorders*, *42*(1), 13–22.

García-Primo, P., Hellendoorn, A., Charman, T., Roeyers, H., Dereu, M., Roge, B., ... Canal-Bedia, R. (2014). Screening for autism spectrum disorders: State of the art in Europe. *European Child and Adolescent Psychiatry*, *23*(11), 1005–1021.

Glascoe, F. P. (2002). Evidence-based approach to developmental and behavioural surveillance   parents' concerns. *Child: Care, Health, and Development*, *26*(2), 137–149.

Harrington, J. W., Bai, R., & Perkins, A. M. (2013). Screening children for autism in an urban   clinic using an electronic M-CHAT. *Clinical Pediatrics*, *52*(1), 35–41.

Hedley, D., Nevill, R. E., Monroy-Moreno, Y., Fields, N., Wilkins, J., Butter, E., & Mulick, J. A. (2015). Efficacy of the ADEC in identifying autism spectrum disorder in clinically referred toddlers in the US. *Journal of Autism and Developmental Disorders*, *45*(8), 2337–2348.

Horovitz, M., & Matson, J. L. (2014). The baby and infant screen for children with autism traits-part 1: Age-based scoring procedures. *Journal of Developmental and Physical Disabilities*, *26*(1), 1–22.

Johnson, C. P., Myers, S. M., & American Academy of Pediatrics Council on Children with Disabilities. (2007). Identification and evaluation of children with autism spectrum disorders. *Pediatrics*, *120*(5), 1183–1215.

Lee, H. Y., Vigen, C., Zwaigenbaum, L., Smith, I. M., Brian, J., Watson, L. R., Crais, E. R., & Baranek, G. T. (2021). Construct validity of the First-Year Inventory (FYI Version 2.0) in 12-month-olds at high-risk for autism spectrum disorder. *Autism*, *25*(1), 33–43.

Lemay, J. F., Amin, P., Langenberger, S., & McLeod, S. (2020). Experience with the Rapid Interactive Test for Autism in Toddlers in an autism spectrum disorder diagnostic clinic. *Journal of Developmental and Behavioral Pediatrics*, *41*(2), 95–103.

Levy, S. E., Wolfe, A., Coury, D., Duby, J., Farmer, J., Schor, E., ... Warren, Z. (2020). Screening tools for autism spectrum disorder in primary care: A systematic evidence review. *Pediatrics*, *145*(S1), S47–S59.

Matson, J. L., Boisjoli, J. A., Hess, J. A., & Wilkins, J. (2010). Factor structure and diagnostic fidelity of the baby and infant screen for children with autism traits-Part 1 (BISCUIT-part 1). *Developmental Neurorehabilitation*, *13*(2), 72–79.

Matson, J. L., Wilkins, J., Sevin, J. A., Knight, C., Boisjoli, J. A., & Sharp, B. (2009). Reliability and item content of the Baby and Infant Screen for Children with autism Traits (BISCUIT): Parts 1–3. *Research in Autism Spectrum Disorders, 3*(2), 336–344.

Moss, J., & Howlin, P. (2009). Autism spectrum disorders in genetic syndromes: Implications for diagnosis, intervention and understanding the wider autism spectrum disorder population. *Journal of Intellectual Disability Research, 53*(10), 852–873.

Nah, Y. H., Young, R. L., Brewer, N., & Berlingeri, G. (2014). Autism detection in early childhood (ADEC): Reliability and validity data for a Level 2 screening tool for autistic disorder. *Psychological Assessment, 26*(1), 215–226.

Ozonoff, S., Young, G. S., Carter, A., Messinger, D., Yirmiya, N., Zwaigenbaum, L., ... Stone, W. L. (2011). Recurrence risk for autism spectrum disorders: A baby siblings research consortium study. *Pediatrics, 128*(3), e488–e495.

Pelphrey, K. A., Sasson N. J., Reznick, S., Paul, G., Goldman, B. D., & Piven, J. (2002). Visual scanning of faces in autism. *Journal of Autism and Developmental Disorders, 32*(4), 249–261.

Petrocchi, S., Levante, A., & Lecciso, F. (2020). Systematic review of level 1 and level 2 screening tools for autism spectrum disorders in toddlers. *Brain Sciences, 10*(3), 180.

Reznick, J. S., Baranek, G. T., Reavis, S., Watson, L. R., & Crais, E. R. (2007). A parent-report instrument for identifying one-year-olds at risk for an eventual diagnosis of autism: The first year inventory. *Journal of Autism and Developmental Disorders, 37*(9), 1691–1710.

Robins, D. L., Casagrande, K., Barton, M., Chen, C. M. A., Dumont-Mathieu, T., & Fein, D. (2014). Validation of the modified checklist for autism in toddlers, revised with follow-up (M-CHAT-R/F). *Pediatrics, 133*(1), 37–45.

Robins, D. L., & Dumont-Mathieu, T. M. (2006). Early screening for autism spectrum disorders: Update on the modified checklist for autism in toddlers and other measures. *Journal of Developmental and Behavioral Pediatrics, 27*(2), S111–S119.

Rutter, M., Bailey, A., & Lord, C. (2003). *The Social Communication Questionnaire.* Western Psychological Services.

Siu, A. L., US Preventive Services Task Force (USPSTF), Bibbins-Domingo, K., Grossman, D. C., Baumann, L. C., Davidson, K. W., ... Pignone, M. P. (2016). Screening for autism spectrum disorder in young children: US preventive services task force recommendation statement. *JAMA, 315*(7), 691–696.

Squires, J., Nickel, R. E., & Eisert, D. (1996). Early detection of developmental problems: Strategies for monitoring young children in the practice setting. *Journal of Developmental and Behavioral Pediatrics, 17*(6), 420–427.

Stone, W. L., Coonrod, E. E., Turner, L. M., & Pozdol, S. L. (2004). Psychometric properties of the STAT for early autism screening. *Journal of Autism and Developmental Disorders, 34*(6), 691–701.

Stone, W. L., McMahon, C. R., & Henderson, L. M. (2008). Use of the Screening Tool for Autism in Two-Year-Olds (STAT) for children under 24 months: An exploratory study. *Autism, 12*(5), 557–573.

Thabtah, F., & Peebles, D. (2019). Early autism screening: A comprehensive review. *International Journal of Environmental Research and Public Health, 16* (18), 3502.

Towle, P. O., & Patrick, P. A. (2016). Autism spectrum disorder screening instruments for very young children: A systematic review. *Autism Research and Treatment, 2016*, 4624829.

Turner-Brown, L. M., Baranek, G. T., Reznick, J. S., Watson, L. R., & Crais, E. R. (2013). The First Year Inventory: A longitudinal follow-up of 12-month-olds to 3-year-old children. *Autism, 17*(5), 527–540.

Vabalas, A., & Freeth, M. (2016). Brief report: Patterns of eye movements in face to face conversation are associated with autistic traits: Evidence from a student sample. *Journal of Autism and Developmental Disorders, 46*(1), 305–314.

Watson, L. R., Baranek, G. T., Crais, E. R., Reznick, J., Dykstra, J., & Perryman, T. (2007). The first year inventory: Retrospective parent responses to a questionnaire designed to identify one-year-olds at risk for autism. *Journal of Autism and Developmental Disorders, 37*(1), 49–61.

Wetherby, A. M., Brosnan-Maddox, S., Peace, V., & Newton, L. (2008). Validation of the Infant-Toddler Checklist as a broadband screener for autism spectrum disorders from 9 to 24 months of age. *Autism, 12*(5), 487–511.

Woodbury-Smith, M. R., Robinson, J., Wheelwright, S., & Baron-Cohen, S. (2005). Screening adults for Asperger Syndrome using the AQ: A preliminary study of its diagnostic validity in clinical practice. *Journal of Autism and Developmental Disorders, 35*(3), 331–335.

Zwaigenbaum, L., Bauman, M. L., Fein, D., Pierce, K., Buie, T., Davis, P. A., ... Wagner, S. (2015). Early screening of autism spectrum disorder: Recommendations for practice and research. *Pediatrics, 136*(S1), S41–S59.

Zwaigenbaum, L., Bryson, S., & Garon, N. (2013). Early identification of autism spectrum disorders. *Behavioural Brain Research, 251*, 133–146.

Chapter 9

Diagnostic Tools

Chapter Contents

Introduction

The classification and diagnoses of medical and mental disorders originated in ancient times. Many cultures attributed mental illnesses to supernatural causes, including demonic possessions. The work and writing of Hippocrates (considered

DOI: 10.4324/9781003336266-12

the father of modern medicine) in the fourth century B.C. in ancient Greece and the writings and practice of Galen of Pergamon (an astute diagnostician) in the second century A.D. contributed immensely to treating afflicted individuals. In our modern era, the work of Emil Kraepelin (a German psychiatrist) in the second half of the 1800s and his publication of a comprehensive classification of psychological disorders and their related symptoms, presumably rooted in physiology, established the modern classification of diseases. Kraepelin established psychiatry as a clinical science based on solid empirical findings (Hoff, 2015). However, his ideas lost their dominance in the years that followed World War II, when psychodynamic perspectives dominated psychiatry.

Individuals in past centuries who displayed eccentric behaviors consistent with current autism diagnostic criteria were not diagnosed with a disorder. They were considered odd. The 20th-century trailblazers whose works I described in Chapter 1 (Sukhareva, Asperger, and Kanner) examined children with atypical behavior and labeled those children's behavior based on their clinical judgment. No diagnostic criteria existed in the first half of the 1900s. The Diagnostic and Statistical Manual of Mental Disorders (DSM) and the International Classification of Diseases (ICD), developed by the World Health Organization (WHO), established diagnostic criteria for diseases and disorders.

The term diagnosis comes from the Greek word *gnosis*, which means knowledge, and the prefix *dia*, which means through or across—i.e., knowledge acquired through investigation. In medical terminology, a diagnosis entails distinguishing or identifying a disease (e.g., ischemic heart disease or diabetes) from its signs and symptoms and distinguishing it from other diseases. Medical diagnoses may require a health history, physical exam, blood tests, biopsies, and imaging tests. Unlike medical diagnoses, diagnosing autism can be challenging. There are no reliable biomarkers to guide the process. Generally, diagnosticians review a child's developmental history and signs, symptoms, and behavior indicative of the condition to make a diagnosis. DSM and ICD diagnostic criteria are based not on objective laboratory measures but on consensus and clinical judgment of a cluster of symptoms.

Signs and symptoms of autism are usually apparent during the first years of life and most reliably during toddlerhood. The median age of diagnosis in the United States is above 4 years (Baio et al., 2018). Early screening allows clinicians to identify infants and toddlers at risk for developing the disorder. The American Academy of Pediatrics recommends universal screening during well-child visits, specifically for autism at 18 and 24 months (Johnson et al., 2007). Surprisingly, the U.S. Preventive Service Task Force published a report (based on limited evidence) not supporting universal screening for autism during well-child visits of infants and toddlers not showing signs of autism (Siu et al., 2016).

The Purpose and Benefit of a Diagnosis

A diagnosis of autism may help a family understand a child's behavior and difficulties navigating the social environment. A formal diagnosis of autism can also ensure that parents have access to available resources and that children receive evidence-based interventions as soon as possible to maximize positive optimal outcomes and take advantage of the developing brain's malleability and **plasticity**. An official diagnosis of autism can help parents understand why their child feels, thinks, communicates, and acts differently to others. The diagnosis can also rule out other conditions, including attention-deficit/hyperactivity disorder, schizophrenia, anxiety, and depression. Moreover, a diagnosis makes obtaining accommodation (e.g., a flexible work schedule) and needed support services more accessible.

Autism from Kanner to DSM

The diagnosis of autism has evolved since Kanner examined 11 children in his clinic in Baltimore in the 1930s and 1940s. Child psychiatry did not exist in the 1800s and the first half of the 1900s. Kanner (1957 [1935]) wrote the first textbook on child psychiatry and was considered the best-known child psychiatrist in the United States. Regarding diagnosis, Kanner (1957 [1935]) wrote:

> Psychiatric diagnosis is no longer the name of a 'disease' or 'condition.' It is no longer an end in itself. It has regained its rightful place between examination and treatment. It does justice to its etymologic origin; diagnosis derives from the Greek and means 'thorough knowledge.' Such knowledge, to be thorough, must include knowledge of the problem, of the factors which have produced it, of the patient who presents it.
>
> (Kanner, 1957 [1935], p. 209)

Donvan and Zucker (2016) documented Donald's (the first child Kanner examined) diagnostic process and Kanner's inability to label what he had observed. The condition did not match any of the labels he described in his textbook, despite examining Donald for the first time in 1938, again in 1939, and subsequently a third and fourth time. Kanner proposed the phrase "autistic disturbances of affective contact" to describe the behavior of the 11 children he observed. Kanner subsequently replaced his initial label of the disorder with "infantile autism"—that the condition is present in early childhood.

The International Classification of Diseases (ICD)

The ICD has evolved from the work of the French physician and botanist Francois Bossier de Sauvages de Lacroix in the 1700s. Recognizing the importance of disease classification, he distinguished 2,400 diseases that he further grouped into ten classes. William Farr, a British physician who pioneered the study of morbidity and mortality, and Jacob Marc d'Espine, a Swiss physician, were tasked during the first International Statistical Congress in 1853 to develop a classification system of causes of mortality that could be used internationally. Their work paved the way for Jacques Bertillon, a French physician and statistician who introduced the Bertillon Classification of Causes of Death in 1893 during a congress of the International Statistical Institute in Chicago. Bertillon's classification became the International List of Causes of Death, which was adopted in North America, updated, and published in 1900, 1910, 1920, 1929, and 1938.

The sixth revision of the manual included morbidity and mortality conditions and contained a section on psychiatric disorders. It was called the *Manual of the International Statistical Classification of Diseases, Injuries, and Causes of Death* (ICD). In 1948, the World Health Organization (WHO) became responsible for revising and publishing the manual. WHO updated and published the seventh and eighth editions in 1957 and 1968, respectively. It was not until the eighth revision and publication of the manual (ICD-8) that "infantile autism" was listed. The ninth (1979), tenth (1999), and eleventh (2019) editions have all included definitions and diagnostic criteria for autism.

ICD-11 Criteria for Autism Diagnosis

According to the ICD-11 (2019), three essential behavioral features must be present for a person to receive a classification of autism. First, the person must display "persistent deficits in the ability to initiate and sustain reciprocal social interaction and social communication," second, "a range of restricted, repetitive, and inflexible patterns of behavior, interests or activities that are clearly atypical or excessive for the individual's age and sociocultural context," and third, "symptoms should result in significant impairment in personal, family, social, educational, occupational or other important areas of functioning." Additionally, the onset of the disorder must have occurred early in development. Unlike the DSM-5, the ICD-11 distinguishes autism with and without an intellectual disability and endorses a medical model of the condition (Greaves-Lord et al., 2022).

The ICD-11, like the DSM-5, uses the term "autism spectrum disorder" and shares similar language and diagnostic criteria. However, there are several significant differences. First, the ICD-11 distinguishes between autism spectrum disorder (ASD) with and without intellectual disability. Second, clinicians are not required to assess a specific number of defining features for a diagnosis. Instead, they have the discretion to determine whether an individual's behaviors or traits align with the criteria for autism. Lastly, the ICD-11 de-emphasizes culturally specific criteria, as the manual is designed for global use.

The Diagnostic and Statistical Manual of Mental Disorders (DSM)

The DSM evolved from the need to classify and collect statistical data on mental disorders in the United States. During the sixth U.S. census in 1840, one single category was used: idiocy/insanity. Census information revealed a prevalence of insanity (among all African Americans), blindness, deafness, and dumbness, making the data questionable and thus useless (Gorwitz, 1974). As a result, the Association of Medical Superintendents of American Institutions for the Insane (aka The Original Thirteen) was formed in 1844. It consisted of 13 members, all affiliated with psychiatric institutions in the U.S. Their primary aim was to combine forces in collecting statistical information about mental illness and improve the treatment of patients in mental institutions. In 1892, the association became The American Medico-Psychological Association (AMA). It developed a new guide titled the *Statistical Manual for the Use of Institutions for the Insane*, which included twenty-two diagnoses. The guide was revised several times, and the *Manual for the Use of Hospitals of Mental Diseases* was re-titled. The AMA became the American Psychiatric Association (APA) in 1921.

During the period preceding World War II, psychiatry dealt with severely ill populations of patients confined in institutions. It became abundantly clear after the war that mental health problems can affect normal individuals. The notion that mental health disorders were reactions to a person's life circumstances was prevalent and promoted by Adolf Meyer (a Swiss psychiatrist), who coined the term psychobiology—the biologic or pathological origins of mental illnesses—to describe maladaptive responses to external stimuli (Scull & Schulkin, 2009). He played an influential role in the development of psychiatry in the U.S., and his ideas guided the development of Medical 203 (Lidz, 1966).

The War Department Technical Bulletin, Medical 203 (aka Medical 203), originated in the office of the Surgeon General of the U.S., William Menninger, a brigadier general and psychiatrist who was appointed head of psychiatry in the army. He played a significant role in promoting psychiatry and other mental health professions after World War II. Menninger's wartime experience and pioneering work assembling teams of psychiatrists, clinical psychologists, and clinical social workers meant he was uniquely qualified to address the mental health issues of soldiers coming home and experiencing combat exhaustion and the horror of war (Houts, 2000). Medical 203 was a reference manual developed to categorize medical and mental health problems.

Medical 203 influenced the development of the DSM-I (APA, 1952). Long before the first publication of the DSM-I, clinicians conceptualized and classified mental disorders, but there was little agreement among classification systems and operational definitions (Stengel, 1959). Neither Medical 203 nor DSM-I included separate sections for childhood disorders in their publications. The Diagnostic and Statistical Manual of Mental Disorders (DSM) became the authoritative guide to diagnose mental disorders and is used by healthcare professionals in the United States and other parts of the world. The manual contains diagnostic criteria for mental disorders that researchers and clinicians commonly use.

The DSM and ICD are produced and revised periodically but not concurrently. There has been little agreement between their diagnostic criteria. Through the years and recent publications, there has been a gradual rapprochement between the two publications. Currently, the DSM-5 and ICD-11 define autism as a spectrum disorder, emphasizing similar characteristics and criteria.

The Evolution of Autism Diagnosis in the DSMs

DSM-I (1952) classified children's odd behaviors under "mental disorder," which was associated with schizophrenia. The condition was coded and described as follows:

> 000-x28 Schizophrenic reaction, childhood type – Here will be classified those schizophrenic reactions occurring before puberty. The clinical picture may differ from schizophrenic reactions occurring in other age periods because of the immaturity and plasticity of the patient at the time of onset of the reaction. Psychotic reactions in children, manifesting primarily autism, will be classified here. Special symptomatology may be added to the diagnosis as manifestations.
>
> (p. 28)

The terminology and understanding of autism have evolved significantly since the DSM-I, reflecting research and clinical practice advancements.

The term "schizophrenia reaction, childhood type" in DSM-I was changed to "schizophrenia, childhood type" in DSM-II (APA, 1968). The word "reaction" was removed because it implied that the symptoms of autism could be temporary and triggered by external stressors rather than being a stable and enduring condition.

> 295.8. Schizophrenia, childhood type – This category is for cases in which schizophrenic symptoms appear before puberty. The condition may be manifested by autistic, atypical and withdrawn behavior; failure to develop identity separate from the mother's; and general unevenness, gross immaturity and inadequacy of development. These developmental defects may result in mental retardation, which should also be diagnosed.
>
> (p. 35)

The first and second editions of the DSM adopted Freud's psychodynamic view that mental disorders result from conflicts between internal drives. Autism was defined as a psychiatric condition manifested as childhood schizophrenia characterized by a detachment from reality. However, the realization that patients with identical symptoms received different diagnoses and treatments prompted some influential U.S. psychiatrists to turn their attention to the categorical approach Kraepelin, a German psychiatrist, developed, such as the classic division between bipolar disorder and schizophrenia. Genetics and brain-imaging research findings support that DSM disorders overlap and lie along a continuum, thus pointing to a dimensional approach to conceptualizing mental conditions rather than a categorical one. DSM diagnostic criteria still split them apart (Adam, 2013).

Feighner Criteria

Feighner and colleagues (1972) developed the Feighner criteria—diagnostic criteria to address the shortcomings of those in the DSM-II that were based essentially upon the dictates of a committee of experts and the "best clinical judgment and experience" of clinicians. Feighner and colleagues proposed a diagnostic classification based on five phases, including (1) a clinical description of the disorder, (2) laboratory findings, (3) delimitation (i.e., the clear boundary from other disorders), (4) follow-up study, and (5) family study. In their view, the clinical description of a disorder is important. Demographic characteristics, age of onset, and precipitating factors may also be considered, including laboratory tests and findings (when possible) that may provide a more reliable picture of the disorder, in addition to psychological testing. The exclusion of other conditions must be specified so that the one being considered is as homogeneous as possible. In addition, preexisting conditions that could have precipitated the manifest disorder must also be considered. Finally, the increased prevalence of the disorder among close relatives of the person being assessed can add to the validity of the diagnosis.

Spitzer and colleagues (1978) developed the Research Diagnostic Criteria (RDC) based on various influential psychiatric diagnostic criteria published in the 1970s (e.g., Robins & Guze, 1970) to address the widely varied diagnoses that existed in psychiatry. The RDC paved the way for the revision of the DSM-II and shaped the development of the DSM-III, which introduced the term "infantile autism" as a diagnosis separate from schizophrenia.

The DSM-III (APA, 1980) marked a significant departure from previous editions regarding aspects such as onset, social interaction, language development, speech patterns, engagement with the environment, and the absence of psychosis. It introduced the term "infantile autism" as a distinct condition, defining the following diagnostic criteria: (a) impairments in social interaction, (b) impairments in communication, and (c) restricted, repetitive patterns of behavior. These impairments must manifest before the age of 30 months. The criteria were based on the *triad of impairments* proposed by Wing and Gould in 1979, drawn from data collected during their epidemiological study published that same year. Their research and subsequent publication (Wing, 1996) led to a definition of the *autism spectrum*, which states that there are no distinct boundaries between autism symptoms in individuals diagnosed with the condition.

DSM-III-TR (APA, 1987) revised the term "infantile autism" to "childhood autism." This change reflected the evolving diagnostic criteria for autism spectrum disorders in highlighting that autism is not limited to infants but can also be diagnosed in children of various ages.

DSM-IV (APA, 1994) classified autism under a broad category of Pervasive Developmental Disorders comprised of five subcategories: (1) Autistic Disorder, (2) Asperger's Disorder, (3) Pervasive Developmental Disorder Not Otherwise Specified (PDD-NOS), (4) Childhood Disintegrative Disorder, and (5) Rett's

Disorder. These subcategories were subsumed under one umbrella term, autism spectrum disorder, in the DSM-5.

DSM-IV-TR (APA, 2000) diagnostic criteria for autism have not changed. However, the criteria format has been refined for clarity, making them more user-friendly for clinicians and improving overall understanding for better diagnostic practices. Additionally, clinicians were encouraged to account for cultural and environmental factors that may influence behavior and development.

DSM-5 (APA, 2013) reduced the triad of impairments to two defining diagnostic criteria: (1) persistent deficits in social communication and social interaction and (2) restricted, repetitive patterns of behavior, interests, or activities and subsumed all four subcategories of autism under one overarching term: "autism spectrum disorder" (ASD). This change in diagnostic criteria, especially the removal of Asperger's syndrome, sparked controversy among parents, researchers, clinicians, and advocacy groups. As an official diagnosis, ASD can be given with or without intellectual disability and with or without language impairment. Additionally, three severity levels were introduced: (1) "requiring support," (2) "requiring substantial support," and (3) "requiring very substantial support."

Although the DSM-5 incorporates some dimensional aspects in diagnosing mental disorders (e.g., specifiers that indicate the severity of a disorder), the manual primary framework is categorical, so individuals are generally diagnosed as fitting into one category or another. However, there is growing interest in a dimensional approach in research and clinical practice that better captures the complexity and variability of mental disorders (Adam, 2013).

One parent, in a newspaper column, sarcastically lauded the DSM-5 diagnostic criteria capacity to cure the condition overnight by a sleight of hand:

> To actually say that the overwhelming majority of persons diagnosed with some form of autism in the last two decades will no longer be considered autistic is Orwellian. How nice that the psychiatric community can somehow cure someone of autism overnight by changing the definition. Goodness, if we parents of autistic children knew that was the way to do it, we would have asked for this definition change decades ago. We did not need to go broke with therapists, doctors, neurologists, and special programs.
>
> (Independent Patriot Westchester County, 2012)

Conversely, Kupfer and Regier (2011) lauded the overall DSM-5 diagnostic classification:

> Beyond keeping pace with the science of psychiatry, many of the DSM-5's proposed changes represent an opportunity to improve the field from clinical and public health perspectives. The proposal for a single "autism spectrum disorder" category that would include the current DSM-IV diagnoses of autism disorder (autism), Asperger's disorder, childhood disintegrative

disorder, and pervasive developmental disorder not otherwise specified was born from data suggesting that these disorders share a pathophysiological substrate. Changes in the wording of the criteria, however, help clarify symptom manifestation and provide diagnosticians with a more accurate example of how these children actually appear in clinics.

(Kupfer & Regier, 2011, p. 673)

DSM-5-TR (APA, 2022) autism diagnostic criteria have not changed, except for the wording clarification of the phrase describing associated autism features, from "manifested by the following" to "as manifested by all of the following," namely (a) social-emotional reciprocity, (b) **nonverbal communication** behaviors used in social interactions, and (c) developing, maintaining, and understanding social relationships. Additionally, clinicians must ascertain whether the autism diagnosis is also associated with another neurodevelopmental, mental, or behavioral problem.

The Research Domain Criteria

The process of diagnosing mental illnesses based solely on symptoms without understanding their underlying causes can often lead to ineffective treatments. The National Institute of Mental Health (NIMH) launched the Research Domain Criteria (RDoC) initiative in 2009 to address this issue, with the primary aim to "transform the understanding and treatment of mental illnesses through basic and clinical research" (Cuthbert, 2015). The RDoC was conceived as a framework that goes beyond the established symptom-based diagnostic systems of the DSM and ICD. The framework incorporates biological, physiological, and behavioral data to capture the full spectrum of mental conditions to guide the classification of mental disorders based on neural circuit disruptions and develop a novel classification of psychopathology (Sanislow et al., 2010). Moreover, it addresses and overcomes the inherent heterogeneity and comorbidity of current diagnostic practices that have hampered research and the development of effective interventions.

Thomas Insel, who led the National Institute of Mental Health (NIMH) from 2002 until 2015, published a blog in 2013 before the publication of the DSM-5 in 2013. In the blog, he highlighted the limitations of the DSM approach in the following terms:

While DSM has been described as a 'Bible' for the field, it is, at best, a dictionary, creating a set of labels and defining each. The strength of each of the editions of DSM has been 'reliability'—each edition has ensured that clinicians use the same terms in the same ways. The weakness is its lack of validity. Unlike our definitions of ischemic heart disease, lymphoma, or AIDS, the DSM diagnoses are based on a consensus about clusters of clinical symptoms, not any objective laboratory measure.

The RDoC conceptualizes mental disorders as multidimensional and addresses two shortcomings of the DSM diagnostic criteria: (1) the DSM's categorical approach to psychiatric disorders and (2) the DSM's primary focus on clinical features (Hakak-Zargar et al., 2022). The goal of the RDoC framework is to identify neural circuit dysfunctions causing similar mental disorders instead of relying solely on overt behavior. Disruptions of neural circuits can either constitute or contribute to the pathophysiology of mental disorders. The RDoC proposed five domains that can support contributing evidence of neural circuits' implication in mental disorders: (1) negative affect, (2) positive affect, (3) cognition, (4) social processes, and (5) arousal/regulatory systems.

Symptom-based diagnoses without a clear understanding of the condition's root cause(s) being assessed seldom lead to the choice of treatment. Cognizant of this impediment to tailoring more precise interventions, the National Institute of Mental Health (NIMH) launched the Research Domain Criteria (RDoC) initiative to incorporate genetics, imaging, and cognitive science to lay the foundation of a new classification system, not to replace the DSM or the ICD but to improve the diagnosis of mental illnesses.

Autism is categorized as a developmental disorder rather than a mental health disorder. However, many individuals diagnosed with autism also face mental health challenges, such as anxiety, depression, and attention-deficit/hyperactivity disorder (ADHD), which can occur alongside autism. Neurodevelopmental disorders are often linked to atypical brain development or functioning, influenced by genetic, environmental, and psychosocial factors. The Research Domain Criteria (RDoC) framework offers a dimensional approach to understanding mental health and developmental disorders by focusing on underlying brain mechanisms rather than adhering strictly to categorical diagnoses. Additionally, the RDoC approach can lead to more personalized interventions and improve our understanding of co-occurring mental health challenges that individuals with autism face.

The Diagnosis Challenges of Autism

Cutting Nature at its Joint, and the Zone of Rarity

Unlike Plato's famous "carving" analogy for the reality of forms: "Like an animal, the world comes to us predivided. Ideally, our best theories will be those which carve nature at its joints" (Slater & Borghini, 2019). "Our best theories" could have been replaced by our best classification of disorders. Stone (2020) argued that the carving allegory, while helpful in differentiating species in the natural environment, does not enable researchers and clinicians to categorize mental disorders neatly. She noted that having a broken leg is not akin to having schizophrenia. The former is about having; the latter is about being.

No diagnostic tests have 100% specificity, so it is not unusual for individuals without a disorder to be diagnosed as having one. Cooper (2013) proposed several approaches to "avoid" **false positives**: the **zones of rarity**, the threshold determination, and the harm criterion. An individual may display some symptoms of a disorder but not enough to meet diagnostic criteria. Additionally, the cut-off points are generally arbitrary and do not show a clear separation between disorder and normalcy. Diagnosticians must ensure that people who depart from the norm are not diagnosed with a disorder. Kendell coined the term "zones of rarity" to describe the natural boundary separating mental disorders from one another and normality. Kendell and Jablensky (2003) argued that natural boundaries do not separate mental disorders as defined by symptom-based psychiatric criteria but overlap. Therefore, they may have diagnostic utility regarding treatment but questionable validity.

The difficulty in diagnosing ASD rests on its heterogeneity. The DSM-5, recognizing that people diagnosed with the condition can present a variety of symptoms, proposed the term "autism spectrum disorder" and specified three severity levels: Level 1 ("requiring support"), level 2 ("requiring substantial support"), and level 3 ("requiring very substantial support"). In other words, a person diagnosed with ASD could be at the lower end of the spectrum and may not need constant care and supervision. In contrast, a student with autism at the higher end of the spectrum who is enrolled in a university may need assistance with managing their class schedules and navigating the social environment. Despite the condition's heterogeneity, two characteristics are common: (1) difficulty in social interactions and (2) restrictive, repetitive patterns of behavior, interest, or activities. Interestingly, The DSM-5 diagnostic criteria mirror the characteristics Kanner observed and described several decades ago: (1) extreme aloneness since the beginning of life and (2) a desire to preserve sameness. Only the child himself can initiate the changes.

Biomarkers and Autism

Unlike biomarkers used in medicine (e.g., blood pressure, x-rays, or blood tests) to identify a disease or condition, no biomarkers exist to diagnose autism. Obtaining an accurate autism diagnosis is a vital step in getting the needed support and services for the condition. Clinicians and diagnosticians base their assessment of the condition not on physical appearance but on an individual's developmental history and the core symptoms of social/communication deficits and restricted, repetitive behavior as delineated in the DSM-5 and ICD-11. Given the heterogeneity of risk factors for autism (i.e., genetic and environmental), it is unlikely that a single biomarker will ever be developed to diagnose autism in all cases reliably (Anderson, 2014). Although the advancement of biomarkers research for autism is promising, many challenges (e.g., the heterogeneity of the condition, gender differences, the presence of co-occurring conditions, sensitivity, and methodological objectivity) must be addressed for biomarkers to have diagnosis utility (McPartland, 2016; Vargason et al., 2020).

Although the serotonin system in autism pathophysiology is not well understood, elevated whole-blood serotonin (hyperserotonemia) was the first biomarker identified in autism. Hyperserotonemia is the most consistent serotonin-related finding in autism. For example, Hranilovic and colleagues (2007) found higher platelet serotonin levels (PSL) in 53 autistic adults compared to 45 health controls. High levels of PSL correlated negatively with the participants' speech development and verbal abilities. Hyperserotonemia is present in more than 25% of children with autism (Muller et al., 2016). Frye and colleagues (2019) conducted a comprehensive review of potential biomarkers for autism. The study evaluated various biomarkers, including physiological, neurological, behavioral, genetic, and gastrointestinal markers. The authors found that these biomarkers show promise in identifying children at risk of developing autism. However, they emphasized that further validation is necessary before these biomarkers can be accurately used for diagnostic purposes.

Autism researchers have investigated various body systems to identify atypicalities that can help in developing potential biomarkers: Immunological (Warren et al., 1991), toxicological (Kern et al., 2011), gastrointestinal, and neurological (Tordjman et al., 2001). Effective biomarkers could identify biological changes specific to autism, a predisposition to developing autism, or identify the presence of the disorder. To date, there are no biomarkers that can reliably diagnose autism. Researchers are still investigating potential biomarkers, but none have been established for routine diagnostic use. The diagnosis of autism primarily relies on behavioral assessments and developmental history rather than biological tests.

Who Can Diagnose Autism?

No medical tests can help diagnose ASD, so clinicians rely primarily on the behaviors of infants (and older individuals) presented to their clinic and parental reports and concerns during well-child visits. Pediatricians are the first clinicians to screen infants and refer them for more comprehensive assessments if warranted. The American Academy of Pediatrics recommends screening all infants during well-child visits at 18 and 24 months for signs of ASD. A reliable autism diagnosis is best achieved with a multidisciplinary approach. Many healthcare professionals can diagnose ASD, including child psychologists, developmental pediatricians, pediatric neurologists, child and adolescent psychiatrists, and psychologists.

In some cases, trained specialists (e.g., speech-language pathologists and occupational therapists) may perform the evaluation. Combining the results of different assessment tools can result in a better-informed application of diagnostic criteria (Risi et al., 2006). ASD shares characteristics with other developmental disorders (e.g., social (pragmatic) communication disorder), so diagnosticians must make a **differential diagnosis**. Because of their training and extensive experience interacting with individuals with the condition, they can distinguish it from other disorders that present characteristics of ASD.

Before diagnosing, a diagnostician should consider three essential criteria: reliability, validity, and clinical utility. A reliable diagnosis must produce consistent results across different diagnosticians and settings (Spitzer et al., 1978). The clinical utility of a diagnosis refers to the valuable information it provides regarding the diagnosed person's characteristics and needs (Jablensky, 2016). Finally, the validity of a diagnosis is of utmost importance, as it determines whether it is accurate and can lead to successful interventions. **Nosology** is the study of the categorization of diseases or disorders. Thus, a valid nosological diagnosis must describe characteristics that arise from a shared underlying neurobiological cause (Kendell & Jablensky, 2003). According to Mandy (2018), the diagnosis of autism is heterogeneous and includes a broad range of individuals whose behavioral manifestations have various underlying mechanisms and causes. Furthermore, treatment approaches treat the condition as a single disorder rather than recognizing it as part of a broader spectrum of neurodevelopmental conditions. Jeste and Geschwind (2014) reviewed the latest technologies used to identify the genetic factors associated with autism and argued that viewing autism as a singular biological entity is unsustainable.

Diagnosis Sensitivity and Specificity

The diagnosis of ASD can be challenging due to the complexity and heterogeneity of the disorder. Typically, researchers and clinicians assess children's behavior based on specific diagnostic criteria in conjunction with concerned caregivers' reports. A diagnostic test examines the presence or absence of a disorder. Therefore, an accurate diagnosis must have sensitivity and specificity. Sensitivity refers to the proportion of true positives that a test correctly identifies. In contrast, specificity is the extent to which a test detects the actual percentage of a particular disease or disorder, not another disease or disorder that shares similar diagnostic characteristics. The terms positive or negative refer to the presence or absence of a specific disease or disorder.

Many screening and diagnostic tools have been developed over the years. However, the properties of many of these instruments have yet to be sufficiently studied or established. Currently, the two instruments most used in research and clinical practice are the Autism Diagnostic Interview-Revised (ADI-R), and the Autism Diagnostic Observation Schedule, second edition (ADOS-2). They are considered gold standard diagnostic tools. A systematic literature review of diagnostic procedures used to determine the presence or absence of ASD found that, among others, the ADI-R and ADOS-2 had the highest sensitivity and specificity, mainly when used in combination (Falkner et al., 2013).

Autism Diagnosis Stability

Although autism can begin in *utero* when cell proliferation and differentiation are disrupted (Courchesne et al., 2019), autism can only be diagnosed postnatally. According to the Centers for Disease Control and Prevention (CDC), parents (and pediatricians) can detect signs and symptoms of autism (e.g., not responding to their names or interacting with others) at 18 months or even younger. Experienced, multidisciplinary professionals using well-authenticated methods of collecting past and present information on the person being assessed can reliably diagnose autism by age two (Lord et al., 2006). However, the mean age of autism detection and diagnosis is between 4 and 5 years of age (Baio et al., 2018). A late age of detection of autism can result in missed opportunities for learning during early optimal brain development (Huttenlocher, 1979).

A diagnosis of autism at around 2 years of age is generally reliable and stable. A newer report examined the stability of an autism diagnosis in a cohort of toddlers and found that the diagnostic stability was 0.50 at 12–14 months but increased to 0.79 by 14 months and by 16 months 0.83 (Pierce et al., 2019). Landa and colleagues (2022) conducted a prospective longitudinal study involving children with and without an elevated risk of autism. The study tracked participants from a mean age of 15 months (Time 1) to 36 months (Time 2) and followed up with them at a mean age of 5.7 years (Time 3). They found that many infants diagnosed with autism at an early age demonstrate diagnostic stability as they grow older.

Autism can be misdiagnosed due to co-occurring conditions that may mimic its symptoms. For instance, children with ADHD, anxiety disorders, intellectual disabilities, and sensory processing issues can complicate the diagnosis of autism. Additionally, the subjective nature of the condition, combined with the possibility of diagnosis substitution, increases the likelihood of misdiagnosing autism. Many adults who were not diagnosed with autism in childhood may still meet the criteria for an autism diagnosis. As social demands increase in adult life, these individuals might find coping more challenging, revealing traits or difficulties that were not apparent earlier.

Autism Diagnostic Instruments

The Autism Diagnostic Observation Schedule (ADOS)

Lord and colleagues (1989) developed the original version of the Autism Diagnostic Observation Schedule (ADOS) as a diagnostic research tool for individuals between 5 and 12 years old. The ADOS has been modified, as younger and nonverbal children needed diagnostic evaluations. The Pre-Linguistic Autism Diagnostic Observation Schedule (PL-ADOS; DiLavore et al., 1995) and the ADOS-Generic (ADOS-G) (Lord et al., 2000) were developed for children younger than five.

The current version of the Autism Diagnostic Observation Schedule-Second Edition (ADOS-2) is an updated version of the original ADOS. It contains new items and revised **algorithms** to enhance autism assessment. As an activity-based assessment, clinicians can administer the instrument to evaluate communication skills, social interaction, and imaginative use of materials in individuals suspected of having autism. The assessment is a semi-structured interview and play-based activity consisting of five modules: (1) a toddler module for those around 12–30 months who do not speak but can walk independently. The module consists of 11 activities (e.g., free play, response to name, and response to joint attention); (2) a module for assessing children 31 months or older who are not entirely verbal. The module has ten activities (e.g., responsive social smile and functional and symbolic imitation); (3) a module for children around six with limited verbal fluency. The module consists of 14 activities (e.g., make-believe play and telling a story from a book); (4) a module for children and young adolescents who are verbally fluent. The module has 14 activities (e.g., joint interactive play and creating a story); and (5) a module for adolescents and adults that assesses responses to questions instead of nonverbal interactions during play (e.g., conversation and reporting and describing emotions). Each module is structured to assess individuals of various developmental levels and ages (Lord et al., 2012). Trained clinicians administer each module in about 45–60 minutes, depending on the person under assessment.

The ADOS-2 is an effective tool for assessing and diagnosing autism due to several important features: (1) it uses a standardized evaluation process that provides a structured format for observing and interacting with the individual being assessed, allowing for a more thorough understanding of behaviors associated with autism; (2) its modules are specifically designed to evaluate various age groups and language abilities; (3) the data collected can reveal social communication and behavioral patterns that are indicative of autism; and (4) the instrument has been extensively researched and validated, demonstrating its effectiveness and reliability in identifying autism.

Researchers and clinicians consider the ADOS and the ADI-R (discussed below) as the "gold standard" tools for diagnosing ASD (Ozonoff et al., 2005), primarily when they use the instruments conjointly. A more recent study (Kamp-Becker et al., 2021) found that combining ADOS and ADI-R can reduce the time-consuming process of administering both instruments and effectively differentiate autism from other mental conditions.

The Autism Diagnostic Interview-Revised (ADI-R)

Le Couteur and colleagues (1989) developed the original version of the DIR to improve the diagnostic criteria of autism and differentiate the disorder from other related developmental conditions. The instrument was designed for administration to children of at least 5 years and others with a mental age of at least 2 years.

The realization that autism emerges in infancy and thus could be diagnosed much earlier prompted Lord, Rutter, and Le Couteur (1994) to revise the instrument for use with infants and others with a mental age of at least 18 months.

Researchers and clinicians use the ADI-R to interview parents of individuals with a mental age of at least 24 months suspected to have autism. The interview consists of 93 open-ended questions that capture the complete developmental history of the person being assessed and information on three domains: (1) language/communication (e.g., pointing to express interest), (2) reciprocal social interactions (e.g., interest in other children), and (3) repetitive behavior/interests (e.g., unusual preoccupations). The interview takes about 90 to 150 minutes to complete. The interviewer uses a scoring algorithm and cut-off scores to diagnose autism.

Reliability

The ADI-R is one of the most widely used instruments among researchers and clinicians to diagnose autism. The originators of the instrument have reported its reliability, validity, and interrater reliability. Other researchers have evaluated its psychometric properties. For example, one study evaluated the ADI-R algorithms in a non-U.S. sample of toddlers and young preschoolers. Although the specificity of the instruments was "satisfactorily high," the sensitivity was moderate and the validity low (de Bildt et al., 2015). Similarly, Fusar-Poli and colleagues (2017) evaluated the sensitivity and specificity of the ADOS and ADI-R in a cohort of adults with an IQ of at least 70. They reported that, unlike ADOS, the ADI-R did not reliably detect autism in adults without an intellectual disability. The ADI-R interrater reliability has been established in research but not clinical settings. One study evaluated the interrater reliability of the tool in a naturalistic clinical multicenter setting and found it concordant with that reported in research settings (Zander et al., 2017).

In sum, the Autism Diagnostic Interview-Revised (ADI-R) offers several features that enhance its effectiveness as a tool for diagnosing autism: (1) it is highly structured and designed for administration to caregivers of individuals across various age groups who may have autism; (2) it is grounded in established diagnostic criteria from the DSM and ICD; and (3) extensive research studies support its reliability as a diagnostic instrument.

The Childhood Autism Rating Scales (CARS)

Schopler and Reichler's (1971) initial work, as part of the TEACCH program (Treatment and Education of Autistic and Related Communication Handicapped Children) at the University of North Carolina, paved the way for the Childhood Autism Rating Scales (CARS) that Schopler and colleagues (1980) developed to detect and diagnose autism. The instrument is structured to observe and rate various domains of an individual under assessment (e.g., imitation, adaptation to change, activity level, verbal communication, object use, and relationship to people). Based on the composite score of the evaluation, the examiner rates and determines a severity continuum ranging from non-autistic to severely autistic. Schopler and colleagues (1988) developed the Childhood Autism Rating Scale.

CARS has been found to have good sensitivity and specificity and is effective in differentiating autistic disorder from PDD-NOS. Additionally, the instrument can distinguish autism from other developmental disorders and typical development (Chlebowski et al., 2010). One study investigated the factor structure of the CARS in a cohort of 2-year-old children (Moulton et al., 2019). Results of the factor analysis indicate three factors (i.e., stereotyped behaviors and sensory sensitivities, social communication, and emotional reactivity), two of which are consonant with the DSM-5 symptom domains and thus relevant in ASD assessment. When administered to a cohort of children from 13 publications, the instrument's summary sensitivity and specificity were 0.80 and 0.88, respectively (Randall et al., 2018).

The Diagnostic Interview for Social and Communication Disorders (DISCO)

Lorna Wing introduced the concept of an "autism spectrum" in the 1980s based on her understanding that autism could be considered dimensionally (not categorically)—i.e., the condition has various causes and affects people of different age groups with varying levels of intellectual disabilities. Wing and colleagues (2002) developed the DISCO based on the notion that autism is a spectrum of related conditions.

The instrument's development originated in the 1970s when Wing and Gould (1979) researched the epidemiology of autism. The DISCO was developed as a research and clinical tool to use with children and adults. As a semi-structured interview schedule, clinicians and researchers use it to collect information on development and behavior. The instrument contains over 300 questions organized into eight parts comprising multiple domains (e.g., family and medical information, developmental skills, repetitive activities and behavior, emotional development, maladaptive behavior, and psychiatric conditions).

The DISCO has several key features: Unlike other interview schedules (e.g., ADI-R) that divide individuals with ASD into non-overlapping (categorical) subgroups, the DISCO adopts a dimensional model of autism. It can be used with children and adults. It collects information on the core characteristics of autism and other co-occurring conditions (e.g., sleep difficulties, maladaptive behavior) that may or may not occur with autism and focuses on developmental progression and delay. The instrument administration takes 2–3 hours and provides a comprehensive profile of an individual's skills. In clinical practice, the DISCO can serve various functions. In addition to providing a clinical description based on information collected during the interview, the instrument can help diagnose autism and other developmental conditions and inform the clinician of recommendations about corrective action (Leekam, 2013).

The DSM-5 (APA, 2013) and the World Health Organization (2019) published revised diagnostic criteria for autism. Diagnostic criteria changes prompted concerns that assessment might not be consistent with those changes. As a result, some individuals previously diagnosed under the DSM-IV-TR or the ICD-10 faced not receiving a diagnosis under the proposed changes. Kent and colleagues (2013) used items from the DISCO, developed a set of DSM-5 ASD algorithms, and used the interview with two independent samples. The results showed that the instrument had good levels of sensitivity and specificity when evaluated on the DSM-5 diagnostic criteria.

The Developmental, Dimensional, and Diagnostic Interview (3Di)

Skuse and his colleagues developed the Developmental, Dimensional, and Diagnostic Interview (3Di) in the early 2000s to assess autism spectrum disorder. Trained professionals can administer the 3Di in about 1–2 hours. The 3Di is a comprehensive, structured diagnostic tool that gathers information across multiple domains, including developmental history, social communication, and repetitive behaviors. The interview with parents consists of 183 items that cover demographics, family background, motor skills, and developmental history. The 3Di has good reliability and validity. The instrument can also assess the severity of autism symptoms.

Santosh and colleagues (2009) developed a short version of the 3Di, the 3Di-sv, which consists of 112 questions. The assessment can be completed in about 45 minutes, and the responses are entered into a computer program. The 3Di-sv has good levels of sensitivity and specificity. Furthermore, the instrument's effectiveness is consistent with that of the full version of the 3Di and the ADI-R. Similarly, Skuse and colleagues (2004) used the 3Di to develop a computerized parental autism interview to measure autistic features dimensionally.

Slappendel and colleagues (2016) conducted a study using the short version of the Developmental Diagnostic Dimensional Interview (3Di-sv) to evaluate its validity and compatibility with the DSM-5 criteria for autism spectrum disorder (ASD). Compared to the ADOS-2, the 3Di-sv demonstrated good sensitivity but low specificity.

Some of the main features of 3Di include the following: (a) computation of the severity of features associated with a diagnosis of autism, (b) completion of an assessment for autism in approximately 45 minutes, (c) generation of a comprehensive report for parents and service providers, (d) excellent reliability and validity, (e) criterion validity established that is consistent with the ADI-R, and (f) provides the means for clinicians and researchers to measure autism traits dimensionally rather than categorically in clinical and normal populations.

Psychometric Properties Evaluation of Diagnostic Instruments

Randall and colleagues (2018) reviewed 13 studies to identify the sensitivity and specificity of various autism diagnostic tools, including ADOS, ADI-R, CARS, DISCO, GARS, and 3Di, and how they most accurately diagnose autism. Additionally, they sought to determine which diagnostic tools most accurately identify ASD in preschool children compared to the clinical judgment of a multidisciplinary team. The authors found that sensitivity and specificity varied significantly across diagnostic instruments, likely due to methodological differences and variations in the characteristics of the participants recruited. Among the instruments tested, the ADOS demonstrated the highest sensitivity, while the specificity was comparable across all diagnostic tools.

Autism Diagnosis Recovery

Autism is generally considered a lifelong condition. Kanner's follow-up report (Kanner, 1971) on the 11 children he described in his seminal paper (Kanner, 1943) showed no improvement in their autistic symptoms. The life history of their conditions indicated that the core autism characteristics persisted. Autism literature has embraced two views of the condition that have guided research and practice: (1) autism and its development are innate, and (2) the characteristics of the condition are inborn.

Autism literature, however, abounds with accounts of some individuals who received an early diagnosis and no longer meet the diagnostic criteria at a later age. For example, Lovaas used the term "recovery" to describe some children in a cohort who received intense behavioral intervention. As a result, their IQs increased in the normal range and were mainstreamed (Lovaas, 1987). Helt and colleagues (2008) described several predictors of "recovery." Children at the more able end of the spectrum with high intelligence, verbal skills, imitative capacity, and motor development are more likely to move into the typical range. Those with chromosomal abnormalities, intellectual disabilities, and seizures are less likely to fare well. However, Fein and colleagues (2013) used the term "optimal outcome" to characterize the diagnosis loss of a group of 34 individuals who subsequently functioned in the typical range after receiving a diagnosis of autism. Another study followed a group of children who "recovered from autism" after receiving behavioral intervention following a diagnosis at around the age of 4. Follow-up interviews with parents about six years later revealed that many of those children had difficulties with attention/activity regulation, speech and language, social interaction, and behavior, and thus needed continuing support (Olsson et al., 2015).

Dawson and colleagues (2012) reported a behavioral intervention that improved the IQ, language, and adaptive behavior of children diagnosed with autism compared to a control group of participants. More significantly, the experimental cohort's electroencephalogram (EEG) indicated more significant cortical activity when presented with human faces, suggesting a normalized pattern of brain activity associated with improved social behavior. A more recent study of 36 children from a cohort of 569 in an early intervention program found that after participating, they no longer met the diagnostic criteria for autism at follow-up about four years later. However, most of those children continued to exhibit behavioral, emotional, and learning problems and thus required continued educational support (Shulman et al., 2019).

Whiteley and colleagues (2019) raised a provocative question: Is autism inborn and lifelong for everyone? Many studies have reported cases of children who developed autism following a period of typical development. Other studies have documented a diminishment of autistic characteristics and their accompanying co-occurring conditions to the point of not meeting the diagnostic criteria in some individuals. Considering that the idea of autism regression is relatively common and various reports have touted the notion of children growing out of autism in the 1980s and 1990s (von Knorring & Hägglöf, 1993), is autism a lifelong condition or is recovery from the disorder possible?

The term "recovery" is controversial as it suggests that autism is a disease that needs a cure. Recovery entails a return to a normal condition. Ozonoff (2013) offered two reasons why using the term *recovery* as a possible outcome should be done responsibly. First, the notion of recovery may lead parents to believe that a particular treatment can automatically make their children whole and indistinguishable from their typically developing counterparts. Second, autism researchers have not fully embraced the notion of full recovery from autism. Losing an autism diagnosis and functioning in the typical range does not necessarily mean that all remnants of the condition have disappeared. Some children on the autism spectrum would make minimal gains even when exposed to various interventions. Lovaas (1987) touted the "recovery" of 47% of children who participated in his early intensive behavioral program for at least two years. Fifty-three percent of the participants did not recover. Should recovery be conceptualized as dichotomous—i.e., either on the autism spectrum or recovered? Perhaps recovery from autism should not be the goal of intervention. Instead, habilitation, skill acquisition, and undesirable behavior reduction should be paramount.

Summary

Diagnostic practices have evolved significantly from Hippocrates, who established a foundation for understanding diseases through careful observation. In more modern times, Emil Kraepelin highlighted the importance of categorizing disorders based on symptoms and empirical observations. He introduced a more structured approach to diagnosis.

Unlike medical diagnoses that can reliably identify a disease or condition, the diagnosis of autism, because of the heterogeneity of the condition, is not as straightforward. An early diagnosis can inform and guide treatment that can be more beneficial if started early. Clinicians and researchers use the diagnostic criteria described in the DSM-5 and ICD-11 and a person's behavioral history to render a diagnosis. There are no reliable biomarkers that can be used to diagnose the condition. Biomarkers that have been developed have explored various body systems (e.g., immunological, toxicological, neurological, and biological) and are promising but must be validated before they can be reliably used to diagnose the condition.

Researchers and clinicians typically use various instruments that are based on the DSM-5 and ICD-11 criteria to diagnose autism. The gold standard instruments for diagnosis are the Autism Diagnostic Observation Schedule (ADOS) and the Autism Diagnostic Interview-Revised (ADI-R). Other instruments like the DISCO, SCARS, and other less frequently used instruments are also available. A diagnosis of autism is typically reliable and stable when conducted by trained professionals using standardized assessment tools.

Autism is a lifelong condition, and a diagnosis made by qualified professionals is considered reliable. Although someone can lose a diagnosis of autism, there is no actual recovery from the condition. Interventions designed to support individuals with autism do not eliminate the characteristics associated with the condition; these traits persist throughout a person's life.

Questions to Ponder for Further Thinking and Learning

1 Discuss the validity of the various assessments and tests used to diagnose autism.
2 Can diagnosticians improve the validity and accuracy of autism diagnosis using artificial intelligence?
3 How reliable are the behavioral observations used in autism diagnosis?
4 In what ways do cultural and societal factors impact the diagnosis of autism?
5 What are the challenges associated with diagnosing autism in individuals with intellectual disabilities?
6 Can a diagnosis of autism be accurately made using standardized questionnaires?
7 Discuss the implications of misdiagnosing a child with autism.
8 Should autism be classified as a disorder for individuals on the higher end of the autism spectrum, including children, adolescents, and adults?

References

Adam, D. (2013). Mental health: On the spectrum. *Nature, 496*(7446), 416–418.
APA (1952). *Diagnostic and statistical manual of mental disorders*. American Psychiatric Association.
APA (1968). *Diagnostic and statistical manual of mental disorders* (2nd ed.). American Psychiatric Association.

APA (1980). *Diagnostic and statistical manual of mental disorders* (3rd ed.). American Psychiatric Association.

APA (1987). *Diagnostic and statistical manual of mental disorders—Text revised* (3rd ed., rev.). American Psychiatric Association.

APA (1994). *Diagnostic and statistical manual of mental disorders* (4th ed.). American Psychiatric Association.

APA (2000). *Diagnostic and statistical manual of mental disorders—Text revised* (4th ed., rev.). American Psychiatric Association.

APA (2013). *Diagnostic and statistical manual of mental disorders* (4th ed.). American Psychiatric Association.

APA (2022). *Diagnostic and statistical manual of mental disorders—Text revised* (5th ed., rev.). American Psychiatric Association.

Anderson, G. (2014). Biochemical biomarkers for autism spectrum disorder. In F. Volkmar, S. Rogers, R. Paul, & K. Pelphrey (Eds.), *Handbook of autism and pervasive developmental disorders* (4th ed) (vol. 2, pp. 457–481). Wiley & Sons.

Baio, J., Wiggins, L., Christensen, D. L., Maenner, M. J., Daniels, J. Warren, Z., ... Dowling, N. F. (2018). Prevalence of autism spectrum disorder among children aged 8 years—Autism and Developmental Disabilities Monitoring Network, 11 Sites, United States, 2014. *MMWR Surveillance Summaries, 67*(6), 1–23.

Chlebowski, C., Green, J. A., Barton, M. L., & Fein, D. (2010). Using the childhood autism rating scale to diagnose autism spectrum disorders. *Journal of Autism and Developmental Disorders, 40*(7), 787–799.

Cooper, R. V. (2013). Avoiding false positive: Zones of rarity, the threshold problem, and the DSM clinical significance criterion. *Canadian Journal of Psychiatry, 58*(11), 606–611.

Courchesne, E., Pramparo, T., Gazestani, V. H., Lombardo, M. V., Pierce, K., & Lewis, N. E. (2019). The ASD living biology: From cell proliferation to clinical phenotype. *Molecular Psychiatry, 24*(1), 88–107.

Cuthbert, B. N. (2015). Research domain criteria: Toward future psychiatric nosologies. *Dialogues in Clinical Neuroscience, 17*(1), 89–97.

Dawson, G., Jones, E. J., Merkle, K., Venema, K., Lowry, R., Faja, S., ... Webb, S. J. (2012). Early behavioral intervention is associated with normalized brain activity in young children with autism. *Journal of the American Academy of Child & Adolescent Psychiatry, 51*(11), 1150–1159.

de Bildt, A., Sytema, S., Zander, E., Bölte, S., Sturm, H., Yirmina, N., ... Oosterling, I. J. (2015). Autism Diagnostic Interview-Revised (ADI-R) algorithms for toddlers and young preschoolers: Application in a non-US sample of 1,104 children. *Journal of Autism and Developmental Disorders, 45*(7), 2076–2091.

DiLavore, P. C., Lord, C., & Rutter, M. (1995). The pre-linguistic autism diagnostic observation schedule. *Journal of Autism and Developmental Disorders, 25*(4), 355–379.

Donvan, J., & Zucker, C. (2016). *In a different key: The story of autism*. Crown Publishers.

Falkner, T., Anderson, K., Falkner, M., & Horlin, C. (2013). Diagnostic procedures in autism spectrum disorders: A systematic literature review. *European Child and Adolescent Psychiatry, 22*(6), 329–340.

Feighner, J. P., Robins, E., Guze, S. B., Woodruff, R. A., Wikonur, G., & Munoz, R. (1972). Diagnostic criteria for use in psychiatric research. *Archives of General Psychiatry, 26*(1), 57–63.

Fein, D., Barton, M., Eigsti, I. M., Kelley, E., Naigles, L., Schultz, R. T., ... Tyson, K. (2013). Optimal outcome in individuals with a history of autism. *Journal of Child Psychology and Psychiatry, 54*(2), 195–205.

Frye, R. E., Vassall, S., Kaur, G., Lewis, C., Karim, M., & Rossignol, D. (2019). Emerging biomarkers in autism spectrum disorder: A systematic review. *Annals of Translational Medicine, 7*(23), 792.

Fusar-Poli, L., Brondino, N., Rocchetti, M., Panisi, C., Provenzani, U., Damiani, S., & Politi, P. (2017). Diagnosing ASD in adults without ID: Accuracy of the ADOS-2 and the ADI-R. *Journal of Autism and Developmental Disorders, 47*(11), 3370–3379.

Gorwitz, K. (1974). Census enumeration of the mentally ill and the mentally retarded in the nineteenth century. *Health Service Reports, 89*(2), 180–187.

Greaves-Lord, K., Skuse, D., & Mandy, W. (2022). Innovations of the ICD-11 in the field of autism spectrum disorder: A psychological approach. *Clinical Psychology in Europe, 4*(Spec Issue), e10005.

Hakak-Zargar, B., Tamrakar, A., Voth, T., Sheikhi, A., Multanil, J., & Schütz, C. G. (2022). The utility of Research Domain Criteria in diagnosis and management of dual disorders: A mini-review. *Frontiers in Psychiatry, 13*, 805163.

Helt, M., Kelley, E., Kinsbourne, M., Pandey, J., Boorstein, H., Herbert, M., & Fein, D. (2008). Can children with autism recover? If so, how? *Neuropsychology Review, 18*(4), 339–366.

Hoff, P. (2015). The Kraepelinian tradition. *Dialogues in Clinical Neurosciences, 17*(1), 31–41.

Houts, A. C. (2000). Fifty years of psychiatric nomenclature: Reflections on the 1943 War Department Technical Bulletin, Medical 203. *Journal of Clinical Psychology, 56*(7), 935–967.

Hranilovic, D., Bujas-Petkovic, Z., Vragovic, R., Vuk, T., Hock, K., & Jernej, B. (2007). Hyperserotonemia in adults with autistic disorder. *Journal of Autism and Developmental Disorders, 37*(10), 1934–1940.

Huttenlocher, P. R. (1979). Synaptic density in human frontal cortex—Developmental changes and effects of aging. *Brain Research, 163*(2), 195–205.

Independent Patriot Westchester County (2012, January 19). New definition of autism will exclude many, study suggests. *New York Times*. http://nytimes.com/2012/01/20/health/research/new-autism-definition-would-exclude-many-study-suggests.html?_r=1&pagewanted=all. Accessed on March 18, 2022.

Insel, T. (2013). Transforming diagnosis. *NIMH*. https://psychrights.org/2013/130429NIMHTransformingDiagnosis.htm. Accessed on September 5, 2024.

Jablensky, A. (2016). Psychiatric classifications: Validity and utility. *World Psychiatry, 15*(1), 26–31.

Jeste, S. S., & Geschwind, D. H. (2014). Disentangling the heterogeneity of autism spectrum disorder through genetic findings. *Nature Reviews Neurology, 10*(2), 74–81.

Johnson, C. P., Myers, S. M., Lipkin, P. H., Cartwright, J. D., Desch, L. W., Duby, J. C., ... Yeargin-Allsopp, M. (2007). Identification and evaluation of children with autism spectrum disorders. *Pediatrics, 120*(5), 1183–1215.

Kamp-Becker, I., Tauscher, J., Wolff, N., Küpper, C., Poustka, L., Roepke, S., ... Stroth, S. (2021). Is the combination of ADOS and ADI-R necessary to classify ASD? Rethinking the "gold standard" in diagnosing ASD. *Frontiers in Psychiatry, 24*(12), 727308.

Kanner, L. (1943). Autistic disturbances of affective contact. *Nervous Child, 2*, 217–250.

Kanner, L. (1957 [1935]). *Child psychiatry* (3rd ed.). C. C. Thomas.

Kanner, L. (1971). Follow-up study of eleven autistic children originally reported in 1943. *Journal of Autism and Childhood Schizophrenia, 1*(2), 119–145.

Kendell, R., & Jablensky, A. (2003). Distinguishing between the validity and utility of psychiatric diagnoses. *American Journal of Psychiatry, 160*(1), 4–12.

Kent, R. G., Carrington, J. S., Couteur, A., Gould, J., Wing, L., Maljaars, ... Leekam, S. R. (2013). Diagnosing autism spectrum disorder: Who will get a DSM-5 diagnosis? *Journal of Child Psychology and Psychiatry, 54*(11), 1242–1250.

Kern, J. K., Geier, D. A., Adams, J. B., Mehta, J. A., Grannemann, B. D., & Geier, M. R. (2011). Toxicity biomarkers in autism spectrum disorder: A blinded study of urinary porphyrins. *Pediatrics International, 53*(2), 147–153.

Kupfer, D. J., & Regier, D. A. (2011). Neuroscience, clinical evidence, and the future of psychiatric classification in DSM-5. *American Journal of Psychiatry, 168*(7), 672–674.

Landa, R. J., Reetzke, R., Holingue, C. B., Herman, D., & Hess, C. R. (2022). Diagnostic stability and phenotypic differences among school-age children diagnosed with ASD before age 2. *Frontiers in Psychiatry, 13*, 805686.

Le Couteur, A., Rutter, M., Lord, C., Rios, P., Robertson, S., Holdgrafer, M., & McLennan, J. (1989). Autism diagnostic interview: A standardized investigator-based instrument. *Journal of Autism and Developmental Disorders, 19*(3), 363–387.

Leekam, S. (2013). Diagnostic interview for social and communication disorders. In F. R. Volkmar (Ed.), *Encyclopedia of autism spectrum disorders*. Springer.

Lidz, T. (1966). Adolf Meyer and the development of American psychiatry. *The American Journal of Psychiatry, 123*(3), 320–332.

Lord, C., DiLavore, P. C., Gotham, K., Guthrie, W. Luyster, R. J., Risi, S., & Rutter, M. (2012). *Autism Diagnostic Observation Schedule, Second Edition (ADOS-2) Manual*. Western Psychological Services.

Lord, C., Risi, S., DiLavore, P. S., Shulman, C., Thurm, A., & Pickles, A. (2006). Autism from 2 to 9 years of age. *Archives of General Psychiatry, 63*(6), 694–701.

Lord, C., Risi, S., Lambrecht, L., Cook, E. H., Leventhal, B. L., DiLavore, P. C., ... Rutter, M. (2000). The autism diagnostic observation schedule-generic: A standard measure of social and communication deficits associated with the spectrum of autism. *Journal of Autism and Developmental Disorders, 30*(3), 205–223.

Lord, C., Rutter, M., Goode, S., Heemsbergen, J., Jordan, H., Mawhood, L., & Schopler, E. (1989). Autism diagnostic observation schedule: A standardized observation of communicative and social behavior. *Journal of Autism and Developmental Disorders, 19*(2), 185–212.

Lord, C., Rutter, M., & Le Couteur, A. (1994). Autism Diagnostic Interview-Revised: A revised version of a diagnostic interview for caregivers of individuals with possible pervasive developmental disorders. *Journal of Autism and Developmental Disorders, 24*(5), 659–685.

Lovaas, O. I. (1987). Behavioral treatment and normal educational and intellectual functioning in young autistic children. *Journal of Consulting and Clinical Psychology, 55*(1), 3–9.

Mandy, W. (2018). The Research Domain Criteria: A new dawn for neurodiversity research? *Autism, 22*(6), 642–644.

McPartland, J. C. (2016). Considerations in biomarker development for neurodevelopmental disorders. *Current Opinion in Neurology, 29*(2), 118–122.

Moulton, E., Bradbury, K., Barton, M., & Fein, D. (2019). Factor analysis of the Childhood Autism Rating Scale in a sample of two-year-olds with an autism spectrum disorder. *Journal of Autism and Developmental Disorders, 49*(7), 2733–2746.

Muller, C. L., Anacker, A. M. J., & Veenstra-VanderWeele, J. (2016). The serotonin system in autism spectrum disorder: From biomarker to animal models. *Neuroscience, 321*, 24–41.

Olsson, M. B., Westerlund, J., Lundström, S., Giacobini, M., Fernell, E., & Gillberg, C. (2015). "Recovery" from the diagnosis of autism—And then? *Neuropsychiatric Disease and Treatment, 11*, 999–105.

Ozonoff, S., Goodlin-Jones, B. L., & Solomon, M. (2005). Evidence-based assessment of autism spectrum disorders in children and adolescents. *Journal of Clinical Child and Adolescent Psychology, 34*(3), 523–340.

Ozonoff, S. (2013). Editorial: recovery from autism spectrum disorder (ASD) and the science of hope. *Journal of Child Psychology and Psychiatry, 54*(2), 113–114.

Pierce, K., Gazestani, V. H., Bacon, E., Barnes, C. C., Cha, D., Nalabolu, S., ... Courchesne, E. (2019). Evaluation of the diagnostic stability of the early autism spectrum disorder phenotype in the general population starting at 12 Months. *JAMA Pediatrics, 173*(6), 578–587.

Randall, M., Egberts, K. J., Samtani, A., Scholten, R. J., Hooft, L., Livingstone, N., ... Williams, K. (2018). Diagnostic tests for autism spectrum disorder (ASD) in preschool children. *The Cochrane Database of Systematic Reviews, 7*(7), CD009044.

Risi, S., Lord, C., Gotham, K., Corsello, C., Chrysler, C., Szatmari, P., ... Pickles, A. (2006). Combining information from multiple sources in the diagnosis of autism spectrum disorders. *Journal of the American Academy of Child & Adolescent Psychiatry, 45*(9), 1094–1103.

Robins, E., & Guze, S. B. (1970). Establishment of diagnostic validity in psychiatric illness: Its application to schizophrenia. *American Journal of Psychiatry, 126*(7), 983–987.

Sanislow, C. A., Pine, D. S., Quinn, K. J., Kozak, M. J., Garvey, M. A., Heinssen, R. K., ... Cuthbert, B. N. (2010). Developing constructs for psychopathology research: Research Domain Criteria. *Journal of Abnormal Psychology, 119*(4), 631–639.

Santosh, P. J., Mandy, W. P., Puura, K., Kaartinen, M., Warrington, R., & Skuse, D. H. (2009). The construction and validation of a short form of the developmental, diagnostic and dimensional interview. *European Child and Adolescent Psychiatry, 18*(8), 521–524.

Schopler, E., & Reichler, R. J. (1971). Parents as cotherapists in the treatment of psychotic children. *Journal of Autism and Childhood Schizophrenia, 1*(1), 87–102.

Schopler, E., Reichler, R. J., DeVellis, R. F., & Daly, K. (1980). Toward objective classification of childhood autism: Childhood Autism Rating Scale (CARS). *Journal of Autism and Developmental Disorders, 10*(1), 91–103.

Schopler, E., Reichler, R. J., & Renner, B. R. (1988). *The Childhood Autism Rating Scale.* Western Psychological Services.

Scull, A., & Schulkin, J. (2009). Psychobiology, psychiatry, and psychoanalysis: The intersecting careers of Adolf Meyer, Phyllis Greenacre, and Curt Richter. *Medical History, 53*(1), 5–36.

Shulman, L., D'Agostino, E., Lee, S., Valicenti-McDermott, M., Seijo, R., Tulloch, D., ... Tarshis, N. (2019). When an early diagnosis of autism spectrum disorder resolves, what remains? *Journal of Child Neurology, 34*(7), 382–386.

Siu, A. L., US preventive Services Task Force (USPSTF), Bibbins-Domingo, K., Grossman, D. C., Baumann, L. C., Davidson, K. W., ... Pignone, M. P. (2016). Screening for autism spectrum disorder in young children: US preventive services task force recommendation statement. *JAMA, 315*(7), 691–696.

Skuse, D., Warrington, R., Bishop, D., Chowdhury, U., Lau, J., Mandy, W., & Place, M. (2004). The Developmental, Dimensional and Diagnostic Interview (3di): A novel computerized assessment for autism spectrum disorders. *Journal of the American Academy of Child & Adolescent Psychiatry, 43*(5), 548–558.

Slappendel, G., Mandy, W., van der Ende, J., Verhulst, F. C., van der Sijde, A., Duvekot, J., ... Greaves-Lord, K. (2016). Utility of the 3Di short version for the diagnostic assessment of autism spectrum disorder and compatibility with DSM-5. *Journal of Autism and Developmental Disorders, 46*(5), 1834–1846.

Slater, M. H., & Borghini, A. (2019). Introduction: Lessons from the scientific butchery. *PhilArchive*, 1–31, https://philarchive.org/archive/SLAILF. Accessed on January 6, 2024.

Spitzer, R. L., Endicott, J., & Robins, E. (1978). Research diagnostic criteria: Rationale and reliability. *Archives of General Psychiatry, 35*(6), 773–782.

Stengel, E. (1959). Classification of mental disorders. *Bulletin of the World Health Organization, 21*(4–5), 601–663.

Stone, L. (2020). Trying to carve nature at its joints: Respecting the complexity of psychiatric diagnosis. *British Journal of General Practice, 70*(689), 504.

Tordjman, S., Gutknecht, L., Carlier, M., Spitz, E., Antoine, C., Slama, F., … Anderson, G. M. (2001). Role of the serotonin transporter gene in the behavioral expression of autism. *Molecular Psychiatry, 6*(4), 434–439.

Vargason, T., Grivas, G., Hollowood-Jones, K. L., & Hahn, J. (2020). Towards a multivariate biomarker-based diagnosis of autism spectrum disorder: Review and discussion of recent advancements. *Seminars in Pediatric Neurology, 34*, 100803.

von Knorring, A.-L., & Hägglöf, B. (1993). Autism in northern Sweden: A population based follow-up study: Psychopathology. *European Child & Adolescent Psychiatry, 2*(2), 91–97.

Warren, R. P., Singh, V. K., Cole, P., Odell, J. D., Pingree, C. B, Warren, W. L., & White, E. (1991). Increased frequency of the null allele at the complement C4b locus in autism. *Clinical and Experimental Immunology, 83*(3), 438–440.

Whiteley, P., Carr, K., & Shattock, P. (2019). Is autism inborn and lifelong for everyone? *Neuropsychiatric Disease and Treatment, 15*, 2885–2891.

Wing, L. (1996). *The autism spectrum: A guide for parents and professionals.* Constable.

Wing, L., & Gould, J. (1979). Severe impairments of social interaction and associated abnormalities in children: Epidemiology and classification. *Journal of Autism and Developmental Disorders, 9*(1), 11–29.

Wing, L., Leekam, S. R., Libby, S. J., Gould, J., & Larcombe, M. (2002). The Diagnostic Interview for Social and Communication Disorders: Background, inter-rater reliability and clinical use. *Journal of Child Psychology and Psychiatry, 43*(3), 307–325.

World Health Organization (WHO) (2019). 6A02 Autism spectrum disorder. In *International statistical classification of diseases and related health problems* (11th ed.). https://icd.who.int/browse11/l-m/en#/http://id.who.int/icd/entity/437815624. Accessed on May 2, 2024.

Zander, E., Willfors, C., Berggren, S., Coco, C., Holm, A., Jifält, I., … Bölte, S. (2017). The interrater reliability of the Autism Diagnostic Interview-Revised (ADI-R) in clinical settings. *Psychopathology, 50*(3), 219–227.

Part IV

Part four describes various interventions practitioners have developed to improve the quality of life and habilitate individuals on the autism spectrum. Chapter 10, *Behavioral Interventions*, focuses on evidence-based practices that have improved the communication, social skills, and everyday functioning of autistic individuals. Chapter 11, *Pharmacologic Interventions*, examines the role of medications in managing co-occurring conditions associated with autism. Chapter 12, *Biomedical and Complementary Alternative Treatments for Autism*, explores nontraditional approaches that have gained popularity among practitioners and parents and the caution they should consider when contemplating using them. Lastly, Chapter 13, *Autism, Then, Now, and Moving Forward*, recapitulates autism diagnostic criteria of the past, present, and future through the lens of the neurodiversity movement and its central tenet: Autism is a natural variation of the human condition, not a deficit or disorder.

DOI: 10.4324/9781003336266-13

Chapter 10

Behavioral Interventions

Chapter Contents

DOI: 10.4324/9781003336266-14

Introduction

In the 1940s, children who were examined and judged "defective" because of various conditions, including Down syndrome, cerebral palsy, or any other conditions that physicians could not diagnose, were sent away to institutions. The first child that Kanner diagnosed in Baltimore with "infantile autism" (Donald T.) spent a year in a preventorium in Mississippi until his parents mustered enough courage to remove him and bring him to Baltimore. A doctor who examined him suggested that his mother had "overstimulated him" (Donvan & Zucker, 2016, p. 13) and recommended a change of environment. Treatment, in those years, was based on addressing psychological and emotional issues thought to be at the root of the condition.

Before the development of behavioral interventions to help children on the autism spectrum, other well-intentioned researchers used LSD to treat the conditions associated with autism. The first study investigating the therapeutic effect of lysergic acid diethylamide (LSD) on autistic children did not yield satisfactory results. Twelve children participated in the study, expecting they would speak and communicate functionally. However, the hope that they could communicate their needs and wants did not happen (Freedman et al., 1962). Other psychiatrists and psychologists jumped on the bandwagon (Simmons et al., 1972), but the methodological soundness of the various studies using LSD was questionable (Sigafoos et al., 2007). The LSD fad fell out of favor when the U.S. government outlawed its possession, except for limited research purposes.

It was not until the 1960s and 1970s that psychologists trained in the experimental analysis of behavior developed behavioral approaches to address autism-related difficulties. Over the years, those approaches have evolved into well-documented, time-tested, and evidence-based interventions that can help individuals on the spectrum acquire skills to improve their quality of life.

Behavior Analysis Before Skinner

Before Burrhus Frederic Skinner formulated the **operant conditioning** principle to study living organisms' behavior, Thorndike (1898) investigated whether animals could learn. He built puzzle boxes where he placed a hungry cat that could escape only by operating latches to access fish scraps. When he put a cat in the box for the first time, there was no evidence of "flashes of insight." The cat's escaping behavior was based on trial and error. Interestingly, each successive **discrete trial** resulted in a shorter and shorter time for the cat to get out of the box. Thorndike believes if an action brings a reward, that action becomes "stamped into the mind." As a result, he formulated the law of effect—i.e., behavior is a function of its consequences.

Ivan Petrovitch Pavlov, a Russian physiologist, serendipitously discovered **classical conditioning**—a learning process involving pairing two stimuli.

Pavlov set out to study dogs' salivary gland and its effect on digestion. Dogs naturally salivate when presented with meat or meat powder. However, Pavlov discovered that salivation could occur with other stimuli paired with food presentation. The stimulus-response (S-R) connection has shaped **Behaviorism**—a school of thought that dominated psychology in the first half of the 20th century. Pavlov's discovery of classical conditioning (aka Pavlovian or respondent conditioning) plays an essential role in many facets of human learning and behavior, including acquiring emotional responses, addiction, counterconditioning, and psychotherapy.

John Broadus Watson is considered the founder of behaviorism. He published a manifesto (Watson, 1913) that influenced psychology as a scientific discipline. Watson argued that for psychology to be on par with the natural sciences (e.g., physics, chemistry, and biology), psychologists must investigate observable and measurable behavior. In Watson's view, introspection, a common practice then, had no place in scientific inquiries. He wrote:

> Psychology as the behaviorist views it is a purely objective experimental branch of natural science. Its theoretical goal is the prediction and control of behavior. Introspection forms no essential part of its methods, nor is the scientific value of its data dependent upon the readiness with which they lend themselves to interpretation in terms of consciousness.
>
> (Watson, 1913, p. 158)

Although Watson's interest was in comparative psychology—the psychological nature of human beings compared to other animals—he wrote: "The behaviorist, in his efforts to get a unitary scheme of animal response, recognizes no dividing line between man and brute" (p. 158). He is best known for his infamous "Little Albert experiment." Like Pavlov's stimulus-stimulus pairing and resulting respondent conditioning, Watson conditioned a 9-month-old infant, Albert, to fear a previously neutral stimulus—a rat—through numerous pairings of the infant's interaction with the animal. When Albert approached the rat, Watson simultaneously banged a metal rod, causing Albert to startle. As a result, Albert became not only afraid of the rat but his fear generalized to anything that had a furry appearance. Watson's experiment demonstrates that people can acquire emotional responses through conditioning. Although Watson embraced the stimulus-response psychology that was prevalent then, he paved the way for what would become the experimental analysis of behavior.

Skinner and the Experimental Analysis of Behavior

Watson's writing on behaviorism influenced Skinner's interest in behavioral psychology. While acknowledging Pavlov's work and the importance of stimulus-response conditioning, Skinner postulated that most human behavior is guided by volitional behavior—i.e., organisms operating in the environment and resulting consequences, making their behavior more or less likely. He developed *operant conditioning*—behavior is a function of its consequences. Skinner wrote extensively on *behaviorism*, the philosophy of the science of behavior. Skinner (1938) set out the parameters of the science of the experimental analysis of behavior.

Skinner devised an apparatus (later termed the operant chamber) to control a hungry rat's lever-pressing responses, which resulted in the delivery of pellets based on specific schedules (i.e., the number of a fixed or variable predetermined number of presses or the passing of a fixed or variable time). Skinner's experiments with rats and pigeons led to his discovery of basic learning principles (e.g., reinforcement, extinction, **punishment**, and so on), which apply to solving significant human problems. As Watson proposed, Skinner argued that behavior analysis is a natural science that can be predicted and studied systematically. He provided a scientific framework for analyzing, understanding, and predicting human behavior (Skinner, 1953). Skinner's (1957) analysis of language forms the basis for therapists to develop and implement interventions for children with autism or other intellectual disabilities with language delays or deficits.

Skinner was primarily interested in the experimental analysis of behavior. However, some writers (Morris et al., 2005) view him as the founder of applied behavior analysis (ABA). In their view, Skinner addressed the central tenets of ABA in his writing, as described and defined by Baer and colleagues (1968).

Applied Behavior Analysis Before Lovaas

Although applied behavior analysis (ABA) is rooted in the experimental analysis of behavior, its evolution has been circuitous. Many researchers who used operant conditioning techniques in the laboratory with rats and pigeons extended those principles to study children with autism or other developmental disabilities. Psychologists trained in the experimental analysis of behavior conducted various studies with human participants to translate what they had discovered in animal laboratories into practical applications. For example, Fuller (1949) published the first report of a study based on operant conditioning with a human subject, whom he described as an 18-year-old "vegetative idiot" confined in a "feeble-minded" institution. The subject had limited body, head, shoulders, and arm movement and had not learned anything in 18 years. Fuller deprived the subject of food for 15 hours and used a syringe full of warm milk-sugar solution. Then, Fuller skirted the solution in the syringe into the corner of the subject's mouth, following any arm movement. As a result, the subject raised his arm 19 times in 16 minutes. After numerous trials, he simultaneously opened his mouth while raising his arm. Fuller extinguished the subject's right arm raising by withholding the reinforcer (sweetened milk). Fuller concluded the report with the following:

> For years, many psychologists have experimented exclusively with infra-human [subjects], and they have expressed a preference for the simple, less variable behavior of the lower organisms in the laboratory. Perhaps by beginning at the bottom of the human scale, the transfer from rat to [hu]man can be effected.
>
> (Fuller, 1949, p. 588)

Other researchers applied operant procedures to address behavior problems of children with autism and other intellectual disabilities. For example, Azrin and Lindsey (1956) manipulated typically developing children's cooperation without prior instructions. Ayllon and Michael (1959) taught a psychiatric nurse to control patients' undesirable behavior in a mental hospital. Ferster (1961) used positive reinforcement to target the behavioral deficits of autistic children. Ferster and Demyer (1962) were among the first researchers to use operant conditioning techniques to teach three severely autistic children who lacked meaningful communication skills. The participants responded to the environmental contingencies and displayed simple responses that gradually became more complex. The experiment demonstrated that operant reinforcement techniques can promote and maintain desirable responses.

Similarly, Wolf and colleagues (1963) taught a 3.5-year-old autistic boy with severe self-destructive tantrums to keep his eyeglasses on because both lenses in his eyes had been removed due to cataracts. Risley and Wolf (1967) used operant techniques, including **shaping**, imitation training, fading, extinction, timeout from reinforcement, and differential reinforcement, to develop speech in echolalic children. Hall and colleagues (1968) investigated the effect of contingent teacher attention on preschool children who exhibited high rates of disruptive behaviors in the classroom. Baer and colleagues (1968) published a paper defining the dimensions of applied behavior analysis.

The Lovaas Method

In the 1960s, there were no effective treatments for autism, so psychiatrists, researchers, and clinicians resorted to outlandish measures, including using **LSD** (Bender et al., 1963; Freedman et al., 1962; Simmons et al., 1966), in their attempts to help parents and their children diagnosed with autism. However, several psychologists with an operant learning orientation at the University of Washington (UW) conducted groundbreaking studies to improve the lives of children with learning disabilities (Wolf et al., 1963).

Lovaas' graduate work was on learning and clinical psychology with an emphasis on psychoanalytic theory and Hullian learning theory. However, his interaction with autistic children at the Neuropsychiatric Institute at the University of Washington and mentors including Donald Baer and Sidney Bijou paved the way for his interest in applied behavior analysis and autism (Larsson & Wright, 2011). Ole Ivar Lovaas' interest in treating and educating children diagnosed with autism originated from his postgraduate training at UW. His initial research on how a person's language could influence other behavior paved the way for his interest in autism at UCLA (Smith & Eikeseth, 2011).

His initial attempts to develop a method to treat autism (Lovaas et al., 1965; Lovaas & Simmons, 1969) centered around using painful electric shocks to modify undesirable behaviors (e.g., repetitive bodily movements, self-stimulatory behavior, and tantrums) in two 5-year-old identical twins diagnosed as childhood schizophrenics. While the shocks effectively eliminated undesirable behaviors, the reduction effect was short-lived without continual shock training. Similarly, he recruited three institutionalized children at the Camarillo and Pacific State hospitals (Donvan & Zucker, 2016) with severe autism who exhibited maladaptive behaviors (e.g., drinking from the toilet, eating feces, and punching their faces). Although Lovaas demonstrated that punishment could reduce undesirable behavior, the children returned to their respective institutions and reverted to engaging in self-destructive behaviors. Public perception of punishment and its long-term ineffectiveness dissuaded Lovaas from continuing its use and instead embraced reinforcement-based tactics.

Lovaas' Young Autism Project originated at the University of California, Los Angeles (UCLA). The philosophy underlying Lovaas' method is that children with autism (and other intellectual disabilities) do not learn as readily as typically developing ones do. Therefore, instruction must be structured in an intense and comprehensive learning environment. The home-based model is designed to take advantage of preschoolers' brain malleability. The treatment entails 40 hours of a child interacting with a team of therapists or a parent for at least three years. Learning opportunities are available during all waking hours and in all learning environments. Lovaas used the term "behavioral engineering" to describe his approach to treating and educating children with autism. His treatment protocol is now known as applied behavior analysis (ABA) or the Lovaas method.

Lovaas trained college students and parents to implement discrete trial procedures, ensuring consistency in his intervention protocol and maintaining acquired skills outside a structured clinical setting. Therefore, instruction must be structured in an intense and comprehensive learning environment. Learning opportunities are available during all waking hours and in all learning environments. Lovaas developed discrete trial training (DTT) as an instructional technique consisting of modeling, prompting, and positive reinforcement to facilitate skill acquisition. DTT breaks down a skill targeted for acquisition into "discrete" simple components that learners acquire independently. Once learners master all the skill parts, they are linked and executed sequentially. For example, teaching a child to hold a pencil and write an

"A" on a sheet of paper entails many steps that she/he must master to complete the task.

Lovaas (1981) wrote the first do-it-yourself handbook for parents of children with autism based on the method he developed in his laboratory at the University of California, Los Angeles (UCLA). He co-founded the Autism Society of America in 1965. He pioneered discrete trial training (DTT), an instructional technique that reduces complex learning tasks to simpler units to instruct children with intellectual disabilities.

Based on the Young Autism Project Lovaas started at UCLA, he published a landmark **quasi-experimental study** (Lovaas, 1987). The data collected across home-based intervention sessions showed that an early intensive behavioral intervention (EIBI), consisting of 40 hours a week of treatment, increased the IQs of nine of the 19 participants by an average of thirty points, making them indistinguishable from their typically developing peers. Lovaas touted that 49% of the participants "recovered" from autism. The popular press substituted the word "recovered" for "cured," a word substitution that generated much-expected scrutiny from his critics. Although his critics viewed the study with skepticism because of the nonrandom assignment of the participants, Lovaas' clinical work greatly influenced the treatment of autism.

Replication of Lovaas' Study

Lovaas' seminal publication (1987) generated optimism and controversy. Optimism because parents could now be hopeful that early treatment would mitigate the condition's debilitating effects. Controversy because many researchers (e.g., Gresham & MacMillan, 1998) questioned whether Lovaas' results could be substantiated and replicated, owing to methodological flaws in the sampling—i.e., he did not randomly assign the participants to the experimental or the control condition. A follow-up of the original study showed that, compared to participants in the control group, eight out of nine participants in the experimental condition who had achieved "best outcomes" maintained their gains and were "indistinguishable" from their typical peers on tests of intelligence and adaptive behavior (McEachin et al., 1993).

Replications of Lovaas' study (1987) found that children with autism who received early intensive behavioral intervention (EIBI)—i.e., 35 or more hours, achieved significant gains in IQ scores and adaptive behaviors compared to their counterparts who received other interventions or no intervention (Eldevik et al., 2010). Cohen and colleagues (2006) replicated Lovaas' findings in community settings by comparing two groups of participants. One group received EIBI for 35 to 40 hours per week, whereas the other group was enrolled in special education classes at local public schools. A randomized trial of intensive early intervention for children with autism (Smith et al., 2000) compared parent training of children with autism with parents whose children received intensive treatment (i.e., an average of 24.5 hours per week). The children who received the intensive treatment outperformed those in the training group regarding intelligence, language, visual-spatial skills, and academics, but not in adaptive functioning of behavior problems.

Similarly, Sallows and Graupner (2005) randomly assigned twenty-four children with autism to two groups: Clinic-directed and parent-directed. The clinic-directed group received the early intensive intervention developed at UCLA, whereas the parent-directed group received similar intensive behavioral interventions by well-trained therapists but less supervision. After four years of treatment, 48% of participants achieved treatment outcomes that were consistent with the results Lovaas (1987) published in his seminal paper. Data from a more recent systematic review of replication studies of the Lovaas model show that it can foster cognitive functioning and adaptive behavior in children diagnosed with autism (Nicolosi & Dillenburger, 2021).

Many variants of applied behavior analysis have been developed and are discussed in detail in the subsequent sections of this chapter. However, applied behavior analysis in its purest form is considered the gold standard of behavioral treatment for several reasons. First, the approach is data-driven and focuses on measurable behavior change. Therapists can assess treatment effectiveness via data inspection and decide whether to continue or modify an intervention. Second, interventions are individually tailored to address the needs of each individual. Third, and most importantly, there is accumulated evidence based on a vast body of literature rooted in the experimental analysis of behavior that supports procedures designed and implemented by well-trained behavior analysts. In 1999, the Surgeon General of the United States, David Satcher, stated in his report on mental health, "Thirty years of research demonstrated the efficacy of applied behavioral methods in reducing inappropriate behavior and in increasing communication, learning, and appropriate social behavior" (Satcher, 1999, p. 164).

In sum, behavior analysts have successfully used ABA to habilitate children, adolescents, and adults with autism. Early intensive behavioral interventions have been most helpful with children, whereas focusing on adaptive and vocational skills has been more appropriate for adolescents and adults (Ivy & Schreck, 2016). The effectiveness of behavioral interventions lies in their adherence to research-supported operant principles.

Discrete Trial Training

Discrete trial training (DTT) is associated with the work of Lovaas; it teaches skill acquisition and reduces problem behavior in children on the autism spectrum. The method is now widely used in applied behavior analysis. The main criticism leveled at DTT is that it is too rigidly structured and implemented in contrived settings. As a result, trained responses may not be generalized to more naturalistic settings (Charlop-Christy et al., 1999; Smith, 2001). Additionally, learners may not be as motivated or engaging as those trained in more natural-istic or child-led approaches. In response to these criticisms, incidental teaching has been developed as an alternative to discrete trial training. Unlike adults de-termining the skills targeted for acquisition in the discrete trial approach, chil-dren in incidental teaching create the activities and "teaching moments" that adults can seize and manipulate to reinforce appropriate language approximation and production.

Incidental Teaching

Incidental teaching is based on applying basic learning principles derived from the experimental analysis of behavior to provide learning opportunities in the natural environment. Incidental teaching is a naturalistic language approach in which children acquire language in the context of typical adult-child interactions. As an instructional method, it uses opportunities that arise during an adult-child interaction to create a teaching moment. Hart and Risley (1975, p. 411) defined incidental teaching as an "interaction between an adult and a single child which arises naturally in an unstructured situation such as free play and which is used by the adult to transmit information or give the child practice in developing a skill."

The environment in which the interaction takes place must be carefully planned and structured. For example, if a child's favorite toy is on display but out of reach, the child is likely to initiate an interaction with a person in the environment. The adult can also prompt the child to request the toy. A therapist, a teacher, or a parent can select an activity in a naturally occurring situation in which a child is interested. Incidental learning strategies are then used to initi-ate the learner's responses. Incidental teaching promotes motivation that can facilitate response generalization. Parents, teachers, and clinicians can structure the environment to lure children into being more motivated to initiate interac-tions with others. Sessions are conducted throughout the day, and children are encouraged to use language in an environment more tightly controlled than one in which discrete trial sessions are implemented. As a result, language acquisi-tion can occur and be generalized in natural contexts.

Hart and Risley (1968) demonstrated the positive effects and word acquisi-tion that disadvantaged children can make when taught language in relevant contexts. For example, they used free-play situations to increase the acquisition rate of color-noun combinations ("red paint"), number-noun combinations ("two blocks"), size-noun combinations ("long time"), and shape-noun combinations ("round circle"). The study paved the way for other studies that shaped the de-velopment of the incidental teaching method. Hart and Risley developed the concept of incidental teaching in the 1970s to increase children's language skills in the natural environment (Hart & Risley, 1974, 1975). The idea was expanded as part of the Walden Early Childhood Program (McGee et al., 1994; McGee et al., 1999, 2000), as a teaching tool to educate toddlers, preschoolers, and pre-kindergarten-age children, including children with autism.

Incidental Teaching Effectiveness

The incidental teaching method has been a long-established and well-documented approach for working with toddlers and children. Various studies have demonstrated the method's effectiveness in promoting language and social skill acquisition in children, including those with autism. One important aspect of incidental teaching is objectively monitoring each child's progress. Alai-Rosales and colleagues (2017) recommended "happy progress" to evaluate the method's effectiveness. Happy progress refers to the positive and observable gains in areas targeted for modification. Happy progress is achieved through the child's happy, uncoerced initiations, motivation, and teaching that promote moments initiated during adult-child interactions.

In addition to incidental teaching, various methods are used to promote language acquisition in autistic children. For example, Goldstein (2002) reviewed various treatment methods (e.g., sign language, discrete trial training, and milieu teaching procedures). Milieu teaching is a variant of incidental teaching and was first described by Hart and Rogers-Warren (1978). Milieu teaching procedures create a language-rich environment that supports a learner's language development. These procedures have been used to promote language acquisition and functional communication in children on the autism spectrum. Similarly, Peterson and colleagues (2024) evaluated the effectiveness of an intervention that combined discrete trial training, mass trial, and naturalistic training in a sample of 93 individuals with autism. Participants who received the combined intervention demonstrated a significant improvement in the behaviors targeted for change.

Pivotal Response Training

The pivotal response treatment (PRT), formerly called the natural language paradigm (Koegel et al., 1987), is a naturalistic, child-directed behavioral approach for helping children (adolescents and adults) diagnosed with autism improve their social interaction, communication, and behavior. "Pivotal" means that specific areas, when targeted, can lead to collateral improvements in other untargeted areas of responding and functioning. Research conducted on PRT has studied five pivotal areas: motivation, self-initiations, self-management, receptivity and responsivity to multiple cues, and empathy (Koegel et al., 1999). PRT emerged in the 1960s and 1970s. Like other behavioral approaches, the model is rooted in operant learning—i.e., stimulus-response-consequence (Skinner, 1953)—and is based on the learner's motivation to respond and initiate contact with the environment. When adequately implemented (Cadogan & McCrimmon, 2015), the PRT can help children improve their communication, behavior, and social interactions.

The guiding principle of PRT is predicated on people's motivation to learn. When their motivation is high, they learn better. Research conducted on PRT and its use as an effective model for learning identified several motivational components: (1) allowing individuals to choose their learning activities; (2) combining easy tasks with difficult ones to avoid monotony and boredom; (3) using natural rewards related to what the individual is learning; and (4) reinforcing an individual's each successive approximation to exhibit desirable behaviors or learn new skills (Koegel & Koegel, 2019).

Contrary to discrete trials in which the outcome is either success or failure, pivotal responses lead to an outcome that can approximate the desired response. In a discrete trial training (DTT), for example, a therapist might prompt a student to touch his nose. The response to the request can either be a success that the therapist reinforces (e.g., the therapist saying "good job") or a failure that the therapist does not reinforce (e.g., the therapist saying "no"). DTT procedures include elevated levels of adult control during all aspects of the interaction. In pivotal response training, however, the child actively guides the therapist during the trials. For example, suppose the child is interested in playing with a toy truck. In that case, the therapist takes advantage of his motivation and integrates playing with a truck into the teaching. The reinforcing consequence is not, say, candy but a truck.

Evaluation of the PRT

Studies conducted to evaluate the PRT have generally found the model effective at improving the communication and social skills of children diagnosed with autism. Many research studies have been replicated using various experimental designs and have shown positive findings across multiple settings (Verschuur et al., 2013). For example, Fossum and colleagues (2018) examined the characteristics of 57 children with autism enrolled in a PRT-based community program. They found that those who made the most progress showed more positive emotions, greater verbal communication, appropriate play with toys, fewer repetitive vocalizations, and less avoidance of people. Lei and Ventola (2017) reviewed several research studies that integrated neuroimaging techniques and behavioral measures and found that the former can help identify children with autism who are more likely to respond and benefit from PRT. Moreover, they found evidence supporting the effectiveness of PRT. Gengoux and colleagues (2019) conducted a 24-week randomized controlled trial to compare the effectiveness of PRT on children diagnosed with autism who received a community-based treatment compared to children who received a pivotal response treatment package (PRT-P) consisting of clinician-delivered in-home intervention and parent training. The results showed that, compared to children who received the community-based intervention, those who received the PRT-P showed marked improvement in social communication skills.

Positive Behavior Support (PBS)

George Sugai and Robert Horner developed the Effective Behavior Support (EBS) at the University of Oregon in the 1990s. Subsequently, EBS became known as Positive Behavioral Interventions and Strategies (PBIS) and, more commonly, Positive Behavior Support (PBS). The underpinning principle of the PBS framework was developed in response to the use of aversive consequences that change agents used with people with intellectual disabilities, hence the term positive behavior support. During the early years of what became applied behavior analysis, Lovaas, a pioneering figure in the development of autism treatment, experimented with various aversive behavior management procedures (Lovaas & Simmons, 1969). Of course, such practice is no longer part of ABA practitioners' behavior change procedures.

Various terms have been included under the umbrella of PBS. For example, positive behavior interventions and support (PBIS) refers to PBS in school-based applications. The term PBIS was introduced in the 1997 amendments to the Individuals with Disabilities Education Act (IDEA), as PBS and functional behavioral assessment played an influential role in school restructuring (Sugai et al., 2000). The positive behavior support approach has been extended as a preventive "school-wide" positive behavior support to address student problem behavior in public elementary and middle schools (Sugai & Horner, 2002, 2006). Program-wide positive behavior support (PWPBS) denotes PBS in early childhood programs. In contrast, school-wide positive behavior support (SWPBS) refers to PBS in schools serving students in kindergarten through grade 12 (Kincaid et al., 2016).

Sailor and colleagues' (2009) Handbook of Positive Behavior Support captured the essence of PBS and how dealing with difficult children in public education in the 1980s guided the approach. Although rooted in applied behavior analysis, PBS moved from a punitive model to one focusing on reinforcing positive behaviors.

Positive Behavior Support (PBS) has been defined in various ways over the years. Carr and Sidener (2002) summarized eight characteristics of the model that comprise the multiple definitions. These characteristics include person-centered planning, functional assessment, focus on the environment, and ecological validity. The PBS characteristics are consistent with those of Applied Behavior Analysis (ABA) despite framing PBS as "The evolution of applied behavior analysis into positive behavior support" (Carr, 1997, p. 208). Horner (2000), one of the originators of the model, defines PBS as follows:

Positive behavior support is the application of behavior analysis to the social problems created by such behaviors as self-injury, aggression, property destruction, pica, defiance, and disruption. It is an approach that blends values about the rights of people with disabilities with a practical science about how learning and behavior change occur.

(Horner, 2000, p. 97)

Kincaid and colleagues (2016) provided the most encompassing definition of PBS:

> PBS is an approach to behavior support that includes an ongoing process of research-based assessment, intervention, and data-based decision-making focused on building social and other functional competencies, creating supportive contexts, and preventing strategies that are respectful of a person's dignity and overall well-being and that are drawn primarily from behavioral, educational, and social services, although other evidence-based procedures may be incorporated. PBS may be applied within a multitiered framework at the level of the individual and the level of larger systems (e.g., families, classrooms, schools, social service programs, and facilities).
>
> (Kincaid, 2016, p. 71)

Does PBS Differ from ABA?

Horner (2000), a prominent figure in the development and implementation of PBS, asserted that

> Positive behavior support is not a new approach; it builds directly from a long experimental history (p. 97) ... There is no difference in the theory or science between positive behavior support and behavior modification. These are the same approaches with different names (p. 99).

Positive behavior support is, at its core, applied behavior analysis branded as a novel approach. Most of the research studies included in meta-analyses in the PBS literature are also published in the ABA literature (Carr & Sidener, 2002; Mulick & Butter, 2005). It is worth noting that the focus and style of many studies published in the *Journal of Positive Behavior Interventions* are comparable to those published in the ABA literature.

PBS distinguishes itself from ABA through its innovative marketing strategies and its proponents' ability to present a model heralded as different, if not superior, to ABA. The success of PBS can be attributed to its emphasis on positive strategies and emphasis on value-laden keywords—including *positive, personal dignity, lifestyle change, and quality of life*—its widespread dissemination as a treatment model instead of a research model, and the support of federal grants, which have facilitated its service delivery within the public school system (Johnston et al., 2006). Carr and Sidener (2002) proposed that "PBS can be characterized as a service-delivery framework within the broader discipline of applied behavior analysis" (p. 251).

Positive Behavior Support Philosophy

The central tenet of PBS is its focus on "fixing environments, not people." The home, school, and community environments are redesigned to minimize and prevent problem behaviors. When settings are effectively structured, problem behaviors are rendered "irrelevant, inefficient, and ineffective" (Horner, 2000, p. 97). According to Carr and colleagues (2002), Positive Behavior Support (PBS) evolved from three primary sources: (1) behavior analysis, (2) person-centered values, and (3) the **normalization/inclusion** movement. As a result, they describe PBS as follows:

> PBS is an applied science that uses educational methods to expand an individual's behavior repertoire and systems change methods to redesign an individual's living environment to first enhance the individual's quality of life and, second, to minimize his or her problem behavior.
>
> (Carr et al., 2002, p. 4)

Horner and colleagues (1990) rejected the term "nonaversive behavior management" based on the notion that what is considered aversive can be objectively blatant. Still, aversion can be subjectively perceived as in the case of a child who believes completing homework or schoolwork is undesirable. Instead, they favored a more socially acceptable term—"positive behavioral support (PBS)"—and proposed several themes that guide the emerging movement: (a) the emphasis is on lifestyle change of individuals and in various aspects of their lives; (b) the minimization of the use of punishment is desirable and can be achieved by withholding the delivery of reinforcers for undesirable behavior and using those reinforcers for promoting the acquisition of more socially acceptable behavior; (c) the reliance on determining the adaptive function(s) of target behaviors through functional analyses, manipulation of antecedents, ecological and setting events, and (d) teaching adaptive behaviors that minimize the recurrence of maladaptive ones.

Positive Behavior Support Effectiveness

How effective is PBS? Donnellan and colleagues (1985) described the effectiveness of a program model that used nonaversive strategies with a diverse group of clients that engaged in maladaptive behaviors, including self-injurious behavior, physical aggression, tantrums, and inappropriate sexual behaviors. Foxx (2005) reviewed the study and thought that the behavior described was not at all "severe" and questioned the efficacy of using an exclusive approach to help people exhibiting severely **challenging behaviors**.

Clarke and Dunlap (2008) reviewed empirical intervention studies conducted with children with intellectual disabilities and published in the *Journal of*

Positive Behavior Interventions in the first seven years of the journal. The authors found that the published articles contained more "high levels of ecological validity, social validity, and assessment-based interventions" (features consistent with the central tenets of PBS) than their peer-reviewed counterparts. For example, the *Journal of Applied Behavior Analysis* also published many articles on intervention with children and youth with disabilities.

The positive behavior support approach is primarily based on operant learning and conditioning. Therefore, applying those principles should effectively manage skill acquisition and reduce maladaptive behaviors. LaVigna and Willis (2012) reviewed the outcomes of 12 studies that used the PBS approach to address several issues that critics of the approach have raised. Namely, how effective is PBS in reducing severe and high-rate behavior problems? How much training is needed for effective service delivery? How affordable are PBS services? Can the administration of its procedures be equally effective in school, community, and institutional settings? They cautioned that their review was based on a few studies, so more research is needed to support the findings of those studies in terms of formal outcome measures.

The School-Wide Positive Behavioral Interventions and Supports (SWPBIS) have proven effective in a study involving over 12,000 elementary school children. Data from randomized controlled trials collected over four years decreased children's concentration and behavioral problems and increased prosocial behavior and social-emotional functioning. In comparison to control groups, children in the SWPBIS program were 33% less likely to be sent to the office for disciplinary actions (Bradshaw et al., 2012).

In sum, positive behavior support emerged in the 1990s in response to aversive procedures that behavior analysts used to reduce undesirable behaviors. Although PBS is rooted in applied behavior analysis, some proponents of the model have framed it as a new approach that should be separated from ABA. Positive Behavior Support (PBS) and Applied Behavior Analysis (ABA) both have their roots in learning principles that originated in experimental behavior analysis. PBS emphasizes understanding the function of the behavior targeted for change through functional assessments and proactive interventions in a supportive classroom environment to teach new skills that can replace undesirable behavior. On the other hand, ABA interventions focus on modifying specific behaviors using reinforcement and consequences. ABA therapists break down complex tasks into smaller teachable units and use mass practice to reduce problematic behaviors and promote desirable ones.

Functional Communication Training

Children diagnosed with autism often have severe limitations in communication skills, and as many as 30% may never develop fluent speech (Wodka et al., 2013). Problem behaviors, including self-injury, tantrums, and aggression, are common among severely developmentally disabled individuals, especially non-verbal ones. Therefore, aberrant behaviors may be a substitute for communicating wants and needs (Carr & Durand, 1985; Durand & Moskowitz, 2015). In such cases, teaching them to communicate by any means possible could mitigate their need to engage in destructive behaviors.

Carr and Durand (1985) first described functional communication training (FCT) as a behaviorally based intervention to address problematic behaviors of four intellectually disabled children who exhibited various behavior problems (e.g., tantrums, aggression, and self-injury). The assessment of the children's behavior showed that a high level of task difficulty and a low level of adult attention in their immediate environment resulted in problematic behaviors. Based on the assessment, Carr and Durand taught the children to request assistance from adults in their environment. As a result, teaching the children a communicative phrase (i.e., a replacement behavior such as "I need a break" or "I do not understand") markedly reduced problematic behaviors.

The implementation of FCT consists of a three-step process. First, the researcher/practitioner must determine the function(s) of the challenging behavior(s) (e.g., sensory, attention, escape, tangible). Second, the researcher/practitioner must identify a communicative response (e.g., verbal response, gesture or signs, picture communication, or assistive technology devices). Finally, implementing the process entails teaching the learner the appropriate communicative response by reinforcing the correct response and extinction of the problematic behavior (Luo et al., 2019).

Tiger and colleagues (2008) defined FCT as

a differential reinforcement procedure in which an individual is taught an *alternative response* that results in the same class of reinforcement identified as maintaining problem behavior. The problem behavior is typically placed on extinction (i.e., reinforcement no longer follows problem behavior).

In other words, therapists implementing FCT identify the function(s) or purpose of individuals' aberrant behavior and teach them more appropriate responses that serve the same purpose. For example, "if you want a break, ask for it instead of biting your hand."

Effectiveness of FCT

The assessment of the effectiveness of FCT has been generally positive. Tiger and colleagues (2008) reviewed 91 studies conducted with 204 participants. They found FCT effective at reducing various problem behaviors (e.g., self-injury, aggression, bizarre vocalization, stereotypy, and self-restraint). Their review indicated that FCT effectively reduced behavior problems maintained by gaining or denying access to environmental and social stimuli. Another review (Muharib & Wood, 2018) found FCT to be moderately effective with children up to 8 years diagnosed with autism, and more research is needed for a "strong level of evidence to support FCT as an evidence-based practice for children with autism." A recent review (Luo et al., 2019) found that FCT can reduce challenging behaviors effectively. However, implementing the model with more children and more rigorous methodologies is needed before FCT meets the standard for treating children with disabilities who display problematic behaviors.

Despite the reviews mentioned above, the initial study (Carr & Durand, 1985) has been replicated in hundreds of other studies dealing with different populations and treating various problem behaviors in individuals across all ages and developmental levels. Moreover, the American Psychological Association deemed FCT as exceeding the criteria for empirically supported treatments and designated the model as a well-established treatment for aberrant behavior of children diagnosed with intellectual disabilities, including autism (Chambless et al., 1996).

The Treatment and Education of Autistic and Related Communication Handicapped Children (TEACCH)

The treatment and education of autistic and related communication handicapped children (TEACCH) is a family-centered lifelong approach to *education* for people with autism. TEACCH (aka structured teaching) originated at the University of North Carolina at Chapel Hill in the 1970s to disseminate community-based services, research, and training programs to improve the quality of life of individuals with autism and their families across the lifespan. The notion that autism was a mental disorder resulting from cold mothering prompted the development of the approach that became TEACCH. Schopler's interactions with children with autism and the data he collected for his dissertation supported a different view of the cause(s) of autism: Individuals with autism have difficulties processing sensory information.

Schopler, who believed parents were an essential part of therapy (Schopler & Reichler, 1971), disagreed with Bettelheim's idea that autism was caused by "refrigerator mothers." Schopler viewed parents as a critical part of the therapeutic process. He emerged as the anti-Bettelheim (the fellow who established the **orthogenic** school at the University of Chicago). Schopler thought autism may be linked to "genetic, constitutional, and biochemical predispositions, not parents." Therefore, parents of autistic children should not be seen as scapegoats (Schopler, 1971) but as co-therapists who can play a pivotal role in developing learning programs for their children.

Donvan and Zucker (2016) provided an account that set the stage for developing what became the TEACCH. Schopler and a newly graduated physician, Reichler, were assigned the *Psychotic Child Group*, a funded program at the University of North Carolina that evaluated the effectiveness of Freudian-inspired group therapy on a cohort of "psychotic" 3- and 4-year-olds. The experience turned out to be an abject failure reminiscent of what Schopler experienced first-hand when Bettelheim invited him to visit his brand of therapy at the Orthogenic School for children with autism.

According to Donvan and Zucker (2016), it all started with David, a 3-year-old boy diagnosed with autism who had no language and was heavily medicated to control his impulsiveness and head banging. Schopler and Reichler dedicated time and effort to connecting with the boy and taught him rudimentary communication skills. Within six months, David became more responsive and acquired a vocabulary of about 1,000 words. After two and a half years of intervention, David made so much progress that he attended a regular kindergarten. Schopler and Reichler turned the recording of video sessions with David into a short film depicting the role of early interaction in mitigating the harmful effects of autism to lead to optimal outcomes. As a result, they received a three-year grant from the National Institute of Mental Health (NIMH). Subsequently, the state of North Carolina funded the program known as TEACCH in 1971.

The TEACCH Philosophy

Despite the heterogeneity of individuals with autism, they share many similarities. For example, many people experience learning, communication, social relationship, sensory processing, and perception difficulties. Therefore, individuals with autism display predictable patterns of behavior. The developers of TEACCH proposed the phrase "culture of autism" (Mesibov et al., 2004) to inform behavior change agents (i.e., therapists, teachers, and parents) of the importance of seeing the natural environment through the lenses of people with ASD (Mesibov et al., 2005). For example, people with autism typically pay attention to details and process visual information relatively more readily. Therefore, tasks must be structured in ways that facilitate learning.

Five core principles guide The TEACCH philosophy. First, students' physical environment where activities will take place (e.g., eating, playing, and learning) is clearly defined by boundaries. Second, the daily activity schedules are depicted in ways that indicate what engagement is expected. Third, activities are structured in ways that establish expectations and promote independence. Fourth, the environment supports consistency and routine in daily activities. Fifth, all cues and reminders are visually based. The flow of activities can proceed uninterrupted and without much verbal prompting.

Effectiveness of TEACCH

Many studies have used the TEACCH method with children on the autism spectrum with high functioning or without intellectual disabilities. Bourgondien and colleagues (2003) evaluated the effectiveness of TEACCH with a group of individuals with autism and severe disabilities. The results showed that participants' independence, communication, socialization, and positive behavior management increased compared to a control cohort. Another research study found that a TEACCH-based approach can foster communication skills in learners with severe disabilities (Butler, 2016). Siu and colleagues (2019) used TEACCH to teach functional skills to young adults with ASD and moderate intellectual disabilities. Participants in the study showed improvements in functional skills compared to their baseline data.

Butler (2016) implemented a TEACCH-based approach to teach communication skills to six adolescents with severe intellectual disabilities enrolled in a special education class. After two years of implementation, the participants showed instances of spontaneous communication above and beyond communication school staff and parents initiated. Sanz-Cervera and colleagues (2018) reviewed 14 studies to assess the effectiveness of TEACCH in reducing the stress levels of parents and teachers interacting with children diagnosed with autism. Results of the studies showed improvements in developmental abilities and a reduction in maladaptive behavior and autistic symptoms. Moreover, five of the 11 studies that evaluated stress among teachers and parents showed a significant reduction.

TEACCH has an established record of providing services to people with autism in their homes, schools, and clinical and residential settings in many parts of the world. Virués-Ortega and colleagues (2013) conducted a meta-analysis of 13 studies consisting of 172 participants with autism. They selected studies that used the TEACCH approach to assess the treatment outcomes of perceptual, motor, adaptive verbal, and cognitive skills. Irrespective of the duration, number of weekly sessions implemented, and implementation settings, results showed "moderate to large gains in social behavior and maladaptive behavior." The effect of the TEACCH approach on communication, motor functioning, and activities of daily living was "within the negligible to small range." Consequently, they concluded that its intervention method does not qualify as an evidence-based, comprehensive treatment model. They further pointed out that the TEACCH approach is not as effective as other current behavioral interventions, namely applied behavior analysis (Virués-Ortega et al., 2017).

The Early Start Denver Model (ESDM)

The Early Start Denver Model (ESDM) is an intensive, comprehensive treatment model based on behavioral and developmental principles for infants, toddlers, and children (12–48 months of age) diagnosed with autism spectrum disorders. Psychologists Sally Rogers and Geraldine Dawson developed the program in the 1980s. The program originated in Denver, Colorado, where Rogers initiated what she then termed the "play school model" with autistic children during their play activities. Over the years, the program became known as the Early Start Denver Model. The program aims to take advantage of young children's developing brains' malleability and plasticity to help them maximize their development potential through interactions with others in various domains: Language development, social skills, imitation, play, cognition, and motor and self-help skills.

Rogers and Dawson (2010) formulated the guiding principles of the ESDM, which consist of two components: (a) the ESDM curriculum checklist and (b) the teaching principles. The curriculum checklist is a 480-item assessment tool covering all developmental domains to assess children when they start the program. The assessment guides the development of a program tailored for each child, with 24–34 objectives evaluated every 12 weeks. Data collection is ongoing and based on the completion of each learned objective. The teaching principles emphasize "joint activity routines" in which children can choose the activity in a dyadic model of child-adult interaction.

Unlike other intervention approaches presented in this chapter (e.g., Incidental Teaching, Milieu Teaching, and Pivotal Response Teaching), the ESDM emphasizes a comprehensive development framework that optimizes the quality of emotions and relationships with others. Although the ESDM has a behavioral orientation, it differs from the traditional ABA in that its approach is more child-centered than adult-centered and focuses on "developmental science rather than operant behavioral models" (Rogers & Dawson, 2010, p. 33). Can the ESDM be consistent with ABA practices? Vivanti and Stahmer (2021) argued that its curriculum and practice are consistent with all the seven characteristics Baer and colleagues (1968) defined, and is thus in line with the behavioral orientation.

Effectiveness of the ESDM

There is accumulating evidence supporting some effectiveness of the ESDM. Various publications examined the effectiveness of the ESDM and found developmental gains in a large group of children with ASD in Denver Model classrooms (Rogers & DiLalla, 1991; Rogers et al., 1986; Rogers & Lewis, 1989; Rogers et al., 1987). Dawson and colleagues (2012) conducted a randomized intervention with forty-eight 18–30-month-old children with autism. Participants were randomly assigned to receive either the ESDM or a community intervention for two years. The ESDM group showed significantly improved language, IQ, and adaptive and social behaviors more than the community training participants. After the intervention, the brain electrical activity of the participants showed different patterns during the presentation of faces versus objects. The ESDM participants showed greater cortical activation when viewing faces. Conversely, participants who received the community intervention showed greater cortical activation when viewing objects. Dawson and colleagues (2012) asserted that their study was the "first trial to demonstrate that early behavioral intervention is associated with normalized patterns of brain activity."

A meta-analysis (Fuller et al., 2020) examined the effectiveness of the ESDM and found that, compared to control groups, children with autism showed improvements in cognition and language development. However, there were no significant gains in social communication or reduction of autism symptoms and repetitive behavior. Holehan and Zane (2019) reviewed a series of studies based on ESDM (e.g., Vismara et al., 2009; Vismara & Rogers, 2008). They concluded that many published studies were not rigorously designed and lacked experimental control. More alarming was that at least one of the two model originators participated in most of the studies, so more systematic replications are needed to evaluate the model's effectiveness. More recently, Tateno and colleagues (2021) conducted randomized control trials to investigate the clinical effectiveness of ESDM in infants diagnosed with autism in a community setting in Japan. They reported that ESDM effectively increased the participants' language and social development and reduced their maladaptive behavior.

Compared to the Lovaas method, how effective is ESDM in helping children on the autism spectrum? Research studies have demonstrated the effectiveness of ESDM in improving language and cognitive skills in children with autism. Unlike the Lovaass model, the ESDM emphasizes naturalistic teaching strategies and focuses on developing social communication skills at an early age.

The Picture Exchange Communication System

Approximately 25% to 30% of children with autism are minimally verbal (i.e., use fewer than 30 words) or have difficulty communicating verbally (Brignell et al., 2018). Various behavioral interventions have been used to remedy such language deficits, including discrete-trial procedures (Lovaas, 1987), pivotal response training (Koegel et al., 1991), and incidental teaching (Hart & Risley, 1980). The Picture Exchange Communication System (PECS) is an **augmentative and alternative communication system** used in applied behavior analysis to facilitate self-initiated communicative interactions with children with autism and related intellectual disabilities who have not acquired functional communication.

Bondy and Frost developed the program in 1985 at the Delaware Autism Program. Subsequently, they formulated the essence of the approach and how it should be taught (Bondy & Frost, 1998, 2001). PECS utilizes only pictures and icons as communication symbols. For example, a child who wants a banana can show and exchange a card depicting a banana to a communication partner to get an actual banana. The advent of computers and specialized speech generation devices has made applying PECS easier.

Phases in Training PECS Protocol

The training protocol consists of six phases that cover teaching a child to request an item of interest and use more advanced multipicture sentences (Bondy &

Frost, 2001). *Phase 1* (How to communicate) targets any indication of a child communicating a preference for an item. During that phase, two trainers facilitate initial communication: One trainer is the child's communication partner (facing the child), and the other (positioned behind the child) prompts and facilitates the child's communication effort. *Phase 2* (i.e., Distance and persistence) requires that the child move toward the communication partners and make more persistent effort in requesting an item of interest. *Phase 3* (i.e., Discrimination between symbols) emphasizes the child's ability to differentiate between a preferred and a non-preferred item using corresponding pictures. *Phase 4* (i.e., Using phrases) involves training the child to use simple phrases. A sequence of at least two pictures is required to initiate a request (e.g., I want juice). *Phase 5* (i.e., Answering a direct question) advances the child's communication capability by prompting him to respond to a verbal prompt (e.g., What do you want?) and the child's presentation of the corresponding pictures in a sentence form of the desired item. During *Phase 6* (Commenting), the last phase, the trainer promotes the child's spontaneous communication, uses sentence forms to request various preferred items, and responds to verbal prompts such as "What do you see?" or "What do you want?"

Effectiveness of PECS

Because PECS uses basic behavioral principles (e.g., shaping, differential reinforcement, **matching to sample**), the approach can be effective if implemented correctly. Eight-five children who learned to use PECS achieved "positive outcomes" (Bondy & Frost, 1994). One study showed that children with limited spontaneous verbal repertoire before PECS training showed a sustained increase in spontaneous vocal repertoire after the training ended (Schwartz et al., 1998). Charlop-Christy and colleagues (2002) examined the effects of PECS on three children with autism. Results of the study indicated that the participants mastered using PECS relatively quickly. More importantly, they displayed the emergence of speech, improved social-communicative behaviors, and decreased problem behavior. Flippin and colleagues (2010) systematically reviewed PECS studies published between 1994 and 2009. The authors reported that the participants (95 children) achieved "small to moderate gains in communication" following treatment. However, they noted that the children showed minor to negative gains in speech. Moreover, they concluded that PECS is a promising approach to teaching language to children on the spectrum but is not yet an established evidence-based practice for promoting communication in children with autism.

In sum, PECS offers many advantages, including a relatively less expensive approach to teaching language. No special training is required because the pictures contain corresponding label words. Conversely, training a child with autism to learn PECS may require much attention on his part. Moreover, communication is limited to the words he has at his disposal. Notwithstanding some of the limitations of the approach, numerous studies have supported the benefits of PECS for facilitating communication in children with communication deficits.

Developmental, Individual-Differences, Relationship-Based (DIR)

A large body of research conducted over many decades has demonstrated the effectiveness of early intensive behavioral intervention (EIBI) for persons diagnosed with autism. Lovaas (1993) was among the first clinicians who developed an approach based on basic learning principles to help children diagnosed with autism acquire adaptive skills and shed maladaptive behaviors that interfered with their daily functioning. Unlike interventions based on the application of basic learning principles, such as applied behavior analysis (ABA) and its variants, which emphasize reinforcement-based procedures to promote adaptive behavior, the Developmental, Individual-differences, Relationship-based (DIR) model (also known as the Greenspan approach) focuses on implementing a developmentally based functional approach to guide the assessment and treatment of autism (Greenspan & Wieder, 1999, 2007, 2009). DIR/Floortime offers an alternative to applied behavior analysis and related models by considering a child's level of interest and building on that interest to motivate the child to interact with others (Hess, 2013).

The DIR/Floortime is a relationship developmental approach that recognizes individual differences and the role emotions play in nurturing the development of the cognitive domain, language acquisition, and social development. The parents and other adults interacting with the child get down on the floor to become the child's peer and capture his interests. Typically developing infants systematically achieve milestones in all three broad domains (i.e., physical, cognitive, and social) by being in the company of parents and other adults, interacting with parents and other adults, and mimicking adaptive social responses that pave further social and cognitive development. Children on the autism spectrum or with an intellectual disability may have difficulties reaching normative developmental milestones without a structured environment.

According to Wieder and Greenspan (2003), the DIR model provides a framework for understanding a child's development and how she/he sees and interacts with the world. Social-emotional development plays a vital role in human development throughout the lifespan. Therefore, understanding the *developmental* process (i.e., "D"), viewing children as individuals *different* from others (i.e., "I"), and cultivating their *relationship* with others ("R") are all necessary facets for healthy development. Additionally, they described six stages of functional developmental, emotional capacities that are the key elements of Floor Time: (1) Self-regulation and shared attention, (2) Engaging and relating, (3) Two-way intentional communication, (4) Purposeful complex problem-solving communication, (5) Creating and elaborating symbols, and (6) Building bridges between symbols. The stages progress from getting the child to connect with a partner via joint attention and pleasurable activities to using pretend play and understanding emotional states such as loneliness, sadness, frustration, and disappointment.

DIR/Floortime Treatment Approach

The DIR/Floortime treatment approach is multidisciplinary and comprises various professionals, including clinical and developmental psychologists, occupational therapists, speech and language pathologists, and physical therapists. Parents play a vital role and are trained by DIR/Floortime therapists to implement Floortime activities. Other specialists, including pediatricians, nutritionists, and neurologists, are consulted as needed.

The central tenet of the DIR/Floortime approach is promoting a child's development by encouraging him to interact with parents and others through play activities. "Floortime" consists of 2–5 hours (repeated sessions of 20 minutes) of adult-child daily interactions, typically on the floor. Finding out what interests a child can be a starting point for engaging him, building his confidence, and teaching him what he wants to learn. The approach aims to promote sensory development, emotional and cognitive development, motor skills, and communication. Therapy sessions begin as early in life as possible. DIR/Floortime certified professionals (e.g., psychologists, speech and language pathologists, occupational therapists) oversee the program and help parents implement it (Greenspan & Wieder, 2009).

Effectiveness of the DIR/Floortime Model

How effective is the DIR/Floortime? A pilot program trained parents of children with autism to use the DIR/Floortime approach. Sixty-eight children participated in the program and interacted with their parents for 15 hours weekly over 8–12 months. Forty percent of the participants progressed developmentally. Notwithstanding "important limitations," results of the study suggest that the model has the "potential to be a cost-effective intervention" for children on the autism spectrum (Solomon et al., 2007).

Wieder and Greenspan (2003) described an account of a boy named Joey, who was diagnosed with autism at 30 months of age. He displayed the telltale signs of the condition (e.g., self-absorption, not responding to his name, lining up toys rather than playing with them, and so on). A series of Floortime interactions consisting of (1) six daily Floortime sessions, (2) four semi-structured and sensory-motor activities, (3) Intensive speech and occupational therapies, (4) 3–5 playdates weekly—i.e., interactions with typically developing children, (5) inclusion in a preschool, and (6) various music, gym, drama, and sports activities. Joey's dad played a vital role in getting on the floor and engaging him in various activities. In a sense, Dad became his play partner as Joey progressed in various stages of his development over three years. Owing to the heterogeneity of autism, would this treatment protocol have been effective with another child? The multidisciplinary approach and various stakeholders' involvement undoubtedly played a role.

A single case design study conducted with a child with autism showed preliminary evidence of the benefit of a DIR/Floortime approach (Dionne & Martini, 2011). Another study found a modest increase in socio-emotional development of children with autism. The authors cautioned that more research based on valid outcome measures and implemented with protocol fidelity is needed to rate the approach as evidence-based (Boshoff et al., 2020). Mercer (2017) reviewed various research articles describing the DIR/Floortime theoretical basis and principles and concluded that more research is needed to establish the approach as an evidence-based treatment.

Ross and colleagues (2018) were the most ardent critics of the DIR/Floortime approach. In their view, the implementation of the approach lacks "experimental control and empirical validity and objective measurement of treatment effects." Owing to the subjectivity of the model, more research is needed to evaluate its effectiveness as a treatment for children with autism. The flexibility of the approach's procedures may not benefit children on the spectrum who tend to adhere to routine activities and are thus unwilling to depart from them.

More recently, Divya and colleagues (2023) systematically reviewed DIR/Floortime articles published from 2010 to 2020 and the effectiveness of their findings in improving the functioning of children with autism. The authors concluded that more randomized clinical trials are needed to assess the approach's benefits on various developmental skills of children with autism. Notwithstanding this caveat, they rated the approach as cost-effective and likely to improve social and emotional development among children when implemented early by trained healthcare professionals.

Summary

Behavioral interventions have a long history characterized by trial and error that ultimately leads to the development of evidence-based treatments. Thorndike's formulation of the law of effect, Pavlov's discovery of classical conditioning, Watson's emphasis on observable behavior, and Skinner's operant conditioning, along with his experimental analysis of behavior, played a crucial role in advancing the science of behavior. Their theories and research laid the foundation for future studies and applications in psychology.

In the 1940s, children who were deemed "defective" due to various conditions, such as Down syndrome, cerebral palsy, or other undiagnosed illnesses, were often sent away to institutions. It was not until the 1960s and 1970s that psychologists who were trained in the experimental analysis of behavior conducted various studies involving human participants to translate findings from animal laboratories into practical applications. Additionally, other researchers used operant procedures to address behavioral issues in children with autism and other intellectual disabilities. Ole Ivar Lovaas' interest in treating and educating children diagnosed with autism originated from his postgraduate training at UW. Lovaas' groundbreaking Young Autism Project at UCLA and his pioneering use of discrete trial training became known as the Lovaas method, commonly called applied behavior analysis. His method focuses on discrete trial training to help children on the autism spectrum reduce maladaptive behaviors and acquire more socially acceptable ones.

Several intervention models based on learning principles have been developed. These include the following: *Positive Behavior Support* focuses on promoting desirable behaviors while preventing inappropriate ones. *Pivotal Response Training* emphasizes enhancing pivotal areas of development, which can lead to improvements in a broad range of behaviors and skills. *Incidental Teaching* encourages the use of everyday situations to promote learning and communication. *Functional Communication Training* replaces challenging behaviors with more appropriate communication methods. *Treatment and Education of Autistic and Related Communication Handicapped Children* (TEACCH) emphasizes using visual supports, structured environments, and individualized strategies to enhance learning and communication skills. *The Early Start Denver Model* combines applied behavior analysis (ABA) techniques with developmental and relationship-based approaches to promote social, communication, and cognitive skills. *The Picture Exchange Communication System* (PECS) facilitates communication challenges through visual symbols. *The Developmental, Individual-differences, Relationship-based* approach highlights the importance of understanding a child's development in the context of their unique individual differences and relationships. Each model offers different strategies and foci to support learning and communication for individuals, particularly those with development and communication challenges.

Questions to Ponder for Further Thinking and Learning

1 How effective are behavioral interventions in treating the symptoms of autism?
2 What is the role of parents in implementing behavioral interventions for their child with autism?
3 What are some potential side effects or drawbacks of behavioral interventions for autism?
4 How do behavioral interventions compare to other types of therapies for individuals with autism?
5 How early should behavioral interventions be started for a child with autism?
6 What are some fundamental principles of behavioral interventions for autism?

7 How do behavioral interventions address challenging behaviors associated with autism, such as self-injurious behavior?

8 Are any new or emerging behavioral interventions being developed for autism?

References

Alai-Rosales, S., Toussaint, K., & McGee, G. (2017). Incidental teaching: Happy progress. In J. B. Leaf (Ed.), *Handbook of social skills and autism spectrum disorder* (pp. 171–185). Springer International.

Ayllon, T., & Michael, J. (1959). The psychiatric nurse as a behavioral engineer. *Journal of the Experimental Analysis of Behavior, 2*, 323–334.

Azrin, N. H., & Lindsley, O. R. (1956). The reinforcement of cooperation between children. *Journal of Abnormal and Social Psychology, 52*(1), 100–102.

Baer, D. M., Wolf, M. M., & Risley, T. R. (1968). Some current dimensions of applied behavior analysis. *Journal of Applied Behavior Analysis, 1*(1), 91–97.

Bender, L., Faretra, G., & Cobrinik, L. (1963). LSD and UML treatment of hospitalized disturbed children. *Recent Advances in Biological Psychology, 5*, 84–92.

Bondy, A. S., & Frost, L. A. (1994). The Picture Exchange Communication System. *Focus on Autistic Behavior, 9*(3), 1–19.

Bondy, A. S., & Frost, L. A. (1998). The Picture Exchange Communication System. *Seminars in Speech and Language, 19*(4), 373–389.

Bondy, A. S., & Frost, L. A. (2001). The Picture Exchange Communication System. *Behavior Modification, 25*(5), 725–744.

Boshoff, K., Bowen, H., Paton, H., Cameron-Smith, S., Graetz, S., Young, A., & Lane, K. (2020). Child development outcomes of DIR/Floortime TM-based programs: A systematic review. *Canadian Journal of Occupational Therapy, 87*(2), 153–164.

Bourgondien, M. E. V., Reichle, N. C., & Schopler, E. (2003). Effects of a model treatment approach on adults with autism. *Journal of Autism and Developmental Disorders, 33*(2), 131–140.

Bradshaw, C. P., Waasdorp, T. E., & Leaf, P. J. (2012). Effects of school-wide positive behavioral interventions and supports on child behavior problems. *Pediatrics, 130*(5), e1136–e1145.

Brignell, A., Chenausky, K. V., Song, H., Zhu, J., Suo, C., & Morgan, A. T. (2018). Communication interventions for autism spectrum disorder in minimally verbal children. *Cochrane Database of Systematic Reviews, 11*(11), CD012324.

Butler, C. (2016). The effectiveness of the TEACCH approach in supporting the development of communication skills for learners with severe intellectual disabilities. *Support for Learning, 31*(3), 185–201.

Cadogan, S., & McCrimmon, A. W. (2015). Pivotal response treatment for children with autism spectrum disorder: A systematic review of research quality. *Developmental Neurorehabilitation, 18*(2), 137–144.

Carr, E. G. (1997). The evolution of applied behavior analysis into positive behavior support. *Journal of the Association for Persons with Severe Handicap, 22*, 208–209.

Carr, E. G., Dunlap, G., Horner, R. H., Koegel, R. L., Turnbull, A. P., Sailor, … Fox, L. (2002). Positive behavior support: Evolution of an applied science. *Journal of Positive Behavior Interventions, 4*(1), 4–16.

Carr, E. G., & Durand, V. M. (1985). Reducing behavior problems through functional communication training. *Journal of Applied Behavior Analysis, 18*(2), 111–126.

Carr, J. E., & Sidener, T. M. (2002). On the relation between applied behavior analysis and positive behavioral support. *The Behavior Analyst, 25*(2), 245–253.

Chambless, D. L., Sanderson, W. C., Shoham, V., Johnson, S. B., Pope, K. S., Crits-Christoph, P., ... McCurry, S. (1996). An update on empirically validated therapies. *The Clinical Psychologist, 49*(2), 5–18.

Charlop-Christy, M. H., Carpenter, M., Le, L., LeBlanc, L. A., & Kellet, K. (2002). Using the picture exchange communication system (PECS) with children with autism: Assessment of PECS acquisition, speech, social-communicative behavior, and problem behavior. *Journal of Applied Behavior Analysis, 35*(3), 213–231.

Charlop-Christy, M. H., LeBlanc, L. A., & Carpenter, M. H. (1999). Naturalistic teaching strategies (NATS) to teach speech to children with autism: Historical perspective, development, and current practice. *Contemporary School Psychology, 4,* 30–46.

Clarke, S., & Dunlap, G. (2008). A descriptive analysis of intervention research published in the Journal of Positive Behavior Interventions: 1999–2005. *Journal of Positive Behavior Interventions, 10*(1), 67–71.

Cohen, H., Amerine-Dickens, M., & Smith, T. (2006). Early intensive behavioral treatment: Replication of the UCLA model in a community setting. *Journal of Development and Behavioral Pediatrics, 27*(2 Suppl), S145–S155.

Dawson, G., Jones, E. J., Merkle, K., Venema, K., Lowy, R., Faja, S., ... Webb, S. J. (2012). Early behavioral intervention is associated with normalized brain activity in young children with autism. *Journal of the American Academy of Child & Adolescent Psychiatry, 51*(11), 1150–1159.

Dionne, M., & Martini, R. (2011). Floor time play with a child with autism: A single-subject study. *Canadian Journal of Occupational Therapy, 78*(3), 196–203.

Divya, K. Y., Begum, F., John, S. E., & Francis, F. (2023). DIR/Floor Time in engaging autism: A systematic review. *Iranian Journal of Nursing and Midwifery Research, 28*(2), 132–138.

Donnellan, A. M., LaVigna, G. W., Zambito, J., & Thvedt, J. (1985). A time-limited intensive intervention program model to support community placement for persons with severe behavior problems. *Journal of the Association for Persons with Severe Handicaps, 10*(3), 123–131.

Donvan, J., & Zucker, C. (2016). *In a different key: The story of autism.* Crown Publishers.

Durand, V. M., & Moskowitz, L. (2015). Functional communication training: Thirty years of treating challenging behavior. *Topics in Early Childhood Special Education, 35*(2), 116–126.

Eldevik, S., Hastings, R. P., Hughes, J. C., Jahr, E., Eikeseth, S., & Cross, S. (2010). Using participant data to extend the evidence base for intensive behavioral intervention for children with autism. *American Journal on Intellectual and Developmental Disabilities, 115*(5), 381–405.

Ferster, C. B. (1961). Positive reinforcement and behavioral deficits of autistic children. *Child Development, 32,* 437–456.

Ferster, C. B., & Demyer, M. K. (1962). A method for the experimental analysis of the behavior of autistic children. *The American Journal of Orthopsychiatry, 32,* 89–98.

Flippin, M., Reszka, S., & Watson, L. R. (2010). Effectiveness of the picture exchange communication system (PECS) on communication and speech for children with autism spectrum disorders: A meta-analysis. *American Journal of Speech-Language Pathology, 19*(2), 178–195.

Fossum, K.-L., Williams, L., Garon, N., Bryson, S. E., & Smith, I. M. (2018). Pivotal response treatment for preschoolers with autism spectrum disorder: Defining a predictor profile. *Autism Research, 11*(1), 153–165.

Foxx, R. M. (2005). Severe aggressive and self-destructive behavior: The myth of the nonaversive treatment of severe behavior. In J. W. Jacobson, R. M. Foxx, & J. A. Mulick (Eds.), *Controversial therapies for developmental disabilities: Fad, fashion and science in professional practice* (pp. 295–310). Lawrence Erlbaum.

Freedman, A. M., Ebin, E. V., & Wilson, E. A. (1962). Autistic schizophrenic children: An experiment in the use of d-lysergic acid diethylamide (LSD-25). *Archives of General Psychiatry, 6*, 203–213.

Fuller, E. A., Oliver, K., Vejnoska, S. F., & Rogers, S. J. (2020). The effects of the Early Start Denver Model for children with autism spectrum disorder: A meta-analysis. *Brain Science, 10*(6), 368.

Fuller, P. R. (1949). Operant conditioning of a vegetative human organism. *The American Journal of Psychology, 62*, 587–590.

Gengoux, G. W., Abrams, D. A., Schuck, R., Millan, M. E., Libove, R., Ardel, C. M., … Hardan, A. Y. (2019). A pivotal response treatment package for children with autism spectrum disorder: An RCT. *Pediatrics, 144*(3), Article e20190178.

Goldstein, H. (2002). Communication intervention for children with autism: A review of treatment efficacy. *Journal of Autism and Developmental Disorders, 32*(5), 373–396.

Greenspan, S. I., & Wieder, S. (1999). A functional developmental approach to autism spectrum disorders. *Journal of the Association for Persons with Severe Handicaps, 24*(3), 147–161.

Greenspan, S. I., & Wieder, S. (2007). The developmental individual-difference, relationship-based (DIR/Floortime) model approach to autism spectrum disorders. In E. Hollander & E. Anagnostou (Eds.), *Clinical manual for the treatment of autism* (pp. 179–209). American Psychiatric Publishing, Inc.

Greenspan, S., I., & Wieder, S. (2009). *Engaging autism: Using the Floortime approach to help children relate, communicate, and think.* Da Capo Press.

Gresham, F. M., & MacMillan, D. L. (1998). Early intervention project: Can its claims be substantiated and its effects replicated? *Journal of Autism and Developmental Disorders, 28*(1), 5–13.

Hall, R. V., Lund, D., & Jackson, D. (1968). Effects of teacher attention on study behavior. *Journal of Applied Behavior Analysis, 1*(1), 1–12.

Hart, B. M., & Risley, T. R. (1968). Establishing use of descriptive adjectives in the spontaneous speech of disadvantaged preschool children. *Journal of Applied Behavior Analysis, 1*(2), 109–120.

Hart, B., & Risley, T. R. (1974). Using preschool materials to modify the language of disadvantaged children. *Journal of Applied Behavior Analysis, 7*(2), 243–256.

Hart, B., & Risley, T. R. (1975). Incidental teaching of language in the preschool. *Journal of Applied Behavior Analysis, 8*(4), 411–420.

Hart, B., & Risley, T. R. (1980). In vivo language intervention: Unanticipated general effects. *Journal of Applied Behavior Analysis, 13*(3), 407–432.

Hart, B., & Rogers-Warren, A. (1978). A milieu approach to teaching language. In R. L. Schiefelbusch (Ed.), *Language intervention strategies* (pp. 193–235). University Park Press.

Hess, E. B. (2013). Dir®/Floortime™: Evidence-based practice towards the treatment of autism and sensory processing disorder in children and adolescents. *International Journal of Child Health and Human Development, 6*(3), 267–274.

Holehan, K. M., & Zane, T. (2019). Is there science behind that?: The Early Start Denver Model. *Science in Autism Treatment, 16*(2).

Horner, R. H. (2000). Positive behavior supports. *Focus on Autism and Other Developmental Disabilities, 15*(2), 97–105.

Horner, R. H., Dunlap, G., Koegel, R. L., Carr, E. G., Sailor, W., Anderson, J., ... O'Neill, R. E. (1990). Toward a technology of "nonaversive" behavioral support. *Journal of the Association for Persons with Severe Handicaps, 15*(3), 125–132.

Ivy, J. W., & Schreck, K. A. (2016). The efficacy of ABA for individuals with autism across the lifespan. *Current Developmental Disorders Reports, 3*, 57–66.

Johnston, J. M., Foxx, R. M., Jacobson, J. W., Green, G., & Mulick, J. A. (2006). Positive behavior support and applied behavior analysis. *The Behavior Analyst, 29*(1), 51–74.

Kincaid, D., Dunlap, G., Kern, L., Lane, K. L., Bambara, L. M., Brown, F., ... Knoster, T. P. (2016). Positive behavior support: A proposal for updating and refining the definition. *Journal of Positive Behavior Interventions, 18*(2), 69–73.

Koegel, R. L., & Koegel, L. K. (Eds). (2019). *Pivotal Response Treatment for autism spectrum disorders*. Brookes Publishing.

Koegel, R. L., Koegel, L. K., & Carter, C. M. (1999). Pivotal teaching interactions for children with autism. *School Psychology Review, 28*(4), 576–594.

Koegel, R. L., Koegel, L. K., & Schreibman, L. (1991). Assessing and training parents in teaching pivotal behaviors. *Advances in Behavioral Assessment of Children and Families, 5*, 65–82.

Koegel, R. L., O'Dell, M. C., & Koegel, L. K. (1987). A natural learning paradigm for nonverbal autistic children. *Journal of Autism and Developmental Disorders, 17*(2), 187–200.

Larsson, E. V., & Wright, S. (2011). O. Ivar Lovaas (1927–2010). *The Behavior Analyst, 34*(1), 111–114.

LaVigna, G. W., & Willis, T. J. (2012). The efficacy of positive behavioural support with the most challenging behaviour: The evidence and its implications. *Journal of Intellectual & Developmental Disability, 37*(3), 185–195.

Lei, J., & Ventola, P. (2017). Pivotal response treatment for autism spectrum disorder: Current perspectives. *Neuropsychiatric Disease and Treatment, 13*, 1613–1626.

Lovaas, O. I. (1981). *Teaching developmentally disabled children: The me book*. University Park Press.

Lovaas, O. I. (1987). Behavioral treatment and normal educational and intellectual functioning in young autistic children. *Journal of Consulting and Clinical Psychology, 55*(1), 3–9.

Lovaas, O. I. (1993). The development of a treatment-research project for developmentally disabled and autistic children. *Journal of Applied Behavior Analysis, 26*(4), 617–630.

Lovaas, O. I., & Simmons, J. Q. (1969). Manipulation of self-destruction in three retarded children. *Journal of Applied Behavior Analysis, 2*(3), 143–157.

Lovaas, O. I., Schaeffer, B., & Simmons, J. Q. (1965). Building social behavior in autistic children by use of electric shock. *Journal of Experimental Research in Personality, 1*(2), 99–109.

Luo, L., Gage, N. A., & Prykanowski, D. A. (2019). Systematic review of functional communication training in early care and education settings. *Education and Training in Autism and Developmental Disabilities, 54*(4), 358–376.

McEachin, J. J., Smith, T., & Lovaas, O., I. (1993). Long-term outcome for children with autism who received early intensive behavioral treatment. *American Journal on Mental Retardation, 97*(4), 359–372.

McGee, G., Daly, T., & Jacobs, H. (1994). The Walden preschool. In S. L. Harris & J. S. Handleman (Eds.), *Preschool education programs for children with autism* (pp. 127–162). PRO ED.

McGee, G. G., Morrier, M. J., & Daly, T. (1999). An incidental teaching approach to early intervention for toddlers with autism. *Journal of the Association for Persons with Severe Handicaps, 24*(3), 133–146.

McGee, G. G., Morrier, M., & Daly, T. (2000). The Walden preschool. In J. S. Handleman & S. L. Harris (Eds.), *Preschool education programs for children with autism* (2nd ed., pp. 157–190). PRO-ED.

Mercer, J. (2017). Examining DIR/FloortimeTM as a treatment for children with autism spectrum disorders: A review of research and theory. *Research on Social Work Practice, 27*(5), 625–635.

Mesibov, G. B., Shea, V., & Schopler, E. (2004). *The TEACCH approach to autism spectrum disorders.* Springer.

Mesibov, G. B., Shea, V., Schopler, E., Adams, L., Burgess, S., Chapman, S. M., … Van Bourgondien, M. E. (2005). *The TEACCH approach to autism spectrum disorders.* Springer.

Morris, E. K., Smith, N. G., & Altus, D. E. (2005). B. F. Skinner's contributions to applied behavior analysis. *The Behavior Analyst, 28*(2), 99–131.

Muharib, R., & Wood, C. L. (2018). Evaluation of the empirical support of functional communication training for children with autism spectrum disorders. *Review Journal of Autism and Developmental Disorders, 5*(11), 360–369.

Mulick, J. A., & Butter, E. M. (2005). Positive behavior support: A paternalistic utopian delusion. In J. W. Jacobson, R. M. Foxx, & J. A. Mulick (Eds.), *Controversial therapies for developmental disabilities: Fad, fashion, and science in professional practice* (pp. 385–404). Lawrence Erlbaum.

Nicolosi, M., & Dillenburger, K. (2021). The University of California at Los Angeles—Young Autism Project: A systematic review of replication studies. *Behavioral Interventions, 37*(2), 415–464.

Peterson, T., Dodson, J., Hisey, A., Sherwin, R., & Strale, F. (2024). Examining the effects of discrete trials, mass trials, and naturalistic environment training on autistic individuals using repeated measures. *Cureus, 16*(2), e53371.

Risley, T., & Wolf, M. (1967). Establishing functional speech in echolalic children. *Behaviour Research and Therapy, 5*(2), 73–88.

Rogers, S. J., Herbison, J. M., Lewis, H. C., Pantone, J., & Reis, K. (1986). An approach for enhancing the symbolic, communicative, and interpersonal functioning of young children with autism and severe emotional handicaps. *Journal of the Division of Early Childhood, 10*(2), 135–148.

Rogers, S. J., & Dawson, G. (2010). *Early Start Denver Model for young children with autism: Promoting language, learning, and engagement.* The Guilford Press.

Rogers, S. J., & DiLalla, D. L. (1991). A comparative study of the effects of a developmentally based instructional model on young children with autism and young children with other disorders of behavior and development. *Topics in Early Childhood Special Education, 11*(2), 29–47.

Rogers, S. J., & Lewis, H. (1989). An effective day treatment model for young children with pervasive developmental disorders. *Journal of the American Academy of Child & Adolescent Psychiatry, 28*(2), 207–214.

Rogers, S. J., Lewis, H. C., & Reis, K. (1987). An effective procedure for training early special education teams to implement a model program. *Journal of the Division for Early Childhood, 11*(2), 180–188.

Ross, R. K., Harrison, K. L., & Zane, T. (2018). Focus on science: Is there science behind that?: Autism and treatment with DIR/Floor time. *Science in Autism Treatment, 15*(1), 20–24.

Sailor, W., Dunlap, G., Sugai, G., & Horner, H. (2009). *Handbook of positive behavior support.* Springer.

Sallows, G. O., & Graupner, T. D. (2005). Intensive behavioral treatment for children with autism: Four-year outcome and predictors. *American Journal on Mental Retardation, 110*(6), 417–438.

Sanz-Cervera, P., Fernández-Andrés, M. I., Pastor-Cerezuela, G., & Tárraga-Mínguez, & R. (2018). The effectiveness of TEACCH intervention in autism spectrum disorder: A review study. *Psychologist Papers*, *39*(1), 40–50.

Satcher, D. (1999). *Mental health: A report of the Surgeon General*. https://ia803202. us.archive.org/12/items/mentalhealthrepo00unit/mentalhealthrepo00unit.pdf. Accessed on 12 January 2024.

Schopler, E. (1971). Parents of psychotic children as scapegoats. *Journal of Contemporary Psychotherapy: On the Cutting Edge of Modern Developments in Psychotherapy*, *4*(1), 17–22.

Schopler, E., & Reichler, R. J. (1971). Parents as co-therapists in the treatment of psychotic children. *Journal of Autism and Childhood Schizophrenia*, *1*(1), 87–102.

Schwartz, I. S., Garfinkle, A. N., & Bauer, J. (1998). The picture exchange communication system: Communicative outcomes for young children with disabilities. *Topics in Early Childhood Special Education*, *18*(3), 144–159.

Sigafoos, J., Green, V. A., Edrisinha, C., & Lancioni, G. E. (2007). Flashback to the 1960s: LSD in the treatment of autism. *Developmental Neurorehabilitation*, *10*(1), 75–81.

Simmons, J. Q., Benor, D., & Daniel, D. (1972). The variable effects of LSD-25 on the behavior of a heterogeneous group of childhood schizophrenics. *Behavioral Neuropsychiatry*, *4*(1–2), 10–16.

Simmons, J. Q., Leiken, S. J., Lovaas, O. I., Schaeffer, B., & Perloff, B. (1966). Modification of autistic behavior with LSD-25. *The American Journal of Psychiatry*, *122*(11), 1201–1211.

Siu, A. M. H., Lin, Z., & Chung, J. (2019). An evaluation of the TEACCH approach for teaching functional skills to adults with autism spectrum disorders and intellectual disabilities. *Research in Developmental Disabilities*, *90*, 14–20.

Skinner, B. F. (1938). *The behavior of organisms*. Appleton-Century.

Skinner, B. F. (1953). *Science and human behavior*. Simon and Schuster.

Skinner, B. F. (1957). *Verbal behavior*. Appleton-Century-Crofts.

Smith, T. (2001). Discrete trial training in the treatment of autism. *Focus on Autism and Other Developmental Disabilities*, *16*(2), 86–92.

Smith, T., & Eikeseth, S. O. (2011). O. Ivar Lovaas: Pioneer of applied behavior analysis and intervention for children with autism. *Journal of Autism and Developmental Disorders*, *41*(3), 375–378.

Smith, T., Groen, A. D., & Wynn, J. W. (2000). Randomized trial of intensive early intervention for children with pervasive developmental disorder. *American Journal on Mental Retardation*, *105*(4), 269–285.

Solomon, R., Necheles, J., Ferch, C., & Bruckman, D. (2007). Pilot study of a parent training program for young children with autism: The PLAY Project Home Consultation program. *Autism*, *11*(3), 205–224.

Sugai, G., & Horner, R. H. (2002). The evolution of discipline practices: School-wide positive behavior supports. *Child and Family Behavior Therapy*, *24*(1–2), 23–50.

Sugai, G., & Horner, R. R. (2006). A promising approach for expanding and sustaining school- wide positive behavior support. *School Psychology Review*, *35*(2), 245–259.

Sugai, G., Horner, R. H., Dunlap, G., Hieneman, M., Lewis, T. J., Nelson, C. M., … Ruef, M. (2000). Applying positive behavior support and functional behavioral assessment in schools. *Journal of Positive Behavior Interventions*, *2*(3), 131–143.

Tateno, Y., Kumagai, K., Monden, R., Nanba, K., Yano, A. Shiraishi, E., … Tateno, M. (2021). The efficacy of Early Start Denver Model intervention in young children with autism spectrum disorder within Japan: A preliminary study. *Journal of the Korean Academy of Child and Adolescent Psychiatry*, *32*(1), 35–40.

Thorndike, E. L. (1898). Animal intelligence: An experimental study of the associative processes in animals. *The Psychological Review: Monograph Supplements*, *2*(4), i–109.

Tiger, J. H., Hanley, G. P., & Bruzek, J. (2008). Functional communication training: A review and practical guide. *Behavior Analysis in Practice*, *1*(1), 16–23.

Verschuur, R., Didden, R., Lang, R., Sigafoos, J., & Huskens, B. (2013). Pivotal response treatment for children with autism spectrum disorders: A systematic review. *Journal of Autism and Developmental Disorders 1*(1), 34–61.

Virués-Ortega, J., Arnold-Saritepe, A., Hird, C., & Phillips, K. (2017). The TEACCH program for people with autism: Elements, outcomes, and comparison with competing models. In J. L. Matson (Ed.), *Handbook of treatments for autism spectrum disorder* (pp. 427–436). Springer International Publishing/Springer Nature.

Virués-Ortega, J., Julio, F. M., & Pastor-Barriuso, R. (2013). The TEACCH program for children and adults with autism: A meta-analysis of intervention studies. *Clinical Psychology Review*, *33*(8), 940–953.

Vismara, L. A., Colombi, C., & Rogers, S. J. (2009). Can one hour per week of therapy lead to lasting changes in young children with autism? *Autism*, *13*(1), 93–115.

Vismara, L. A., & Rogers, S. J. (2008). The Early Start Denver model: A case study of an innovative practice. *Journal of Early Intervention*, *31*(1), 91–108.

Vivanti, G., & Stahmer, A. C. (2020). Can the early start Denver model be considered ABA practice? *Behavior Analysis in Practice*, *14*(1), 230–239.

Watson, J. B. (1913). Psychology as the behaviorist views it. *Psychological Review*, *20*, 158–177.

Wieder, S., & Greenspan, S. I. (2003). Climbing the symbolic ladder in the DIR model through floor time/interactive play. *Autism*, *7*(4), 425–435.

Wodka, E. L., Mathy, P., & Kalb, L. (2013). Predictors of phrase and fluent speech in children with autism and severe language delay. *Pediatrics*, *131*(4), e1128–e1134.

Wolf, M., Risley, T., & Mees, H. (1963). Application of operant conditioning procedures to the behaviour problems of an autistic child. *Behaviour Research and Therapy*, *1*(2), 305–312.

Chapter 11

Pharmacologic Interventions

Chapter Contents

Introduction

The management and treatment of autism and its co-occurring conditions often necessitates a comprehensive approach that may include behavioral therapies and, in many cases, medications. Behavioral interventions are the mainstay for treating behavior problems associated with autism. Medications can help manage symptoms associated with autism, including aggression, anxiety, hyperactivity, and sleep problems. However, medications (and complementary and alternative medicine—CAM) can be an adjunct to treating autism.

It is not uncommon for children diagnosed with autism to receive a combination of medications to address various behavioral problems. The practice of **polypharmacy** requires (a) careful oversight and understanding of the medication side effects and drug interaction and (b) monitoring the effectiveness of the treatment regimen. It is worth noting that medications are not intended to cure autism.

DOI: 10.4324/9781003336266-15

However, they may help alleviate autism symptoms and improve the quality of life of autistic individuals. Medication effectiveness varies from person to person.

The chapter provides a comprehensive review of various medications and their potential benefits and potential secondary effects. Additionally, the chapter delves into drugs that have gained public acceptance without enough scientific support for their effectiveness. The final section of the chapter discusses the growing popularity of medical marijuana and warns parents of autistic children to be cautious when considering its use. The aim is to offer parents of children on the autism spectrum valuable insights that can empower them and help them make informed decisions about medication use for autism.

Medication Approval in the United States

Developing and approving a new medication is a complicated and time-consuming process. The drug company must first submit to the Food and Drug Administration (FDA) an investigational new drug (IND) application, along with documented laboratory evidence of the drug's effectiveness and safety in animal and human clinical studies to determine the potential toxicity of the drug. **Clinical trials** are designed to establish new drug safety, **efficacy**, and effectiveness and consist of many phases (Van Norman, 2016). *Phase 0* studies are exploratory and evaluate the lowest dose of the drug on a small number of participants to ensure that it is not harmful to humans. *Phase I* studies are conducted with healthy participants or those with the disease. The studies can last several months, and the primary objective is to determine the safety and dosage of the drug and the best way to administer it (i.e., orally, topically, or intravenously). *Phase II* studies are conducted with a more sizable number of participants (usually several hundred) who have the disease for which the drug is being developed. The investigators carefully monitor the data collected with each participant and the drug's potential side effects. During *phase III* studies, a large group of participants (up to 3,000) are enrolled, and the efficacy of the drug is compared to other approved drugs that were developed to treat the same disease. Participants are randomly assigned to different conditions (FDA, 2018).

Randomized controlled trials (RCT) are considered the gold standard of clinical research. Some participants receive the treatment under investigation (i.e., the experimental group). However, other participants (i.e., the control group) receive either a **placebo** or a current approved treatment. In a double-blind study, neither the experimenter dispensing the drug, nor the participants know who is receiving any particular treatment. In a single-blind study, only the experimenter dispensing the drug knows which participants receive the experimental drug. In an open-label trial, the researchers and the participants know which treatment has been administered. Open-label trials are often conducted to gather data on participants' long-term exposure to a new drug or to compare the safety and effectiveness of two existing treatments (FDA, 2018).

Because of the more considerable number of participants and the long duration of *phase III*, adverse reactions to the drug are more likely to become evident. Upon successful completion of *phase III* clinical trials, the drug developer
can file a new drug application (NDA) with the FDA. The FDA will then ap-
prove the medication if the investigators demonstrate that it is at least as safe and
effective as other approved medications treating the same disease. The drug can
then be manufactured and sold. *Phase IV* studies (aka post-approval surveillance
or open-label trials) are conducted with many participants and can go on for
many years. The studies are designed to evaluate the drug in diverse participant
populations to establish its long-term safety and effectiveness.

When the FDA approves a drug (i.e., when clinical studies demonstrate its
efficacy), it is to treat a specific condition. Therefore, drugs are approved for
specific indications, even though most can treat many conditions. Physicians
usually prescribe medications "off label"—i.e., dispensing a drug to treat conditions for which the manufacturer did not seek approval.

Medications for Autism

People diagnosed with autism are at considerable risk for comorbid disorders,
including attention-deficit/hyperactivity disorder (ADHD), anxiety, seizures, depression, phobia, sleep difficulties, aggressive behavior, self-injurious behavior,
restrictive food intake, and gastrointestinal problems (Aishworiya et al., 2022).
Gastrointestinal problems (e.g., diarrhea, constipation, and heartburn) are common among people diagnosed with autism and can be treated with probiotics or
digestive enzymes (Patusco & Ziegler, 2018). To date, there is no known cure for
autism, and no medications are approved to treat the core symptoms of autism
(i.e., impairments in social interactions and communication, and the presence
of restrictive and repetitive behaviors). Medications are typically prescribed to
manage the symptoms of the disorder, not its underlying causes. The Food and
Drug Administration (FDA), so far, has approved two specific drugs for treating
autism-related irritability in children and adolescents 5–16 years of age: Risperidone (*Risperdal®*) and Aripiprazole (*Abilify®*) (Biospace, 2006). Both risperidone and aripiprazole are atypical antipsychotics (aka second-generation drugs)
that were developed in the 1990s. Compared to the first-generation drugs (e.g.,
haloperidol, aka typical antipsychotics) developed in the 1950s, atypical antipsychotics are believed to induce fewer **extrapyramidal side effects** and less
drowsiness. Second-generation drugs, however, can potentially result in more
weight gain (Leucht et al., 2009).

In addition to behavioral therapy (the mainstay of autism treatment), medications are commonly used as adjuncts to treat the symptoms of autism (Blankenship et al., 2011). Spencer and colleagues (2013) reviewed the use of medications
in more than 30,000 children with ASD in the United States. They found that
64% of children have received at least one psychotropic medication, and 35%
have received more than one psychotropic medication (aka polypharmacy),

particularly older children and those who presented with comorbid conditions including anxiety, seizures, ADHD, depression, or bipolar disorder. There is a limited evidence base for the effectiveness of psychotropic medications, especially in younger children, when the brain is developing (Mandell et al., 2008). Nevertheless, psychiatrists and psychopharmacologists are usually the healthcare professionals who prescribe and manage medications for autism and mainly prescribe them "off-label"—i.e., for conditions other than the specific ones for which the drugs were developed and approved. The medications fall into four basic categories: (a) antidepressants, (b) antipsychotics, (c) mood stabilizers, and (d) stimulants (Sandberg & Spritz, 2012).

Antidepressants and Anxiolytics

Selective serotonin reuptake inhibitors (SSRIs) are a class of drugs the FDA approved to treat symptoms of moderate to severe depression, anxiety disorders, and obsessive-compulsive disorder. **Serotonin** is one of the neurotransmitters that facilitate communication among nerve cells. SSRIs facilitate the availability of serotonin by selectively blocking its reabsorption (reuptake) in the brain. Although approved to treat the symptoms of depression, SSRIs have also been used to treat anxiety, which is common among children and adolescents diagnosed with autism. Van Steensel and colleagues (2011) performed a meta-analysis on the prevalence of anxiety. They found that 40% of children and adolescents with autism meet the diagnostic criteria for at least one anxiety disorder, with phobia being the most prevalent.

In addition to non-pharmacological treatments, SSRIs are commonly prescribed off-label to treat autism-related symptoms that may include the following: increased repetitive behavior and/or vocalizations, disruptive behavior, tantrums, irritability, aggression, self-injurious behaviors, and sleep difficulties. Fluoxetine (*Prozac®*), Sertraline (*Zoloft®*), Citalopram (*Celexa®*), Fluvoxamine (*Luvox®*), and Escitalopram (*Lexapro®*) are the most commonly prescribed antidepressants. There is compelling evidence of SSRIs' effectiveness in treating anxiety disorders in typically developing children. However, there is a lack of consensus regarding their effectiveness in youth diagnosed with autism. The research studies on autism-related anxiety were primarily open-label or retrospective chart reviews with small sample sizes (Lucchelli & Bertschy, 2018). A review of nine randomized control trial studies of the effectiveness of SSRIs in children and adults with autism yielded inconclusive results (Williams et al., 2013). Thus, researchers need to conduct randomized control trial research studies to assess the safety and effectiveness of SSRIs with children and adolescents with autism (Mouti et al., 2014). More recently, Thorkelson and colleagues (2019) conducted a chart review of children and adolescents treated with SSRI monotherapy (i.e., not receiving any other medication). Based on the Clinical Global Impression Improvement scores, 55% of those who received the medication were deemed "improved," even at a nine-month follow-up.

Considering that the FDA has not approved any of the SSRIs to treat autism-related issues and the medications are prescribed off-label, the Autism Speaks Autism Treatment Network Anxiety Workgroup has made several recommendations regarding the use of SSRIs (Vasa et al., 2016). First, youth suffering from anxiety disorders and their families must be educated about the symptoms of anxiety disorders and possible treatment outcomes; second, modified cognitive behavioral therapy (i.e., restructuring the interplay among dysfunctional emotions, thoughts, and behavior) can be considered, particularly with high-functioning children and adolescents; third, the administration of medications can be considered if non-pharmacological approaches have not been effective. Given the FDA black box warning (i.e., the strictest warning placed in the labeling of drug prescriptions) of possible suicidal thoughts or behavior and the potential adverse effects (e.g., nausea, gastrointestinal disturbances, weight gain, agitation, anxiety, and insomnia) of people using antidepressants, dosages must be individualized and carefully monitored to assess the SSRIs' effectiveness and their potential adverse effects.

Although SSRIs are commonly prescribed to treat anxiety in children and adolescents diagnosed with ASD, anxiolytics such as buspirone (*BuSpar®*) have shown some efficacy in alleviating anxiety symptoms in youth diagnosed with ASD. Ceranoglu and colleagues (2019) conducted a retrospective chart review with children and adolescents (ages 8–17 years) diagnosed with ASD who were treated with buspirone. Results showed that buspirone had no apparent adverse effects; it was well tolerated and decreased anxiety symptoms in patients who received the medication, despite the commonly reported side effects, including drowsiness, insomnia, and nausea. While the drug showed some effectiveness in managing anxiety symptoms, the authors cautioned that further prospective research with randomized controlled trials is warranted.

Antipsychotics

Antipsychotics are the most commonly prescribed medications to treat some symptoms of ASD (Jobski et al., 2017). While the medications are seldom used to treat actual **psychosis** in children, they have helped manage the irritability associated with autism, including self-injurious behaviors and aggression. In addition to risperidone (*Risperdal®*) and aripiprazole (*Abilify®*), approved in 2006 and 2009, respectively, to manage some symptoms of ASD, other second generations of antipsychotics, including clozapine (*Clozaril®*) and quetiapine (*Seroquel®*) are also used as adjunct treatments. More studies, however, are needed to evaluate their effectiveness and long-term effects.

Risperidone (*Risperdal®*) was first developed and approved to treat schizophrenia and bipolar mania in adolescents and adults. Risperidone is a serotonin and dopamine receptor **antagonist**—i.e., it blocks the brain's receptors for the neurotransmitters serotonin and dopamine. Serotonin receptors regulate mood, sleep, memory, and social behavior, whereas dopamine receptors play a significant role in emotions, motivation, thinking, and addiction. Autism researchers have conducted numerous studies, including double-blind, placebo-controlled (e.g., McDougle et al., 2008; Shea et al., 2004), multisite, randomized, double-blind trials (McCracken et al., 2002), and open-label trial studies with risperidone (e.g., Troost et al., 2005). Risperidone effectively reduced repetitive behavior, aggression, tantrums, and irritability in children diagnosed with autism. Consequently, the FDA approved its use (ages 5–16) to treat the symptoms of irritability related to autism. The most commonly reported side effects were increased appetite, weight gain, anxiety, drowsiness, and fatigue.

Aripiprazole (*Abilify®*; *Aripiprex®*) is an FDA-approved medication used to treat the symptoms of schizophrenia and bipolar disorder in adolescents and adults. Aripiprazole is a partial receptor agonist (i.e., it initiates the action of brain receptors) to restore the correct balance of dopamine and serotonin. The effectiveness of aripiprazole in reducing the irritability associated with autism has been well established. Aman and colleagues (2010) conducted a randomized, double-blind study to evaluate the efficacy and flexibility of various drug doses. Aripiprazole was found to be effective in treating irritability in children and adolescents with ASD, especially the symptoms related to tantrum behavior. Aripiprazole has also effectively treated challenging behavior in adults with ASD (Jordan et al., 2012). More recently, Bartram and colleagues (2019) reviewed the evidence supporting the use of aripiprazole for treating the irritability associated with ASD. Many studies have shown the benefit of aripiprazole (compared to a placebo) in alleviating the common irritability in individuals diagnosed with ASD. The most commonly reported adverse effects may include weight gain, tremors, sedation, and fatigue.

Mood Stabilizers

In addition to irritability, children and adolescents diagnosed with autism have higher rates of comorbid psychiatric disorders than the general population. Mood disorders are particularly common (e.g., mania, paranoia, euphoria—the feeling of intense excitement) or sleeplessness (Siegel et al., 2014). Lithium citrate (*Cibalith-S®*), valproic acid (*Depakote®*), lithium carbonate (*Eskalith®; Lithobid®*), and carbamazepine (*Tegretol®*) are the most common mood stabilizers psychiatrists prescribe (Sandberg & Spritz, 2012).

There is scant research on the effectiveness of mood stabilizers in treating mood symptoms related to autism. Both carbamazepine and valproic acid have been approved to treat seizures and have also been used "off-label" to control mania in patients who do not respond to antipsychotics. Research studies have not established their effectiveness and safety in children and adolescents diagnosed with autism. Lithium is used to treat manic episodes of bipolar disorder in adults. Siegel and colleagues (2014) performed a retrospective review of children and adolescents with autism who were prescribed lithium. Forty-three percent of the 30 participants in the study responded to the medication and showed improvement. The most common adverse reactions reported were vomiting, tremors, fatigue, irritability, and enuresis (bed wetting).

Similarly, Findling and colleagues (2015) performed a study with children and adolescent participants to assess the effectiveness of lithium in managing the symptoms of bipolar disorder. Compared to the control group, participants who received the drug showed a significant reduction in manic symptom scores based on the Young Mania Rating Scale. Lithium was not associated with any significant weight gain and was well tolerated.

Stimulants

Methylphenidate (e.g., *Ritalin®* and *Concerta®*) is a central nervous system stimulant used to manage attention-deficit/hyperactivity disorder (ADHD) symptoms. According to the Centers for Disease Control and Prevention (CDC), 14% of children with autism also have ADHD. Unlike the previous editions of the DSM, the DSM-5 now allows for a dual diagnosis of ADHD and ASD. Although ASD and ADHD are distinct conditions, they typically co-occur, suggesting they may share some common genetic causes (Leitner, 2014). The co-occurrence of both disorders is usually associated with poorer adaptive functioning and lower quality of life than when only one condition is present. Methylphenidate stimulates the central nervous system by increasing the level of dopamine. As a result, methylphenidate may improve attention and reduce distractibility in tasks that do not typically capture the attention of children diagnosed with ASD (Volkow et al., 2001). The most common side effects associated with methylphenidate are loss of appetite, irritability, and insomnia.

While typically developing children and adolescents with ADHD respond well to methylphenidate (Greenhill et al., 2002), studies that evaluated the effectiveness of the stimulant medication in treating ADHD comorbid with autism have been inconclusive. The Research Unit on Pediatric Psychopharmacology (RUPP Autism Network, 2005) conducted the largest randomized, placebo-controlled trial with methylphenidate in children diagnosed with autism. Compared to typically developing children, the results of the study indicated that children with ASD were less likely to respond to methylphenidate and more likely to experience adverse reactions associated with the medication.

Other non-stimulants (e.g., guanfacine and atomoxetine) with stimulant-like effects have been used to treat ADHD associated with ASD. Scahill and colleagues (2015) performed a multisite trial study to investigate the effectiveness of extended release guanfacine (*Intuniv®*; *Tenex®)* in reducing the symptoms of ADHD in a sample of school children. Compared to the placebo control group, guanfacine was safe and effective in the experimental group for reducing distractibility, impulsiveness, and hyperactivity. The most common side effects associated with the drug were decreased appetite, drowsiness, and fatigue. Similarly, Arnold and colleagues (2006) conducted a double-blind, placebo-controlled study of atomoxetine (*Strattera®*) in children with ASD and symptoms of ADHD. Atomoxetine was safe and effective in controlling hyperactivity in children diagnosed with ASD. Like methylphenidate, atomoxetine yielded a lower response rate in children diagnosed with ASD than typically developing ones but with fewer adverse reactions.

Melatonin

Melatonin, a hormone secreted by the pineal gland in response to darkness, helps regulate biological cycles, including sleep and wake cycles. Insomnia affects 50% to 75% of children diagnosed with neurodevelopmental or psychiatric conditions (Elrod & Hood, 2015). Currently, no medications are approved for treating insomnia in children and adolescents. There is growing evidence from research (e.g., Rossignol & Frye, 2011) indicating an abnormal melatonin secretion in children diagnosed with neurodevelopmental disorders. The synthetic form of melatonin, which can be purchased as a nutritional supplement, has been found to help regulate the sleeping pattern of most people with autism, particularly when a behavioral intervention is added to the melatonin treatment (Cortesi et al., 2012). Melatonin has a short half-life of 40 minutes, so its concentration and potency in the blood plasma are reduced to 50% after 40 minutes. A more recent study investigated the effect of a pediatric-appropriate prolonged-release melatonin 3 mm mini-tablet (dubbed PedPRM and designed for ease of swallowing) in a sample of 125 children and adolescents (Gringras et al., 2017). The authors reported that 2–5 mg/day of the prolonged-released medication was safe and efficacious for treating insomnia in children with ASD with/without ADHD. The most common side effects of PedPRM were fatigue, headache, and somnolence.

Promising Drugs for Autism Treatment

Oxytocin

Oxytocin (*Pitocin®*) is a hormone produced by the hypothalamus and released by the pituitary gland. Oxytocin (OXT), dubbed the "love hormone," plays a role in social bonding, trust, lactation, parturition (i.e., childbirth), and maternal behavior (Lee et al., 2009). Given that individuals diagnosed with ASD show a marked deficit in social interaction and the recognition of others' emotions, autism researchers have been particularly interested in OXT as a potential treatment agent. Consequently, Preti and colleagues (2014) conducted a systematic review of randomized controlled trial studies from 1990 to 2013 to assess the effectiveness of OXT as a potential treatment for ASD. They reported that the most consistent findings were "potentially promising" regarding participants' eye gaze and emotion recognition. Guastella and colleagues (2010) conducted a study in which they administered intranasal oxytocin (OT) to 16 adolescent males diagnosed with ASD. Oxytocin significantly improved their performance on the "Reading the Mind in the Eyes Task," a test that is widely used to assess emotion recognition.

Arginine Vasopressin

Arginine Vasopressin (AVP), like oxytocin, is a neuropeptide associated with regulating the social behavior of humans and animals (Bolognani et al., 2019). Experimental manipulation and disruption of AVP cellular functioning have resulted in social impairments in rodent models (Carson et al., 2015). Therefore, there has been a growing interest in investigating the modulation of vasopressin as a possible treatment for autism. Carson and colleagues (2015) found that the concentration of AVP in the blood plasma could be used as a biomarker of social functioning in children with autism. In a recent study, Parker and colleagues (2018) developed a rhesus monkey model of social impairments among primates with low and high sociality. The cerebrospinal fluid concentration of arginine vasopressin (CSF AVP) was a key indicator of the group difference among the rhesus monkeys. Lower CSF AVP concentration was associated with lower sociability. Consistent with the animal model results, Parker and colleagues (2019) extended their findings to children with autism and found that those with autism had a lower vasopressin cerebral fluid concentration than a control group of age-matched typical male children.

Bolognani and colleagues (2019) conducted a phase II clinical trial with an experimental drug (balovaptan). The drug works as a vasopressin receptor antagonist (i.e., it blocks the action of vasopressin in the brain). The participants (223 men diagnosed with autism without an intellectual disability) showed no significant gain when their behavior was evaluated on the Social Responsiveness Scale, Second Edition. However, the participants showed significant improvements in social competence when tested on the Vineland-II socialization and communication scores. In addition, the orally administered drug was well tolerated and no side effects or safety concerns were identified.

Based on preliminary evidence of the potential effectiveness of the medication (Bolognani et al., 2019), the FDA has granted Roche Pharmaceutical a "breakthrough therapy" designation (i.e., a process designed to accelerate the development and approval of a new drug that shows marked effectiveness over existing ones) for Balovaptan, an experimental drug believed to increase social interaction and alleviate the core deficits of people diagnosed with autism (Diament, 2018; Roache, 2018).

Medical Marijuana and Autism

Current medications can alleviate a few symptoms associated with autism but are unable to target the root causes of the condition. Many families trust anecdotal evidence suggesting cannabis can help relieve some symptoms in individuals with autism. Therefore, it is fitting to review the literature and review the evidence of the potential benefits and risks of using cannabis as a treatment for autism.

The term "medical marijuana" refers to the use of extracts or compounds (e.g., nabilone, dronabinol, and cannabidiol) of the marijuana plant for therapeutic purposes. Although medical marijuana has been legalized in several states, the U.S. Food and Drug Administration (FDA) has not approved marijuana for any medical purpose. Because of marijuana's high potential for abuse, the federal government has classified it as a Schedule 1 drug (Gregario, 2014). Therefore, marijuana use is illegal under federal law, even for medical purposes. Schedule 1 drugs are categorized as substances that have a high potential for abuse and no recognized medical value. Schedules 2 through 5 drugs are classified as substances that have some therapeutic value, but their ranking differs and depends on their potential for abuse.

Marijuana contains over one hundred cannabinoids—i.e., chemical compounds (Pertwee, 2008). Two of those chemical compounds, THC and CBD, have interested researchers and users (Freeman et al., 2019). Tetrahydrocannabinol (THC) is the psychoactive marijuana plant that leads to euphoria (Crane & Phan, 2021) and can also affect coordination and perception. Cannabidiol (CBD) is not psychoactive but can interact with cannabinoid receptors CB1 and CB2 in the human body. Compared to CBD, THC carries a higher risk of adverse effects (Freeman et al., 2019). The endocannabinoid system consists of cannabinoid receptors in the brain, nervous system, and various organs throughout the body. CB1 and CB2 are two main types of cannabinoid receptors that are responsible for distinct functions (Zou & Kumar, 2018). The presence of these receptors in the body facilitates the effects of cannabinoids such as THC and CBD.

The endocannabinoid system plays a significant role in the development of the central nervous system and synaptic plasticity (Lu & Mackie, 2016). Moreover, it regulates various physiological and cognitive processes, including mood, appetite, and memory. Endocannabinoids are cannabinoids the body produces naturally. Cannabinoids such as THC (tetrahydrocannabinol) have psychoactive properties and are responsible for the "high," including symptoms of euphoria, memory loss, and effects on perception and coordination associated with cannabis use. Other cannabinoids, such as CBD (cannabidiol), are non-psychoactive and have been studied for their potential therapeutic benefits. When cannabinoids, those found in cannabis, are consumed, they can interact with the body's endocannabinoid system and influence its physiological and cognitive processes.

The use of CBD has become widespread, leading to claims that it is a cure-all. It is marketed as a treatment for everything from infections to neurodegenerative diseases. Neuroimaging studies suggest that CBD may affect brain activity and connectivity in the brain, which are relevant for psychosis and anxiety. Such findings could be an indication of CBD's therapeutic effects (Batalla et al., 2021). Conversely, CBD can have adverse effects and toxicity. In animal research, CBD has been linked to embryo-fetal mortality, hypotension, central nervous system inhibition, and neurotoxicity. In humans, CBD studies for epilepsy found it associated with induced drug-drug interactions, diarrhea, vomiting, fatigue, and sleepiness (Huestis et al., 2019).

The FDA recently approved Epidiolex (Abu-Sawwa & Stehling, 2020), a pharmaceutical grade of CBD for treating epilepsy for patients two years and older with Dravet syndrome or Lennox-Gastaut syndrome. The FDA approval of CBD for treating epilepsy has generated lots of enthusiasm among parents of autistic children, considering that seizures are common among children diagnosed with autism. However, the American Academy of Child and Adolescent Psychiatry does not support the use of medical marijuana or cannabinoids to treat the core symptoms or co-occurring conditions in children and adolescents with autism. Nevertheless, many parents of autistic children have turned to alternative medicine, including using cannabinoids as a treatment option, even in the absence of evidence-based effectiveness. Wilkinson and D'Souza (2014) have argued that marijuana prescribed for medical purposes should be subjected to more rigorous regulatory oversight (e.g., randomized, double-blind, and placebo-controlled clinical trials) as other medications physicians prescribe and not based on anecdotal evidence of therapeutic value.

Medical marijuana has gained much popularity in recent years due to a growing body of research that suggests that cannabinoids (active chemical components) found in cannabis have therapeutic benefits for various medical conditions. Although the use of cannabis as a medical treatment is unregulated, there is anecdotal evidence that some parents of autistic children are turning to cannabis as a treatment option. Research on the use of cannabis to alleviate various conditions associated with autism (e.g., anxiety, self-injurious behavior, and aggression) is not conclusive. Rapin and colleagues (2021) conducted a retrospective study on the effectiveness of CBD. Their findings suggest that CBD has beneficial effects on pain, depressive symptoms, anxiety, and overall well-being for patients experiencing moderate to severe symptoms but no effects on those experiencing mild symptoms. However, Bortoletto and Colizzi (2022) cautioned about a higher risk of autistic individuals developing psychosis due to their increased vulnerability to the pro-psychotic effects of cannabinoid exposure. In their views, cannabis exposure seems to have adverse epigenetic effects on the brains of individuals with autism, specifically in areas that play a role in the development of schizophrenia and the onset of psychosis in later life.

Similarly, Silva and colleagues (2022) conducted a thorough review of studies that examined the impact of cannabis and cannabinoid use on ASD symptoms. They found that cannabis products had a positive effect on reducing the intensity and frequency of various symptoms such as hyperactivity, self-mutilation, anger, sleep disorders, anxiety, restlessness, psychomotor agitation, irritability, aggressiveness, and depression. Additionally, cannabis improved cognitive abilities, sensory sensitivity, attention, social interaction, and language. However, some common side effects of using cannabis were sleep disorders, restlessness, nervousness, and appetite changes. Based on these findings, the authors cautioned that cannabis and cannabinoids could be a promising therapeutic alternative for alleviating ASD symptoms. However, further randomized, blind, placebo-controlled clinical trials are required to confirm the efficacy of cannabis and its cannabinoids in individuals with ASD.

In sum, the medical establishment does not support the use of cannabis for autism because research conducted on its effectiveness for treating autism is limited, and studies conducted have yielded conflicting findings. For example, some studies suggest that the use of cannabis can alleviate symptoms of autism, such as anxiety, hyperactivity, and aggression. However, other studies indicate that the use of cannabis may even aggravate symptoms of autism, including cognitive deficits and social withdrawal. Although the use of cannabis to treat autism has gained much attention, there is currently not enough scientific evidence to support its use and effectiveness as a treatment option.

Summary

Medications are commonly prescribed as adjunctive treatments to behavioral therapy for people diagnosed with autism. Currently, there are no drugs that can treat the core symptoms of autism. The FDA has approved two antipsychotic medications to manage irritability (e.g., aggression, tantrums, self-injurious behavior) associated with autism: risperidone and aripiprazole. Other classes of medications (not FDA-approved but prescribed off-label) address comorbid conditions associated with autism: Antidepressants, antipsychotics, mood stabilizers, and stimulants. Antidepressants (e.g., fluoxetine) have been found to reduce self-injurious behavior and irritability. Antipsychotic medications (e.g., risperidone) do minimize irritability. Side effects include weight gain, fatigue, and insomnia. Despite limited research, mood stabilizers (e.g., lithium) have shown some effectiveness in treating mood disorders in children and adolescents diagnosed with ASD. Stimulants (e.g., methylphenidate) reduce inattention, hyperactivity, and impulsivity.

The most commonly reported side effects of medications are irritability, decreased appetite, weight loss, social withdrawal, and restlessness. Melatonin has been a treatment of choice to treat insomnia. Gastrointestinal problems are common among people diagnosed with autism and can be treated with probiotics or digestive enzymes. Clinical trials for developing medications and their approval to treat the core symptoms of autism are currently underway. Medical marijuana has gained popularity as a treatment for various medical conditions. However, there is no scientific evidence to support the effectiveness of CBD for treating autism. Although anecdotal reports claim that CBD can alleviate the symptoms of autism, research is inconclusive. Further studies are needed to determine the effectiveness of using CBD to treat autism and its accompanying conditions.

Questions to Ponder for Further Thinking and Learning

1 What are the benefits and potential risks of using medications to manage autism symptoms?
2 How does medication interact with other therapies and interventions for autism?
3 Are there any long-term effects of medication use for individuals with autism?
4 How can healthcare professionals work with individuals with autism and their families to make informed decisions about medication use?
5 Are there alternative or complementary treatments that could be used in conjunction with medications to manage symptoms of autism?
6 How can parents be better informed about potential drug interactions?
7 Given advances in drug development and artificial intelligence, will pharmaceutical companies be able to develop drugs that could address specific aspects of autism?

References

Abu-Sawwa, R., & Stehling, C. (2020). Epidiolex (cannabidiol) primer: Frequently asked questions for patients and caregivers. *Journal of Pediatric Pharmacology and Therapeutics*, *25*(1), 75–77.

Aishworiya, R., Valica, T., Hagerman, R., & Restrepo, B. (2022). An update on psychopharmacological treatment of autism spectrum disorder. *Neurotherapeutics 19*(1), 248–262.

Aman, M. G., Kasper, W., Manos, G., Mathew, S., Marcus, R., Owen, R., & Mankoski, R. (2010). Line-item analysis of the aberrant behavior checklist: Results from two studies of aripiprazole in the treatment of irritability associated with autism disorder. *Journal of Child and Adolescent Psychopharmacology, 20*(5), 415–422.

Arnold, L. E., Aman, M. G., Cook, A. M., Witwer, A. N., Hall, K. L., Thompson, S., & Ramadan, Y. (2006). Atomoxetine for hyperactivity in autism spectrum disorders: Placebo-controlled crossover pilot trial. *Journal of the American Academy of Child & Adolescent Psychiatry*, *45*(10), 1196–1205.

Bartram, L. A., Lozano, J., & Coury, D. L. (2019). Aripiprazole for treating irritability associated with autism spectrum disorders. *Expert Opinion on Pharmacotherapy*, *20*(12), 1421–1427.

Batalla, A., Bos, J., Postma, A., & Bossong, M. G. (2021). The impact of cannabidiol on human brain function: A systematic review. *Frontiers in Pharmacology*, *11*, 618184.

Biospace (2006, October 9). FDA approves the first drug to treat irritability associated with autism, Risperdal. https://www.biospace.com/article/releases/fda-approves-risperdal-r-for-treatment-of-irritability-associated-with-autistic-disorder-/. Accessed on July 15, 2022.

Blankenship, K., Erikson, C. A., Stigler, K. A., Posey, D. J., & McDougle, C. J. (2011). Psychopharmacological treatment of autism. In D. G. Amaral, G. Dawson, & D. H. Geschwind (Eds.), *Autism spectrum disorder* (pp. 1196–1214). Oxford University Press.

Bolognani, F., Del Valle, M., Squasssante, L., Wandel, C., Derks, M. Sevigny, J., … Fontura, P. (2019). A phase 2 clinical trial of a vasopressin V1a receptor antagonist shows improved adaptive behaviors in men with autism spectrum disorder. *Science Translational Medicine, 11*(491), eaat7838.

Bortoletto, R., & Colizzi, M. (2022). Cannabis use in autism: Reasons for concern about risk for psychosis. *Healthcare, 10*(8), 1553.

Carson, D. S., Garner, J. P., Hyde, S. A., Libove, R. A., Berquist, S. W., Hornbeak, K. B., … Parker, K. J. (2015). Arginine Vasopresin is a blood-based biomarker of social functioning in children with autism. *PLOS ONE, 10*(7), e0132224.

Ceranoglu, T. A., Wozniak, J., Fried, R., Galdo, M., Hoskova, B., DeLeon, F. M., … Joshi, G. (2019). A retrospective chart review of buspirone for the treatment of anxiety in psychiatrically referred youth with high-functioning autism spectrum disorder. *Journal of Child and Adolescent Psychopharmacology, 29*(1), 28–33.

Cortesi, F., Giannotti, F., Sebastiani, T., Panunzi, S., &Valente, D. (2012). Controlled-release melatonin, singly and combined with cognitive behavioural therapy, for persistent insomnia in children with autism spectrum disorders: A randomized placebo-controlled trial. *Journal of Sleep Research, 21*(6), 700–709.

Crane, N. A., & Phan, K. L. (2021). Effect of Δ9-Tetrahydrocannabinol on frontostriatal resting state functional connectivity and subjective euphoric response in healthy young adults. *Drug and Alcohol Dependence, 221*, 108565.

Diament, M. (2018). FDA grants 'breakthrough therapy' status to potential autism drug. https://www.disabilityscoop.com/2018/01/30/fda-breakthrough-autism-drug/24649/. Accessed on November 4, 2024.

Elrod, M. G., & Hood, B. S. (2015). Sleep differences among children with autism spectrum disorders and typically developing peers: A meta-analysis. *Journal of Developmental and Behavioral Pediatrics, 36*(3), 166–177.

FDA (2018). Step 3: Clinical research. U.S. Food and Drug Administration. Retrieved from fda.gov/ForPatients/Approvals/Drugs/ucm405622.htm. Accessed November 16, 2023.

Findling, R. L., Robb, A., McNamara, N. K., Pavuluri, M. N., Kafantaris, V., Scheffer, R., … Taylor-Zapata, P. (2015). Lithium in the acute treatment of bipolar I disorder: A double-blind, placebo-controlled study. *Pediatrics, 136*(5), 885–894.

Freeman, T. P., Hindocha, C., Green, S. F., & Bloomfield, M. A. P. (2019). Medicinal use of cannabis based products and cannabinoids. *BMJ, 365*, 1141.

Greenhill, L. L., Pliszka, S., Dulcan, M. K., Bernet, W., Arnold, V. Beitchman, J., … Stock, S. (2002). Practice parameter for the use of stimulant medications in the treatment of children, adolescents, and adults. *Journal of the American Academy of Child & Adolescent Psychiatry, 41*(2 Suppl), 26S–49S.

Gregario, J. (2014). Physicians, medical marijuana, and the law. *Virtual Mentor, 16*(9), 732–738.

Guastella, A. J., Einfeld, S. L., Gray, K. M., Rinehart, N. J., Tonge, B. J., Lambert, T. J., & Hickie, I. B. (2010). Intranasal oxytocin improves emotion recognition for youth with autism spectrum disorders. *Biological Psychiatry, 67*(7), 692–694.

Gringras, P., Nir, T., Breddy, J., Frydman-Marom, A., & Findling, R. L. (2017). Efficacy and safety of pediatric prolonged-release melatonin for insomnia in children with autism spectrum disorder. *Journal of the Academy of Child & Adolescent Psychiatry*, *56*(11) 948–957.e4.

Huestis, M. A., Solimini, R., Pichini, S., Pacifici, R., Carlier, J., & Busardò, F. P. (2019). Cannabidiol adverse effects and toxicity. *Current Neuropharmacology*, *17*(10), 974–989.

Jobski, K., Höfer, J., Hoffmann, F., & Bachmann, C. (2017). Use of psychotropic drugs in patients with autism spectrum disorders: A systematic review. *Acta Psychiatrica Scandinavica*, *135*(1), 8–28.

Jordan, L., Robertson, D., Catani, M., Craig, M., & Murphy D. (2012). Aripiprazole in the treatment of challenging behavior in adults with autism spectrum disorder. *Psychopharmacology*, *223*(3), 357–360.

Lee, H. J., Macbeth, A. H., Pagani, J. H., & Young W. S. 3rd (2009). Oxytocin: The great facilitator of life. *Progress in Neurobiology*, *88*(2), 127–151.

Leitner, Y. (2014). The co-occurrence of autism and attention deficit hyperactivity disorder in children—What do we know? *Frontiers in Human Neuroscience*, *8*, 268.

Leucht, S., Corves, C., Arbter, D., Engel, R. R., Li, C., & Davis, J. M. (2009). Second-generation versus first-generation antipsychotic drugs for schizophrenia: A meta-analysis. *The Lancet*, *373*(9657), 31–41.

Lu, H. C., & Mackie, K. (2016). An introduction to the endogenous cannabinoid system. *Biological Psychiatry*, *79*(7), 516–525.

Lucchelli, J. P., & Bertschy, G. (2018). Low-dose fluoxetine in four children with autistic spectrum disorder improves self-injurious behavior, ADHD-like symptoms, and irritability. *Case Reports in Psychiatry*, *2018*, 6278501.

Mandell, D. S., Morales, K. H., Marcus, S. C., Stahmer, A. C., Doshi, J., & Polsky, D. E. (2008). Psychotropic medication use among Medicaid-enrolled children with autism spectrum disorders. *Pediatrics*, *121*(3), e441–e448.

McCracken, J. T., McGough, J., Shah, B., Cronin, P., Hong, D., Aman, M. G., ... McMahon, D. (2002). Risperidone in children with autism and serious behavioral problems. *New England Journal of Medicine*, *347*(5), 314–321.

McDougle, C. J., Stigler, K. A., Erickson, C. A., & Posey, D. J. (2008). Atypical antipsychotics in children and adolescents with autistic and other pervasive developmental disorders. *Journal of Clinical Psychiatry*, *69*(suppl 4), 15–20.

Mouti, A., Reddihough, D., Marraffa, C., Hazell, P., Wray, J., Lee, K., & Kohn, M. (2014). Fluoxetine for autistic behaviors (FAB trial): Study protocol for a randomized controlled trial in children and adolescents with autism. *Trials*, *15*, 230.

Parker, K. J., Garner, J. P., Oztan, O., Tarara, E. R., Li, J., Sclafani, V., ... Capitanio, J. P. (2018). Arginine vasopressin in cerebrospinal fluid is a marker of sociality in nonhuman primates. *Science Translational Medicine*, *10*(439), eaam9100.

Parker, K. J., Oztan, O., Liboye, R. A., Mohsin, N., Karhson, D. S., Sumiyoshi, R. D., ... Hardan, A. Y. (2019). A randomized placebo-controlled pilot trial shows that intranasal vasopressin improves social deficits in children with autism. *Science Translational Medicine*, *11*(491), eaau7356.

Patusco, R., & Ziegler, J. (2018). Role or probiotics in managing gastrointestinal dysfunction in children with autism spectrum disorder: An update for practitioners. *Advances in Nutrition*, *9*(5), 637–650.

Pertwee, R. G. (2008). The diverse CB1 and CB2 receptor pharmacology of three plant cannabinoids: Delta9-tetrahydrocannabinol, cannabidiol and delta9 tetrahydrocannabivarin. *British Journal of Pharmacology*, *153*(2), 199–215.

Preti, A., Melis, M., Siddi, S., Vellante, M., Donnedu, G., & Fadda, R. (2014). Oxytocin and autism: A systematic review of randomized controlled trials. *Journal of Child and Adolescent Psychopharmacology, 24*(2), 54–68.

Rapin, L., Gamaoun, R., El Hage, C., Arboleda, M. F., & Prosk, E. (2021). Cannabidiol use and effectiveness: Real-world evidence from a Canadian medical cannabis clinic. *Journal of Cannabis Research, 3*(1), 19.

Roche (2018). FDA grants breakthrough therapy designation for Roche's balovaptan in autism spectrum disorder. https://www.roche.com/investors/updates/inv-update-2018-01-29.htm. Accessed on July 15, 2021.

Rossignol, D. A., & Frye, R. E. (2011). Melatonin in autism spectrum disorders: A systematic review and meta-analysis. *Developmental Medicine and Child Neurology, 53*(9), 783–792.

RUPP Autism Network (2005). Randomized, controlled, crossover trial of methylphenidate in pervasive developmental disorders with hyperactivity. *Archives of General Psychiatry, 62*(11), 1266–1274.

Sandberg, E. H., & Spritz, B. L. (2012). *A guide to autism treatment.* Jessica Kingsley.

Scahill, L., McCracken, J. T., King, B. H., Rockhill, C., Shah, B., Politte, L., ... McDougle, C. J. (2015). Extended-release guanfacine for hyperactivity in children with autism spectrum disorder. *The American Journal of Psychiatry, 172*(12), 1197–1206.

Shea, S., Turgay, A., Carroll, A., Schulz, M., Orlik, H., Smith, I., & Dunbar, F. (2004). Risperidone in the treatment of disruptive behavioral symptoms in children with autistic and other pervasive developmental disorders. *Pediatrics, 114*(5), e634–e641.

Siegel, M., Beresford, C. A., Bunker, M., Verdi, M., Vishnevetsky, D., Karlsson, C., ... Smith, K. A. (2014). Preliminary investigation of lithium for mood disorder symptoms in children and adolescents with autism spectrum disorder. *Journal of Child and Adolescent Psychopharmacology, 24*(7), 399–402.

Silva, E. A. D., Medeiros, W. M. B., Torro, N., Sousa, J. M. M., Almeida, I. B. C. M., Costa, F. B. D., ... Albuquerque, K. L. G. D. (2022). Cannabis and cannabinoid use in autism spectrum disorder: A systematic review. *Trends in Psychiatry and Psychotherapy, 44*, e20200149.

Spencer, D., Marshall, J., Post, B., Kulakodlu, M., Newschaffer, C., Dennen, T., ... Jain, A. (2013). Psychotropic medication use and polypharmacy in children with autism spectrum disorders. *Pediatrics, 132*(5), 833–840.

Thorkelson, G., Laughlin, S. F., Turner, K. S., Ober, N., & Handen, B. L. (2019). Selective serotonin reuptake inhibitor monotherapy for anxiety disorders in children and adolescents with autism spectrum disorder: A chart review. *Journal of child and Adolescents Psychopharmacology, 29*(9), 705–711.

Troost, P. W., Lahuis, B. E., Steenhuis, M. P., Ketelaars, C. E. J., Buitelar, J, K., van Engeland, H., ... Hoekstra, P. J. (2005). Long-term effect of risperidone in children with autism spectrum disorders: A placebo discontinuation study. *Journal of the American Academy of Child & Adolescent Psychiatry, 44*(11), 1137–1144.

Van Norman, G. A. (2016). Drugs, devices, and the FDA: Part 1: An overview of approval processes for drugs. *JACC: Basic to Translational Science, 1*(3), 170–179.

van Steensel, F. J., Bögels, S. M., & Perrin, S. (2011). Anxiety disorders in children and adolescents with autistic spectrum disorders: A meta-analysis. *Clinical Child and Family Psychology Review, 14*(3), 302–317.

Vasa, R. A., Mazurek, M. O., Mahajan, R., Bennett, A. E., Bernal, M. P., Nozzolillo, A. A., ... Coury, D. L. (2016). Assessment and treatment of anxiety in youth with autism spectrum disorders. *Pediatrics, 137*(S2), S115–S123.

Volkow, N. D., Wang, G., Fowler, J. S., Logan, J., Gerasimov, M., Maynard, L., ... Franceschi, D. (2001). Therapeutic doses of oral methylphenidate significantly increase extracellular dopamine in the human brain. *The Journal of Neuroscience, 21*(2), 1–5.

Wilkinson, S. T., & D'Souza, D. C. (2014). Problems with the medicalization of marijuana *JAMA, 311*(23), 2377–2378.

Williams, K., Brignell, A., Randall, M., Silove, N., & Hazell, P. (2013). Selective serotonin reuptake inhibitors (SSRIs) for autism spectrum disorders (ASD). *The Cochrane Database of Systematic Reviews, 8*, CD004677.

Zou, S., & Kumar, U. (2018). Cannabinoid receptors and the endocannabinoid system: Signaling and function in the central nervous system. *International Journal of Molecular Science, 19*(3), 833.

Chapter 12

Biomedical and Complementary Alternative Treatments for Autism

Chapter Contents

Introduction

Although autism results from genetic and environmental causes, its specific etiology is unknown, and to date, there is no cure for the disorder. Consequently, families of children with autism may turn to biomedical treatments or **complementary and alternative medicine** (Levy & Hyman, 2015) and therapies with no scientifically proven effectiveness yet widely promoted by some professionals to be beneficial. Biomedical treatments, in the true sense of the term, entail various practices, including medications, surgeries, and other treatments that are

DOI: 10.4324/9781003336266-16

based on scientific evidence and used in modern medicine to treat various ill-nesses and health conditions. However, biomedical therapies for autism (e.g., herbal supplements and chelation) are commonly considered complementary al-ternative medicines (CAM) that are not part of conventional medicine. Although some alternative therapies have shown promising efficacy in clinical studies, others lack scientific evidence to support their therapeutic effectiveness.

Many children with autism often have underlying medical issues, including immune system dysregulation, gastrointestinal problems, and nutritional defi-ciencies that can aggravate their condition. Biomedical treatments for autism are commonly viewed as complementary and alternative medicines and treatments in comparison to well-established conventional therapies and evidence-based treatments. Biomedical treatments are based on the idea of using medications (discussed in Chapter 11), supplements, and dietary modifications to alleviate those underlying medical conditions.

Bernard Rimland, an autism researcher and the father of an autistic son, founded the Autism Research Institute (ARI), a non-profit organization, in 1967. In 1995, members of the Autism Research Institute (ARI) established the Defeat Autism Now! (DAN!) project due to the perceived ineffectiveness of traditional autism treatments. The project advocates for a specific protocol for diagnosing and treating autism (Levy & Hyman, 2003). Defeat Autism Now! (DAN!) op-erates on the belief that autism is caused by genetic and environmental factors and can be treated through dietary changes, nutritional supplements, and other alternative medicine approaches.

Although the DAN approach was popular in the 2000s, it was viewed as contro-versial within the medical community. In 2011, the American Academy of Pediat-rics warned practitioners and parents about using the DAN protocol, stating, "There is no scientific evidence to support the use of any of the interventions promoted by the DAN protocol." ARI remains a prominent organization in autism research and advocacy, supporting various initiatives to improve understanding and treatment.

There is no cure for autism, and there is a lack of evidence that biomedical therapies can improve the functioning of children with autism. Nevertheless, parents of autistic children commonly turn to unproven treatments on the ba-sis that something done is better than nothing done. More concerning is that the originators of those treatments make unfounded claims, luring parents into investing valuable time and resources into deceptive practices which can some-times be harmful (Singer & Ravi, 2015).

Biomedical Treatment for Autism

Biomedical interventions target the underlying medical problems that may re-sult in the presentation of the core symptoms of autism. Although medications for treating the core symptoms are considered biomedical interventions, they are listed separately and discussed in Chapter 11 as *Pharmacologic Interventions*.

Instead, the chapter will focus on other biomedical interventions and complementary and alternative medicine (CAM), which has recently gained much popularity.

Given the complex etiology of autism and the need to find effective interventions, parents of children with autism have turned to biomedical treatments and complementary and alternative medicine (CAM). There are no established guidelines regarding the use of CAM therapies. The American Academy of Pediatrics has published guidelines for physicians interacting with families using CAM treatment. Physicians must be conversant with CAM treatment, open to discussing various options with families regarding evidence-based therapeutic interventions and safety issues, and not be outright dismissive of what families are willing to explore (Committee on Children with Disabilities, 2001).

Although there is limited scientific evidence supporting the effectiveness of CAM therapies, families of autistic children have embraced them as alternative treatments, possibly because those treatments are considered safe and "natural" with fewer side effects than conventional medications (Perrin et al., 2012). Biomedical treatments for autism are rooted in established pathophysiological processes (e.g., immune dysregulation, neuroinflammation, and mitochondrial dysfunction). There is evidence that biomedical interventions can be beneficial if they are based on personalized and evidence-based medicine (Pacheva & Ivanov, 2019).

Li and colleagues (2017) reviewed 22 randomized controlled trials on eight different dietary supplements targeting the core symptoms of autism. They found little evidence supporting their effectiveness for children on the autism spectrum. Similarly, Brondino and colleagues (2015) conducted a comprehensive review of 80 studies. They found no scientific evidence supporting the effectiveness of CAM, except for some promising results for sensory integration therapy, music therapy, and acupuncture.

Celiac Disease and Gluten-Free and Casein-Free Diet (GFCF)

Celiac disease is an inherited, autoimmune disorder of the digestive system triggered by consuming gluten, a protein found in wheat, barley, or rye. As a result, the immune response leads to inflammation and damage to the small intestine, which means affected children cannot absorb nutrients despite adequate food consumption. Celiac disease's symptoms include bloating, diarrhea, and fatigue. Fortunately, treatment consisting of a gluten-free diet can repair the small intestine damage and restore proper food absorption. Children with autism may also have gastrointestinal problems, but not necessarily celiac disease. Gastrointestinal symptoms are common in children with autism, raising the possibility of an association with celiac disease or gluten sensitivity (Lau et al., 2013). Although the association between celiac disease and autism cannot entirely be ruled out, most studies did not find any convincing link between the two conditions (Quan et al., 2021). Parents of children diagnosed with autism have increasingly turned to gluten-free and casein-free diets to alleviate their children's symptoms (Genuis & Bouchard, 2010). Casein is a protein found in milk that shares some similarities to gluten. Both are proteins found in certain foods and can be difficult for some individuals to digest.

Restricted food diets as a treatment option for autism originated in the postulates of the "opioid-excess theory" (Panksepp, 1979) or "leaky-gut syndrome" (Shattock & Whiteley, 2002). According to the opioid-excess theory of autism, opioid **peptides** present in certain foods can enter the bloodstream and cross the **blood-brain barrier**, where they may bind to opioid receptors, affect brain function, and cause autism symptoms. The leaky gut theory posits that the permeability of the intestinal lining allows harmful substances to leak into the bloodstream, thus triggering an immune response that may contribute to the development of autism. However, the notion of "leaky gut syndrome" is controversial and has not been widely accepted by the medical establishment.

The gluten-free casein-free (GFCF) diet is an elimination diet that removes specific proteins, specifically gluten and casein, from a regular diet. However, research demonstrating the benefits of the GFCF on autistic individuals is limited. The GFCF diet has gained popularity among some parents of autistic children. One online survey of parents of autistic children found that 27% of those parents reported using GFCF diets (Green et al., 2006).

Can celiac disease present itself as autism? Genuis and Bouchard (2010) documented the case of a 5-year-old child with autism who recovered from the condition after being diagnosed with celiac disease and, as a result, consumed a gluten-free diet. Another study found that the immune system of some children on the autism spectrum appears to respond to gluten atypically in comparison to how the immune system of individuals with celiac disease reacts to gluten (Lau et al., 2013). However, a nationwide study conducted in Sweden examined the association between celiac disease and autism. The study found no evidence to suggest a link between autism and celiac disease (Ludvigsson et al., 2013).

Effectiveness of a GFCF Diet

Although some parents have reported improvements in their children's behavior, communication, and gastrointestinal issues due to consuming a GFCF diet, the scientific evidence supporting their claims is weak. The evidence supporting the DGCF diet is primarily based on self-report rather than direct measurement and comes from clinicians, educators, and parents (Seung et al., 2007). There are limited studies demonstrating the beneficial effect of the GFCF diet and explaining its mechanism (Baspinar & Yardimci, 2020). Despite the popularity of CFGF diets for children with autism, research on its efficacy is limited (Elder, 2008). Johnson and colleagues (2011) conducted a three-month prospective, **open-label**, randomized design comparing a GFCF diet with a healthy, low-sugar one for children on the autism spectrum. Although participants in both groups showed some gains on measures of behavior and language, there were no significant nutritional differences between the two diets. Similarly, Piwowarc-zyk and colleagues (2018) systematically reviewed the effectiveness of a gluten-free and casein-free (GFCF) diet as a treatment for ASD in children. They found little evidence that GFCF diets reduce the symptoms associated with autism in children.

Harrison and Zane (2017) questioned the scientific basis of the GFCF diet. Additionally, they suggested that the GFCF should be considered only if a child is allergic to gluten and casein. Additionally, they cautioned parents about the financial cost associated with a GFCF diet and the need for children on such a diet to be closely monitored by a physician.

Chelation Therapy

Chelation is a process that removes some heavy metals (e.g., mercury and lead) from the bloodstream. Chelation therapy is approved to treat patients with heavy metal poisoning (e.g., lead poisoning in painters exposed to lead-based paint). When the chelating agent is ingested, it binds to heavy metals and is then ex-creted during urination. However, in the 1990s, when the prevalence of autism had risen and the notion that thimerosal, a mercury-based compound used as a preservative in vaccines, was a likely culprit that caused the rapid increase of au-tism, chelation seemed a novel practice worth trying. The idea of using chelation gained momentum when Bernard Rimland, the autism researcher who debunked the notion that cold parenting causes autism, created the Autism Research Insti-tute (ARI). Rimland instituted Defeat Autism Now! (DAN!). His rationale was that autism could be cured through biomedical interventions. Owing to contro-versies surrounding the treatment, the Autism Research Institute discontinued the DAN treatment protocol in 2011.

The Food and Drug Administration has approved chelation therapy for spe-cific uses, such as treating lead poisoning and iron overload, but not for treating autism. Chelation agents should only be used under professional supervision. Removing essential minerals that the body needs can lead to severe and life-threatening outcomes.

Brown and colleagues (2006) reviewed the practice of chelation with autistic children from 2003–2005 and reported that three persons died of "cardiac arrest caused by **hypocalcemia** during chelation therapy." Consequently, they cau-tioned that healthcare providers contemplating chelation therapy should consult an expert. The rationale for using chelation to treat autism is that elevated levels of toxic heavy metals in the bloodstream positively correlate with the severity of autism symptoms. Therefore, the use of chelation agents to remove those heavy metals can result in the reduction of ASD symptoms.

James and colleagues (2015) reviewed a study on chelation therapy involving 77 children who were randomly assigned to receive seven days of glutathione (a chelation agent) or a placebo. The study found no supporting evidence that chelation therapy improves autism symptoms. Moreover, considering the potential risks associated with this treatment, its use is strongly discouraged for treating autism symptoms. Similarly, Davis and colleagues (2013) evaluated five studies that used chelation to treat symptoms of autism. They did not support using chelation agents as a treatment for autism.

In sum, the notion that heavy metal may cause autism is not supported by research. Chelation is not a treatment modality that has been approved to treat autism. Research has not found it to be an effective treatment for autism symptoms, as there is no scientific evidence supporting its use. Considering potential severe adverse side effects, including renal impairment, gastrointestinal problems, and hypocalcemia (Kosnett, 2010; Morgan et al., 2002), chelation is not recommended to treat autism symptoms.

Vitamins and Supplements

Vitamins play an essential role in the functioning of the body. For example, they support growth and development, help with energy production, and boost the immune system. Adequate food consumption is the primary means to obtain the necessary vitamins needed for the body's optimal functioning. Some children with autism experience difficulties with food consumption (e.g., aversion to smell, color, or texture of food). As a result, they may become picky eaters, develop a liking for a specific dish, and refuse to consume anything else. Additionally, some may have gastrointestinal issues that can complicate their food intake. Consequently, they may be deprived of essential vitamins. Some studies support the idea of adding to diets some specific vitamins and supplements to boost vitamin deficiencies that some children with autism may have. This review is not exhaustive, given the wide variety of vitamins and supplements used for their potential role in managing autism symptoms. However, it does focus on the most commonly used ones.

Vitamin D

Vitamin D, in addition to its role in the absorption of calcium and the maintenance of strong bones and teeth, has been found to play a role in brain development. Low levels of vitamin D have been linked to various psychiatric conditions, including autism (Eyles et al., 2013). Vitamin D deficiency has been proposed as a possible risk factor for autism because of its role in cell proliferation and differentiation (Ali et al., 2018) and its capacity to reduce the risks of autism through its anti-inflammatory properties (Cannell & Grant, 2013). Low levels of vitamin D during pregnancy have also been suggested as a risk factor for autism (Grant & Soles, 2009; Vinkhuyzen et al., 2018).

Some studies have suggested vitamin D benefits children with autism (e.g., Jia et al., 2015). However, there is no agreement on the therapeutic effect of vitamin D, owing to inconsistent results and methodology and the lack of randomized controlled trials. Despite the overwhelming interest in suggesting a link between vitamin D deficiency and autism, only one randomized controlled trial (RCT) has been conducted and published (Saad et al., 2018). Based on the findings, the authors suggested that vitamin D could improve autism core symptoms, particularly in children with vitamin D deficiency. It is worth noting that the Committee on Publishing Ethics (COPE) and Wiley's Best Practice Guidelines on Publishing Ethics retracted the article. The authors could not provide all the data on request.

Omega-3 Fatty Acids

Adequate nutrition plays a vital role in development. Our body does not synthesize omega-3; its intake depends on food consumption and dietary supplements (Simopoulos, 2010). Therefore, malnutrition can lead to vitamin deficiency, including omega-3 fatty acids. Omega-3 plays a substantial role in optimal development and neurodevelopment (Gow & Hibbeln, 2014; Shulkin et al., 2016). There is empirical evidence supporting the benefits of Omega-3 on the brain, cognitive processes, and neuropsychological performance (Reyes et al., 2019).

In addition to omega-3 fatty acids' role in reducing inflammation, lowering the risk of heart disease, and supporting cognitive functions, they have been studied for their benefits in alleviating autism symptoms. Various randomized controlled trials have been conducted. For example, Amminger and colleagues (2007) conducted a double-blind randomized, placebo-controlled pilot study. Compared to the placebo control group, omega-3 showed preliminary evidence of effectiveness for reducing stereotypy and hyperactivity over the placebo condition. Similarly, Mankad and colleagues (2015), in a randomized, placebo-controlled study, found no positive effects of omega-3 in ameliorating autism symptoms. Li and colleagues (2017) reviewed the effectiveness of various supplements in treating the symptoms of autism based on those supplements' deficiencies in autistic individuals, anecdotal evidence, and probable causal theories of autism. The authors found no compelling scientific evidence but promising evidence of effectiveness.

In sum, omega-3 fatty acid consumption has many benefits. Considering that the body does not synthesize omega-3, consuming it via food or supplements can be beneficial. Various research studies, including randomized controlled ones, do not support its effectiveness in alleviating autism core symptoms. More rigorous clinical trials are needed to assess the benefits of omega-3 for treating symptoms associated with autism.

Methyl B-12

Methyl B-12 (aka methylcobalamin—a natural form of vitamin B-12) is an essential nutrient that serves various bodily functions (e.g., the synthesis of DNA, the formation of red blood cells, and the maintenance of the nervous system).

Compared to other forms of B-12, methylcobalamin is more readily absorbed and retained in the body (Allen, 2012; Paul & Brady, 2017).

Studies have shown that some children with autism have impaired **methylation** capacity (James et al., 2004) and reduced antioxidant capacity (Han et al., 2015). Methyl B-12 can mitigate the effect of the pollutant nitrous oxide, a risk factor for autism (Fluegge, 2016). Vitamin B-12 has been used to increase methylation capacity and restore the balance between the levels of oxidants and antioxidants in the body—i.e., the **redox status** (Li et al., 2017). Therefore, it has been considered as a potential treatment for autism symptoms.

Hendren and colleagues (2016) examined whether methyl B-12 could improve autism symptoms. Fifty autistic children (ages 3–7) completed the study. One group received injections of methyl B-12 every three days for eight weeks. The placebo-controlled received a saline solution. The experimental group performed statistically significantly on measures of the Clinical Global Impressions-Improvement (CGI-I), Aberrant Behavior Checklist (ABC), and Social Responsiveness Scale (SRS). The authors cautioned that the "findings are preliminary ... holds the potential to improve [autism] symptoms. A larger randomized controlled trial with greater power and greater control over laboratory assessments should be a high priority" (p. 782).

More recently, Rossignol and Frye (2021, p. 1) systematically reviewed 17 studies that assessed methyl B-12 effectiveness for treating autism symptoms. Methylcobalamin (mB12) was administered orally or subcutaneously in most reviewed studies. The authors reported that "preliminary clinical evidence suggests that B12, particularly subcutaneously injected mB12, improves metabolic abnormalities in ASD along with clinical symptoms." Despite suggesting that B-12 is a promising treatment for autism, they cautioned on the need to conduct large multicenter placebo-controlled studies to corroborate their data.

In sum, methyl B-12 has shown evidence of being effective in treating autism symptoms, particularly in children with unfavorable biochemical profiles. B-12 is safe and well-tolerated with no unpleasant side effects. Although B-12 taken orally as a dietary supplement is effective and convenient (Andrès et al., 2010), subcutaneous injection of B-12 appears to be the most effective mode of administration. Still, the latter mode of administration is invasive and may lead to poor compliance among recipients. Due to the heterogeneity of ASD, more randomized controlled trials with larger groups of participants are needed to obtain compelling scientific evidence of the effectiveness of B-12.

Probiotics and Digestive Enzymes

Many individuals with autism suffer from gastrointestinal symptoms. Numerous studies have established a connection between the microbiota-gut-brain axis and how it can influence the development of many neurological disorders, including autism (Taniya et al., 2022; van De Sande et al., 2014). Research suggests that probiotics and digestive enzymes might help reduce some autism symptoms.

According to the Merriam-Webster dictionary, *probiotics* are microorganisms that maintain or restore beneficial bacteria to the digestive tract when consumed (as in a food or a dietary supplement). Because probiotics can help keep the optimal balance of beneficial balance in the gut and reduce bacterial overgrowth (Quigley & Quera, 2006), they are called good or friendly bacteria that can support digestive health and overall well-being (Ohland & MacNaughton, 2010). Gastrointestinal issues are common among autistic individuals, resulting in higher rates of diarrhea and abdominal pain (Chaidez et al., 2014; McElhanon et al., 2014).

A review of studies that addressed the connection between autism and gastrointestinal abnormalities in autism found that probiotic administration might reduce gastrointestinal issues, decrease inflammation, and restore the intestinal gut-brain barrier (Feng et al., 2023). Another systematic review and meta-analysis of seven studies assessed the merits of probiotics in children with autism (He et al., 2023). They found limited effectiveness for their effectiveness in reducing behavioral symptoms. The authors cited the small sample sizes, variety of probiotics used, short intervention duration, and poor methodology as probable causes for non-significant findings.

Digestive Enzymes

Unlike probiotics, *digestive enzymes* break down ingested food into more easily absorbable components. Like probiotics, they have been targeted as a possible treatment for autism symptoms. Saad and colleagues (2015, p. 188) conducted a double-blind, randomized clinical trial on 101 children with ASD (ages 3–9 years). The authors reported "significant improvement in emotional response, general impression autistic score, general behavior and gastrointestinal symptoms." Another double-blind randomized controlled trial conducted with 43 children (ages 3–8) assessed whether digestive enzymes can improve language and autism symptoms. The authors reported that consuming digestive enzymes showed no significant benefits (Munasinghe et al., 2010).

In sum, although many studies have investigated the effectiveness of probiotics and digestive enzymes in treating autism symptoms, the results of those studies are inconclusive. Although probiotics and digestive enzymes can alleviate the discomfort associated with gastrointestinal issues, research has not provided convincing scientific evidence that they can ameliorate autism symptoms.

Complementary and Alternative Medicine (CAM)

Hyperbaric Oxygen Therapy

Hyperbaric Oxygen Therapy (HBOT) has been around since the 1930s and was initially used to treat decompression sickness of deep-sea divers. In recent years, however, its use has been extended to treat other medical conditions, including smoke inhalation, carbon monoxide poisoning, and wound healing (Leach et al., 1998; Thom, 2011). In the past two decades, clinicians and healthcare practitioners dealing with autism have promoted the use of HBOT for (supposedly) treating autism, owing to the therapy's positive effects on language, cognition, anxiety, and socialization (Harrison & Zane, 2016). The rationale for using HBTO is that pressurized oxygen can reduce gut or brain inflammation that is common in people with autism (Levy & Hyman, 2015) and possibly mitigate the problematic behaviors associated with autism. During an HBTO session, the person breathes 20% to 100% oxygen in a pressurized chamber. There are no guidelines regarding the number of sessions required to achieve a desired therapeutic outcome. Each session lasts 60 minutes, once or twice daily, five days a week. The therapy can cost more than $15,000 per person when conducted in specialized clinics. Parents can opt to purchase a chamber for home use calibrated at 1.3 ATA and 21% to 40% oxygen concentrations (Lerman et al., 2008).

We typically breathe 21% oxygen at sea level (i.e., a pressure of 14.7 pounds per square inch or one atmosphere absolute—ATA). At higher altitudes, the percentage of oxygen in the air is still 21%, but breathing becomes problematic. In a hyperbaric chamber, the pressure can be elevated up to three times greater than the normal pressure, and inhalation of pure oxygen can be up to 100%. Most people tolerate HBOT sessions well but not without various side effects that are mild and temporary. The most common ones reported are the middle ear and sinus barotrauma—i.e., discomfort or injury caused by changes in air pressure (Heyboer, 2016). Other potential side effects include changes in vision, fatigue, lightheadedness, and claustrophobia. Moreover, more severe and rare side effects include oxygen toxicity, seizures, and pressure injury to the lungs in individuals with underlying lung problems.

Autism researchers and clinicians have investigated the effectiveness of HBOT in treating autism using **case series studies**, open-label studies, and randomized controlled trials. One major drawback of case series and open-label studies is that they do not include comparison groups, and their efficacy is based on parent ratings (Sakulchit et al., 2017). Rossignol and Rossignol (2006) reported a time series study in which six children diagnosed with autism showed improved clinical symptoms based on parent ratings after receiving 40 one-hour sessions of HBOT. Similarly, another time series study (Chungpaibulpatana et al., 2008) showed improvement in language and social development, motor and eye-hand coordination, and gross motor development of five out of seven children who received ten sessions of HBOT at 1.3 ATA and 100% oxygen. Lerman and colleagues (2008) evaluated the effectiveness of HBOT in three children who received 40 one-hour sessions at 1.3 ATA with 88% oxygen. The three children also received an intensive behavioral intervention. There was no evident benefit of the HBOT "beyond those obtained through the behavioral intervention alone."

A randomized controlled trial was conducted with 60 children diagnosed with autism who received 20 one-hour sessions over ten weeks (Sampanthavivat et al., 2012). The experimental group received HBOT at 1.15 ATA and 100% oxygen. The control group inhaled 21% of oxygen at 1.15 ATA. Parents and trained clinicians who were blind to each group's treatment used the Autism Treatment Evaluation Checklist (ATEC) to assess improvement in behavioral problems, cognitive function, and social interaction and communication. They found no significant differences in improvement between groups. Similarly, Ghanizadeh (2012) reviewed two randomized controlled trials with 89 participants diagnosed with autism who received HBOT and concluded that more rigorous studies must be conducted to determine the effectiveness of HBO therapy. One study (Granpeesheh et al., 2010) found no significant improvement in autism symptoms in children who received HBOT at 1.3 ATA and 24% oxygen. Conversely, Rossignol and colleagues (2009) reported significant improvements in functioning (i.e., eye contact, receptive language, social interaction, and sensory/cognitive awareness) of 62 children diagnosed with autism who were either assigned to the control or experimental group. A more recent review of 14 studies (Podgórska-Bednarz & Perenc, 2021) found no evidence of the effectiveness of HBOT in treating autism.

In sum, research studies conducted with HBOT as an intervention for autism have yielded mixed results at best. Consistent with the lack of sufficient scientific evidence supporting the use of various complementary medicine treatments for autism, the Food and Drug Administration (FDA, 2019) has published caution about the misleading and false claim of potentially dangerous products and therapies that claim to treat autism. Consequently, it has issued words of caution about their use as a form of treatment.

Sensory Integration

All the senses are present at birth but not fully developed. Infants can hear, taste, smell, feel, and see. To some extent, the sensory system functions in an integrated way at birth. For example, infants will orient to incoming sounds, suggesting that vision and hearing are linked. Infants' sensory abilities will become more refined with time, brain maturation, and experience with environmental stimulation. As the brain develops, the ability to process multiple pieces of information and draw on past experiences to understand the meaning of various inputs also develops (Burr & Gori, 2012).

The nervous system plays a crucial role in processing and combining sensory information from the environment. *Sensory integration* is the process by which the brain organizes sensory input from various environmental sources to create a sense of order. For typically developing children, the ability to process sensory input is essential for their socialization, communication, and learning skills. Difficulties with sensory integration are common among individuals with autism, leading to hypersensitivity and hyposensitivity to sensory inputs. This difficulty in processing and integrating sensory information can result in challenges in everyday interactions and social situations, impacting communication, socialization, and learning. Sensory integration therapy aims to assist individuals with autism in managing and integrating their sensory experiences to enhance their daily functioning.

Sensory Integration Treatment for Autism

For Anna Jean Ayres, an occupational and educational psychologist, her interactions with children with various disabilities and her interest in the relationship between the brain and behavior led to the development of the *sensory integration* model in the 1960s and 1970s. Her work aimed at understanding how the brain processes information and how difficulties processing sensory information can result in daily challenges for affected individuals. She developed the Ayres Sensory Integration (ASI) as a therapeutic approach that helps individuals with sensory processing challenges by providing sensory experiences in a structured, repetitive way.

During ASI procedures, therapists and children engage in play interactions in a sensory-rich environment. The goal is to provide opportunities for the child to engage with and adapt to various sensory stimulations through various activities that integrate multiple senses.

Effectiveness of Sensory Integration Therapy

A review of sensory integration conducted in the 1990s raised some serious doubts about the validity and utility of the model, particularly the notion of "sensory integrative dysfunction" children with learning disabilities experience. The authors concluded that SI is "not merely an unproven, but a demonstrably ineffective unproven and demonstrably ineffective treatment" for children with learning disabilities (Hoehn & Baumeister, 1994, p. 338). The American Academy of Pediatrics (AAP) questioned whether children with sensory-based problems have an actual disorder that is associated with developmental and behavioral issues. Furthermore, the AAP cautioned parents about the limited and inconclusive research regarding the effectiveness of SI (Zimmer et al., 2012).

A pilot study evaluated the effectiveness of sensory integration (SI) by comparing two groups of children randomly assigned to two conditions: A fine motor group and an SI treatment group. Targeted measures were social responsiveness, sensory processing, functional motor skills, and social-emotional factors. Compared to the fine motor group, the SI group showed a significant decrease in autistic mannerisms (Pfeiffer et al., 2011).

Despite the lack of agreement regarding the effectiveness of Sensory Integration Therapy (SIT), Schoen and colleagues (2019) used the Council for Exceptional Children Standards for Evidence-based Practices in Special Education to evaluate the effectiveness of research conducted on SIT from 2006 to 2017.

The authors concluded that SIT is an evidence-based practice for 4- to 8-year-old children with autism when consistently implemented, as described by Ayres (1972, 1979, 1989).

Weighted Vest

Sensory processing disorder is common among children with autism (Baranek, 2002). The weighted vest has been developed as a sensory tool to aid children with sensory processing difficulties, including those with autism, by helping them manage their issues (Lane et al., 2019). The use of weighted vests has gained popularity, and healthcare professionals recommend their use to assist individuals with autism spectrum disorder in managing sensory input and promoting calmness.

Ayres Sensory Integration (ASI) is a common approach occupational therapists use for autistic children. Occupational therapists implement sensory integration therapy to help with inattentiveness, hyperactivity, stereotypic behaviors, and clumsiness in children with sensory issues. This therapy involves using weighted vests, which add extra weight (usually between 5 and 10% of a person's body weight). The homeostatic theory of stereotyped behaviors suggests that these behaviors regulate arousal. Weighted vests provide **proprioceptive** input and deep touch pressure to help individuals regulate their sensory systems. Therefore, the vests could help reduce stereotyped behaviors in individuals with autism because they provide the same type of input that serves a homeostatic function.

Weighted Vest Effectiveness

Research conducted on the effectiveness of weighted vests for autism is limited. Many parents, teachers, therapists, and autistic individuals have reported positive effects of weighted vests on individuals with autism. However, anecdotal evidence cannot substitute well-designed research studies that are the basis for evidence-based practice. Some studies have suggested that weighted vests help reduce sensory-seeking behaviors and improve attention and focus. In contrast, other studies have found no benefit associated with weighted vests (Hodgetts et al., 2011; Stephenson & Carter, 2009).

One study conducted with five preschool children with pervasive developmental disorders used an A-B-A design (A—not wearing the vest, B—wearing the vest, and A—not wearing the vest). Except for one participant, when wearing the vest, the other four participants showed a decrease in the number of distractions and self-stimulatory behavior and an increase in the duration of focused attention. The authors cautioned that more research is needed to ascertain the effectiveness of weighted vests in reducing problem behaviors (Fertel-Daly et al., 2001). Another study used an alternating treatment design with three conditions:

a weighted vest, a vest without weight, and no vest. Participants showed no difference in engagement across the three conditions (Reichow et al., 2010).

VandenBerg (2001) found that weighted vests (owing to the deep-pressure sensory input) increased on-task behavior for four children diagnosed with ADHD. A pilot study examined the effectiveness of sensory integration in treating autistic children. The study measured improvements in social responsiveness, sensory processing, functional motor skills, and social-emotional support. The study's findings suggest that sensory integration can help reduce autism mannerisms (Pfeiffer et al., 2011). Another self-report study involving 514 occupational therapists assessed the effectiveness of weighted vests in modifying the behaviors of school-aged children diagnosed with autism and ADHD. A response rate of 68% of the participants reported that staying in their seats and having an increased attention span were the most improved behaviors (Olson & Moulton, 2004).

Taylor and colleagues (2017) reviewed weighted vests with individuals with autism. The review findings indicate that the utilization of weighted vests with individuals diagnosed with autism spectrum disorder is not an evidence-based practice. Coined initially as *evidence-based medicine* (Sackett et al., 1996), the term has been expanded to other areas of healthcare and referred to as *evidence-based practice*, meaning that practitioners use research and scientific evidence to inform clinical decision-making to ensure the patient or client receives the most effective and appropriate care based on the available evidence.

In sum, research on the effectiveness of weighted vests is mixed. The added weight may have a calming effect, which can vary individually. Temple Grandin, a prominent figure in the field of animal science and autism advocacy, has disclosed building a squeezing machine to get comfort from the soothing pressure.

Animal-Assisted Therapy

Animal-assisted therapy (AAT) is not a novel approach to treatment but has gained popularity in recent years as an alternative therapy approach. In addition to other complementary and alternative medicine therapies, AAT has been proposed as an alternative approach for people with autism (Braun et al., 2009). *Canine-assisted therapy* (interactions with specialized trained dogs), *dolphin-assisted therapy* (swimming and interacting with dolphins in a controlled environment), and *equine therapy* (horseback riding and other equine activities) can help improve the social and emotional development of children with autism. Dogs are the animals most commonly used in therapy with autistic children, as they provide a sense of security and help reduce anxiety in social interactions.

Animal-assisted therapy is a form of therapy that incorporates animals in the therapeutic process (Chandler, 2017). The animal facilitates the therapist-client relationship and can foster the necessary trust for the client to disclose information. Sigmund Freud, the Viennese neurologist and founder of psychoanalyst, included his dog, Jodi, in therapy sessions. He realized that the dog functioned as a social lubricant, making an uncomfortable conversation between therapist-client more effortless (VanFleet & Faa-Thompson, 2014).

AAT can effectively reduce anxiety in neurotypical children (Tahan et al., 2022). Can AAT be effective for autistic children? Research on the use of animal therapy with autistic children has been found to be effective. Research increasingly suggests that autistic children can form intimate bonds with animals (Grandin et al., 2015). Compared to other quantitative studies, Ang and MacDougall (2022) used structured interviews with three therapists and four parents to understand AAT better through their perspectives. Therapists and parents highlighted the physical, sensory, and emotional benefits of AAT while also pointing to its limitations. One therapist interviewed stated:

> Children with autism who participated in therapeutic horseback riding showed greater **sensory seeking**, sensory sensitivity, and less irritability and hyperactivity. While riding a horse, restless children are distracted, which makes them less jumpy. Therapy animals enjoy being petted by children, which increases feelings of affection in children with autism. Cuddling and touching animals cause the release of oxytocin, which calms the child.
>
> (Ang & MacDougall, 2022, p. 76, my emphasis)

Similarly, London and colleagues (2020) explored parent perspectives on the effectiveness of AAT using trained dogs with their autistic children and adolescents. Parents unanimously indicated their support for using trained dogs, as the dogs facilitated their children's engagement, enjoyment, and motivation.

Rehn and colleagues' (2023) review of seven randomized clinical controlled trials reported overall positive gains in social, cognitive, behavioral, and physical domains in children and adolescents with autism. However, the authors recommended standardizing the implementation of the AAT treatment protocol and the need for future research to address the existing literature's methodological concerns. A recent review and meta-analysis found AAT effective in specific areas, including improving social communication and language skills and reducing irritability and hyperactivity. The authors cautioned about generalizing improvements in other areas and highlighted the need to assess the long-term benefits of treatment (Xiao et al., 2024).

Music Therapy

Music therapy (MT) involves using music in various forms to address individuals' emotional, social, and cognitive needs. The American Music Therapy Association, based on the clinical and evidence-based intervention, has established music therapy as a *bona fide* treatment modality. Music can promote relaxation and stress reduction and be an effective medium for creativity and self-expression, especially for individuals who have difficulty expressing themselves verbally. Music can also be beneficial for individuals experiencing emotional and psychological problems.

Bruscia (1998, p. 20) defined music therapy as "a systematic process of intervention wherein the therapist helps the client to promote health, using musical experiences and the relationships that develop through them as dynamic forces of change." Therapists with specialized academic and clinical training, not parents, conduct the application and implementation of music therapy.

Can MT benefit individuals on the autism spectrum? Despite the socioemotional impairments that characterize their condition, individuals with autism can process the emotional aspects of music (Caria et al., 2011). Importantly, music therapy is a non-invasive and easy-to-implement intervention with most autistic individuals, regardless of the severity of the disorder (De Vries et al., 2015).

Why might music therapy be effective for individuals on the autism spectrum? Many individuals on the autism spectrum have a strong sensitivity to sound and a deep appreciation for music. As a result, they may find enjoyment and an emotional connection through music (Heaton, 2009). There are similarities in how the brain processes and understands music and language (Patel, 2003). For example, studies have shown that the processing of rhythm in music and the rhythm of speech occurs in overlapping neural areas. It has been found that music can activate Broca's and Wernicke's brain areas, which are responsible for language production and comprehension, respectively (Moreno, 2009).

It has been suggested that the **mirror neuron system** (MNS), which is somewhat impaired in autism, is responsible for some of the condition's characteristics. Various forms of music engagement, such as singing, playing a musical instrument, and listening to music, activate brain regions associated with the MNS. Wan and colleagues (2010) propose that music therapy can engage these brain regions, potentially fostering cognitive development and language skills. Additionally, music can be a powerful tool for improving the social skills of children with autism (Ghasemtabar et al., 2015).

Music therapy has been extensively reviewed. Ke and colleagues (2022) investigated the effectiveness of music therapy (MT) in a meta-analysis comprising 608 participants. They found that MT increases social skills in autistic children, but the benefits appear to be short-lived. A Cochrane Database of Systematic Reviews of ten studies with 165 participants assessed the effectiveness of music therapy for individuals with autism (Geretsegger et al., 2014). Notably, Cochrane systematic reviews use a rigorous methodology to identify, select, and critically appraise relevant research. The review found that music therapy positively affects initiations of social interaction, nonverbal communication skills, communication skills, and the quality of the parent-child relationship. None of the studies reviewed reported any aversive reaction to the interventions. A literature review of the relationship between music and language found that they share some common characteristics. Music components, including rhythm and melody perception, play an essential role in early language development

(Pino et al., 2023). Thompson and colleagues (2014) expanded music therapy to the entire family, connecting and engaging children and parents with active music-making activities. Twenty-three toddlers with severe autism participated in the study. The findings showed that social interaction and parent-child relationships, not language skills or general responsiveness, improved in the home and community.

A more recent review and meta-analysis of 18 randomized controlled trial (RCT) studies with 1,457 children with ASD found that music therapy can improve the symptoms of children with autism—i.e., language social skills, behavior, sensory perception, and self-help (Shi et al., 2024). Despite the effectiveness of music therapy, the authors emphasized the need to conduct more rigorous research with larger sample sizes and control groups to assess the long-term sustainability of music therapy.

In sum, music therapy consists of various activities tailored to an individual's needs, including singing, listening to music, and playing musical instruments. Research has consistently supported the benefits of using music therapy with individuals with autism. Music therapy can facilitate language production and comprehension for individuals with autism. As a nonverbal outlet for self-expression, music can improve social interactions, emotional expression, and communication skills and enhance the quality of life of individuals with autism.

Yoga

Yoga originated in ancient India as a physical, mental, and spiritual practice. According to the American Heritage Dictionary, "Yoga is a Hindu discipline aimed at training the consciousness for a state of perfect spiritual insight and tranquility." Yoga involves breathing exercises, physical posture, and relaxation techniques that have been shown to reduce stress and anxiety, improve flexibility and balance, increase strength and endurance, and promote overall physical and mental well-being (Goldberg, 2013; Woodyard, 2011). There is some evidence to suggest that yoga can be an effective complementary therapy for individuals with autism.

It has been found that practicing yoga can positively impact the symptoms associated with autism and significantly improve health outcomes and quality of life in children with ASD (Sotoodeh et al., 2017). Shanker and Pradhan (2022) investigated the effect of a yoga program on the severity of autism in children with ASD who attend special schools. They found that compared to a control group, the children who received 12 weeks of yoga intervention showed significant improvements in the reduction of the symptomatology of autism. Other studies have found numerous benefits associated with yoga practice for children on the autism spectrum, including amelioration of gastrointestinal distress and sleep disorders (Narasingharao et al., 2017), reduction of hyperactivity and aggression (Rosenblatt et al., 2011), and promotion of calmness, resilience, and self-regulation (Goldberg, 2013).

Yoga Effectiveness for Autism

Based on the findings of several studies reporting the use of yoga and mindful-ness-based interventions for autism, Semple (2019) reviewed the effectiveness of yoga and mindfulness-based interventions for children with ASD in eight empirical research studies. Although the studies reported social, emotional, and behavioral improvements, they had several limitations, including small sample sizes, a lack of measures to assess the intervention's effectiveness, and no con-trol groups. The empirical evidence to support the efficacy of yoga still needs to be improved. These early findings are encouraging and suggest the need for further research.

More recently, Ju and colleagues (2024) conducted a randomized controlled trial (RCT) with 17 children with autism. The study shows that practicing yoga can help reduce problem behaviors and improve motor coordination in autistic children. The results also indicate that yoga intervention significantly reduces ir-ritability and social withdrawal in children with autism. In summary, implement-ing a yoga intervention can be an effective approach to improving the well-being of children with autism.

In summary, yoga therapy is generally safe as a supplementary intervention for individuals on the autism spectrum, and its benefits tend to outweigh its short-comings. However, compared to evidence-based treatments that can be more ef-fective, allocating time and limited resources to a safe but less effective therapy may result in missed opportunities for skill acquisition and possible reduction of problem behaviors that are prevalent in individuals on the autism spectrum. Ad-ditionally, some individuals with autism may struggle with the social aspects of a yoga class, such as being near others, following group instructions, or perform-ing certain poses or movements that may be uncomfortable or challenging. Yoga interventions might not be suitable for individuals on the autism spectrum due to the level of concentration and self-control required. Autistic individuals might have difficulties focusing, and their speech, communication, body language, and breathing deficits may make a yoga intervention challenging and ineffective.

Acupuncture

Acupuncture treatment is common in China and other parts of the world. Its use has been pilot-tested in autistic children (Warren et al., 2017). Hanson and colleagues (2007) reviewed the prevalence of various therapies used in autism. They found that 74% of parents reported using CAM and found the practice to be either helpful or ineffective but not harmful, compared to the side effects of medications.

Scalp acupuncture treatment (SAT) is a variant of acupuncture that consists of inserting fine needles into different lines or zones in the scalp (Lu, 1991). SAT is believed to be effective in treating various conditions. One study shows that SAT can improve certain hormone levels and cerebral blood flow (Xiang et al., 1996). Another research that evaluated the effectiveness of SAT on autistic individuals found that their language comprehension and self-care ability improved significantly (Allam et al., 2008). Lee and colleagues (2018) reviewed 27 studies that support the safety and effectiveness of treating children with autism.

SAT has not been evaluated systematically. To that end, Liu and colleagues (2019) used the Childhood Autism Rating Scale, the Autism Behavior Checklist, and the Psychoeducational Profile scores as outcome measures. Compared to behavioral and educational interventions, SAT reduced the scores on all three outcome measures, suggesting the effectiveness of the treatment modality. However, the authors cautioned that although SAT may be an effective intervention for autism, given the heterogeneity of the disorder, "randomized controlled trials of higher quality and design" are necessary before embracing SAT as an evidence-based therapy for autism.

Summary

Biomedical treatments encompass a range of practices such as medications, surgeries, and other evidence-based interventions used in modern medicine to address various illnesses and health conditions. It is important to note that biomedical therapies for autism, such as herbal supplements and chelation, are often viewed as complementary alternative medicines (CAM) that fall outside the scope of conventional medicine.

Gastrointestinal symptoms are common in children with autism, raising the possibility of an association with celiac disease or gluten sensitivity. As a result, parents of children diagnosed with autism have increasingly turned to gluten-free and casein-free diets to alleviate their children's symptoms. Chelation therapy, yoga, hyperbaric oxygen therapy, weighted vest, sensory integration, animal-assisted therapy, and music therapy are also commonly used to treat autism symptoms. Similarly, parents of autistic children have championed using a wide variety of vitamins and supplements, including vitamin D, omega-3 fatty acids, methyl B-12, probiotics, and digestive enzymes, for their potential role in managing children's autism symptoms. Although many families of autistic children have reported positive outcomes with biomedical treatments and CAM, the evidence supporting their effectiveness is often limited, and some may carry risks and be unsafe.

Questions to Ponder for Further Thinking and Learning

1 What are the potential benefits (if any) of biomedical treatments for autism?
2 What are the potential risks or side effects (if any) of these treatments?
3 Have these treatments been scientifically proven to be effective?

4 How do healthcare providers determine which biomedical interventions are appropriate for a child with autism?
5 What role do parents play in pursuing biomedical treatments for their autistic child?
6 What is the cost of these treatments, and does insurance cover them?
7 Are there any alternative treatments or therapies that may be more appropriate or effective for a child with autism?
8 How can parents ensure their child receives safe and effective CAM treatments for their autism symptoms?

References

Allam, H., Eldine, N. G., & Helmy, G. (2008). Scalp acupuncture effect on language development in children with autism: A pilot study. *Journal of Alternative and Complementary Medicine, 14*(2), 109–114.

Ali, A., Cui, X., & Eyles, D. (2018). Developmental vitamin D deficiency and autism: Putative pathogenic mechanisms. *The Journal of Steroid Biochemistry and Molecular Biology, 175*, 108–118.

Allen, L. H. (2012). Vitamin B-12. *Advances in Nutrition, 3*(1), 54–55.

Amminger, G. P., Berger, G. E., Schäfer, M. R., Klier, C., Friedrich, M. H., & Feucht, M. (2007). Omega-3 fatty acids supplementation in children with autism: A double-blind randomized, placebo-controlled pilot study. *Biological Psychiatry, 61*(4), 551–553.

Andrès, E., Fothergill, H., & Mecili, M. (2010). Efficacy of oral cobalamin (vitamin B12) therapy. *Expert Opinion on Pharmacotherapy, 11*(2), 249–256.

Ang, C. S., & MacDougall, F. A. (2022). An evaluation of animal-assisted therapy for autism spectrum disorders: Therapist and parent perspectives. *Psychological Studies, 67*(1), 72–81.

Ayres, A. J. (1972). *Sensory integration and learning disabilities.* Western Psychological Services.

Ayres, A. J. (1979). *Sensory integration and the child* (1st ed.). Western Psychological Services.

Ayres, A. J. (1989). *Sensory integration and praxis tests* (SIPT). Western Psychological Services.

Baranek, G. T. (2002). Efficacy of sensory and motor interventions for children with autism. *Journal of Autism and Developmental Disorders, 32*, 397–422.

Baspinar, B., & Yardimci, H. (2020). Gluten-free casein-free diet for autism spectrum disorders: Can it be effective in solving behavioural and gastrointestinal problems? *Eurasian Journal of Medicine, 52*(3), 292–297.

Braun, C., Stangler, T., Narveson, J., & Pettingell, S. (2009). Animal-assisted therapy as a pain relief intervention for children. *Complementary Therapies in Clinical Practice, 15*(2), 105–109.

Brondino, N., Fusar-Poli, L., Rocchetti, M., Provenzani, U., Barale, F., & Politi, P. (2015). Complementary and alternative therapies for autism spectrum disorder. *Evidence-Based Complementary and Alternative Medicine, 2015*, 258589.

Brown, M. J., Willis, T., Omalu, B., & Leiker, R. (2006). Deaths resulting from hypocalcemia after administration of edetate disodium: 2003–2005. *Pediatrics, 118*(2), e534–e536.

Bruscia, K. E. (1998). *Defining music therapy* (2nd ed.). Barcelona Publishers.

Burr, D., & Gori, M. (2012). Multisensory integration develops late in humans. In M. M. Murray & M. T. Wallace (Eds.), *Frontiers in neuroscience: The neural bases of multisensory processes.* CRC Press/Taylor & Francis.

Cannell, J. J., & Grant, W. B. (2013). What is the role of vitamin D in autism? *Dermatoendocrinology*, *5*(1), 199–204.

Caria, A., Venuti, P., & de Falco, S. (2011). Functional and dysfunctional brain circuits underlying emotional processing of music in autism spectrum disorders. *Cerebral Cortex*, *21*, 2838–2849.

Chaidez, V., Hansen, R. L., & Hertz-Picciotto, I. (2014). Gastrointestinal problems in children with autism, developmental delays or typical development. *Journal of Autism and Developmental Disorders*, *44*(5), 1117–1127.

Chandler, C. K. (2017). *Animal-assisted therapy in counseling*. Taylor & Francis.

Chungpaibulpatana, J., Sumpatanarax, T., Thadakul, N., Chantharatreerat, C., Konkaew, M., & Aroonlimsawas, M. (2008). Hyperbaric oxygen therapy in Thai autistic children. *Journal of the Medical Association of Thailand*, *91*(8), 1232–1238.

Committee on Children with Disabilities (2001). American Academy of Pediatrics: Counseling families who choose complementary and alternative medicine for their child with chronic illness or disability. Committee on children with disabilities. *Pediatrics*, *107*(3), 598–601.

Davis, T. N., O'Reilly, M., Kang, S., Lang, R., Rispoli, M., Sigafoos, J., ... Mulloy, A. (2013). Chelation treatment for autism spectrum disorders: A systematic review. *Research in autism Spectrum Disorders*, *7*(1), 49–55.

De Vries, D., Beck, T., Stacey, B., Winslow, K., & Meines, K. (2015). Music as a therapeutic intervention with autism: A systematic review of the literature. *Therapeutic Recreation Journal*, *49*(3), 220–237.

Elder, J. H. (2008). The gluten-free, casein-free diet in autism: An overview with clinical implications. *Nutrition in Clinical Practice*, *23*(6), 583–588.

Eyles, D. W., Burne, T. H., & McGrath, J. J. (2013). Vitamin D, effects on brain development, adult brain function and the links between low levels of vitamin D and neuropsychiatric disease. *Frontiers in Neuroendocrinology*, *34*(1), 47–64.

FDA (2019). Be aware of false or misleading claims for treating autism. Food and Drug Administration. https://www.fda.gov/consumers/consumer-updates/be-aware-potentially-dangerous-products-and-therapies-claim-treat-autism. Accessed on June 10, 2024.

Feng, P., Zhao, S., Zhang, Y., & Li, E. (2023). A review of probiotics in the treatment of autism spectrum disorders: Perspectives from the gut-brain axis. *Frontiers in Microbiology*, *14*, 1123462.

Fertel-Daly, D., Bedell, G., & Hinojosa, J. (2001). Effects of a weighted vest on attention to task and self-stimulatory behaviors in preschoolers with pervasive developmental disorders. *American Journal of Occupational Therapy*, *55*(6), 629–640.

Fluegge, K. (2016). The role of air pollution exposures in mediating nutritional biochemical profiles in autism: A reply to Jory (2015). *Nutrition*, *32*(10), 1163.

Genuis, S. J., & Bouchard, T. P. (2010). Celiac disease presenting as autism. *Journal of Child Neurology*, *25*(1), 114–119.

Geretsegger, M., Elefant, C., Mössler, K. A., & Gold, C. (2014). Music therapy for people with autism spectrum disorder. *Cochrane Database of Systematic Reviews*, *2014*(6), CD004381.

Ghanizadeh, A. (2012). Hyperbaric oxygen therapy for treatment of children with autism: A systematic review of randomized trials. *Medical Gas Research*, *2*, 13.

Ghasemtabar, S. N., Hosseini, M., Fayyaz, I., Arab, S., & Poudineh, Z. (2015). Music therapy: An effective approach in improving social skills of children with autism. *Advanced Biomedical Research*, *4*, 157.

Goldberg, L. (2013). *Yoga therapy for children with autism and special needs*. W. W. Norton & Company.

Gow, R. V., & Hibbeln, J. R. (2014). Omega-3 fatty acid and nutrient deficits in adverse neurodevelopment and childhood behaviors. *Child and Adolescent Psychiatric Clinics of North America, 23*(3), 555–590.

Grandin, T., Fine, A. H., O'Haire, M. E., Carlisle, G. & Bowers, C. M. (2015). The roles of animals for individuals with autism spectrum disorder. In A. H. Fine (Ed.), *Handbook on animal-assisted therapy: Foundations and guidelines for animal-assisted interventions* (4th ed., pp. 225–236). Elsevier Academic Press.

Granpeesheh, D., Tarbox, J., Dixon, D. R., Wilke, A. E., Allen, M. S., & Bradstreet, J. J. (2010). Randomized trial of hyperbaric oxygen therapy for children with autism. *Research in Autism Spectrum Disorders, 4*(2), 268–275.

Grant, W. B., & Soles, C. M. (2009). Epidemiologic evidence for supporting the role of maternal vitamin D deficiency as a risk factor for the development of infantile autism. *Dermatoendocrinology, 1*(4), 223–228.

Green, V. A., Pituch, K. A., Itchon, J., Choi, A., O'Reilly, M., & Sigafoos, J. (2006). Internet survey of treatments used by parents of children with autism. *Research in Developmental Disabilities, 27*(1), 70–84.

Han, Y., Xi, Q. Q., Dai, W., Yang, S. H., Gao, L., Su, Y. Y., & Zhang, X. (2015). Abnormal transsulfuration metabolism and reduced antioxidant capacity in Chinese children with autism spectrum disorders. *International Journal of Developmental Neuroscience, 46*, 27–32.

Hanson, E., Kalish, L. A., Bunce, E., Curtis, C., McDaniel, S., Ware, J., & Petry, J. (2007). Use of complementary and alternative medicine among children diagnosed with autism spectrum disorder. *Journal of Autism and Developmental Disorders, 37*(4), 628–636.

Harrison, K. L., & Zane, T. (2016). Focus on science: Is there science behind that?: Hyperbaric oxygen therapy. *Science in Autism Treatment, 13*(4), 28–33.

Harrison, K. L., & Zane, T. (2017). Is there science behind that? Gluten-free and casein-free diets. *Science in Autism Treatment, 14*(2), 32–36.

He, X., Liu, W., Tang, F., & Chen, X., & Song, G. (2023). Effects of probiotics on autism spectrum disorder in children: A systematic review and meta-analysis of clinical trials. *Nutrients, 15*(6), 1415.

Heaton, P. (2009). Assessing musical skills in autistic children who are not savants. *Philosophical Transactions of the Royal Society of London. Series B, 364*(1522), 1443–1447.

Hendren, R. L., James, S. J., Widjaja, F., Lawton, B., Rosenblatt, A., & Bent, S. (2016). Randomized, placebo-controlled trial of methyl B12 for children with autism. *Journal of Child and Adolescent Psychopharmacology, 26*(9), 774–783.

Heyboer, M. (2016). Hyperbaric oxygen therapy side effects—Where do we stand? *Journal of the American College of Clinical Wound Specialists, 8*(1–3), 2–3.

Hodgetts, S., Magill-Evans, J., & Misiaszek, J. E. (2011). Weighted vests, stereotyped behaviors and arousal in children with autism. *Journal of Autism and Developmental Disorders, 41*(6), 805–814.

Hoehn, T. P., & Baumeister, A. A. (1994). A critique of the application of sensory integration therapy to children with learning disabilities. *Journal of Learning Disabilities, 27*(6), 338–350.

James, S., Stevenson, S. W., Silove, N., & Williams, K. (2015). Chelation for autism spectrum disorder (ASD). *Cochrane Database of Systematic Reviews, 5*(5), CD010766.

James, S. J., Cutler, P., Melnyk, S., Jernigan, S., Janak, L., Gaylor, D. W., & Neubrander, J. A. (2004). Metabolic biomarkers of increased oxidative stress and impaired methylation capacity in children with autism. *The American Journal of Clinical Nutrition, 80*(6), 1611–1617.

Jia, F., Wang, B., Shan, L., Xu, Z., Staal, W. G., & Du, L. (2015). Core symptoms of autism improved after vitamin D supplementation. *Pediatrics, 135*(1), e196–e198.

Johnson, C. R., Handen, B. L., Zimmer, M., Sacco, K., & Turner, K. (2011). Effects of gluten free/casein free diet in young children with autism: A pilot study. *Journal of Developmental and Physical Disabilities, 23*, 213–225.

Ju, X., Liu, H., Xu, J., Hu, B., Jin, Y., & Lu, C. (2024). Effect of yoga intervention on problem behavior and motor coordination in children with autism. *Behavioral Science, 14*(2), 116.

Ke, X., Song, W., Yang, M., Li, J., & Liu, W. (2022). Effectiveness of music therapy in children with autism spectrum disorder: A systematic review and meta-analysis. *Frontiers in Psychiatry, 13*, 905113.

Kosnett, M. J. (2010). Chelation for heavy metals (arsenic, lead, and mercury): Protective or perilous? *Clinical Pharmacology & Therapeutics, 88*(3), 412–415.

Lane, S. J., Mailloux, Z., Schoen, S., Bundy, A., May-Benson, T. A., Parham, L. D., ... Schaaf, R. C. (2019). Neural Foundations of Ayres Sensory Integration®. *Brain Sciences, 9*(7), 153.

Lau, N. M., Green, P. H., Taylor, A. K., Hellberg, D., Ajamian, M., Tan, C. Z., ... Alaedini, A. (2013). Markers of celiac disease and gluten sensitivity in children with autism. *PLoS One, 8*(6), e66155.

Leach, R. M., Rees, P. J., & Wilmshurst, P. (1998). ABC of oxygen: Hyperbaric oxygen therapy. *British Medical Journal, 317*(7166), 1140–1143.

Lee, B., Lee, J., Cheon, J. H., Sung, H. K., Cho, S. H., & Chang, G. T. (2018). The efficacy and safety of acupuncture for the treatment of children with autism spectrum disorder: A systematic review and meta-analysis. *Evidence-Based Complementary and Alternative Medicine, 2018*, 1057539.

Lerman, D. C., Sansbury, T., Hovanetz, A., Wolever, E., Garcia, A., O'Brien, E., & Adedipe, H. (2008). Using behavior analysis to examine the outcomes of unproven therapies: An evaluation of hyperbaric oxygen therapy for children with autism. *Behavior Analysis in Practice, 1*(2), 50–58.

Levy, S. E., & Hyman, S. L. (2003). Use of complementary and alternative treatments for children with autistic spectrum disorders is increasing. *Pediatric Annals, 32*(10), 685–691.

Levy, S. E., & Hyman, S. L. (2015). Complementary and alternative medicine treatments for children with autism spectrum disorders. *Child and Adolescent Psychiatric Clinics of North America, 17*(4), 803–820.

Li, Y. J., Ou, J. J., Li, Y. M., & Xiang, D. X. (2017). Dietary supplement for core symptoms of autism spectrum disorder: Where are we now and where should we go? *Frontiers in Psychiatry, 8*, 155.

Liu, C., Li, T., Wang, Z., Zhou, R., & Zhuang, L. (2019). Scalp acupuncture treatment for children's autism spectrum disorders: A systematic review and meta-analysis. *Medicine, 98*(13), e14880.

London, M. D., Mackenzie, L., Lovarini, M., Dickson, C., & Alvarez-Campos, A. (2020). Animal-assisted therapy for children and adolescents with autism spectrum disorder: Parent perspectives. *Journal of Autism and Developmental Disorders, 50*(12), 4492–4503.

Lu, S. (1991). Scalp acupuncture therapy and its clinical application. *Journal of Traditional Chinese Medicine, 11*(4), 272–280.

Ludvigsson, J. F., Reichenberg, A., Hultman, C. M., & Murray, J. A. (2013). A nationwide study of the association between celiac disease and the risk of autism spectrum disorders. *JAMA Psychiatry, 70*(11), 1224–1230.

Mankad, D., Dupuis, A., Smile, S., Roberts, W., Brian, J., Lui, T., ... Anagnostou, E. (2015). A randomized, placebo controlled trial of omega-3 fatty acids in the treatment of young children with autism. *Molecular Autism, 6*(1), 18.

McElhanon, B. O., McCracken, C., Karpen, S., & Sharp, W. G. (2014). Gastrointestinal symptoms in autism spectrum disorder: A meta-analysis. *Pediatrics, 133*(5), 872–883.

Moreno, S. (2009). Can music influence language and cognition? *Contemporary Music Review, 28*, 329–345.

Morgan, B. W., Kori, S., & Thomas, J. D. (2002). Adverse effects in 5 patients receiving EDTA at an outpatient chelation clinic. *Veterinary and Human Toxicology*, *44*(5), 274–276.

Munasinghe, S. A., Oliff, C., Finn, J., & Wray, J. A. (2010). Digestive enzyme supplementation for autism spectrum disorders: A double-blind randomized controlled trial. *Journal of Autism and Developmental Disorders*, *40*(9), 1131–1138.

Narasingharao, K., Pradhan, B., & Navaneetham, J. (2017). Efficacy of structured yoga intervention for sleep, gastrointestinal and behaviour problems of ASD children: An exploratory study. *Journal of Clinical and Diagnostic Research, 11*(3), VC01–VC06.

Ohland, C. L., & MacNaughton, W. K. (2010). Probiotic bacteria and intestinal epithelial barrier function. *American Journal of Physiology Gastrointestinal and Liver Physiology*, *298*(6), G807–G819.

Olson, L. J., & Moulton, H. J. (2004). Use of weighted vests in pediatric occupational therapy practice. *Physical and Occupational Therapy in Pediatrics*, *24*(3), 45–60.

Pacheva, I., & Ivanov, I. (2019). Targeted biomedical treatment for autism spectrum disorders. *Current Pharmaceutical Design*, *25*(41), 4430–4453.

Panksepp, J. (1979). A neurochemical theory of autism. *Trends in Neuroscience*, *2*, 174–177.

Patel, A. D. (2003). Language, music, syntax and the brain. *Nature Neuroscience, 6*, 674–681.

Paul, C., & Brady, D. M. (2017). Comparative bioavailability and utilization of particular forms of B12 supplements with potential to mitigate B12-related genetic polymorphisms. *Integrative Medicine*, *16*(1), 42–49.

Perrin, J. M., Coury, D. L., Hyman, S. L., Cole, L., Reynolds, A. M., & Clemons T. (2012). Complementary and alternative medicine use in a large pediatric autism sample. *Pediatrics*, *130*(2), S77–S82.

Pfeiffer, B. A., Koenig, K., Kinnealey, M., Sheppard, M., & Henderson, L. (2011). Effectiveness of sensory integration interventions in children with autism spectrum disorders: A pilot study. *American Journal of Occupational Therapy*, *65*(1), 76–85.

Pino, M. C., Giancola, M., & D'Amico, S. (2023). The association between music and language in children: A state-of-the-art review. *Children*, *10*(5), 801.

Piwowarczyk, A., Horvath, A., Łukasik, J., Pisula, E., & Szajewska, H. (2018). Gluten- and casein-free diet and autism spectrum disorders in children: A systematic review. *European Journal of Nutrition*, *57*(2), 433–440.

Podgórska-Bednarz, J., & Perenc, L. (2021). Hyperbaric oxygen therapy for children and youth with autism spectrum disorder: A review. *Brain Sciences*, *11*(7), 916.

Quan, J., Panaccione, N., Jeong, J., Underwood, F. E., Coward, S., Windsor, J. W., … King, J. A. (2021). Association between celiac disease and autism spectrum disorder: A systematic review. *Journal of Pediatric Gastroenterology and Nutrition*, *72*(5), 704–711.

Quigley, E. M., & Quera, R. (2006). Small intestinal bacterial overgrowth: Roles of antibiotics, prebiotics, and probiotics. *Gastroenterology*, *130*(2), S78–S90.

Rehn, A. K., Caruso, V. R., & Kumar, S. (2023). The effectiveness of animal-assisted therapy for children and adolescents with autism spectrum disorder: A systematic review. *Complementary Therapies in Clinical Practice*, *50*, 101719.

Reichow, B., Barton, E. E., Sewell, J. N., Good, L., & Wolery, M. (2010). Effects of weighted vests on the engagement of children with developmental delays and autism. *Focus on Autism and Other Developmental Disabilities*, *25*(1), 3–11.

Reyes, V. P., Capps, J. W., Méndez, Y. L., Leal, G. R., & Avitia, G. (2019). Omega-3 and cognition in children with malnutrition. In R. R. Watson & V. R. Preedy (Eds.), *Omega fatty acids in brain and neurological health* (2nd ed., pp. 143–159). Elsevier Academic Press.

Rosenblatt, L. E., Gorantla, S., Torres, J. A., Yarmush, R. S., Rao, S., Park, E. R., ... Levine, J. B. (2011). Relaxation response-based Yoga improves functioning in young children with autism: A pilot study. *Journal of Alternative and Complementary Medicine, 17*(11), 1029–1035.

Rossignol, D. A., & Frye, R. E. (2021). The effectiveness of cobalamin (B12) treatment for autism spectrum disorder: A systematic review and meta-analysis. *Journal of Personalized Medicine, 11*(8), 1–22.

Rossignol, D. A., & Rossignol, L. W. (2006). Hyperbaric oxygen therapy may improve symptoms in autistic children. *Medical Hypotheses, 67*(2), 216–228.

Rossignol, D. A., Rossignol, L. W., Smith, S., Schneider, C., Logerquist, S., Usman, A., ... Mumper, E. A. (2009). Hyperbaric treatment for children with autism: A multicenter, randomized, double-blind, controlled trial. *Pediatrics, 9*, 21.

Saad, K., Abdel-Rahman, A. A., Elserogy, Y. M., Al-Atram, A. A., El-Houfey, A. A., Othman, H. A., ... Abdel-Salam, A. M. (2018). Randomized controlled trial of vitamin D supplementation in children with autism spectrum disorder. *Journal of Child Psychology and Psychiatry, 59*(1), 20–29. Retraction in: *Journal of Child Psychology and Psychiatry* (2019), *60*(6), 711.

Saad, K., Eltayeb, A. A., Mohamad, I. L., Al-Atram, A. A., Elserogy, Y., Bjørklund, G., ... Nicholson, B. (2015). A randomized, placebo-controlled trial of digestive enzymes in children with autism spectrum disorders. *Clinical Psychopharmacology and Neuroscience, 13*(2), 188–193.

Sackett, D. L., Rosenberg, W. M., Gray, J. A., Haynes, R. B., & Richardson, W. S. (1996). Evidence based medicine: What it is and what it isn't. *British Medical Journal, 312*(7023), 71–72.

Sakulchit, T., Ladish, C., & Goldman, R. D. (2017). Hyperbaric oxygen therapy for children with autism spectrum disorder. *Canadian Family Physician, 63*(6), 446–448.

Sampanthavivat, M., Singkhwa, W., Chaiyakul, T., Karoonyawanich, S., & Ajpru, H. (2012). Hyperbaric oxygen in the treatment of childhood autism: A randomised controlled trial. *Diving and Hyperbaric Medicine, 42*(3), 128–133.

Schoen, S. A., Lane, S. L., Mailloux, Z., May-Benson, T., Parham, L. D., Roley, S. S., & Schaaf, R. C. (2019). A systematic review of Ayres sensory integration intervention for children with autism. *Autism Research, 121*(1), 6–19.

Semple, R. J. (2019). Review: Yoga and mindfulness for youth with autism spectrum disorder: Review of the current evidence. *Child and Adolescent Mental Health, 24*(1), 12–18.

Seung, H., Rogalski, Y., Shankar, M., & Elder, J. (2007). The gluten-free and casein-free diet and autism: Communication outcomes from a preliminary double-blind clinical trial. *Journal of Medical Speech-Language Pathology, 15*(4), 337–345.

Shanker, S., & Pradhan, B. (2022). Effect of yoga on children with autism spectrum disorder in special schools. *Industrial Psychiatry Journal, 31*(2), 367–369.

Shattock, P., & Whiteley, P. (2002). Biochemical aspects in autism spectrum disorders: Updating the opioid-excess theory and presenting new opportunities for biomedical intervention. *Expert Opinion on Therapeutic Targets, 6*(2), 175–183.

Shi, Z., Wang, S., Chen, M., Hu, A., Long, Q., & Lee, Y. (2024). The effect of music therapy on language communication and social skills in children with autism spectrum disorder: A systematic review and meta-analysis. *Frontiers in Psychology, 15*, 1336421.

Shulkin, M. L., Pimpin, L., Bellinger, D., Kranz, S., Duggan, C., Fawzi, W., ... Mozaffarian, D. (2016). Effects of omega-3 supplementation during pregnancy and youth on neurodevelopment and cognition in childhood: A systematic review and meta-analysis. *The FASEB Journal, 30*(1 Suppl), 295.5.

Simopoulos, A. P. (2010). Genetic variants in the metabolism of omega-6 and omega-3 fatty acids: Their role in the determination of nutritional requirements and chronic disease risk. *Experimental Biology and Medicine, 235*(7), 785–795.

Singer, A., & Ravi, R. (2015). Complementary and alternative treatments for autism part 2: Identifying and avoiding non-evidence-based treatments. *AMA Journal of Ethics, 17*(4), 375–380.

Sotoodeh, M. S., Arabameri, E., Panahibakhsh, M., Kheiroddin, F., Mirdoozandeh, H., & Ghanizadeh, A. (2017). Effectiveness of yoga training program on the severity of autism. *Complementary Therapies in Clinical Practice, 28*, 47–53.

Stephenson, J., & Carter, M. (2009). The use of weighted vests with children with autism spectrum disorders and other disabilities. *Journal of Autism and Developmental Disorders, 39*(1), 105–114.

Tahan, M., Saleem, T., Sadeghifar, A., & Ahangri, E. (2022). Assessing the effectiveness of animal-assisted therapy on alleviation of anxiety in pre-school children: A randomized controlled trial. *Contemporary Clinical Trials Communications, 28*, 100947.

Taniya, M. A., Chung, H. J., Al, M. A., Alam, S., Aziz, M. A., … Xiao, J. (2022). Role of gut microbiome in autism spectrum disorder and its therapeutic regulation. *Frontiers in Cellular and Infection Microbiology, 12*, 915701.

Taylor, C. J., Spriggs, A. D., Ault, M. J., Flanagan, S., & Sartini, E. C. (2017). What is evidence based practice? A systematic review of weighted vests with individuals with autism spectrum disorder. *Research in Autism Spectrum Disorders, 37*, 49–60.

Thom, S. R. (2011). Hyperbaric oxygen—its mechanisms and efficacy. *Plastic and Reconstructive Surgery, 127*(1), 131S–141S.

Thompson, G. A., McFerran, K. S., & Gold, C. (2014). Family-centred music therapy to promote social engagement in young children with severe autism spectrum disorder: A randomized controlled study. *Child: Care, Health and Development, 40*(6), 840–852.

VandenBerg, N. L. (2001). The use of a weighted vest to increase on-task behavior in children with attention difficulties. *American Journal of Occupational Therapy, 55*(6), 621–628.

van De Sande, M. M., van Buul, V. J., & Brouns, F. J. (2014). Autism and nutrition: The role of the gut-brain axis. *Nutrition Research Reviews, 27*(2), 199–214.

VanFleet, R., & Faa-Thompson, T. (2014). Animal assisted play therapy to empower vulnerable children. In G. Green and A. Myrick (Eds.), *Play therapy with vulnerable populations: No child forgotten* (pp. 85–103). Rowman & Littlefield.

Vinkhuyzen, A. A. E., Eyles, D. W., Burne, T. H. J., Blanken, L. M. E., Kruithof, C. J., Verhulst, F., … McGrath, J. J. (2018). Gestational vitamin D deficiency and autism-related traits: The generation R study. *Molecular Psychiatry, 23*(2), 240–246.

Wan, C. Y., Demaine, K., Zipse, L., Norton, A., & Schlaug, G. (2010). From music making to speaking: Engaging the mirror neuron system in autism. *Brain Research Bulletin, 82*(3–4), 161–168.

Warren, L. R., Rao, P. A., & Paton, D. C. (2017). A pilot observational study of an acupressure/acupuncture intervention in children with autism spectrum disorder. *Journal of Alternative and Complementary Medicine, 23*(11), 844–851.

Woodyard, C. (2011). Exploring the therapeutic effects of Yoga and its ability to increase quality of life. *International Journal of Yoga, 4*(2), 49–54.

Xiang, L., Wang, H., & Li, Z. (1996). [TCD observation on cerebral blood flow dynamics inference of cerebral palsy with scalp therapy]. *Zhen Ci Yan Jiu, 21*(4), 7–9.

Xiao, N., Bagayi, V., Yang, D., Huang, X., Zhong, L., Kiselev, S., … Chereshnev, V. A. (2024). Effectiveness of animal-assisted activities and therapies for autism spectrum disorder: A systematic review and meta-analysis. *Frontiers in Veterinary Science, 11*, 1403527.

Zimmer, M., Desch, L., Rosen, L. D., Bailey, M. L., Becker, D., Culbert, T. P., … Wiley, S. E. (2012). Sensory integration therapies for children with developmental and behavioral disorders. *Pediatrics, 129*(6), 1186–1189.

Chapter 13

Autism Then, Now, and Moving Forward

Chapter Contents

Introduction

The signs and characteristics associated with autism spectrum disorder, as diagnosed in the DSM-5 and ICD-11, have likely been present throughout history, even before clinicians and researchers formally recognized and diagnosed the condition. The conceptualization of autism has evolved over the decades with each new publication of the DSM and ICD, transforming it from a misunderstood condition into a spectrum of neurodevelopmental differences. In this chapter, I will review the historical contexts that have shaped our understanding of autism, both in the past and in recent times, and consider their implications for the near future.

Each formulation of the Diagnostic and Statistical Manual of Mental Disorders (DSM) since its first publication in 1952 and that of the International

DOI: 10.4324/9781003336266-17

Classification of Diseases (ICD) creation in 1948 by the World Health Organization has proposed diagnostic criteria that have refined the understanding of ASD. The Research Domain Criteria (RDoC) framework, initiated by the National Institute of Mental Health (NIMH) in 2009, unlike the DSM and ICD, emphasizes a dimensional approach to understanding psychological conditions, including autism. This approach differs from the DSM and ICD by avoiding the categorization of autism symptoms into predetermined binary views of having or not having autism. The RDoC encourages researchers and clinicians to consider the underlying mechanisms of ASD rather than relying solely on traditional diagnostic categories.

The concept of **neurodiversity**, which advocates for recognizing and appreciating neurological differences as a natural variation of human diversity rather than a disorder, will likely shape the diagnosis and treatment of autism in various ways. For example, treatment could focus on the strengths rather than individuals' challenges and deficits. Additionally, research could seek to understand the diversity within neurological profiles rather than conformity to the preconceived neurotypical standard. Finally, the acceptance of **neurodivergent** individuals as not in need of a cure but rather acceptance could reduce the stigma and promote a more accommodating environment where autistic individuals can thrive.

Autism Then

Signs, symptoms, and behaviors associated with those consistent with autism spectrum disorder have been around long before Kanner and Asperger clinically described the condition in the 1940s. The cases of Hugh Blair, an 18th-century landowner, Victor, the wild boy of Aveyron, and Pelagija Serebrenikova, a woman in old Russia considered a "blessed fool" (described in Chapter 1), depicted behaviors that would likely warrant a diagnosis of autism. However, in earlier centuries, manifestations of autism signs were not recognized as a distinct condition. They were misinterpreted due to a lack of understanding of developmental disorders and attributed to various incorrect assumptions, including madness or feeble-mindedness.

Before the 20th century, no treatments were available for individuals exhibiting unusual behaviors. There was a lack of understanding and treatment for mental health conditions, including what we now recognize as autism. Many people displaying eccentric behaviors were marginalized, misunderstood, or often confined to mental institutions, where they received little to no appropriate care. During this time, autism was not well-defined or recognized, which contributed to the stigma surrounding behaviors that deviated from the norm. In the 1940s, children who were examined and judged defective because of various conditions, including Down syndrome, cerebral palsy, or any other conditions physicians could not diagnose, were sent away to institutions. Donvan and Zucker (2016) provide a list of terms that physicians used to describe children and adults that displayed a "disparity from normal functioning," including having a defective heart valve:

> Throughout the first half of the twentieth century, the lexicon of disability also included 'cretin,' 'ignoramus,' 'simpleton,' 'maniac,' 'lunatic,' 'dullard,' 'dunce,' 'demented,' 'deranged,' 'schizoid,' 'spastic,' 'feebleminded,' and 'psychotic'.
>
> (Donvan & Zucker, 2016, p. 14)

The best medical advice in those days for children whose behavior departed considerably from the norm was to institutionalize them. The well-documented case of Donald T., the first child diagnosed with autism, highlights the emerging understanding and treatment options available in the mid-20th century.

Donvan and Zucker (2016) provide a detailed overview of Donald's early life, beginning with his time at a preventorium in Mississippi at the age of 3. He spent a year there before his parents took him to Baltimore for an examination by Kanner at the Harriet Lane Home for Invalid Children, an extension of Johns Hopkins Hospital, in the hope of receiving a more psychiatric-based diagnosis. Donald's discharge document from the preventorium, which he received after over a year of stay, consisted of a brief half-page note. In this document, the director of the establishment suggested that Donald's condition was some form of "glandular disease" (p. 33).

Kanner, upon examining Donald, could not formulate a diagnosis after the boy's first two-week visit in 1938. Despite a second visit in 1939, a third, and the fourth one in subsequent years, Kanner did not have a formal diagnosis of Donald's condition in 1942. Kanner's examination of ten more children who exhibited behaviors somewhat like those of Donald informed the title of his seminal paper "Autistic disturbances of affective contact" (Kanner, 1943) and the first few words he wrote:

> Since 1938, there have come to our attention a number of children whose condition differs so markedly and uniquely from anything reported so far, that each case merits—and I hope, will eventually receive—a detailed consideration of its fascinating peculiarities.
>
> (Kanner, 1943, p. 217)

Donald Tripplett, the first boy diagnosed with autism by Kanner, died on June 15, 2023, at the age of 89. He defied all odds by living a long life, well beyond the life expectancy of about 79 years for neurotypicals in the United States. How was Donald able to graduate high school, attend college, hold a job, and learn to drive? His mother, Mary, taught him to drive when he was 27. All these accomplishments were possible because his parents and the people around him understood that he was different and embraced him. Donvan and Zucker (2016,

p. 534) described Donald as a "happy man." Donald's family wealth and influence in Forest, Mississippi, undoubtedly contributed to his thriving and finding his place in the world. Donald spent one year in an institution before his parents took him to Baltimore for Kanner to examine him. How would life have turned out for him had he remained in that institution?

Autism Now

Current Autism Research

Research conducted in the past several decades has not found a singular underlying genetic cause for autism but a wide variation of brain deficits. Waterhouse (2013) asserted that the heterogeneity of the condition makes it impossible to be reduced to one disorder because "No unitary **pathogenesis** exists for autism. No unitary pathophysiology exists for autism. No consistent unitary phenotype exists for autism" (Waterhouse, 2013, p. 428, my emphasis).

Research on autism causes and treatments has progressed significantly over the years. Genetic studies have found various risk factor genes that interact with other genes or environmental variables contributing to autism. The Human Genome Project (HGP), which mapped the entire human genome, provides a comprehensive reference for researchers to identify genetic variations associated with various conditions, including autism. Identifying genes that increase susceptibility to autism can improve the development of better treatment aimed at enhancing the health and neurodevelopment of children with autism and facilitating more accurate perinatal diagnosis (Hu-Lince et al., 2005). Furthermore, The HGP's technologies (e.g., Microarray) have promoted new research to identify specific genes and chromosomal regions associated with the condition.

To date, no single gene has been found to cause autism. Instead, research has found several genes that can contribute to an individual's risk of developing the condition. For example, the SHANK3 gene plays a role in synaptic function (Pagani et al., 2019). Its mutation and deletion have been linked to autism and other neurodevelopmental disorders. The CHD8 gene plays a role in brain development (Jiménez et al., 2020). Mutations in this gene have been associated with an increased risk of autism. **Copy number variations (CNVs)** and mutations across other genes may also contribute to the disorder.

Current Autism Diagnosis

Eighty years have passed since Kanner and Asperger identified and described autism. The diagnosis of autism still depends on the assessment of behavioral observations. To date, there are no reliable biomarkers that can unequivocally diagnose autism. Owing to the heterogeneity of the condition and ongoing research, the diagnostic criteria for autism have been changing over time. They will likely continue to change as more genetic research findings emerge. With each publication of the DSM, the conceptualization of autism has evolved. In the DSM-I (APA, 1952), autism was referred to as "Schizophrenia reaction, childhood type." The DSM-II (APA, 1968) labeled it "Schizophrenia, childhood type." In 1980, the DSM-III introduced "Infantile autism" and identified three areas of impairment: (1) social and communication deficits, (2) repetitive behavior, and (3) restricted interests (APA, 1980). The DSM-III-R (APA, 1987) revised the criteria, expanding the symptoms to include a broader range of characteristics. In the DSM-IV (APA, 1994), the term Asperger's disorder was introduced. Finally, the DSM-5 (APA, 2013) removed separate diagnoses of autism-related disorders and replaced them with the umbrella term "autism spectrum disorder" (ASD) to capture the diverse range of symptoms and severity levels associated with autism. This evolving trajectory highlights the shift from a more categorical perspective to a recognition of the spectrum and dimensionality of autism.

Autism Causes and Interventions

The causes of autism (see Chapter 6) are complex and not fully understood. Research indicates that several factors may interact to influence its development, including (a) genetic factors, which encompass gene variants, *de novo* mutations, polygenic risk factors, and copy number variations; (b) neurological development, which involves brain structure and connectivity, neural development, neurotransmitter dysregulation, and mirror neuron dysfunction; and (c) environmental factors such as advanced parental age, maternal immune response during pregnancy, birth complications, and exposure to environmental toxins. Overall, while considerable progress has been made in understanding autism, the precise causes are still unclear.

Current interventions for autism are multifaceted, encompassing various approaches tailored to individual needs. Behavioral therapy, primarily applied behavior analysis and its variants (see Chapter 10), has been widely recognized as an effective method for treating autism. Pharmacological therapy (see Chapter 11), is used as an adjunct to behavioral treatment to help manage symptoms of co-occurring conditions, including anxiety, depression, sleep issues, and attention-related problems. Given that there are no medications developed to treat autism *per se* and those that physicians prescribed are associated with adverse side effects, parents of autistic children have turned to complementary alternative medicine (see Chapter 12) that often lacks rigorous scientific support but offers less severe adverse reactions.

Autism and the Neurodiversity Movement

According to the DSM-5 and the ICD-11, autism spectrum disorder is a neurodevelopmental condition marked by deficits in social communication and interaction, as well as restricted and repetitive patterns of behavior, interests, or activities. However, proponents of the neurodiversity movement view autism as a form of neurodivergence—i.e., the natural variation in the human brain, nervous system, and the way some people interact with and experience the world. Although the socialization, communication, learning, and behavior of individuals on the autism spectrum may be viewed as eccentric, neurodiversity advocates do not consider autism an illness that needs to be cured.

Since Kanner and Asperger's first description of autism, the condition has been rooted in a medical model of child psychiatry, a model that focuses on disability and deficits. A new model of autism has emerged as an alternative—neurodiversity, the view that autism is one form of variation of brain wiring akin to the biodiversity existing in the natural environment. Autism advocates and researchers who promote the notion of neurodiversity are stepping away from the medical model of disability and its emphasis on deficits and approaching autism in a fundamentally novel way.

Countless individuals who have lived in previous centuries and various parts of the world have shown signs, symptoms, and behaviors that would call for a diagnosis of autism. Silberman (2015) described two eccentric individuals who, despite their peculiarities, excelled in the sciences and, thus, advanced our understanding of the natural world: Henry Cavendish, an 18th-century chemist and physicist, most notably known for his discovery of Hydrogen, and Paul Dirac, a 20th-century theoretical physicist who won a Nobel Prize for his formulation of new productive forms of atomic theory. Cavendish and Dirac displayed behaviors that their contemporaries found odd (e.g., social anxiety, shyness, awkwardness in social situations, poor motor coordination, and so on). James (2003) speculated about well-known scientists, such as Newton, Einstein, and Cavendish, who may have had autism owing to behaviors that were consistent with DSM-5 current autism diagnostic criteria (APA, 2013) and Kanner's (1943) two core deficits: a desire to be alone and the preservation of sameness.

Judy Singer coined the term "neurodiversity" in her sociology honors thesis at the University of Technology in Sydney in 1998. The idea of the term germinates from her personal experience and the difficulties she faced growing up with an eccentric mother. Judy thought of herself and her daughter as eccentric—i.e., they had peculiarities typically associated with individuals on the autism spectrum. Three generations of women on the autism spectrum fueled the consideration of her family as neurodivergent. Judy Singer and the journalist Harvey Blume's (1998) interest in autism led them on the same path—that of viewing autism as differences, not disabilities. Because of mutual interest in autism, journalist Harvey Blume corresponded with Singer on the subject matter and popularized the term in an article in The Atlantic (1998). "Neurodiversity may be every bit as crucial for the human brain as biodiversity is for life in general. Who can say what form of wiring will prove best at any given moment?" Blume wrote. No two human brains are wired similarly, so the distinction between what is normal or pathological is somewhat subjective (Armstrong, 2015).

The Social Model of Disability

The disability rights movement of the 1970s, the disenchantment of people with disabilities, and the prevailing view of their condition as a medical problem (the medical model of disability) that needed a cure to make individuals more normal gave rise to the social model of disability. People are not disabled because of their impairments; they are disabled because of the barriers they face in society (Oliver, 1990). A disability is typically defined according to the medical model—the result of a physical condition within an individual. A so-called disability necessarily places people at a disadvantage and thus reduces the quality of their lives, but it does not necessarily result in a disability *per se* (Brisenden, 1986). Conversely, the social model of disability differentiates "impairment" from "disability." For example, a person unable to walk has an impairment that can be disabling if the societal view of disability and the environmental structure do not somehow alter the individual's physical environment (a wheelchair with accessible ramps). Oliver (2013) coined the phrase *social model of disability* as a tool and not an "all-encompassing framework within which everything that happens to disabled people could be understood or explained" (Oliver, 2013, p. 1024).

Is Autism a Disability or a Disorder?

A disability denotes a physical or mental condition that limits a person's activities or senses. As a result, a disability can result in a disadvantage or handicap. According to the U.S. Department of Labor (Office of Disability and Employment Policy), autism is a neurological developmental disability that is highly heterogeneous. Symptom presentations vary widely for everyone diagnosed with the disability. Consistent with the heterogeneity of the disorder, the DSM-5 (APA, 2013) changed all previous diagnostic criteria to "autism spectrum disorder" with various levels of needed support: Level one ("Requiring support"), level two ("Requiring substantial support"), and level three ("Requiring very substantial support"). While it is unclear what "requiring support" entails, the phrase elicits a specific question. Had Cavendish or Dirac received a diagnosis of autism spectrum disorder, what types of support would they have required?

Jaarsma and Welin (2012) proposed a compelling argument supporting the concept of neurodiversity with respect to low-functioning and high-functioning autistic individuals:

> Some autism inside the narrow conception of neurodiversity can be seen as a natural variation on par with, for example, homosexuality. (Lower-functioning autism is also part of natural variation but may rightly be viewed as a disability) ... in the case of high-functioning autists, society should not stigmatize these persons as being disabled, or as having a disorder or use some other deficit-based language to refer to these people.
>
> (Jaarsma & Welin, 2012, p. 28)

Asperger, in his thesis, lauded some autistic individuals he observed. He wrote:

> Able autistic individuals can rise to eminent positions and perform with such outstanding success that one may even conclude that only such people are capable of certain achievements. It is as if they had compensatory abilities to counter-balance their deficiencies. Their unswerving determination and penetrating intellectual powers, part of their spontaneous and original mental activity, their narrowness and singlemindedness, as manifested in their special interests, can be immensely valuable and can lead to outstanding achievements in their chosen areas.
>
> (Frith, 1991, p. 88)

Is autism a disorder? In medical terminology, the term disorder denotes a disturbance of normal functioning of the mind or body that may be caused by genetic factors, disease, or trauma. Baron-Cohen (2017, p. 746) proposed that "disorder should be used when there is nothing positive about the condition, or when despite trying different environmental modifications, the person is still unable to function." The DSM (1952) listed 106 disorders in its first publication. The number has grown to three hundred disorders in the DSM-5 (APA, 2013). Same-sex attraction was once listed as a disorder in the DSM-I (APA, 1952) and DSM-II (APA, 1968) until civil rights advocates successfully petitioned its declassification from the DSM-III (APA, 1980). Eighty-five to 90% of people are right-handed. Should children be discouraged from using their left hand and forced to use their right hand, as is the case in various cultures? Baron-Cohen (2017) argued that ample evidence from genetic, neural, cognitive, and behavioral research suggests differences and signs of disability, but not a disorder. Moreover, "disability" and "disorder" conceptualize autism differently: The former requires societal and environmental support, while the latter promotes a cure or treatment.

The Neurodiversity Paradigm

The main argument of the neurodiversity perspective is that autism and other developmental disorders (e.g., attention-deficit/hyperactivity disorder, dyslexia, or dyspraxia) are brain differences that should not be viewed as pathological but as natural brain variations akin to the concept of biodiversity. The notion of neurodiversity has gained traction in recent years and has fueled various perspectives, mainly that autism is not a disorder. As a result, the movement became the darling of autistic self-advocates and the autism rights movement. It embraced autism as inseparable from a person's identity. Consistent with this identification, many autistic people prefer identity-first (i.e., autistic person) instead of person-first (i.e., person with autism) designation. Sinclair (1993) captured what it means to be autistic in a speech and publication that is considered the neurodiversity movement's first manifesto.

> Autism isn't something a person has, or a "shell" that a person is trapped inside. There's no normal child hidden behind the autism. Autism is a way of being. It is pervasive; it colors every experience, every sensation, perception, thought, emotion, and encounter, every aspect of existence. It is not possible to separate the autism from the person—and if it were possible, the person you'd have left would not be the same person you started with.
>
> (Sinclair, 1993, p. 1)

The neurodiversity movement has gained momentum in recent years. Advocates of the movement believe that certain neurological conditions such as autism and ADHD are akin to the biodiversity existing in the natural environment and that these "disorders" offer adaptive advantages that should be celebrated instead of stigmatized and pathologized. To support neurodiverse individuals, society and the medical establishment should dedicate significant resources to research and promote and advocate for changes in education, employment, and social policies. Leadbitter and colleagues (2021) wrote:

> With close attention to the needs, preferences and priorities of autistic people, we can move beyond historical divides, misunderstandings and wrongdoings to a place where we value the expertise of autistic people, embrace practices that respect and accept individual neurotypes, and ensure our interventions address the things that matter most to the recipients.
>
> (Leadbitter et al., 2021, p. 5)

Will autism be removed from the DSM and ICD owing to the claims of the neurodiversity movement? It is unlikely because, unlike those at the higher end of the spectrum, individuals at the lower end face significant challenges in daily life and require substantial support.

Arguments For and Against the Neurodiversity Movement

One of the main arguments of the neurodiversity movement is that autism is not a disorder. Thus, the symptoms and behaviors considered pathological in autistic individuals and, therefore, need fixing or curing are typical human differences in behaviors rather than disorders that warrant a diagnosis and treatment. Another argument of the neurodiversity perspective is that it adds value to society, akin to that of biodiversity, for the ecosystem to survive and thrive, and is thus normal and natural (Hughes, 2021). The neurodiversity framework, however, has its critics. One criticism leveled at the neurodiversity movement is that its proponents present a diluted view of what autism can be like for those functioning on the milder end of the spectrum while deflecting attention and much-needed resources from those severely affected by the condition (Hughes, 2021). The odd child who prefers to be alone and is fascinated with planets and stars is clearly different from another highly sociable one. However, a child with no functional communication and engaging in self-injurious behavior cannot be celebrated as exhibiting desirable variations of human behavior. In such a case, habilitation (not treatment) would be highly desirable.

In sum, the neurodiversity movement has implications for research and practice. Autism researchers and clinicians must engage with autistic people and be attentive to the neurodiversity framework. Doing so can allow them to develop an agenda that best fits the interests of autistic people (Leadbitter et al., 2021). One online survey that examined opposing characterizations of the medical view and neurodiversity found that participants who identified as autistic and were conversant with the neurodiversity perspective viewed autism as a positive identity that needs no cure (Kapp, 2012). Autism researchers should also describe autism not as a defect that must be corrected. Instead, they should characterize and investigate it as a variant of the human gene pool that may have adaptive and maladaptive values and not conceive it as an error of nature that should be remedied (Mottron, 2011). The hope is that the neurodiversity paradigm will serve as a springboard toward a more holistic view of autism in terms of its neurological differences and not shortcomings or disabilities.

Autism Diagnosis Criteria and Moving Forward

DSM and ICD Future Autism Diagnosis Criteria

The diagnostic criteria for autism in the DSM-5 and ICD-11 have evolved due to ongoing research, clinical insights, and a better understanding of mental health conditions. As new editions of the DSM and ICD are published, the diagnosis of autism will continue to change. It is unlikely that clinicians and researchers will ever discover a single, definitive cause of autism. As Boucher (2022, p. 4) eloquently stated, "What is published and read about autism today will take its place in the story of autism tomorrow."

The perspective that neurodivergence is a difference rather than a disorder may influence how autism is diagnosed and how treatments are designed and implemented. Rather than focusing solely on naming the condition (such as one autism or many autisms), the priority should be on supporting individuals who have already been diagnosed. By prioritizing the needs and experiences of those with autism, clinicians can develop more effective interventions and foster a supportive community instead of getting caught up in terminology.

According to the DSM-5 and the ICD-11, autism is a neurodevelopmental disorder marked by deficits in social communication and interaction, as well as restricted and repetitive patterns of behavior, interests, or activities.

However, proponents of the neurodiversity movement view autism as a form of neurodivergence—i.e., the natural variation in the human brain, nervous system, and the way some people interact with and experience the world. As a result, the socialization, communication, learning, and behavior of individuals on the autism spectrum are considered eccentric. Being autistic is not an illness that needs to be cured.

The diagnostic criteria and treatment for autism will likely evolve due to ongoing research, more targeted interventions, and advancements in precision medicine. New versions of the DSM and ICD will be introduced, and, as a result, the diagnostic criteria for autism will once again change. Hopefully, parents, autism advocates, and those at the least severe end of the spectrum will have their voices included in the crafting of new diagnostic criteria instead of autism experts, who have so far dictated what the condition is, how it should be treated, and how to habilitate those the disorder affects. *Nothing about us without us* will finally enter the equation.

Zosia Zaks, a notable figure in the field of autism advocacy and support to promote understanding and acceptance of neurodiversity, wrote:

> We need all hands on deck to right the ship of humanity. As we sail into an uncertain future, we need all forms of human intelligence on the planet working together to tackle the challenges we face as a society. We cannot afford to waste a brain.

Paul Collins, a parent of an autistic child, wrote: "Autists are the ultimate square pegs, and the problem with pounding a square peg into a round hole is not that the hammering is hard work. It's that you're destroying the peg."

Anderson-Chavarria (2022, p. 1321) recently proposed a predicament model of autism that goes beyond the traditional "low-to-high functioning" classification. She argues that the medical model primarily focuses on what individuals with autism cannot do rather than what they can achieve. In contrast, the social model of autism highlights a person's unique way of being, which often leads to marginalization and exclusion. The predicament model emphasizes the individuality of each autistic person's experience, avoiding comparisons to a standard notion of normality.

RDoC and Future Autism Diagnosis Criteria

The Research Domain Criteria (RDoC) framework can potentially influence the future of autism diagnosis in several ways. First, RDoC focuses on a dimensional approach to understanding mental and brain disorders instead of a categorical one. As a result, its approach can lead to a more personalized and precise autism diagnosis that focuses on individual symptoms and functioning levels rather than placing individuals in predetermined categories. Second, RDoC promotes a holistic perspective—i.e., the integration of biological, behavioral, and environmental factors that can lead to a more comprehensive diagnosis and enhance our understanding of autism. Third, RDoC encourages an interdisciplinary approach that can improve diagnostic tools and identification of the disorder. Fourth, the RDoC approach to understanding autism can lead to a better understanding of the underlying mechanisms, leading to more effective targeted interventions that can result in more optimal outcomes for individuals on the autism spectrum.

Summary

Behaviors, signs, and symptoms associated with autism spectrum disorder existed long before Kanner and Asperger clinically described the condition in the 1940s. In earlier centuries, signs of autism were not recognized as a distinct condition. Before the 20th century, no treatments were available for individuals displaying unusual behaviors. Understanding and treatment for mental health conditions, including what we now recognize as autism, were severely lacking. The prevailing medical advice at that time was to institutionalize children whose behavior significantly deviated from the norm.

The current autism diagnostic criteria and the designation of autism spectrum disorder (ASD) have evolved from various revisions of the Diagnostic and Statistical Manual of Mental Disorders (DSM) and the International Classification of Diseases (ICD). Over the years, these classifications have changed to reflect new understandings of autism. Although no single gene contributing to autism has been found, research is still ongoing, and researchers continue to explore the genetic basis of autism, aiming to uncover the various genetic factors and their interactions that contribute to the condition. The etiology of autism is complex and involves a combination of genetic predispositions, neurological differences, and environmental influences. Research continues to explore these interactions better to understand their roles in the development of autism. Current interventions for autism are multifaceted, incorporating behavioral therapies and, in some cases, pharmaceutical treatments to address specific symptoms or challenges associated with the disorder.

The concept of neurodiversity challenges the view that autism needs to be cured. Instead, neurodivergent individuals should be viewed and treated as variations in brain wiring, like the diversity found in the natural environment. Advocates and researchers who support the concept of neurodiversity are moving away from the traditional medical model of disability, which emphasizes deficits. Instead, they are approaching autism from a fundamentally new perspective.

The conceptualization and diagnosis of autism will evolve with each new DSM and ICD edition. Although significant progress has been made in understanding the several factors associated with autism, a single definitive cause remains elusive. The Research Domain Criteria (RDoC) framework focuses on a dimensional approach to understanding brain disorders. This framework emphasizes integrating biological, behavioral, and environmental factors and interdisciplinary collaboration. Such an approach can potentially lead to more effective targeted interventions, resulting in better outcomes for individuals on the autism spectrum.

Questions to Ponder for Advanced Thinking and Learning

1   What are some of the biggest challenges facing individuals with autism and their families?
2   What are some of the most promising research areas for improving the lives of individuals with autism?
3   What resources and support are available for individuals with autism and their families?
4   What can individuals without autism do to understand better and support those with autism?
5   What role can educators and employers play in creating a more inclusive environment for individuals with autism?
6   How has technology impacted the lives of individuals with autism?
7   How has the understanding and awareness of autism changed over time?
8   Will the neurodiversity movement change the way society and the medical establishment view autism?
9   The conceptualization of autism will continue to evolve in response to advances in genetic research. Will the DSM and ICD eventually remove autism as a disorder in their manuals and view the condition as a variation of the human condition that needs not be pathologized?

References

Anderson-Chavarria, M. (2022). The autism predicament: Models of autism and their impact on autistic identity. *Disability & Society, 37*(8), 1321–1341.

APA (1952). *Diagnostic and statistical manual of mental disorders.* American Psychiatric Association.

APA (1968). *Diagnostic and statistical manual of mental disorders* (2nd ed.). American Psychiatric Association.

APA (1980). *Diagnostic and statistical manual of mental disorders* (3rd ed.). American Psychiatric Association.

APA (1987). *Diagnostic and statistical manual of mental disorders—Text revised* (3rd ed., rev.). American Psychiatric Association.

APA (1994). *Diagnostic and statistical manual of mental disorders* (4th ed.). American Psychiatric Association.

APA (2013). *Diagnostic and statistical manual of mental disorders* (5th ed.). American Psychiatric Association.

Armstrong, T. (2015). The myth of the normal brain: Embracing neurodiversity. *AMA Journal of Ethics, 17*(4), 348–352.

Baron-Cohen, S. (2017). Editorial perspective: Neurodiversity—A revolutionary concept for autism and psychiatry. *The Journal of Child Psychology and Psychiatry, 58*(6), 744–747.

Blume, H. (1998). Neurodiversity: On the neurological underpinnings of geekdom. *The Atlantic.* https://www.theatlantic.com/magazine/archive/1998/09/neurodiversity/305909/. Accessed on June 17, 2023.

Boucher, J. (2022). *Autism spectrum disorders: Characteristics, causes, and practical issues* (3rd ed.). SAGE Publications.

Brisenden, S. (1986). Independent living and the medical model of disability. *Disability, Handicap, and Society, 1*(2), 173–178.

Donvan, J., & Zucker, C. (2016). *In a different key: The story of autism.* Crown Publishers.

Frith, U. (1991 [1944]). 'Autistic psychopathy' in childhood. In U. Frith (Ed. & Trans.), *Autism and Asperger syndrome* (pp. 37–92). Cambridge University Press.

Hughes, J. A. (2021). Does the heterogeneity of autism undermine the neurodiversity paradigm? *Bioethics, 35*(1), 47–60.

Hu-Lince, D., Craig, D. W., Huentelman, M. J., & Stephan, D. A. (2005). The Autism Genome Project: Goals and strategies. *American Journal of Pharmacogenomics, 5*(4), 233–246.

Jaarsma, P., & Welin, S. (2012). Autism as a natural human variation: Reflections on the claims of the neurodiversity movement. *Health Care Analysis, 20*(1), 20–30.

James, I. (2003). Singular scientists. *Journal of the Royal Society of Medicine, 96*(1), 36–39.

Jiménez, J. A., Ptacek, T. S., Tuttle, A. H., Schmid, R. S., Moy, S. S., Simon, J. M., & Zylka, M. J. (2020). *Chd8* haploinsufficiency impairs early brain development and protein homeostasis later in life. *Molecular Autism, 11*, 74.

Kanner, L. (1943). Autistic disturbances of affective contact. *Nervous Child, 2*, 217–250.

Kapp, S. K., Gillespie-Lynch, K., Sherman, L. E., & Hutman, T. (2012). Deficit, difference, or both? Autism and neurodiversity. *Developmental Psychology, 49*(1), 59–71.

Leadbitter, K., Buckle, K. L., Ellis, C., & Dekker, M. (2021). Autistic self-advocacy and the neurodiversity movement: Implications for autism early intervention research and practice. *Frontiers in Psychology, 12*, 1–7.

Mottron, L. (2011). The power of autism. *Nature, 479*, 33–35.

Oliver, M. (1990). *The politics of disablement.* Macmillan.

Oliver, M. (2013). The social model of disability: Thirty years on. *Disability & Society, 28*(7), 1024–1026.

Pagani, M., Bertero, A., Liska, A., Galbusera, A., Sabbioni, M., Barsotti, N., ... Gozzi, A. (2019). Deletion of autism risk gene Shank3 disrupts prefrontal connectivity. *Journal of Neuroscience, 39*(27), 5299–5310.

Silberman, S. (2015). *NeuroTribes: The legacy of autism and the future of neurodiversity.* Avery.

Sinclair, J. (1993). Don't mourn for us. *Autism Network International, 1*(3), 1–5.

Waterhouse, L. (2013). *Rethinking autism: Variation and complexity.* Academic Press.

Glossary

Adaptive behavior: A valuable and appropriate behavior for functioning and thriving in an environment.

Affect: The term psychologists use to describe a broad range of emotions and moods that people can experience.

Affective empathy: A person's capacity to partake in the emotions of others.

Alexithymia: A person's difficulty identifying and expressing emotions.

Algorithm: A step-by-step procedure for solving a problem in a finite number of steps. Diagnosticians use algorithms to score responses to a test to establish a diagnosis.

Amygdala: The almond-shaped mass of gray matter in the interior portion of the temporal lobes involved with experiencing emotions.

Analytic intelligence: The capacity to answer questions in traditional intelligence tests based on information-processing skills and concepts that are essential for the use and understanding of language.

Angelman syndrome: A genetic disorder caused by a mutation on chromosome 15. The condition affects the nervous system and is characterized by delayed development, speech impairment, intellectual disability, and problems with balance and movement.

Animal/murine model: The use of non-human animals in the investigation of human diseases, conditions, and disorders. Murine models use mice to study diseases, conditions, and disorders due to their physiological similarities to humans and the ease with which researchers can manipulate their genetics.

Anoxia: A condition in which oxygen is deficient in the body's tissues. This can lead to damage to organs and brain functions.

Antagonist: A substance that interferes with or inhibits the action of another.

Anterograde amnesia: A medical condition characterized by the inability to form new memories.

Applied Behavior Analysis (ABA): A science that uses learning principles to improve socially significant behaviors, focusing on assessment, intervention, and data-driven decision-making to understand and modify behaviors.

Arginine Vasopressin (AVP): A hormone that plays an essential role in memory, social behavior, and stress response. AVP is also crucial in regulating the body's water balance and blood pressure.

Attachment: An emotional bond infants form with their primary caregivers, usually their mothers.

Attention-Deficit/Hyperactivity Disorder (ADHD): A disorder characterized by attentional difficulties coupled with impulsivity and overactivity. ADHD commonly co-occurs with ASD.

Augmentative and alternative communication (AAC) system: Methods and tools therapists use to assist individuals who have difficulties with verbal communication, including picture boards and electronic devices that produce speech.

Autobiographical memory: Memory of everyday personal events that a person has experienced.

Axon: The elongated part of the nerve cell along which impulses are conducted from one cell to other cells.

Basal ganglia: A subcortical brain structure located deep within the brain that is responsible primarily for motor control and other functions such as motor learning.

Basic/primary emotions: Emotions that are innate and universal in humans (i.e., fear, anger, joy, sadness, contempt, disgust, and surprise) and are the foundation for the development of more complex emotions.

Behaviorism: A psychological approach that emphasizes the study of observable behaviors over mental processes. Its central tenet is that all behaviors are acquired through learning and interactions with the environment.

Biomarker: A measurable substance in an organism whose identification indicates a disease, condition, or environmental exposure.

Blood-brain barrier: A network of semi-permeable blood vessels and tissues that help keep harmful substances from reaching the brain.

Brain lateralization: Specialization of the right and left sides of the brain resulting in attending to and processing sensory inputs differently.

Brain oscillations: Rhythmic and/or repetitive electrical activity occurring spontaneously in response to stimulation of neural tissue in the central nervous system.

Brain stem: The lower part of the brain that is connected to the spinal cord and responsible for regulating most of the body's automatic functions, including breathing and heartbeat.

Broader autism phenotype (BAP):   A term that describes a cluster of traits associated with autism but considered subclinical or not debilitating enough to warrant a diagnosis of autism.

Broca area: A brain region located in the left hemisphere of the frontal lobe. It is primarily associated with speech production and language processing. Damage to Broca's area can lead to difficulties in forming coherent speech.

Candidate genes: Genes suspected to be related to a particular trait, disease, or physical attribute.

Case series studies: Description of the characteristics and outcomes among a group of individuals with a disease. Data in case series are collected retrospectively or prospectively without randomization or a control group.

Central coherence: Our capacity to derive meaning from a mass of details. A weak central coherence describes a person who focuses on minute details rather than the overall meaning and global information processing.

Central nervous system: The part of the vertebrate nervous system consisting of the brain and the spinal cord.

Cerebellum: A brain structure (meaning little brain) located at the base of the brain, near the back of the head. The cerebellum is responsible for motor control, balance, and movement.

Cerebral cortex: The brain's outer layer of gray matter that lies on top of the cerebrum.

Cerebral hemispheres: The left and right half of the cerebrum.

Challenging behavior: Pattern of behaviors (e.g., temper tantrums, self-injurious behaviors, hitting, and biting) that interferes with a child's learning and engagement in social activities with others.

Childhood psychosis: An extreme mental state that is very rare in children. Affected children experience impaired thinking and emotions that cause them to lose contact with reality.

Chronological age: A person's age that is based on their birth year and date.

Classical conditioning: A learning process in which a neutral stimulus is paired with an unconditioned (unlearned) stimulus. After repeated pairings, the neutral stimulus becomes a conditioned stimulus capable of eliciting a conditioned response like that of the unconditioned stimulus.

Clinical trials: Research studies conducted to evaluate the safety and effectiveness of new medical treatments, drugs, or devices on human participants.

Cognitive empathy: Knowing how other people feel and think.

Common variants: The most common type of genetic variation among people.

Comorbid/comorbidity: The co-occurrence of two or more psychiatric conditions affecting an individual.

Complementary and alternative medicine (CAM):   Nonmedical treatments that are outside of mainstream healthcare.

Concordance rate: The percentage of pairs of twins or other blood relatives exhibiting a particular trait or disorder.

Connectome: The complete neural connections within an organism's brain or nervous system.

Copy number variations (CNVs):   A deleted or duplicated DNA stretch. CNVs can either be inherited from one parent or happen spontaneously, resulting in higher rates of diseases and disorders.

Corpus callosum: The thick membrane of nervous tissue that connects and allows communication between the two hemispheres of the brain.

Creative intelligence: Responses to novel experiences or situations requiring active and conscious information processing.

Cytokines: Various substances that some immune system cells secrete and affect other cells. They control the migration of cells in the immune system.

Dendrites: A branched extension of a neuron that receives nerve impulses from another adjacent neuron.

De novo mutation: A spontaneous alteration in an organism's genome that was not inherited from their parents.

Developmental trajectory: The progression and attainment of expected milestones at individual ages.

Devereux School: Helena Devereux founded the school in 1912 to provide specialized education and support for students with emotional, behavioral, and developmental challenges.

Differential diagnosis: A diagnosis differentiating between two or more conditions with similar signs or symptoms.

Differential reinforcement: A technique used in applied behavior analysis consisting of selectively reinforcing (i.e., rewarding) a desired behavior and not an undesired one.

Discrete Trial Training (DTT):   A structured teaching method commonly used in behavioral therapy, particularly with individuals on the autism spectrum. It involves breaking down skills into small, discrete steps and teaching these skills through repetitive practice.

Dizygotic (DZ) twins: Twins that develop from separate fertilized eggs and thus have nonidentical genotypes.

Dominant gene: A gene variant that will express its trait even when only one copy is present in an individual.

Dopamine: A neurotransmitter formed in the brain and essential for the optimal functioning of the central nervous system and the brain's reward system (i.e., feeling good). Dopamine is also associated with motor functions (e.g., Parkinson's disease—dopamine concentration reduction).

Downcast gaze: The act of looking downwards to avoid direct eye contact with others as in the case of being shy, submissive, or sad.

Down syndrome: (aka trisomy 21) A chromosomal abnormality involving an extra chromosome in the 21st pair. Affected individuals have mild to moderate intellectual disabilities, short stature, and a flattened facial profile.

Dyadic interaction: An interaction between two individuals, as in a mother and a child or a husband-and-wife social exchange.

Dysmorphic features: Physical characteristics that are abnormal in shape or appearance compared to typical or average features.

Echolalia: Speech involving the meaningless repetition of words just spoken by another person. Echolalia can be immediate or delayed and is often a symptom of autism.

Efficacy study: A scientific study to determine the effectiveness of a drug or intervention under controlled laboratory conditions.

Embryo: A human offspring during the prenatal period from approximately the second week to the eighth week after fertilization.

Emerging Adulthood: A period of the life span, more so in Western societies, extending from about age 18 to about 25.

Emotional contagion: Occurs when individuals mimic and adopt the emotions of others (e.g., facial expressions, body language, or vocal tones), often subconsciously. Emotional contagion plays a significant role in social interactions.

Emotional empathy: The ability to feel and understand another person's emotions.

Emotion regulation: The capacity of an organism to initiate, maintain, and alter emotional responses.

Empathizing-systemizing system: A theory proposed by Baron-Cohen to describe how males and females respond differently to others. Males tend to display systematic thinking, whereas females exhibit more empathic thinking.

Empathy: Identifying and understanding another person's situations, feelings, and motives.

Endophenotype: Measurable variables related to an organism's phenotypes that narrow the heterogeneity of a complex disorder.

Entorhinal cortex: The brain region located in the medial temporal lobe. It acts as a bridge between the hippocampus and the neocortex, facilitating the transfer of information.

Epidemiology: The study of prevalence, distribution, and control of diseases in a population.

Episodic memory: Conscious recollection of personal experiences associated with the context in which they occurred.

Etiology: The branch of medicine that studies the origins or causes of a condition or a disease.

Excitatory neurons: Neurons in the central nervous system that produce electrical signals that stimulate other neurons to fire and transmit signals.

Executive function: Set of cognitive processes, including working memory, self-control, and flexible thinking, which are necessary for selecting and monitoring behaviors that facilitate the achievement of chosen goals.

Explicit memory: Conscious recollection of previously learned information.

Extrapyramidal side effects: Drug-induced movement disorders (e.g., irregular, jerky movements) that can occur because of taking certain antipsychotic medications.

Extreme male brain theory: A theory that seeks to explain why ASD is more common in males than females. People with autism process the world through a male lens and thus are more likely to systematize than empathize.

False belief test: A test designed to measure the understanding that people can have incorrect beliefs that can guide their behavior.

False negative: Incorrectly misidentifying the presence of a condition or disorder during the screening or diagnosis process.

False positive: Incorrectly identifying the presence of a condition or disorder during the screening or diagnosis process.

Fetus: An offspring of a human during the fetal stage of prenatal development, which begins during the ninth month of gestation.

Fine motor skills: The coordination of the hands, small muscles, and fingers necessary for performing tasks, including writing and manipulating small objects.

Fluid intelligence: Facets of intelligence associated with active thinking and reasoning to solve novel problems.

Fragile X syndrome: An X-chromosome abnormality resulting in behavioral characteristics associated with autism. It affects males and females differently. FXS is the most known cause of inherited intellectual disability.

Frontal lobe(s):   The lobe that is located at the front of each cerebral hemisphere.

Functional magnetic resonance imaging (fMRI):   A brain-imaging technique that shows increased blood flow in the brain, indicating areas that are activated during a cognitive task.

General intelligence: A broad mental capacity (aka the general or 'g' factor) that is the basis for learning, reasoning, and problem solving.

Genetic variant/variation: Any changes within a gene, including mutations, copy number variations, or single nucleotide polymorphisms.

Genome: The complete number of genes or genetic material present in a cell or organism.

Genome-Wide Association Studies (GWAS):   Comparing the genomes of many individuals to find variations associated with a particular disorder or disease. The information can be used to treat and prevent disease.

Genotype: The genetic endowment an individual inherits.

Glia/Glial cells: Non-neuronal cells that support and protect neurons in the central and peripheral nervous system. They insulate neurons, provide nutrients, and help remove dead neurons.

Global processing: The ability to process complex stimuli and information in a general, holistic manner.

Gray matter: Brain tissue consisting of high concentrations of cell bodies, axon terminals, and dendrites.

Gross motor skills: Skills necessary to coordinate large muscle and whole body movement (e.g., walking, jumping, and maintaining balance).

Gyrus/Gyri: The cerebral cortex's pattern of folds or bumps.

Head lag: Infants' delay in the ability to control the head in relation to the body (e.g., keeping the head aligned with their body).

Heterogeneity: The quality or state of being diverse or dissimilar.

Hippocampus: A seahorse-shaped structure in the inner fold of the temporal lobes associated with forming new memories.

Human Genome Project (HGP):   An international scientific project aimed at mapping and sequencing all the chemical bases of DNA (adenine [A], cytosine [C], guanine [G], and thymine [T]) and identifying the gene pairs in the genome.

Hypersensitivity: An increased sensitivity to sensory input, characterized by being easily overwhelmed by sensory experiences.

Hypocalcemia: A condition characterized by a lower than normal level of calcium in the blood, which can lead to various health issues.

Hyposensitivity: A reduced sensitivity to sensory input, characterized by not noticing pain or changes in temperature.

Idiopathic autism: Autism that develops in an individual in the absence of any known causes.

Implicit memory: Non-declarative memory that occurs unconsciously and automatically such as waking.

Incidence: The occurrence of new cases of a disease or disorder in a specified population during a defined period of time.

Inclusion: The practice of providing equal opportunities for people with intellectual disabilities or for members of minority groups who might otherwise be excluded or marginalized.

Infantile Amnesia: The inability of adults to recall personal memories that occurred during the first few years of life (usually 0–3 years).

Insistence on sameness: A strong tendency to resist changes in daily routine or the repetitive-restricted behavior of children diagnosed with autism.

Intellectual disability: A condition defined by below-average intellectual functioning (i.e., IQ<70), lack of adaptive functioning, and originating before age 18.

Internal working model: A cognitive template that infants develop based on their interactions (positive or negative) with their primary caregiver. The model has implications for the individual's future relationships.

In *utero*:   A period during which a fetus is developing inside a pregnant individual's womb or uterus.

Joint attention: The ability to share a perceptual experience with another person, as when a baby responds to a parent's cue to look at a clock on a wall.

Left inferior frontal gyrus: A brain region located within the frontal lobe and involved in various cognitive processes, including language production, speech fluency, semantic processing, and decision making.

Life expectancy: The expected average age members of a population may live (77–78 years in the United States).

Local processing: Attending to and processing specific information in a complex stimulus rather than viewing it as a whole.

Longitudinal study: A study in which the same participants are observed or tested over time to understand developmental changes and continuities.

Long-term memory: Unlimited capacity of the brain to store information for extended periods, ranging from hours to a lifetime.

LSD (lysergic acid diethylamide):   A hallucinogenic drug that can alter thoughts, perceptions, mood, and a person's state of consciousness.

Macrocephaly: A condition in which the head is abnormally large.

Maladaptive behavior: Inappropriate behavior that interferes with a person's activities of daily living. Maladaptive behavior can lead to instant gratification but result in adverse consequences when displayed consistently.

Matching to sample: A technique behavior analysts use to assess and teach discrimination skills (e.g., an individual is presented with a sample stimulus and must select the correct matching stimulus from a set of options).

Mental age: A measure of cognitive development determined by an intelligence test. When the mental age is divided by the chronological age, it yields an intelligence quotient (IQ) or score.

Meta-analysis: A statistical procedure that analyzes findings of various research studies that investigated the same phenomenon.

Methylation: A biochemical process involving the addition of a methyl group (CH_3) to a DNA molecule. This process can affect gene expression and regulation without altering the DNA sequence itself.

Microarray technology: A high-throughput method used to analyze the expression of many genes simultaneously.

Microcephaly: A condition characterized by an abnormally small head size relative to the rest of the body. Microcephaly can be associated with various developmental delays, intellectual disabilities, and other neurological issues.

Mirror neuron system: A distinctive group of neurons that fire when a person performs a motor act or when that person observes someone else perform the same action. Mirror neurons were first discovered in monkeys' brains.

Molecular syndrome: A set of clinical symptoms resulting from a specific genetic mutation or alteration at the molecular level, including multiple systems or signs observed together due to a shared underlying genetic cause.

Monogenic: Genetic inheritance in which a pair of genes (an allele) determines a particular trait or characteristic.

Moro/startle reflex: A primitive reflex observed in infants to sudden movements or noises. As a result, infants throw their arms and legs outward, arch their back, and bring their arms back towards their body.

Multiplex autism: Families in which more than one person is diagnosed with autism.

Murine/mouse model: The use of strains of mice explicitly bred to study a human disease or condition and effective development of prevention and treatment.

Mutations: Changes in the DNA sequence of an organism that occur naturally due to errors during DNA replication or because of environmental factors.

Myelination: The production of the myelin sheath that covers the axons in the central and peripheral nervous systems.

Myelin sheath: A white fatty material composed of lipoproteins that wraps around the axons of the neurons to increase the electrical communication between neurons.

Negative predictive value: The probability that a patient with a negative (normal) test result does not have a disease or a condition.

Neocortex: The most recently evolved part of the cerebral cortex. It is vital for higher cognitive functions.

Neurodevelopmental disorder: A condition involving some disruption in brain development and functioning. A neurodevelopmental disorder (e.g., autism) can range from mild impairments to more debilitating ones.

Neurodivergent: A term used to describe individuals whose neurological development and functioning differ from what is considered typical or neurotypical.

Neurodiversity: The view that many conditions regarded as pathological (e.g., ASD) are normal variations of the human brain akin to environmental biodiversity.

Neurogenesis: The process by which new neurons are generated. This process is crucial during prenatal development, laying the foundation for the brain's structure and function.

Neuron: A nerve cell consisting of a cell body with one or more dendrites and a single axon.

Neuropeptide: Small protein-like molecules neurons use to communicate with each other. They can influence the activity of neurotransmitters, affecting mood, behavior, and several bodily functions.

Neurotransmitter: A chemical substance (e.g., dopamine) released by a neuron when activated to stimulate or inhibit the firing of other neurons.

Neurotypical: A term used to describe individuals whose neurological functioning and development are typical of the general population.

Nonverbal communication: A system of communication (e.g., hand gestures, facial expression) that conveys information without the use of words.

Noradrenaline/norepinephrine: A neurotransmitter and hormone the adrenal gland produces. It is part of the sympathetic nervous system and is the hormone that triggers the body's emergency response to flight or fight.

Normalization/inclusion: A movement that originated in Scandinavia. It promotes the guiding principle that people with a disability, or those who are marginalized, should receive the opportunity and the resources to participate in normal daily activities.

Nosology: The branch of medicine or psychiatry that deals with the classification of diseases.

Nuchocephalic reflex: Also known as the head-righting reflex, which describes the phenomenon where, when the head is turned to one side, the body also turns to the same side.

Obsessive-compulsive disorder: A disorder characterized by anxiety and persistent compulsions and rituals.

Occipital lobe(s): Lobes of the cerebrum that are located at the back of the skull. They play a vital role in visual perception.

Oligodendrocytes: A type of glial cell in the central nervous system whose primary function is to produce myelin.

Open-label studies: Clinical trials in which both the researchers and participants are aware of the treatment being administered.

Operant conditioning: A learning process through which behaviors are modified by their consequences. Behaviors that are rewarded are more likely to be repeated, whereas those that are punished are less likely to occur again.

Optimal outcome: The term used to describe instances when a person previously diagnosed with ASD no longer meets the diagnostic criteria of the disorder.

Orbitofrontal cortex: The brain region in the frontal lobes, just above the eyes. It plays a critical role in various functions, including decision-making, emotional processing, and social interactions.

Orthogenic: A concept that promotes proper development or growth. In psychology, it relates to intervention approaches that foster healthy psychological development.

Oxytocin: Also dubbed the love hormone, it is produced in the hypothalamus and secreted by the pituitary gland. Oxytocin facilitates contractions during labor, lactation, social bonding, and positive physical contact.

Parietal lobe(s): Lobes of the cerebrum that are located near the back and top of the head. They play a primary role in the experience of pain, pressure, touch and the position of our body parts and movement.

Pathogenesis: The development of a disease or disorder and the factors that contribute to its initiation and progression.

Pathognomonic: Signs or symptoms that are uniquely characteristic of a particular disease or disorder.

Peptide: Short chains of amino acids linked together by peptide bonds. Peptides involve various biological functions, such as hormone regulation, immune response, and cell signaling.

Peripheral nervous system (PNS): The part of the nervous system not within the brain and the spinal cord (i.e., the central nervous system). The PNS connects the central nervous system with other parts of the body.

Phenotype: The set of an individual's observable characteristics resulting from the interaction of their genotype with the environment.

Placebo: A substance with no active therapeutic effect, often used in clinical trials as a control.

Plasticity: The capacity of an organism's brain to change due to positive and negative experiences.

Pleiotropic: A term used in genetics to refer to genes that influence more than one phenotype.

Polygenic: Genetic inheritance (aka multiple factors inheritance) that involves the workings of various genes characterizing an individual.

Polypharmacy: The regular use of five or more medications simultaneously. The practice can lead to potential drug interactions and adverse effects.

Positive predictive value: The probability that a patient with a positive (abnormal) test result has the disease or the condition.

Practical intelligence: The ability to solve problems encountered in everyday life.

Precision medicine: (aka personalized medicine) A novel approach to designing the prevention and treatment of diseases and conditions based on differences in people's genes and environments.

Predictive validity: The degree to which a test predicts the occurrence of a condition or disease in a general population.

Prefrontal cortex: The part of the brain that covers the front part of the frontal lobe of the cerebral cortex.

Pretend play: A type of play in which children use their imagination to act out different roles, express their creativity, and develop social skills.

Prevalence: The total number of cases of a disorder or disease in a population at a specific time.

Primacy criterion: A standard for assessing a theory since the cause always precedes the effect.

Primitive reflexes: Involuntary movements that are controlled by the brainstem and spinal cord. They are present in infants and generally lost as their nervous systems mature.

Prognosis: A prediction of the probable cause and outcome of a disease.

Prosody: The intonation, loudness variations, pausing, rhythm, and the melody of speech patterns.

Prospective studies: Studies of participants selected on the grounds of likely risk before they show any signs of a disorder or disease and followed over time to detect the emergence of the disorder or disease.

Proprioceptive: Our ability to sense our body's location, movements, and actions.

Protective factor: Factor (or factors) that can mitigate those more likely to cause a disease or a condition.

Protodeclarative pointing: Pointing intended to show something of interest to another person.

Protoimperative pointing: Pointing to obtain something of interest from another person.

Psychosis: A mental state characterized by a loss of touch with reality, often manifested as delusions, hallucinations, and disorganized thinking and speech.

Punishment: A consequence that follows a behavior and decreases the likelihood of that behavior occurring in the future. Punishment can be administered by presenting an aversive stimulus or removing a pleasurable stimulus.

Purkinje cells: Densely branching neurons located in the cortex of the cerebellum. They play a fundamental role in controlling motor movement.

Qualitative study: A non-numerical data research method, including interviews, open-ended questionnaires, observations, and focus groups used to obtain an in-depth understanding of human behavior and experiences.

Quasi-experimental study: A type of study in which the effect of an intervention or treatment is evaluated without random assignment of participants to either the experimental or the control group.

Randomized Controlled Trials: A study design in which participants are randomly assigned to either an experimental group or a control group.

Rapid Eye Movement (REM): One of the four stages of sleep, associated with vivid dreams. During this stage, the brain is highly active, which plays a role in memory consolidation and emotional processing.

Rare variants: Genetic variations that occur infrequently in a population, which can include single nucleotide polymorphisms (SNPs) among other types of mutations.

Recessive gene: A gene variant that only expresses its trait when two copies are present in an individual.

Redox status: The overall balance between oxidants and antioxidants in a biological system. Disruption of the redox system can lead to oxidative stress and damage to cells and tissues.

Reliability: The consistency and stability of screening or diagnostic instruments when assessing individuals for autism, producing the same results over time.

Retrospective studies: Studies based on past events and existing recorded data to identify the earliest signs and risk factors relevant to the condition or disorder being investigated.

Rett syndrome: A rare female degenerative disorder characterized by hand stereotypies, loss of language, and some degree of social withdrawal.

Risk Factor: A factor (or factors) that increases the chance of someone developing a disease or a condition.

Savant ability: (aka splinter skills) The phenomenon in which individuals with an intellectual disability demonstrate extraordinary talents in various domains, including the arts, music, mathematics, and more.

Screening: An investigative process in medicine to determine the risk marker of a condition or disease. Screening can be performed on one individual or a whole population.

Selective serotonin reuptake inhibitors (SSRIs): A class of drugs that increase the levels of serotonin in the brain, improve mood, and reduce anxiety.

Self-injurious behavior: Behaviors (e.g., head banging, hand biting) that are maladaptive and can result in physical injury or death.

Semantic memory: A long-term memory in which people can recall words and concepts essential for language use and understanding.

Sensitivity: The extent to which a test accurately and correctly identifies a condition it is designed to detect.

Sensory register/memory: A component of memory that captures and holds sensory information for a very brief period, usually less than a second.

Sensory seeking: A tendency to seek out sensory experience across the five senses.

Serotonin: A neurotransmitter that carries messages between neurons in the brain and throughout the body.

Shaping: A technique used in applied behavior analysis to gradually teach a behavior to a learner using reinforcement (i.e., rewarding) until the behavior is learned.

Shared attention: Another term used for joint attention.

Short-term memory: A temporary storage system that holds a limited amount of information for a brief period, typically from a few seconds to a minute.

Simplex autism: Families in which only one person has autism.

Single nucleotide polymorphisms (SNPs): The most common type of genetic variation among people, consisting of a genomic variant at a single base position in the DNA.

Social (Pragmatic) Communication Disorder: A neurodevelopmental condition marked by significant difficulties in using verbal and nonverbal communication socially.

Social brain: A network of multiple brain regions that supports social interaction.

Social orienting: Young babies' innate preference to attend to social stimuli, particularly human voices and faces.

Socioeconomic status: Social standing or class of a person or group of individuals, including their education, occupation, and income.

Specificity: (screening tests) A test's capacity to correctly identify people with a disorder or disease.

Specificity criterion: The view that a sufficient and necessary causal factor must lead to a single effect, not multiple effects. For example, a sufficient and necessary causal factor for autism should result in autism only and not in anxiety disorders.

Speech-language pathologists (SLP):   Healthcare professionals who evaluate, diagnose, and treat individuals of all ages with communication disorders.

Stereotyped behavior: See Stimming.

Stimming: A term that describes individuals with autism engaging in self-stimulating behaviors, repetitive body movements, or repetitive movements of objects.

Sulcus/Sulci: The cerebral cortex's deep, narrow furrow or groove.

Survival reflexes: Automatic responses (e.g., breathing) that are built into the nervous system and play a crucial role in ensuring survival. These reflexes are generally present throughout life and protect individuals from harm.

Susceptibility genes: Genes that increase the probability of a person developing a particular characteristic or condition.

Synapse: The tiny gap where the axon or dendrite of one neuron connects with another. The sending neuron releases neurotransmitters at the synaptic gap to bind with receptors of the receiving neuron.

Synaptic pruning: The brain's automatic disconnections of networks that are no longer being used.

Synaptogenesis: The formation of new connections in the brain in response to an organism's interaction with the environment.

Syndrome: A group of signs or symptoms that consistently occur together.

Syndromic autism: Autism that results from known genetic or congenital medical syndrome (e.g., Fragile-X syndrome).

Temperament: A person's patterns of thinking and behaving that are influenced by genetic and environmental factors. One's temperament plays an essential role in shaping one's personality.

Temporal lobe(s):   One of the four major lobes of the cerebral cortex that sit behind the ears. The temporal lobes play a role in memory, the processing of sound and vision, and the recognition of objects and language.

Theory of Mind: The understanding that people have mental states (e.g., desires, beliefs, and intentions) that can guide and explain their behavior.

The tonic labyrinthine reflex: A primitive reflex observed in infants that helps them develop balance and coordination. It involves the body's response when the baby's head position is changed relative to gravity.

Thimerosal: An organic mercury compound that has been used since the 1930s as a preservative in some vaccines.

Tonic/asymmetric tonic neck reflex: When an infant's head is turned to one side, the arm and leg typically extend, while the opposite arm and leg flex. This reflex is thought to help with motor development and hand-eye coordination.

Transcriptomic changes: Alterations in the complete set of RNA transcripts that are produced by the genome of a cell or a group of cells.

Tuberous sclerosis: A rare genetic disease that causes benign tumors to grow in the brain and other parts of the body (e.g., spinal cord, lungs, heart, and kidneys).

Typical development trajectory: The predictable pathway or progression an individual follows over time due to maturation and environmental input.

Unitary disorder: A disorder resulting from a singular cause or closely related causes and symptoms that are typically homogeneous.

Universality criterion: A standard for assessing the validity of a theory. For example, if a factor causes autism, the factor must be present in all autistic individuals.

Validity: The extent to which a concept, test, or assessment is well-founded and conforms to reality. The validity of an assessment is the degree to which it measures what it purports to measure.

Valproic acid: An anticonvulsive drug that is also used to treat the manic phase of bipolar disorder and the prevention of migraine headaches.

Vasopressin (arginine vasopressin):   A hormone secreted by the pituitary gland that constricts blood vessels, raises blood pressure, and reduces urination.

White matter: Brain tissue consisting of a concentration of axons covered with a whitish myelin sheath.

Working memory: Memory with a limited capacity that temporarily holds and manipulates information necessary for cognitive tasks such as learning, reasoning, and comprehension.

X chromosome: A female sex chromosome located on the 23rd pair.

Zone of rarity: The idea that there can be a continuum between normal functioning and a clearly defined mental disorder (e.g., an individual may exhibit some symptoms of a disorder but not enough to meet the diagnostic criteria).

Index

treatment 242–243; Positive Behavior
Support 244–247; replications of
Lovaas' study 239–240; Skinner and
the experimental analysis of 235–236;
before Skinner, B. F. 234–236;
treatment and education of autistic and
related communication handicapped
children 249–251
Bernier, R. 177
Bertillon, Jacques 208
Besler, F. 74
Betancur, C. 171
Bettelheim, B. 147
Beversdorf, D. Q. 179
Bhasin, T. K. 29
Bijou, S. 238
Binet, A. 95
biomarkers 187, 215–216
biomedical treatment for autism 283–285;
celiac disease and GFCF diet 285–287;
chelation therapy 287–288; vitamins
and supplements 288–291
birth weight, autism and 39
Bleuler, E. 4
blood-brain barrier 286
Blume, H. 314
Bolognani, F. 274
Bondy, A. S. 253
Bonnaterre, P-J. 7
Bortoletto, R. 276
Bouchard, T. P. 286
Boucher, J. 94, 142
Bourgondien, M. E. V. 250–251
Bowlby, J. 65–66
Bracken, M. B. 154
Bradshaw, J. 90
brain development 28–33; brain
lateralization 32–33; brain myelination
30–31; cerebral cortex 28; gestational
age 29–30; neurogenesis 28, 31–32;
neurons 28; synapses 28
brain lateralization 27, 32–33
brain myelination 30–31
brain oscillations 44
brain stem 40
brain structure implications for autism
34–38; amygdala 35–36; cerebellum
34–35; cerebral cortex 35; corpus
callosum 36–37; dopamine pathways
36; hippocampus 36; pineal gland 38
Brewer, N. 195

Brignell, A. 100
Broadbent, D. 91
broader autism phenotype (BAP) 177
Broca 32
Broca, P. 99
Bromley, R. L. 156
Brondino, N. 285
Brown, M. J. 287
Brun, L. 33
Bruscia, K. E. 298
buspirone (*BuSpar®*) 270
Butler, C. 251

Campbell, D. B. 154–155
Campos, J. J. 63
Canine-assisted therapy 296
cannabidiol (CBD) 275
carbamazepine *(Tegretol®)* 271
Carmody, D. P. 87
Carr, E. G. 248
Carr, J. E. 244–246
casein 286
case studies 292; Alfred L. 14, 115;
Barbara K. 13, 113–114; Charles N.
14–15, 115–116; David 250; Donald
T. 11–12, 111–112, 125, 169–170, 311;
Elaine C. 15, 116–117; Ernst K. 9–10;
Frederick W. 12, 112; Fritz V. 8–9;
Harro L. 9; Hellmuth L. 10; Herbert B.
14, 114–115; John F. 15, 116; Paul G.
12–13, 113; Richard M. 12, 112–113;
Serebrenikova P. 310; Victor 310;
Virginia S. 13, 114
Cattell, R. B. 96
Cavendish, H. 314
celiac disease 285–287
Centers for Disease Control and
Prevention (CDC) 19, 120, 189, 218,
272; Autism and Developmental
Disabilities Monitoring (ADDM)
Network 20
central coherence, weak 142–143
Ceranoglu, T. A. 270
cerebellum 34–35
cerebral cortex 28
cerebral hemispheres 32
challenging behaviors 246
Challis, N. 6
Chan, M. M. Y. 146
Charlop-Christy, M. H. 254
CHD8 gene 312

For Product Safety Concerns and Information please contact our EU
representative GPSR@taylorandfrancis.com
Taylor & Francis Verlag GmbH, Kaufingerstraße 24, 80331 München, Germany

www.ingramcontent.com/pod-product-compliance
Lightning Source LLC
Chambersburg PA
CBHW050332270326
41926CB00016B/3416

9 781032 372860